The Author in Garter mantle, worn for Order of the Garter ceremonies. The insignia on the table: sceptre ex officio, *along with those of a King of Arms, gold collar of S's and crown; the latter, as with all such crowns, inscribed on the rim,* Miserere mei Deus secundum magnam misericordiam tuam – *a prudential insurance in view of Original Sin, n'est ce pas?! Credit: Charles Mackinnon: Sir Conrad Swan, KCVO, PhD, FSA, Garter Principal King of Arms. Courtesy of Andrew Swan, Esq., BSc.*

A King From Canada

A King From Canada

by

CONRAD SWAN

The Memoir Club

First published in 2005 by
The Memoir Club
Stanhope Old Hall
Stanhope
Weardale
County Durham

British Library Cataloguing in
Publication Data.
A catalogue record for this book
is available from the
British Library.

ISBN: 1 84104 072 X

Typeset by George Wishart & Associates, Whitley Bay.
Printed by CPI Bath.

Dedicated to my Grandchildren

*Alice, John, Thomas, Rafe Herring, Elizabeth, Thomas, Edward,
Nicholas, Alexander, Frederick Galvin, Hugh, Eleanor, Francis Walters, Isabelle,
Amelia, Alexandra, Cecily Swan, Alexander, Alicia and Benedict Hatvany.*

Contents

Illustrations

Acknowledgments

A POET, known to all of us once said, 'No man is an island'. How true that is especially when he is an author, for such often needs help, especially when historical facts need verification.

In this regard, as in others, I acknowledge with particular gratitude, much assistance received when writing this book from the following in:

Australia, Michael Bryce, FRAIA, LEDIA, FRSA, of Brisbane, and Mrs Diana Morgan of Toorak, Melbourne;

Canada, Mrs Muriel Jarvis Auckinclose, of Saanichton, BC; the Hon. David Crombie, PC, BA, Secretary of State of Canada (1986-88); my cousin Mrs Sylvia Dyer, of Victoria, BC; Mrs Prescilla Lowe, Curator/Manager, Cowichan Valley Museum; Charles R. Maier, Head of Ceremonial and Protocol for the Federal Government; my *confrères* in the Order of Malta, Maria Teresa McCullough and F.G.A. McCullough; R. G. Mcpherson, Niagara Herald Extraordinary; David P. Marshall; Dr Robert Pichette, *D. és L., Héraut Dauphin éxtraordinaire*; my brother, the Reverend Dr P. J. M. Swan, CSB, PhD, LLD, DD, Vice-Chancellor Emeritus of the University of St Michael's College, Toronto; Auguste Vachon, *Héraut Outaociais émerite,* and Robert D. Watt, Chief Herald of Canada, who has also kindly written the foreword to this book;

Lithuania: His Excellency Justas Vincas Paleckis, Deputy Minister of Foreign Affairs, lately Lithuanian Ambassador to the Court of St James's, and Madame Liamute Paleckiene; Dr Algis Tomas Geniušas, President of the United Nations Association of Lithuania, and Dr Isolde Gabriele Geniušiene, of the University of Vilnius;

New Zealand, Philip O'Shea, MVO, New Zealand Herald of Arms Extraordinary;

Poland: my *confrère* in the Orders of Malta and Constantine St George, Professor Andrew Count Ciechanowiecki, Knight of the Order of the White Eagle, PhD, FSA, and Professor dr. hab. Stefan K. Kuczynski, Prezes, Polskie Towarzystwo Heraldyczne;

Russia: Dr W. Tarasaw, of the Main Archival Administration under the Council of Ministers, Moscow, and Dr Stanislaus Dumin of the Historico Genealogical Society of Moscow;

The United Kingdom: F.S. Andrus, LVO, Beaumont Herald of Arms Extraordinary; Michael Ball, of the National Army Museum; H.E. Anthony Bailey, Delegate, Delegation of the Order of Constantine St George in Great

Britain and Ireland; Sandra Curtis, Manager, Sudbury, Suffolk, Library and her colleagues; Holly Downer, Assistant Librarian Royal Naval Museum, Portsmouth; E.J. Edgerley-Harris, Assistant Curator, Gurkha Museum, Winchester; Oliver Everett, CVO, Assistant Keeper of the Royal Archives, Windsor Castle; the Reverend Russell G. Frost, MA(Oxon), STh(Lambeth; R.S. Harrison, Archives Officer, House of Lords' Archives; my grandson Edward Galvin; A.E Haydon, MA; Sir Malcolm Innes of Edingight, KCVO, lately Lord Lyon King of Arms; Cecil R. Humphrey-Smith, OBE, FSA, founder and Principal of the Institute of Genealogical and Heraldic Studies, Canterbury; Max Marnau; R.J.B. Noel, MPhil, Lancaster Herald of Arms; the Reverend Francis Owen, CJ, of St George's College, Weybridge, and Major David Rankin-Hunt, MVO, MBE, TD, Norfolk Herald of Arms Extraordinary, and Administrator, Royal Collection;

the **West Indies**: His Excellency Sir James Carlisle, GCMG, Governor-General of Antigua & Barbuda; Miss Vincene Bachelor, BEM, Chancellor of the Chivalric Orders of Antigua & Barbuda, and Alison Insley-Madson, British Vice-Consul, Port au Prince, Haiti;

and **elsewhere**: Philippe de Chasteleux, *Directeur de la Documentation, Bibliotheque Généalogique d'Histoire Sociale, 'Centre de Recherches', Paris*; my cousin Dr Jo Anne Davis, Ed.D, of Edmond, Oklahoma; Professor Leon-François Hoffman, Department of French, Princeton University; Fergus Gillespie, Deputy Chief Herald of Ireland, and the Most Reverend Abune Berhaneyesus Souraphael, Metropolitan Archbishop of Addis Ababa (of the Ethiopic-Coptic Rite in union with Rome); my brother officers in the Indian Army and the Gurkhas (some of whom subsequently served in the regular British Army) R. Boxall, A. C. Buckingham, Peter Burger, Alan D. Burnett, I.J. Cowen, OBE, the Reverend G. E. Fooks, MA(Cantab), L.A. Lambert, K.P. Murphy, Major S.R.O'R. Shearburn, M.G.M. Simmons, Lieutenant Colonel Donald Stone, J.L. Vickers, David Wade, Barrister-at-Law and Member of the Inner Temple, and the late Reverend Roger Whitehead, MA(Oxon).

With the generous assistance had of those mentioned above, I was then able to ask my eldest daughter, Elizabeth Herring, to type up the text of this book – again and again – as I incorporated the information so provided, and modified the text accordingly. This she has done with a professional skill matched only by her patience and good humour in assisting with the accouchement, so to speak, of this brain child – not forgetting, of course, *gratia mea Sancto Antonio Olisiponis et Padovae.*

A note on Polish pronunciation and symbols
with reference to words used in this text

The vowels are probably best rendered in English as
a – hard as in 'far'
e – 'Ben'
i – soft as in 'lit'
o – 'slot'
u – 'nook'
y – 'nip'

Consonants mostly behave as in English except
c – if without an 'h' following, the 'c' is pronounced as 'ts' as in English with
the word 'tsar'(in Polish 'car'); but if followed by an 'h' is pronounced as
an 'h' is in English.
j – is soft as in 'yes'
w – is the same as the English v

Some letters are accented and combined in ways peculiar to Polish
ˎ – beneath a letter, as with a or e renders it nasal
cki – 'tski' as with ski (see below)
ł – is pronounced 'w' in English
rz – as with the French j in 'je'
ś – sounds almost as the s in 'sure' (sh)
ski – 'tski' as in cki – both pronounced as 'tski' with a soft i as in 'lit'
and so with parliament which in Polish is, sejm and is pronounced (same)
General Władysław (v-wad-is-wav) Sikorski (shi-kor-tski)
Lech (le-h) Wałęsa (va-wen-sa)
Jastrzębiec (yast-jen-biets)
Święcicki (sh-vien-chee-tski)

Once the variations are mastered, Polish pronunciation is consistent.

However, it must be admitted that, as a result, one does not experience the thrill
of the chase, as in English, where all too often the correct pronunciation is
unknown until tutored, as with:
Cholmondeley, which ends up as 'Chum-ley'; and
the Cornish village, Mousehole – 'Maw-zul'!

Foreword

WHEN I FIRST had the pleasure of visiting the College of Arms in 1971, Sir Conrad Swan, then Conrad Swan, York Herald was my host. I will never forget that visit when he kindly gave me a thorough taste of the beauties of the building and the treasures of its historic and priceless records. He also introduced me to some aspects of the day-to-day practice of a herald and I began my long education in the art and science of heraldry. He was thoughtful, considerate and a thorough gentleman. It was intriguing to learn that we were fellow British Columbians, he more than I, as he was born to a gentry family on southern Vancouver Island.

For more than thirty years, our professional lives have intersected with regular frequency and I have always valued his insights and advice.

But are we not intrigued by the evolution, the character of the lives of our friends, of notable public figures and by their inner thoughts?

In this autobiography, Sir Conrad gives us a vivid and intimate look at his childhood, his parents, his fascinating mixed Canadian, English, Polish and Lithuanian ancestry, his school life in Canada and England, his career as an army officer in India, his work as a professor and as a herald (ultimately Garter Principal King of Arms) and his rich family life from childhood on, culminating in the tragic loss of his beloved wife.

Several sections are extended extracts from diaries, which deepen the immediacy of the picture he paints. His characteristic flashes of humour come through clearly as does his deep Catholic spirituality. There are extensive genealogical charts which amplify his unique multicultural heritage.

Canadian heraldists and historians will be fascinated by his recounting of his part in the development of the Order of Canada, our national flag and the establishment of the Canadian Heraldic Authority. Students of the long history of the College and its heralds will gain a clear sense of the experiences and ideas that have formed him and some of the things he has considered significant along the way.

Heraldry, while central to his life is by no means all of it. You will enjoy his story very much. As a herald and historian, I would like to salute his courage and determination in setting out so much revealing material and giving us his impressions of who and what he encountered and providing the opportunity to view him as a completely rounded human being.

Thank you Conrad, for this special memoir.

Robert D. Watt, AIH, FRHSC, (HON)FHS   *Chancellery of Honours, Rideau Hall*
Chief Herald of Canada   *January 2004*

CHAPTER I

Gentry in the Sticks:
Cowichan – Cricket – Curry and *Country Life*
or
more succinctly
DISPERSIO GENTIS BRITANNICAE

'WHAT SHALL I WEAR for the Coronation?' asked my mother, thinking aloud. 'We shall be out in the open, seated in stands, but it can still rain in May in England.' I am not sure why she had asked us, as her dress sense was unerring. Her formula was: quality plus simplicity of line and detail equals chic; and she was always right. 'A navy blue matching frock and hat,' she answered herself 'and a silk rain coat to match – rolls up into nothing and goes in one's handbag.' So the ensemble for that great occasion was settled and it was soon time for me to go upstairs. It was one of those airless evenings that slouch along the West Coast in summer. To counter this, we had been sitting in the garden under the Maple tree near the rose pergola having a cool drink after dinner.

Soon I lay on my bed with the top covers turned well down, wearing only my pyjama bottoms. It was sometime between 9p.m. and 10p.m., and following the custom of a kind yet regulated family, I had kissed both my parents and gone upstairs at 9p.m. Hasty ablutions had been followed by equally hasty prayers; off went the day clothes, on the pyjamas and so to bed. I was 12 years old.

My bedroom – we always called it the Nursery – had been my whole world for long periods of my childhood, as I had congenital rheumatic fever which kept me in bed for weeks on end. To counteract the pain, one of the medicines prescribed for me by my medical father was called 'Dovers'. It was tipped into a glass of water and drunk by the patient; the basic ingredient was opium. A small bottle of Guinness every day was also prescribed, to put some flesh on my skinny frame. It may be that starting so young on such excellent medicines prevented me from becoming either a drug addict or an alcoholic. I am happy to admit, though, to a long-standing friendship with the distillations of the Highlands and the fermentations of many a vineyard which, with Aquinas, I hold conducive *pro convivialitatem*. But that was an appreciation yet to be developed, and did not concern the boy who lay on his bed on this particular evening.

His current thoughts were filled by something coming from the Indian

Reservation nearby: the monotone chanting of the Somena Tribe. This conspired with the sweaty air to delay the onset of sleep. The Indians – always so referred to at the time (the terms, First Nations/Peoples came much later) – were having a 'Potlatch' – as we Whites called it. Technically, these had been forbidden/banned by the Federal Government in 1884 because of their ruinous expense. So it was simply a ceremony, possibly a name-giving or the formal remembering of a past elder in one of their 'Big Houses' – the name they gave to the buildings used for such events. During these ceremonies Canadian Quarters (25 cent pieces), blankets and other items were handed out to the guests – sometimes again and again – so as to ensure their witness and remembrance of the event.[1] The dull, continual chant insisted: no sleep for now, no sleep for now… So I just lay awake and thought.

The old King (George V) had died some six or more months before[2]. He had been succeeded by his debonair son as Edward VIII. Mother, I knew, had danced with him at the Government House Balls in Victoria given for the Prince of Wales, as he then was, during his several tours of Canada after World War I. She was an ideal partner for such occasions being statuesque, not beautiful but definitely handsome and with great presence. With all this she combined a feminine charm, which concealed a rare ability to organize. Men ate out of her hand; but she always remembered marriage required chastity. Her resultant unattainability made her all the more attractive.

So everyone's 'Prince Charming' was to be crowned next year in May, 1937. Father had decided that Mother and I should go to England to take part in that great occasion. Afterwards I was to be sent to a boarding school there.

I was aware that these would be my last few months for some time in The Nursery. I understood that I would be coming back for the long summer holidays – a journey of about two weeks by boat and train – but the better part of the next five or six years I was to spend at school. For the shorter holidays I would stay with relations in England. A great adventure lay before me. My imagination was fired. There was no temptation now to stick my head between the bars of my old iron bedstead. I had often done that in the past – I found it fun for some reason – until one evening we had one of those occasional tremors caused by the geological fault which runs all along the Pacific Coast of North America. When that happened I could not get my head out: the bars kept moving from left to right – then, after a while, all was still again. At last I extracted myself.

So, as I lay on my bed my eyes passed round the room. Near the head of the bed, to my right, was the wide-open window, letting in the Reservation's ceaseless monotone. Directly opposite, on the far side, was the door onto the

---

[1] This is an essential element in an oral-based culture – as it was with the Celtic Irish and Welsh, and is to this day with the Maoris.
[2] 20 January, 1936

landing. Later on, my parents would poke their heads round that door and, if I was awake, wish me good night and 'God bless you' before they retired. They usually appeared as a silhouette against the light on the landing which shone all night.

On the right of that door, as I faced it, the wall was filled with shelves. On these was my 'museum', crammed with exhibits – all neatly labelled. They included some local Indian artefacts such as a small Totem Pole, coloured with vegetable dyes and not modern paint, some basketwork and a canoe-bailer made of bark: so different to those plastic so-called Indian pieces (made in Japan!) for the tourists.

Then there were my coins: among them a Queen Victoria Diamond Jubilee Shilling with the old Queen's effigy – double chin and all – on the obverse, and a shield of the Royal Arms ensigned by the Imperial Crown on the reverse – a beautiful piece in mint condition. It was a gift from my maternal grandmother. Yet again, there were a dozen or so *pice*: a minute silver former coin each about the size of half my finger-nail (worth 1/64 of a Rupee!) which had been given to me by the wife of an Indian Army officer retired to Cowichan, Lieutenant-Colonel James Hodding. He conducted on his property there one of the several local establishments where young gentry from Britain learned about farming in the Province prior to buying their own farms. They were known as Mud Pups – and generally added a touch of dash to local society. Mrs Hodding used to thrill me with tales of life down on the maidans, and up in the hill stations of India.

Passing the door to the left was the toy cupboard. Usually, it was crammed to bursting in complete disarray. However, from time to time a *diktat* would emanate from Mother that the mess *must* be tidied up. There was no room for discussion.

Finally, past the toy cupboard was the altar – the top of a chest of drawers – where my brother, Peter, and I 'celebrated Mass'. At least, he was always the celebrant (being five years my senior; there is such a thing as precedence) and I was a species of deacon, as everything was madly Tridendine and pre-Vatican II. Fortescue, (the author of the then standard work on the Roman liturgy,[3]) would have been proud of that alter: gradines, three candles on either side, vases for flowers and in the centre a tabernacle. This latter had been made from one of those beautiful cigar boxes, with all its gold tin-foil inside, which had been presented to Peter and me by our maternal grandfather (an Anglican and Mason!). Inside the tabernacle we had a large silver egg-cup which served as a Ciborium. The hosts – made of flour and water – were a little tacky, but we took such details in our stride.

Peter went on to become a distinguished priest, survived the (now past) upheavals of Vatican II, and distinguished himself as an academic administrator

---

[3] Fortescue, Adrian, *The Mass. A Study of the Roman Liturgy*. Longmans, Green & Co. London. New York, Toronto 1912.

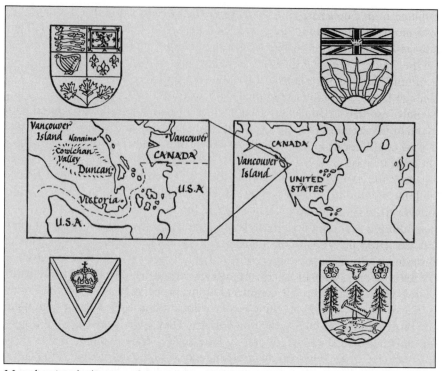

Map showing the location of the Cowichan Valley and Duncan on Vancouver Island. The arms are: upper left, Canada; upper right, British Columbia; lower left, Victoria, the Provincial capital; lower right, Duncan, the civic centre of the Valley.

and a Thomistic philosopher specializing in medical ethics – which with a father like ours was surely highly appropriate.

Little did I realize, but what then passed before my eyes as they scanned the room on that evening was, in a sense, an earnest of my future life: concern with, and devotion to, monarchy, heraldry, numismatics, and India, as well as a spirituality in accordance with the Roman tradition.

I was soon to leave that room, never, as it turned out, to return; but clearly etched for me there was a map of the years to come.

★   ★   ★

Home and Father

Home for us was a large, old frame house built about 1910. It stood in extensive grounds and garden and was surrounded by a close boarded, stout wooden fence 6ft high. It was called *Harrow Weald,* after some property owned by my maternal grandfather in England in Middlesex. The house was situated on Kenneth Street in Duncan. In Cowichan, at that time, there was none of that Napoleonic mania for numbering houses as if they were all identical and occupied by people of a sausage-like sameness!

The City of Duncan, incorporated in 1912, was, in fact, a very pleasant, small community in our day, consisting of some 2,000 'with or without souls', as Stephen Leacock would have said. The centre of the social and commercial life of the Cowichan Valley, it was situated in the southeastern part of Vancouver Island in the Province of British Columbia.

One could not describe Duncan as a mistake, exactly, but it certainly was not intended to exist, by some at least. When the Esquimalt and Nanaimo Railway was built the nearest station was to be elsewhere. However, on 11 August 1886 Sir John A Macdonald, the Prime Minister of Canada, drove the last symbolic spike of that railway at a spot near Shawnigan Lake. Sir John, Robert Dunsmuir (the owner of the railway) and their party then climbed back into the train on this inaugural passenger run and proceeded towards Nanaimo. However, at Duncan's Crossing the train was brought to a halt by a concourse of local residents, their ladies, their Indian neighbours, the Sisters of St Ann and their school children and the pupils of Miss Monk's school.

The strength of their welcome was equalled only by the force of their representations that Duncan's Crossing should be a regular stop. Hurried conferring took place between the Prime Minister (doubtless not unaware of such a clutch of potential votes) and Dunsmuir (ever on the look out for future business possibilities). A decision was taken, and, as the train moved off again the latter called out from the observation platform to the assembled gathering, 'You'll get your station, boys!'

Our house, as so often the case in that part of the world, was covered with cedar shingles, painted dark brown with cream trim. Oblong bay windows fronted the house: to the right was that of the music room; that to the left, Father's Waiting Room for his patients. Hanging in the windows of the latter bay were oblong pieces of plate glass inscribed in gold letters, to the left, 'H P Swan, MD' (HP for Henry Peter) and to the right, 'Physician and Surgeon'. Having arrived on the porch by wide shallow steps, there was a choice of doors: that straight ahead led into the house; the one on the left to the patients' Waiting Room which, in turn, led into the Consulting Room and so on into the Surgery where minor operations could be carried out.

Above this area – where people came to seek consultations, examinations, diagnoses and prescriptions in the face of those ills of the flesh to which man is heir – there was a *secret* known only to our parents and us boys: our play room. On its floor, my brother's beautiful electric train was set up permanently. It was a Hornby of the *Orient Express* variety, correct in every detail. It ran through countryside, where little leaden sheep, horses and cows grazed (these were mostly mine, as I have always tended towards the bucolic); and on through

*A university Vice-Chancellor and a King of Arms in potencia: left, Peter Julian Michael
Swan and right, his brother the Author, aged 8 and 3, respectively. 1927.*

towns complete with miniature houses; through *papier mâché* ravines, valleys and
mountains; over level crossings and bridges; came to and stopped at stations – or,
if the train was an express, raced through them; went off into sidings, obeyed
signals (always!) and so on. It gave us measureless pleasure and kept us busy for
hours, especially in the cold or wet – to which the Coast is no stranger.

A brick chimney stack from the Consulting Room fire rose through the room
at a point about two thirds of the way across the floor. This made a convenient
and suitable frontier for Peter's 'country' – after all he was the elder. The
remaining third was mine. We devised a constitution for each, and he and I were
sovereign heads of contiguous but independent countries.

Now obviously, with patients baring their minds, souls and bodies in the
rooms beneath us, the yelling and chaos of boys at play was definitely not on. So
Peter and I learned how to have an uproarious time, but quietly: it taught us
discipline.

While *Harrow Weald* was not situated among the shops it was near the centre of town. As a result, its drawing room was frequently lent by my parents for receptions when dignitaries visited Duncan and the local people wished to attend upon them: such included the personal representative of the Sovereign, the Lieutenant-Governor, the two Bishops of the Island, Catholic as well as Anglican, and other persons of eminence.

Further persons who availed themselves of my parents' co-operation in this regard were the Officers of the 16th Canadian Scottish – a Militia Unit. Their receptions usually preceded balls held in the Agricultural Hall: that centre not only of agricultural and horticultural shows, but also of theatricals and all manner of social events in the extremely social Cowichan Valley.

Father's Duties as MO

My father was the Medical Officer of this Regiment, being a Major in the Royal Canadian Army Medical Corps. It was not, however, the custom for medical officers to wear a Corps uniform, but rather that of the Regiment. Father, about 6ft tall, with a build most useful in a rugby scrum, looked terrific in his kilt. Like many well built men, he was extremely light on his feet at ballroom and highland dancing. The only trouble with the kilt for him, as he used to say, was the fact that no sooner had he put it on, along with boiled shirt and Mess kit coat, and had stuck his Skean-do firmly in his stocking, than Mrs X, Y or Z would throw herself into labour! This happened so frequently that a subaltern had always to be detailed to look after the MO's lady if he had to pick up his bag and attend an *accouchement*, or some other emergency.

On mornings after such nights before, when Mother had danced away the hours, while Father – in the manner of a Greek chorus – had been saying 'push', breakfast was a little later than usual. Accordingly, at the appointed hour Peter and I would appear and take that meal with our parents, as we did all meals (except during term time, when we had a packed lunch at school, or when Father had been called out on a case). This almost invariable eating together meant table talk had an almost limitless range. This included medical topics. Father would recount these and many other episodes of a busy practice. This table talk education could hardly have been better.

Then, naturally at the same time, manners were inculcated: having the courtesy to see that everyone else had what they needed; and learning to wait patiently until everyone had finished, whereupon Mother would ring the little silver bell from Birks to let the maid know that it was time to serve the next course. Grace was always said before and after each meal from which one learned the importance of saying, 'Please' and 'Thank you'. At the time this reminded us that one could not expect three square meals a day to appear inevitably: we were in the middle of the Great Depression.

Groups of men, desperate for work, roamed from town to town. Not infrequently, one would go into the Consulting Room and ask my father for money for a meal. This was always refused. However, the man was told that at meal times, if he went round the side of the house to the kitchen door at the back, he would be provided with a meal.

My father always paid his bills so promptly the local tradesmen quipped, 'Dr Swan pays before the ink is dry!' Accordingly, he expected his patients to meet his accounts promptly, if not with quite such dispatch. In this connection one must recall at this time all medicine was Private, there being no Medicare or other universal Health Service. If, however, a patient – because of the Depression, or for some other reason – had little or no money, some way had to be found whereby he could meet his financial obligations. Father considered it essential for the patient's self respect that he discharge his debts in one way or another: in kind or service, if necessary. As a result, we had the garden tended by a patient who, so to speak, had several green thumbs. Another knew how to make bread so our supply of that commodity came from her, usually in the form of cottage loaves. The two magnificent silver fox furs which Mother would sling over her shoulders, when it was highly fashionable for ladies to wear them, told the silent story that twins had been delivered of the wife of a local fox farmer; and so on. There was no end to this barter.

Father's Faith

Father had a great appreciation of the dignity of each human being – be he prince or peasant – holding him created by God with a particular destiny which he, and he alone, could fulfil, and for whom Christ had died in the great act of redemption: all perfectly straightforward, orthodox, Christian theology. Such were among the principles he held and applied throughout his life and, never more so than when faced with the practical problems of the Great Depression.

As to my father's formal religious position, he was a Catholic, holding Christ's Vicar on earth to be the Bishop of Rome.

To my father all this was as plain as a pikestaff, and he acted accordingly. It could be said of him that he had *cette foi granitique des Polonais* (about which see more in Chapter III). In his religious observance he was as meticulous as in his medical practice he was prophylactic – and I use that term in its strict medical, clinical meaning of sterilized cleanliness. As a result of this rock-solid devotion to Catholicism he was in no way diffident in what today would be called the ecumenical. This attitude is all the rage nowadays. However, during the first half of the twentieth century such a stance was regarded with grave suspicion by most English-speaking Catholics as a misleading Anglican idea, even if Continental Catholics, French in particular, were much more sympathetic. The English Catholics said that the latter did not fully understand the actual position within the theologically inclusive Church of England. Be that as it may, mercifully Vatican II reminded the Faithful that the Holy Ghost was not restricted as to his movements. If he were, then the Fathers of the Church, when putting together the various writings we now call the Bible, would have had to miss out everything from Genesis to Maccabees – in other words over three-quarters of the total text.

One example of his spiritual position was that Father never charged a Protestant minister of religion, nor his wife, nor his children – when living under the parental roof – a single cent in respect of his medical attendance. The reason for this was that he admired these ministers as men of principle who loved Our Blessed Lord so much that they sacrificed what otherwise could have been highly profitable careers in the world. Yet again, he would willingly acknowledge and applaud those tenets of their doctrine that accorded with those of the Apostolic See and so taken as orthodox. On the other hand, if pressed – and he was in no sense aggressive in religion – he would sadly point out their heterodox views. Naturally, he included the local RC priests and nuns in this arrangement of holding what might be called, 'honorary accounts' with him. Little wonder that he seemed to have cornered the clerical market!

China Town
and
Other Exotic Patients

This was all very well and good, but he had a wife and two children to support so let us now pass to consider – indeed cherish! – some of the other patients who made such charity possible. The practice was large, not unlucrative, and the list of patients exotic in parts. These included a number of Chinese who, after their own custom – so well described in Denise Chong's *The Concubine's Children*[4] – maintained their own area, up near Duncan's Police Station. We always referred to it as 'China Town'.

The headman in the local China Town was named Sue Lam Bing. He had come to Duncan in 1910 and became prominent in business there. My father relied upon him for translations when in attendance upon the Chinese patients. He and Father got on well together, and upon occasion, if my parents felt like a Chinese meal of an evening, a telephone call to the redoubtable Mr Sue Lam Bing, of a thousand interests, produced a marvellous assortment of dishes brought round to the house on a felt covered tray.

From time to time, Peter and I would be taken by our father to shop in China Town. There were one or two emporia that seemed to sell everything. Once having stepped over the threshold of one of these shops one entered another world: tea was in large lacquered containers, spices in innumerable drawers in cabinets behind the counters, over which hung meat – what parts of the animal's anatomy were they?, we wondered – obviously cured by some form of smoking; root ginger, in squat, earthenware jars, glazed on the inside and sealed with a

---

[4] Penguin Books Edition 1996

bung that kept in the ginger amid a mass of rich syrup, was available; as well as delicious lychee nuts – both favourites with our family. When Halloween approached, a stock of fireworks had to be got from these disciplined and masterly pyromaniacs.

There was, without exception, a wonderful aroma – oriental, inviting, mysterious – about these shops which doubtless the owners did not notice at all. On the other hand, it is probable that they immediately noted how we Europeans smelt – to them, we are told on the best authority, most unpleasantly – but they were far too polite to allude to that. Being in commerce, they probably would have agreed with the Roman Emperor Vespasian[5] who, when his courtiers expostulated with him over his taxing lavatories replied, 'The money doesn't smell'!

The service was attentive and efficient, though the faces of those who served were inscrutable. In one corner there was, without exception, someone working out the complicated finances of the establishment on an abacus with the balls flying up and down their threaded rods at lightening speed.

Loath as one was to leave these shops, one was always relieved to be able to walk out in the reassuring presence of Father – whom all the attendants seemed to know. He regarded them with a benign and understanding smile. But, so intoxicating was the atmosphere that I could see myself being whisked off in one of those beautifully carved Chinese chests aboard a junk, and ending up a tea boy in some Mandarin's palace – or even in an opium den. It was not that I had – or have to this day – ever had the honour of being presented to a Mandarin, nor the experience of penetrating an opium den, but a child's imagination can be fertile, and mine certainly was.

Further Exotic Patients
Japanese and Sikhs

I do not recall my father having many Japanese patients, though one of our maids, Tenaka – about whom more later – naturally, was one.

The first Sikhs arrived in 1904, attracted by the opportunities in lumbering. Almost without exception, everyone in the Cowichan Valley referred to them as Hindus. Genealogically, they descended from Hindus but Sikhism is completely different from Hinduism being, among other points, monotheistic and with no caste system.

In my time the leader of the community in the Cowichan Valley was Mayo Singh from the Punjab. He was the owner of the Mayo Mill which had been founded in 1917 and located to the west of North Cowichan (since 1936 called Paldi after his native village in the Punjab – from which part of India most of the Sikhs come.). Here were developed great logging and milling operations, from

---

[5] Emperor, AD 69-79

the profits of which Mayo Singh was a generous benefactor to local worthy causes, especially hospitals.

My father had many Sikh patients including Mr Mayo Singh, and from time to time we boys would visit the mill, when Father was on one of his rounds. We would see there great logs being thrown about like matchsticks by large and ingenious machines.

At one point, we acquired a wonderful fancy dress of a raja's costume which I wanted to wear when riding my horse in a charity carnival. Obviously, if I was to be a proper raja I must have a turban – but how? Mr Mayo Singh came to the rescue. He dispatched an old Sikh to *Harrow Weald* to be my turban guru[6]. He arrived with yard upon yard of fine muslin and patiently practised me again and again in tying a turban correctly until I got it right.

My guru also taught me that beautiful greeting of the Sikhs: 'Sat Siri Akal' (God is truth), which is used on those occasions when we might say: 'How do you do?' 'Good evening', and so on. Some 45 years later, in 1982, I had the honour of being a Gentleman-in-Waiting upon His Holiness Pope John Paul II during his visit to Great Britain. It fell to me, upon one occasion, to help explain to some Sikh religious leaders what the form would be when the Holy Father entered the room in Archbishop's House, Westminster – the residence of Cardinal Hume – where the Pope was to greet them. I remembered to start off what I had to say with, Sat Siri Akal – smiles broke out amid luxuriant black beards worn close to the chin in the Sikh manner. Urdu, learnt when I was in the Indian Army was then available for the detailed instructions. They all conducted themselves thereafter as if they had been in Papal circles for years – thanks to my turban guru.

More Patients
The Indians – The Cowichan Peoples

Though not 'the Indian doctor', as the phrase went, meaning the medical practitioner provided by the Government for the local Cowichans, Father had a number as patients.

Their home, Cowichan – Quwutsun – the name of a river, valley and bay means, 'the warm land' – and had been so for those people for something like 25 times the age of the European presence in North America. Judging by archaeological remains that means something in the order of 5,000 years. In other words, when the Pyramids were being built in Egypt, the Cowichan peoples were living on their ancestral acres.

My father's patients among the Cowichan peoples were mainly from the Quamichan, the Khenipsin and the Somena tribes. He had a great advantage

---

[6] 'guru' simply means 'teacher' – one can have a tennis guru, a mathematics guru and so on. It does not inevitably mean a spiritual teacher though that is what some western people who have just discovered oriental spirituality, would have us believe.

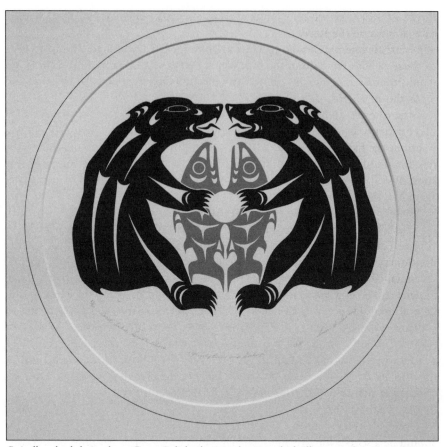

Spindle whorl design by a Coast Salish aboriginal artist which illustrates the aim common to both totemic as well as heraldic artists of capturing the quiddity of the subject, and so in this case: ursine of the Grizzly and piscatorial of the Sockeye.

when attending them in that he spoke fluent Chinook[7] which he had learned as a boy when spending his summer holidays at Coquitlam on the mainland near New Westminster. It is, in reality, a *lingua franca*, intended for use between Indians who spoke different languages, as well as between Indians and Whites. It has a short vocabulary and simple syntax. It is not exactly the best vehicle for discussing the more esoteric insights of theology, but excellent for telling the doctor whether the pain is in one's gut or some other part of the anatomy.

At times the Indian patients would come to my father in his surgery at *Harrow*

[7] Technically Chinook Jargon, but during the 19th century, and on into the middle of the 20th century, it was common usage in British Columbia to refer to it simply as, Chinook. The language of the Chinook Indians (the core of Chinook Jargon) is a very difficult one and different from Chinook Jargon.

Weald, at others he would, as was common practice at the time, visit, them in their homes on the Reservations. When there with him on such visits I came to admire their totemic carvings. Later I realized the common aim of their artists as of those of Western heraldry in that both seek the quiddity – the aquilinity, the leoninity and so on – of the subject and not zoological reproduction.

As these patients had the availability of the Indian Doctor without charge, by coming to my father they were private patients on an equal footing with all his other patients, be they of whatever hue. As a result, one aspect of the professional relationship had to be settled, without exception, before the attendance: the consultation fee. One could not sue an Indian for non-payment of debts, being a ward of the government. The Indians understood this completely.

White Advent

The first White person to come to the Cowichan Valley was almost certainly the Oblate Father, the Reverend H. Lempfirt, who included Cowichan Bay in a missionary tour in April, 1850. Nine years later, the Reverend Peter Rondeault was detailed, at his own request, to take charge of the mission to the 'murderous' Cowichans, as they were described at the time. He departed from Victoria with a sack of flour, his breviary and his gun[8]. Far from threatening him with death, the Indians received him in a friendly manner and even built him a log church and a house in which he conducted a school – the first in the Cowichan Valley. Further, he was instrumental in the building of the church on Comiaken Hill at Cowichan Bay, long known as the Old Stone Church (1869-70): the oldest stone building in the whole of the Province.

The Catholic Ordinary of the whole of the Island, the Right Reverend Modeste Demers, 1st Bishop of Victoria (1847-71)[9] was anxious that there should be a school for girls in Cowichan. To that end he approached the recently formed Sisters of St Ann of Montreal who were already in his Diocese. As a result, two of the sisters were sent up from Victoria to make a reconnaissance. They went both overland and by canoe to Tzouhalem, the projected site for the school. Bearing in mind the voluminous religious habits (uniforms) of the period – which reached right to the ground – to get a nun, so clothed, into a canoe must have been akin to asking a Guardsman of the Governor General's Foot Guard – in full uniform, bearskin and all – to squeeze into an Austin Mini. However, the report the Sisters brought back was favourable, and their Order duly opened an Indian boarding school in Cowichan in 1864.

---

[8] Boshauwers, Rev. Francis, SMM, 'Early Cowichan Valley' *The Orphans Friend*, Victoria, BC, Vol. 25 no 10, 29 October, 1939 p.3

[9] From 1847-63 the Diocese included not only Vancouver Island but also the whole of present day British Columbia as well as Russian America (Alaska). By an Apostolic Brief of 14 December, 1863 a Vicariate Apostolic was created on the mainland and the Diocese of Victoria reached its present confines of Vancouver Island and the adjacent islands.

Among the domestic skills taught to the pupils was knitting. This was later to prove advantageous in the production, by the local Indians, of their famous sweaters. It will be recalled how that Beau Brummell of the time, the Prince of Wales, later King Edward VIII, was happy to wear one such when out golfing; the lanolin not being completely removed from the wool of these sweaters made them ideal as rain repellents. The local IODE, when my mother was Regent, arranged for this addition to the prince's wardrobe. My father had as patients the successors of these intrepid ladies who came to our area in 1864.

Two years before the founding of this Indian boarding school, on 18 August, 1862 HMS *Hecate* sailed out of Victoria and landed the first party of European settlers at Cowichan Bay on the same day at about 4 o'clock. They comprised some 78 who formed the original nucleus of the White inhabitants of Cowichan. These have grown to several thousands during the intervening one and a half centuries down to the present day. They were brought by the Governor, Sir James Douglas, KCB[10] who, by and large, was an outstanding administrator. However, his arrangements over the entry of White settlers into the Cowichan Valley – or more accurately in certain respects the lack of them – have been a source of difficulties for both the local tribes and the Whites ever since[11].

The problem of aboriginal land rights is not new, and has exercised some great minds, like that of the Dominican Bishop, Bartolome de las Casas (1474-1566) who wrote on this subject as it affected Spanish America some three centuries before the Cowichan problems[12] appear to have arisen. However, this matter did not prevent Cowichans of our day seeking out as patients my father's aid, nor our personal friendly relations with them.

Life for these early settlers was incredibly hard. Rolling well-tilled fields had to be created out of the dense West Coast forests.

The man, after a day's hard toil, would come home exhausted, to be met by a wife equally worn out from trying to make a home out of one or two rooms in a log house. She would cook him his dinners on a fieldstone fireplace with its stick and clay chimney; running water was in her dreams. Meals had to be prepared for all, and these could include not only husband and children but also servant help as well as the hired hands who lived with them. Coming in from sweating all day on the land, the nearest thing to a bath would be to strip off behind the barn and get one of the lads to empty from its roof a bucket of cold water or two over one's aching body. Crawling into bed at night after such labours, it is

---

[10] Governor of Vancouver Island, 1851-63 and of British Columbia, 1858-64. He was an early Knight Commander of the Most Honourable Order of the Bath in its recently reconstituted form under its Great Master, Albert the Prince Consort.

[11] For a most scholarly presentation of the Indian case *Vide,* Dr Daniel P. Marshall's, *Those Who Fell from the Sky*. Cultural and Education Centre, Cowichan Tribes, Duncan, British Columbia, 1999.

[12] De las Casas, Bartolome. *La Historia de Las Indias*. Originally published in 5 volumes, Madrid, 1875-76; modern editions (2 volumes) Madrid, 1958 and 3 volumes, Mésàco, 1951 & 66.

remarkable that they had the energy for anything but sleep. Fortunately, God had other ideas and the race continued!

The sometime Cowichan resident and later Bard of the Yukon, Robert Service, captured so often in verse the qualities of perseverance needed if those early hard-pressed, pioneers were to succeed – poems my father could recite from memory, one after the other. Possibly, the last verse of *The Quitter* sums up what was needed:

> But to fight and to fight when hope's out of sight –
> Why that's the best game of them all
> And though you come out of each gruelling bout
> All broken and beaten and scarred,
> Just have one more try – it's dead easy to die.
> It's the keeping-on-living that's hard.[13]

I have some idea myself how gruelling work out of doors in the country can be, not simply under the blazing sun of India when in the Army there, but even here where I write this, on a property in Suffolk occupied and tilled since before its recording in Domesday Book, 1086.

When I come in, exhausted after such a day, a hot bath – with a glass of Black Label on a table nearby, followed by a glass or two of Chardonnay or Chateauneuf du Pape, does wonders – and so to bed. Whereupon Hilda, my late wife – blissful creature – used to say that I was at my best after a hard day's physical work. Having admitted that, humility and truth contend, but delicacy trumps them!

So before saying more that's best not said in the drawing room, let us turn to other matters and note that the greater part of the 1862 White settlers were Protestants – including Methodists and Presbyterians – though probably the majority were as we would say nowadays, Anglicans. Following their arrival itinerant Clergy of that communion visited Cowichan from time to time.

In 1866 these matters were put on a firm basis by the Right Reverend George Hills, Bishop of British Columbia – his *sedes* was in Victoria – with the appointment as resident clergyman of the Reverend William Sheldon Reece, one of Hills' promising young men. Next year the first St Peter's Church – of logs – was built at Quamichan on the site of the present church, under his direction. Mr Reece was also instrumental in the founding not only of the Cowichan and Salt Spring Island Agricultural Society, but also the Lending Library and Library Institute – several features of the future intellectual, social and scientific life of the Cowichan Valley were thus beginning to take shape. These foundations were typical of the contributions made to the general life of a community by so many of the Anglican Clergy of the day in Canada.

Those who came from Britain were characteristic of the period: almost always

---

[13] *Collected Verse of Robert Service*. Ernest Bern of London, 1960, Vol I p. 283.

the younger sons of the gentry and the products of some of the best public schools (in the English sense of private, fee-paying schools) of the time. They had a good idea of what amenities helped to contribute to a civilized social order, and as often as not were in the forefront in obtaining them.

Among the pioneer families who were patients of my father, possibly it was the Castleys I knew best. Doubtless, this stemmed from the fact that one of them, Edna, married my mother's brother, Claude Alfred John Green, and in time became my favourite aunt. As a result, I had ample opportunity to learn about the family when sharing with her a love of antiques, as well as learning much about horticulture, of which she was one of the cognoscenti.

Her extensive garden at their home, *Pentrilew* on Grieve Road which sloped down and led the eye towards a magnificent view of Somenos Lake, was known among the many luxuriant gardens up and down the West Coast for, among other flora, its collection of every known species of daffodil.

There was something special about this good-looking, knowledgeable, well-dressed lady who, for as long as I can remember, was topped with a mass of well-groomed white hair. Her dark eyebrows added definition to a face full of character, but one which immediately put people at ease – often with an engaging smile.

One of my earliest childhood memories (I was rising 5) was attending her and my uncle Claude's wedding in July 1928 in Christchurch Cathedral, Victoria.

After the wedding, my parents and I accompanied the bride and groom to Seattle for their honeymoon. Later in life I came to think what odd things some people do! It is to be hoped that the young couple were left alone upon occasion during that visit. Certainly, all four of them – my parents, aunt and uncle – got on marvellously for the rest of their lives after that, so presumably the bridal pair did not object to what some might have called an intrusion.

Another of my Seattle memories is of driving with my parents – and Claude and Edna were definitely not with us then – when something caught my eye and I called out, 'Oh, look there's Jesus in gumboots'. It was in fact, one of those innumerable statues one sees in the United States of its first President, George Washington, in full military uniform, complete with Wellingtons. Up to that time, my main experience of iconography had been confined to statues of Christ, Our Lady and so on in churches, convents and at home.

I was quickly put right, and it was explained that as far as we were concerned, the statue was of an arch rebel who had led about one third of the population of the American Colonies to deny their natural allegiance[14]. It was a classic case of the old ditty:-

---

[14] Benjamin Franklin calculated that about 1/3 supported those we regarded as rebels (Patriots to themselves), 1/3 (Tories to the rebels) supported the Crown (and later became the United Empire Loyalists and founders of new Brunswick and Upper Canada (Ontario)) while the balance 'sat on the fence' in Philadelphia (the rebel headquarters) and elsewhere to see which way to jump.

Treason doth never prosper, what's the reason?
For if it prosper, none dare call it treason![15]

My Aunt's family of Castley descends from Thomas Castley (born 1669) through his son John (born 1698) of *The Thorn*, Rosgill in the Eastern part of the Lake District of Westmoreland (now Cumbria) in North West England. It was Henry Thomas Castley (b. 1833 – fifth in descent from Thomas) who came to Cowichan in 1887 soon after the railway was put through. The fourth son of Henry was Elias – to whom the early development of Cowichan and beyond owes an immense debt of gratitude – was the father of my aunt Edna[16].

★　　★　　★

This brings us to consider, briefly, the largest contingent of my father's practice who were also part of my family's and so my own social life: the Gentlemen Emigrants. They were a phenomenon of Canadian history which stretched back to the post Napoleonic War period when half-pay officers were settled round Lake Ontario. Similarly, and still more important for the West, were those who came following the Crimean war and, finally, those attracted by the discovery of gold in British Columbia in 1858. As a result of this continuing movement, by about 1890, the largest contingent in Canada of the Gentlemen Emigrants was to be found in the Cowichan Valley.

Their contribution to the development of Canada – economic, administrative and generally establishing a civilized style of life wherever they settled – was incalculable.

In Cowichan, where my father fought the good fight with scalpel and stethoscope, the Kings Daughters Hospital was erected to a great extent through the efforts of a classic example of this group, Frederick Maitland-Dougall, of the Earls of Lauderdale[17], and his Southern Belle wife, Bessie[18].

It was he who also founded the South Cowichan Lawn Tennis Club (1886) –

---

[15] Sir John Harington (1561-1612)

[16] In writing about the Castleys, in addition to what my aunt, Edna Castley (Mrs Claude Green) told me, I am also much indebted to the paper written by her husband, my uncle, in July, 1982 for the 95th anniversary of the arrival in the Cowichan Valley of Henry Thomas Castley and his wife, Eliza, and the reunion of all their living descendants held on July 24th of that year to mark this occasion. This paper is preserved in the SSA: *misc. papers.*

[17] The earliest entry concerning the Maitlands, Earls of Lauderdale at the Court of the Lord Lyon in the Public Register of all Arms and Bearings in Scotland is Vol. 1 folio 34 (*c*.1672); and concerning the Arms *vide* also *Roll of Scottish Arms* (1969) p.236 concerning James (Maitland) 8th Earl of Lauderdale and the matriculation of Arms, 29th July, 1790, Vol. 1 pp34 & 35. *Burkes Peerage and Baronetage*, 1999 Vol. 2 pp. 1642-46. Although by the time Frederick arrived in Cowichan the full name of the family was Heriot-Maitland-Dougall he was always known as Maitland-Dougall.

[18] *Memories Never Lost – Stories of the pioneer women of the Cowichan Valley and a brief history of the Valley 1850-1920*. Compiled by the Pioneer Researchers. 1986 pp. 134, 142, 194, 248-250.

second only in age, throughout the whole of the Empire, to Wimbledon, founded nine years earlier. On its courts my parents passed many happy hours.

Watching cricket matches is another of my earliest memories. One of these was on 17 June, 1932. It was one of those brilliant occasions with the Australian XI led by the greatest batsman of all time, Sir Donald Bradman – actually on his honeymoon. My maternal grandfather, Alfred Edward Green contributed in the glory of that day for the Cowichan Cricket Club (CCC). Stan McCabe – second only to Bradman as a batsman – already having scored 150 runs, hit the ball with tremendous force and sent it almost out of sight. Yet it was caught with ease by my grandfather standing in the outer field: to have thus invited such a brilliant player off the field was the high point of his cricketing career. The CCC was founded by EW Carr-Hilton and has had matches now for almost 100 years, two World Wars alone interrupting play[19].

Post 1867 the federal Government much encouraged Gentlemen Emigrants to come to Canada as a counter balance to the increasing immigration from Eastern Europe.

The one thing that all Gentlemen Emigrants had in common was that they were gentlemen. Nowadays, this word frequently means nothing more than male as distinct from female, or a lavatory for men. For the period referred to it meant that they were either armigerous, or had been educated in schools for the education of such gentry, and so moved easily in those circles of society.

All regarded themselves, and were known, as Gentlemen Emigrants not Immigrants. They were British and always remained so. As Sir Clive Phillips-Wolley[20] – of Cowichan and Woodhall, Oak Bay, Victoria – expressed it, carved over the entrance of the latter this quotation from Horace, *Caelum non animum mutant qui trans mare currant*, for which, I trust you will agree with my running translation, 'Those who cross the seas change their sky but not their soul.' They saw themselves as British Subjects who had simply moved from one area of the Crown's jurisdiction to another.

Early on, the Statute of Westminster (1931) was still a long way off. Nevertheless, even after its passage onto the Statute Books, this was a general attitude in Cowichan right down to World War II. It was well expressed in the 1930s by my mother when, upon landing in Seattle for a day's shopping, she was

---

[19] During World War II, with the younger members away fighting, although there were no matches nevertheless the taxes on the CCC grounds had to be met so my maternal grandfather, uncle Claude Green and W.T. Corbishley shared this between them.

[20] One might describe him as a 'Renaissance Man and Big Game Hunter'. He was a man of many parts: poet, author (*One of the Broken Brigade*, Smith, Elder, London 1897; *The Trottings of a Tenderfoot*, Richard Bentley & Son, London, 1884 etc); had copper mine interests in northern B.C.; a steam paddle-wheeler and pack train into the Klondike gold fields, and so on. Upon the recommendation of the Canadian Prime Minister he was made a Knight Bachelor (1915) particularly for his work on behalf of the Navy League. For his genealogical and armorial registrations, *vide* C.A.R., 1.65/260 and Grs LIX.264 respectively.

asked by the US Immigration Official, 'Are you an immigrant?' At that, Mother pulled herself up to her full height, and looking this wretched man in the eye replied, 'Most certainly not, Officer, I am a British Subject by birth.' The reaction of the poor man is not recorded!

> Life in Cowichan was extremely active what
> With bridge and teas and tennis too
> There really is a lot to do,
> And every week we have a dance;
> It doesn't give a man a chance
> To get the little chores done...
> A chap must have a little fun[21]

as Mud-Pup told his chum. The dances referred to were usually those of this or that athletic club and often held at their own premises. If one enjoyed equitation – I developed a life-long interest in this in Cowichan – there was much of that, including gymkhanas, amateur races and polo, with its own grounds just south of Duncan. Oddly enough one could not ride to hounds in that area. The nearest pack that I can remember was the Fraser Valley Hunt, on the mainland, but that was just a little far if one had to be home for dinner. Fishing could be had for the asking. At Mill Bay, where we often took a house for part of the summer, I had hours of pleasure fishing. With a line over the stern of a dinghy, and one of us rowing while the others played the line with its spoon, bright beads and baited hook, we would be back at the house in an hour or so with the main course for dinner. It was usually young small salmon. When gutted, cleaned and grilled one could almost taste the salt! For the more venturesome there were Cohos, Bluebacks and Springs available in tidal waters, with Steelhead and other trout in the rivers and lakes.

Although later in life I developed a liking for shooting, as befitted a future Master of the Gunmakers Company (one of the Livery Companies of the City of London), none of us shot when living in the Cowichan Valley. It was not that we were against shooting. Rather, I think that the number of men wounded when out shooting in the woods who were brought to the surgery at *Harrow Weald* tended to put us off. However, game was plentiful: buck along with willow grouse, pheasants, duck and geese. Elk, the largest game on The Island, was to be sought around Cowichan Lake and, in my day, there was a bounty on cougars.

The annual Cowichan Bay Regatta was much enjoyed, with all manner of aquatic sports. The races included the Indians in their great war canoes making a magnificent spectacle. The first Agricultural Hall was built in Duncan in 1890 and it, and its successor, were the scenes of agricultural and horticultural shows,

---

[21] Mutter, Jean. *Mud-Pups* (privately printed). From internal evidence this was some time between 1939 and 1945. The authoress was a resident of Cowichan.

theatricals and balls. Of the latter, Mud-Pup tells us of one which was an annual event, observing:

> The New Year's ball is quite the thing,
> We'll all be there to dance and sing
> The old year out and the new year in
> And make a really rousing din.
> But come along we'd better dress –
> Tails, of course, and heaven bless
> The ladies, they're a real delight;
> They'll wear their gayest gowns to-night.
> Even the smartest will be there
> With jewels flashing; old Mayfair
> Couldn't put on a finer show…
> It will be jolly don't you know[22]

Garden parties were not unusual in season. They were held in many a garden that would make the Royal Horticultural Society sit up – blessed as they are with a climate and soil that encourage luxurious growth. Dinner parties (always black tie) were frequent, and weddings called for morning coats, of course. Majhong parties were another favourite and would be held in houses often filled with family antiques – some of them of museum standard. And if the host and hostess had lived, at one time, in the Orient then domestic furnishings included *objets d'art et de vertu* reflective of India, China and points East. In the summer there were picnics and clam-bakes (at Cowichan, Maple and Mill Bays – excellent seafood available on this Coast). In short, one had almost every sort of diversion the Gentleman Emigrant considered conducive to a civilized existence. Up to World War II, at the least, everyone in Cowichan would have described life there as definitely gay – (*in sensu antiquam*[23] – of course!)

★   ★   ★

These memoirs can not be a detailed enquiry into the Gentlemen Emigrant phenomenon in Canada and Cowichan in particular, fascinating though it is. Nevertheless, let me mention that in broad strokes it is dealt with in Patrick A. Duane's excellent *Gentlemen Emigrants*[24]

May I therefore content myself with simply selecting two representatives of

---

[22] Ibid p.14

[23] Being the victims of a living language, perhaps one ought to point out that the use of that particular adjective had nothing to do with the activities condemned by St Paul in that licentious seaport of Corinth; (Corinthians, 6:9-11); it must be understood *in sensu antiquo*! Such a pity. It was a lovely and complimentary word with which to describe a party: one full of life, thoroughly enjoyable and basically innocent – even if, at times a little frivolous.

[24] *Gentlemen Emigrants. From the British Public Schools to the Canadian Frontier*. Douglas & McIntyre, Vancouver & Toronto, 1981.

this historical phenomenon who were an important formative influence upon me as a boy: the co-Founders and co-Headmistresses of

Queen Margaret's School Duncan
– for which Father was the doctor, and for Peter and me our first school after kindergarten

Following service during World War I in the QAIMNS, and decorated with the Royal Red Cross, Nora Creina Denny came to Cowichan. Her father's first cousin, Sir Cecil Denny, 6th Bt, had been Inspector of the Royal Canadian Mounted Police. They were Dennys of Cheshunt, Hertfordshire, and of Tralee Castle, co Kerry, descending from Sir Anthony Denny, executor of Henry VIII's Will and guardian of the boy King, Edward VI[25] – in short, Anglo-Irish.

Another to come to Cowichan at about the same time was Dorothy Geoghan (BA, of the first graduating class of UBC). She was the daughter of an RN surgeon descending from the Mac Geoghagans, the Hereditary Marshalls of Meath, and so was Native Irish. Both the Dennys and the Geoghans were of the Protestant Ascendancy and, if I may say so, examples of the very best sort of that group important in Irish history.

Each having started a small school in Duncan, they decided to pool their resources. Accordingly, on 4th April, 1921 as co-founders and Headmistresses they opened the doors of Queen Margaret's School[26] which was to become one of the outstanding girls' boarding schools in all Canada and an ornament to that distinguished corps.

As they also took boys up to the age of 10 – possibly considered a danger after that to the girls' virtue?! – both my brother and I had the privilege of attending Queen Margaret's School, and have always looked back on our time there with gratitude: the tuition was excellent, and the atmosphere civilized. While there, and in a number of succeeding schools Peter became a school chum of the future V.C., Charles Ferguson Hoey[27] – of the four from Canada in World War II, the one from Vancouver Island.

When a school chapel was built – finished in 1934 and constructed of fir logs lined and floored with hemlock – much of the furnishing was presented by parents, old girls and other well-wishers. Peter and I gave a chair for the sanctuary made of maple and yellow cedar – a somewhat early ecumenical gesture, *n'est ce pas*? It was, nevertheless, completely in accord with the firm

---

[25] C.A.R. Records of Ulster King of Arms. 178-162 (12.782) and for printed details *vide Burkes Peerage and Baronetage*, 1999 Vol. I. pp 809-810 and Fox Davies, Arthur. *Armorial Families* 7th edition. London, Hurst and Blackett Ltd., 1929 Vol. I pp 532-533.

[26] The Queen in question was St Margaret, the Anglo-Saxon princess (great niece of St Edward the Confessor, the penultimate Anglo-Saxon King) who married Malcolm III of Scotland. For further details see Appendix I.

[27] *London Gazette* citation of 18 May 1944; *Queen Margaret's School Magazine*, Summer Edition, No. 20, 1944.

Henry Peter Swan, MD, CM (McGill), LMCC, DRCOG, LM (Rotunda),
Major RCAMC and RAMC. Father of the Author.

Roman Catholic position of our family, as described earlier, and was somewhat akin to Pope Paul VI giving an historic episcopal ring to Archbishop Ramsey of Canterbury. We were delighted to do so: it was a small token of gratitude for much kindness received.[28]

That the Chapel should be built of logs was the suggestion of Mr C Stone[29] – head of the local Hillcrest Lumber Company, one of the largest such concerns in the whole of the Province. He, together with Mrs Stone as well as their family of six children, five boys and a girl, were church-going Anglicans.

My father was their doctor and our families were friends. I used to play with the young Stones – the 'pebbles' we called them – at their attractive home built on the outskirts of Duncan, and set in its own grounds.

---

[28] For further information, *vide, Beyond all Dreams. A History of Queen Margaret's School for Girls.* The QMS. History Committee, Duncan, 1975
[29] *Op. Cit.* p. 50

In these, the boys had made *not* a tree house but a subterranean bunker, about six feet underground. Access was by a vertical ladder, and at the bottom one found oneself in a room all duly supported, as in a mine, with wooden pillars and cross beams. We spent hours there talking and playing games – imagining that the adults did not know where we were.

Then one day an antique grandfather clock arrived from Britain and was duly installed on the lower landing of the staircase in the hall of the house. With my love of old things I thoroughly approved. The wooden case in which it had travelled was soon made into a car, fitted with wheels from an old perambulator – with a family of that size there was bound to be one if not more in some out-house. As I was somewhat thin and very light, the others would ask me to sit in the seat and steer, shoving into my hand a stop-watch with which I was to time the speed. The boys gathered round the rear and provided the necessary 'boy power' for propulsion and off we went down the drive. Faster and faster we would go with the wind racing through our hair. – Sir Donald Campbell had nothing on us. Then we would reach the slope which went down past the lake at the bottom, and real speed would be achieved with me racing ahead and the boys running after the car yelling and laughing until Newton's law put a stop to all this fun as the car gradually came to rest on the flat part of the drive by the lake. Then we would pull the car back – in which operation I hopped out of the seat and added traction – up to where we started near the house and did it all again. It was great fun!

The boys' sister was called Auriol. I was at Honours school at the time (about which more later). We had been to Queen Margaret's together earlier and I liked her. In fact she was the first girl I kissed, with all the delicate sensitivity of an eleven year old boy! It was a 'chaste kiss' of the kind to which St Paul refers as he finishes off so many of his letters. When I called next time and asked if Auriol could come out and play I was told that she was not available. This happened on every succeeding occasion I called until I received the message: I was disconsolate, and if my heart was shattered, my feet were like lead as they pressed down the pedals of my bicycle with just enough force to keep the machine upright homeward bound. There were at least two possible reasons for this cutting me off after so many happy hours of play together. Possibly she objected to this osculation by me – but surely that could not be so, I thought – humility has never been my strong point! On the other hand, it could have been that once her parents heard of this sudden advance, they decided that they did not want to face the possibility of a shot-gun marriage with a Papist at some time in the future if this boy was encouraged. (It will be recalled that all this happened well before Vatican II, and a mixed marriage was only permitted provided the non-Catholic signed an agreement that any child of these marriages would be raised a Catholic – an arrangement I still feel had much in its favour). To the pious, Anglican Stones such a fate would have been worse than death – quite understandably from their point of view.

For me the experience was seismic, and my parents could not understand why I was so quiet and withdrawn. This lasted about seventy-two hours, after which I brightened up, dusted myself off and remembered all my other playmates. Yet in after years, I sometimes wondered who Auriol married. Was it some muscle-bound logger from Hillcrest? Or again, was it a pin-striped barrister making straight for the bench? Amazing thought, when she could have had me – a further lapse of humility! Whatever happened, I do hope that he was kind to her and she loving to him, and that they had bliss together co-operating with God in producing a platoon of children who were sent to Queen Margaret's School and so had the benefit of attending that inestimable institution.

★　　★　　★

These few observations, one hopes, give some idea of those who constituted a major section of society in Cowichan Valley up to World War II, and so during the first thirteen years of my life.

They gave the area that particular character which was quintessential of the Gentlemen Emigrant phenomenon in the Canadian scene. It has now past into history, but without those who comprised it much of the country – particularly in the West – would not be as it is today to the great benefit and distinction of Canada.

Mother

The one person about whom I have said little so far is my mother Mrs H.P. Swan, Edna Hanson Magdalen Green – known to the family as, 'EHS'. The enunciation of those combined initials signified respect and the acknowledgement of someone not to be regarded lightly. She was a person of such character, drive, charm and ability that she played a great part not only in the lives of our immediate family, but also of the community at large.

I have already noted her looks and dress sense. Not academic, she was eminently practical, embodying the old saying: 'If you want something done, ask the busiest person in the village.' Her organizational competence, combined with her ability to get blood out of a stone over fund-raising, soon became apparent following her arrival in Cowichan and she put them to good use. EHS was a social animal and thoroughly enjoyed the company of others; there was nothing of the recluse about her. In addition to tennis and golf, bridge and mahjong, she was a competent amateur dramatist, sang well; was a versatile pianist, and an accomplished water-colour artist of several one-man shows. As already noted, she took an active part in the Imperial Order of the Daughters of the Empire (IODE); was the Regent of the local Chapter and founded another, the 'Duncan Dogwoods'. Any cause that needed help could call on her and she would make time to put her shoulder to its wheel.

It is difficult to point to any one endeavour as her major contribution to Cowichan life. Nevertheless, it is beyond doubt that one of these was the building of a spacious church during the depth of the Great Depression for the relatively small Catholic community of Duncan and its environs. What is more, the entire mortgage was entirely paid off despite the harsh economic conditions of that period.

Brought up as an Anglican, Mother had been educated at the convent of Chemay in Belgium. When during World War I she was to marry a Catholic, my Mother decided she wanted to become one as well. She took to Catholic life with an ease and sincerity which was complete. It answered her every spiritual need and, like most converts, she set an example in attempting to live out the tenets of her new faith. There was nothing 'pi' about her, as the Catholic saying goes; her religion was to her simply a part of the woof and warp of life.

The Catholics of Cowichan

In 1902 the local Bishop of Victoria (the Right Reverend Bernard Orth) decided that Duncan needed a parish of its own as otherwise Tzouhalem and Mill Bay were the nearest places for Mass. Accordingly, a small church was built on Station Road with St Edward the Confessor[30]named as its patron – the number of English Catholics of the area having been noted.

In 1910 the St Edward's Altar Society was founded and Mother joined it some eleven years later, soon after her arrival, my father having set up his practise in Duncan upon demobilization following World War I. It was through this Society, as its President, that she was to make her major contribution in building the new church when it became necessary. She was the colonel; its members the loyal troops.

By 1926 the old church (where, two years before, I had been baptized) had become too small. Accordingly, two lots were brought on Redingley Road (Coronation Avenue) as the site for the new one[31].

To pay for the land, church building and furnishings would require more money than the small Catholic community (50 families) could raise. This was where Mother with her wide-ranging connections with, and service to almost every local organization, was able to call in her chips, so to speak.

This she did: 'with Mrs Swan, President, there was a relentless drive' – a (?)

---

[30] Reigned 1042-66; Canonized by Pope Alexander III in 1161

[31] The Parish Priests of St Edwards concerned with the new church were: The Rev. Paul Jensen, SMM who, having decided on the new site, was moved by his order (the de Montfort Fathers); The Rev. Henry Lemmens, SMM replaced him and had the shock of finding a laywoman (Mother) quite prepared to disagree with him over purely prudential matters(!) but became her greatest ally before being appointed Assistant General of his order which necessitated his move to France in 1934, one year before the celebrations upon the completion of the project; he was replaced by the Québecois cricketer, The Rev. Joseph Latour, SMM.

lapsus calami – slip of the pen – according to the author of a history of the Altar Society[32].

Almost every form of fund raising was pursued[33], even if it meant throwing Peter and me onto the stage in some skit!

In the end, despite the thick, wet blanket of the Great Depression, all expenses were paid off and the mortgage redeemed. As a result, on 24 April, 1935 civic dignitaries, representatives of those generous Protestant neighbours and those of the parish who had supported the fund-raising were invited to a grand banquet, during which the mortgage papers were ceremonially burnt.

The church produced by all this effort was both dignified and capacious. Of its fittings, its stone altar, made to order in France, was the *pièce de resistance*: the only one of its kind in the Province (not even St. Andrew's Cathedral in Victoria could boast such).

Generally speaking, the parishioners were cut from the same cloth as the remainder of the Cowichan community. There were also some who might be likened to angostura bitters in gin: an added interest. These included the only two gentry families of non-British descent, that is to say our family (for more about whom see Chapter III) and that of Manuel de las Casas, North Devon Huzzars and veteran of the Boer and First World Wars. His Spanish-born father, Juan, had been *en poste* at the Court of St James's as Cuban Ambassador. On retirement, as he liked the country so much, he stayed on in England[34]. They were of the same family as the 16th century Bishop Bartolome de las Casas, (already mentioned as the author of important writings on aboriginal rights).

Yet again, there was the family of Colliard, the patriarch, of whom Alfred Joseph, was a noted conchologist with an important collection of shells. I was so much interested in the Colliard collection that, in later life, I made one of my own, starting in Queensland with its Great Barrier Reef – a treasure-house of shells.

Of particular interest from the historical point of view was the reflection in the parish of that phenomenon Canada experienced of being a refuge for Irish Catholic Unionists following the establishment of the Irish Free State in the early twenties. They had become *personae non gratae* to the new rulers of southern Ireland. For the Southern Unionist, both Catholic and Protestant, this disastrous turn of events meant, in the words of the psalmist, 'their familiar world taken away... and ...folded up like a shepherd's tent'[35]. Without a doubt the most famous of these was Sir Bertram (Coghill Alan) Wendle, MD, DSc, FRS, the

---

[32] Hogan, Frances. *St Edward's Altar Society, 1910-1944 – 50 – Catholic Women's League of Canada, St Edward's Council, 1944-1960 – A Story about Fifty Glorious Years,* 1960 p. 14

[33] Ibid, pp 13-15.

[34] For further details, see the obituary of Capt. De las Casas in *The Cowichan Leader* (Duncan) 26 Nov. 1931.

[35] *Canticum ezechiae.* (Isaias XXXVIII:12).

celebrated anthropologist, who became Professor of that speciality at St Michael's College in the University of Toronto. He was the grandson, through his mother, of Vice-Admiral Sir John Coghill, 3rd Bt., whose male-line ancestor was settled in Ireland with the estate of Ballyfoile, co. Killarny by Cromwell – a further example of the fact that *dans la généalogie on ne jamais dit jamais!*

Fellow Irish Catholic Unionist refugees of Sir Bertram, in St Edward's Parish, were: Major William Robert Russell and his family – generally referred to as the 'W R Russells', – and that of his brother, Major Francis Xavier Russell, DFC, similarly referred to as the ' F X Russells'. Their parental home in Ireland was Drumcullin House, Balldugan, co. Down, though they also had property at Downpatrick co. Louth where each was born. They both went to Hodder Place, the preparatory school for Stonyhurst, Lancashire, and then on to that College. These Russells descended from the eighteenth century George Russell of Ballystew co. Down. They were thus of the same family as the Russells of Killowen and so of the first Catholic Lord Chief Justice since the Reformation (appointed 1894) Lord Russell of Killowen, GCMG, PC.

Major William Robert Russell graduated from Trinity College, Dublin in 1905 and served in Lord Strathcona's Horse in World War I, during which in 1917 he was wounded when on service in Flanders. Major Francis Xavier Russell, DFC, served in the Royal Munster Fusiliers. His decoration attests to his having been an early member of the Royal Flying Corps – the forerunner of the Royal Air Force – in the days when aeroplanes were little more than thin slats of wood and canvas, and the pilots took to the air in their riding breeches(!)

Both the Major and his wife were very kind to me as a boy. Accordingly when, many years later, in Windsor Castle I would be one of the heralds leading the procession of the Sovereign and Knights of the Order of the Garter out of St George's Hall and so down the Grand Staircase on our way, eventually, to St George's Chapel, at about half way down, upon reaching the landing, we would slacken the pace a little to allow the older KGs to catch up. At that point I would always glance to my right and have a look at the colours hanging there of the South Irish Regiments disbanded after the establishment of the Irish Free State in 1922. These included both Colours of the Royal Munster Fusiliers. I remembered the Russells, and mentally saluted all that service, loyalty and valour over the years of those many and mainly Irish Catholic Unionists who, along with their Protestant compatriots, had been members of these regiments.

One could not help but wonder why in the 19th century, when every Home Rule meeting under Daniel O'Connell and his colleagues ended with the singing of *God Save the Queen*, Westminster – that council so brilliant at handling many areas further overseas – had seemed capable only of 'home goals' on Home Rule. After all, the Home Rulers were asking for little more than what most English counties have today. Had some accommodation been achieved then, the Irish leaders who by birth, education and experience had been running the country for centuries, would have been left in charge, and by a process of gradual, organic evolution Ireland would have developed. It is much easier for a duke to be generous than for a plebeian whose sole grasp of power depends upon the whim of a fickle electorate. Instead, in the end in 1922 sordid compromises were made with enemies, and friends were forgotten. All such thoughts passed through my mind as we turned left on the landing and started to descend the rest of the stairs to the Guard room and out into the open, and so on down, on our way to St George's Chapel.

★   ★   ★

It was into such a community, I have described above, that I first opened my eyes at the King's Daughters' Hospital, Duncan, at about 9 in the morning on 13 May, 1924. I weighed 9 lbs. Within a few hours of the delivery, our Japanese maid, Tenaka, on seeing me for the first time became almost hysterical. It was not my resemblance to an extra-crushed rugger ball (although, as we all know, except to their mother, all new-born babies look like that) but the fact that I was lying in broad day-light. At that time, in Japan newborn babies were kept in the dark at first and only gradually introduced to the light. Following an explanation Tenaka was reassured that this custom of the barbarians was not so barbarous after all. I was assured, at least, of one ally – whose countrymen, strangely enough, within not so many years, when in the Indian Army, I fought and came to regard as my least favourite enemy: the compatriots of she who had nursed me.

★   ★   ★

CHAPTER II

My Mother's Family:
The Greens –
Hard-Boiled Baptists and 'Men of Straw'

B Y HIS BERLIN DECREE of 21 November 1806, Napoleon put into effect his decision to strangle Britain economically. The exportation of any of her produce to Continental Europe was forbidden. This policy has come to be known as 'the Continental System' or 'Continental Blockade'. The British Government countered with the Orders in Council of 7 January and 11 November, 1807, prohibiting trade with ports occupied by the French. Now precious few were open for business.

In the end, Bonaparte was hoist with his own petard, as local industry increased and flourished in Britain. This included the manufacture of straw plait, which greatly increased the fortunes of my mother's paternal family of Green of Tring in Hertfordshire.

Tring is a small, pleasant and rural community about 50 miles to the north west of London. It is situated in that curious 'pan handle' of the county which stretches up into Buckinghamshire, near Aylesbury – home of the celebrated breed of duck of that name. It is also in the Chilterns – a range of chalk hills once covered with thick forest, which at one time became infested with robbers. To protect the surrounding countryside from their depredations, an officer, known as the Steward of the Chiltern Hundreds[1], was appointed. This office of the Crown still exists – though now purely titular – but all British students of political science know that if a Member of Parliament wishes to retire from the House of Commons at Westminster that person must apply to hold this Office, otherwise he or she is 'locked' into the session until Parliament is dissolved for a General Election.

This area of Hertfordshire, and the contiguous counties of Bedford, Buckingham and Essex were, from the early 17th century the heart of the English straw-plaiting industry from which hats were made for both men and women. The towns of Luton and Dunstable – both in Bedfordshire – were the centres for such hat-making. Early references include one to Iris's 'ryestraw hat' in

---

[1] A division of the County originally of Danish origin and so called it is supposed, from it containing 100 families at the time the Counties were originally divided in about 897. It will be recalled that at this time the Danish influence in England was strong.

Shakespeare's *Tempest*; and Lady Wroth's 'wheaten hat', about which Ben Jonson speaks in 1630, could well have been a product of either town.

The industry of straw-plaiting has now passed completely from the English economic scene and little is generally known about it. However, my maternal ancestors were much concerned with it, and through its efficient organization they enabled bread to be put on the tables of many a country labourer and his family during a particularly difficult period in British agriculture. One must always show due respect for one's ancestors for, in nature, obviously, without them one would not exist. Yet I feel that in view of the beneficial social effects of the work of the Green family a few further observations about this industry might be appropriate *in piam memoriam*.

Before the Napoleonic Wars, the finest straw plait was imported from Italy, from Leghorn (as the English called Livorno), but once that supply was cut off, the making of high quality plait in England was encouraged. This coincided with several fundamental changes to the life of rural England: parliamentary enclosures, alterations in land ownership, rapid population growth as well as altered farming practices; all these combined to make life for a good number of agricultural labourers extremely difficult. Straw plaiting provided alternative employment and could be engaged in by the whole family. It was an industry that required practically no capital and could be carried out in the home. So while its products were enjoyed by society in general – as straw hats were very fashionable – it provided useful employment for the poor. Had they not had this available they would have become a burden 'on the parish', that is to say, the somewhat grim ecclesiastical arrangements for looking after the poor, unchanged since Elizabethan times. During the first decade or so of the 19th century plait produced greater financial reward than agricultural labour. Indeed, so successful was this industry that at this time there was a shortage of female farmworkers as they could earn, in a week, as much as 30/- (i.e. £1-10-0 (one and half pounds) which in AD 2000 terms = £90.00 = $ Can. 180.00 approximately) – a good wage at that time.

The 1841 Census recorded 9,800 male and female straw plaiters in England and Wales, 84% of whom were concentrated in the contiguous counties of Bedfordshire, Buckinghamshire, Essex and Hertfordshire.

In all this the Green family – the John Greens, Senior (1808-80) and Junior, (1833-1923) [see the genealogical chart at pp 42-46] – developed a substantial business as manufacturers and dealers. They would arrange with cottagers to produce whatever type and quantity of plait was needed, collect it when ready and pay on the spot for the produce. Straw was used not only for ladies' hats but also for those of labourers. Later on in the century the summer helmets of the police were made of straw, though rendered in some dark colour to achieve that necessary air of *gravitas*. Other male attire made of this material were boaters for schools – the Greens supplied the plait hats to such schools as Harrow when

Winston Churchill was there; not that they seemed to have improved his academic performance, though we all thanked God for him in World War II. Such hats were equally popular with the schoolboys' older brothers, when, cutting a dash in striped blazers and flannels, they punted their current lady friend on the Isis or the Cam; she too could have one perched jauntily on the front of her head. That royal Beau Brummell, Edward, Prince of Wales, and later VIIth of that name as King, apparently highly approved of the boaters made from plait supplied by the Greens.

All in all, it was a major and lucrative family business if carefully managed, and this was the case with the Greens of Tring. Indeed, so proud were they of their devotion to this local trade that the arms of the family bear as the principal and central device three thin vertical bands plaited with a like number of horizontal bands and so in the form of a cross – all gold – and all against a green background as a pun upon the family name. (p. 47)

The Greens and the 'Hard-Boiled Baptists'

From the point of view of religion, the early nineteenth century found England in a state of flux, and so it was at the time that John Green, Sr, comes within our historical view in 1808.

The Anglican Church was at a low ebb. Gone were Lancelot Andrewes, Richard Hooker and the like. Wesley and his followers had come forward from within, advocating the practice of a virile evangelism. The Baptists joined in this crusade to feed the souls of a population largely bereft of spiritual inspiration from the Established Church, which was losing members at an alarming rate[2].

Buckinghamshire, Hertfordshire and other contiguous counties, in addition to being the principal areas for straw plaiting in England, were also places where the spirit of Oliver Cromwell still lived. They were in fact among the heartlands of English dissent, and so of Baptist strength. Indeed, a very important grouping within that church, known as the Northamptonshire Association, founded 1764, had extended its influence into Hertfordshire.

Notwithstanding these local circumstances, John Green, Sr, had been born and brought up an Anglican; having been baptized as an infant on 3 January, 1808 in the Parish Church of Wendover, some 8 miles from Tring.

However, as a young man he did not find what he sought as far as the spirit was concerned among his early co-religionists. Influenced by the vigorous evangelism of the Baptists, coupled with a move to Tring, he joined the Particular[3] wing of that communion and became a member of the New Mill

---

[2] Perkin, Harold. *The Origins of Modern English Society* 1969, pp. 196-197

[3] There are two wings in the Baptist Church: Particular, signifying that individuals are pre-destined to Salvation in a Calvinist manner, and General, signifying that Christ died for all, and all can be saved in an Arminian manner.

Church, eventually serving as its deacon[4] from 1842-58. Similarly, his son, John Green, Jr, was the Precenter of the Akeman Street Baptist Church (also Particular Baptist) 1861-85. It is because of this very close and long association of these two with the chapels of the area that they and their children have been referred to – in an affectionate manner – by the family in general as 'Hard-Boiled Baptists.'

New Mill is the historic mother chapel of the area. It was founded in 1656: halcyon days for the extreme Puritans during the Commonwealth. Cromwell had just become Lord Protector for life, and all looked set fair for his supporters – be they Baptists or Congregationalists, those two closely connected churches[5].

For these, all was shattered by the Restoration of 1660. They were particularly galled by the Conventicle Act, 1663, whereby all of 16 years and over had to adhere to the religious practices of the Church of England. Penalties were laid down for infringement; a third conviction meant banishment 'to some of the American plantations.' Three years later the Five Mile Act forbade a Nonconformist minister to go within 5 miles of the last place in which he had ministered. The dissenting communities of New Mill now went into the woods at night for worship. This situation is reflected in one of the New Mill hymns which runs, in part:-

> When oft oppressed, and tested sore,
> By persecution tried,
> They fain forsook their meeting-house
> In nearby wood to hide.
> And there, in tranquil prayerfulness,
> Their Saviour they adored,
> Until religious liberty
> To England was restored.

Their hiding place was discovered and their Pastor, Richard Sutton, imprisoned in Hertford Gaol until the death of Charles II and the accession of his brother, the Catholic James II. He granted liberty of conscience, and released all imprisoned for reasons of religion (It is singular how often in Baptist histories James II gets a good press – unlike that of his Whig traducers).

The Cromwellian chapel continued to serve for the next one and a half centuries, during which time Bunyan apparently preached there. Ultimately, on

---

[4] One who is elected by the particular chapel to assist in the day-to-day administration of the church. Just as the pastor of a Baptist church has no authority *ex officio* (as does a priest in a sacerdotal system) but has authority only by being *Called* by the members of a church to be its minister, so with a Deacon.

[5] For further details *vide* Payne, Ernest A. General Secretary of the Baptist Union of Great Britain and Ireland, 'Baptist-Congregational Relationship' in *Free Churchmen, Unrepentant and Repentant*. The Carey Kingsgate Press, Ltd, London, 1965 p.93 ff

the same site the present chapel was built in 1818. The general atmosphere of the time was one of relief and of reconstruction: the Napoleonic Wars were over and Bonaparte was safely under guard on St Helena; the border between Canada and the United States was agreed from the Lake of the Woods[6] Westwards to the summit of the Rockies (the 49th parallel); Jane Austen wrote *Northanger Abbey,* and the Duchess of Kent was pregnant, for the last months of the year, with a future great Queen[7].

The style of the new chapel was, as one would expect, *à l'epoque*: confidently Regency but solid and plain. It contains a commodious schoolroom, classrooms, vestry and church. Until recently there was a large stable to accommodate the horses, carts and chaises which brought the worshippers for a series of services on a Sunday – 100 to 200 having their midday meal in the vestry. Earlier there had been a millpond near the church where adult baptisms by immersion took place – one can only trust these were performed between July and September, when England often has warm weather! The last record of an outdoor baptism was in 1798, for 5 men and 1 woman. The pond was filled in when a canal was built nearby twelve years later.

Upon opening the door of the church itself, one is immediately struck by the symbolic declaration that 'God is in his word': an enormous, high pulpit situated on the far end wall dominates the scene. It is the Protestant version of the Catholic arrangement in, say, a convent of Perpetual Adoration, where above the high altar is a 'throne' upon which is placed a monstrance containing a consecrated communion host. To the theologically orthodox (in Aristotelian-Thomist terms) the latter is the substance of the body of Christ under the accidents of bread.

Confronted with either arrangement, one instinctively wants to kneel, in the presence of such a manifestation of faith. Such living monuments of devotion can only be admired by us utterly unworthy mortals as we stumble towards a declaration of dependence. Perhaps *faith* is best defined as a relationship with God, and *religion* as the encounters that nourish that relationship? It was here at New Mill that some of my Protestant ancestors built their own 'Jerusalem/In England's green and pleasant land.'

The present church could seat 500 people – using ground floor and galleries – and exhibits, as Sir John Betjeman would have it, the character of a well-scoured farmhouse kitchen. Originally it met all the needs of its theologically literate congregation, providing a great contrast with those enormous preaching stadia built at the turn of the eighteenth and nineteenth centuries in order to accommodate the uneducated masses of the industrial revolution as they congregated beneath the sounding-board of the gospel[8].

---

[6] i.e., Westward from the South East corner of what is now Manitoba.

[7] Princess Alexandrina Victoria, born 24 May, 1819.

[8] Betjeman, Sir John. *First and Last Loves.* 1952 pp 97–105.

New Mill must have appealed to those of the older view of their church as a local gathering, which was so identified with the manifestation of Christ's body that its acts became His acts. By contrast, the great preaching houses reflected the other view, which saw the church as a great missionary society. This difference caused much tension between Baptists.

As for those who became Baptists in the nineteenth century, they appear to have included all classes, from great industrialists to yeomen, from professionals to artisans, only excluding Peerage families and the brute end of the labouring classes. They numbered among the baptised such men as Sir Egerton Lleigh, Bt., who served as a minister at Rugby, Sir Joseph Bright, a solicitor, important in connection with developing certain legal aspects of Baptist chapels, Sir George Goodman, MP, for Leeds, Judge Willis and Sir Nathaniel Barnaby, both of the same church at Lee in South London[9], to name but a few of the more exotic. Generally speaking, a baronet, a knight and a judge were rare birds among Baptists.

Those of that communion tended to favour reform: as in the Reform Bill of 1832. This was drafted by Joseph Parkes who, with the John Greens, Senior and Junior, shares 20 first cousins as descendants[10]; anti-Slavery and pro Free Trade. A resolution of the Yorkshire Baptist Association even supported Catholic Emancipation – very generous in view of the Catholic strength in the North – and, at the same time, added the Jews for good measure[11].

In many areas the Baptist church appealed to those who were independent minded, good organizers, leaders and capable of making their way in the world. While it has been said – with a degree of justification – that in the nineteenth century, in particular, the Church of England was the Tory Party at prayer, so with equal partial justice it could be said that the Baptist position, at the same period, was that of 'laissez-faire politico-economics on its knees'[12].

While Catholic Emancipation (1829) was supported in theory by some Baptists, when Puseyism and the Tractarian Movement within the Church of England began to flourish, and the Second Spring for the Catholics came into bud, the reaction was predictable. The voluntarism of the Baptists regarded all idea of hierarchy, of the sacerdotal, of eucharistic sacrifice, of ritual and so on, as anathema. As a result, when the Government proposed in 1845 to increase the grant to Maynooth, the Anti-Maynooth Committee found a more than sympathetic ear among the Baptists: it was bad enough that there should be such a seminary of Popery, but that it should be financed by the Government was intolerable!

---

[9] McLeod, Hugh. *Class and Religion in the late Victorian City*, 1974 p. 143.

[10] Vide the genealogical chart showing descendants of Dr Joseph Priestley, FRS. Appendix III.

[11] Briggs, J.H.Y. *The English Baptists of the nineteenth Century*. The Baptist Historical Society, 1944 p. 207.

[12] Ibid., p. 11.

Such was the religious, social and political position of both John Green, Sr, and of his son, John, Jr.

And such was the general atmosphere in which the latter had grown up and in which he raised his four sons and five daughters. Both father and son were men of principle, and they stuck to it through thick and thin. They were doughty Protestants and lived according to their consciences. I may not be able to agree with all their theological conclusions, but I cherish them for being able to share with them those I can. They had the honesty and intelligence to consider their position *sub specie aeternitatis,* and for this I salute them, and am proud to count them among my ancestors.

In the course of time, the religious position of their branch of the family gradually evolved, so that today one finds that many of the descendants of the two Johns have either returned to the Anglican fold or are Roman Catholics. Yet a good number, especially in the southern part of the United States, have remained Baptists. What either John would have said had they anticipated one of their blood (and, in fact looking very much like them) – fourth in descent from the Deacon of New Mill – concelebrating the Holy Sacrifice of the Mass with the Holy Father, His Holiness John-Paul II, Bishop of Rome, Prince of the Apostles and Servant of the Servants of God, in the latter's private chapel in the Vatican – as did my brother, Peter, on 2 April, 1985 – one finds it difficult to imagine[13]. If they were wise, it would possibly have been, as said before: *'dans la généalogie, on ne....'*! As for my description of the august celebrant – Polish, and so very close to us – the two Johns might have extracted one or two choice pieces from the Book of Revelations. Bless them – *requiescant in pace.*

The Greens of the Diaspora

When the time came to leave The White House, Tring – for many years the home of John Green, Junior, and his family – the advice of the time was, 'Go West young man, go West' – it was part of that contemporary movement already noted. In the end all four sons did so, but this was not accomplished until Herbert, the eldest, had pitted himself against those redoubtable warriors, the Zulus. His service was in the Zulu Wars which lasted from January to July, 1879. He was just 18 years of age, and served in the Stranger Mounted Rifles, a Natal and East Griquland volunteer regiment[14].

If that was not enough excitement, dust and heat, we find him lining up on 16 September, 1893 with thousands of others on the starting line for the last Land Run in American history. This was onto the Cherokee Outlet – that 200 mile long by 57 mile deep strip of land (hence its common name of Cherokee Strip)

---

[13] The other three concelebrants were a brace of Papal Secretaries and a Vietnamese Bishop – catholic and Catholic to say the least!

[14] WO 100/49 and Hurst, G.T. *Volunteer Regiments of Natal and East Griquland.* Durban, 1946, p. 52.

which ran due East-West south of Colorado and Kansas, North of Texas and bordering onto New Mexico.

160-acre farms had been marked out with a marker-stake driven into the centre of each. The first to reach a marker and write his name on it was the owner – formal registration at the government land office, followed by the issue of a patent, confirmed the land to the owner upon the payment of $14.00 per acre.

No rain had fallen in the area for some 6 months, so everyone was ankle deep in dust as they foregathered for the Run. The scene along the starting lines – both the northern and southern borders of the Strip – was one of fidgeting, impatience and noise as riders, or wagons, hacks, surreys, buckboards, carts or prairie schooners – stripped of all excess weight – jostled for position among, it is estimated, something between 30,000 and 115,000 homesteaders. The US Cavalry patrolled the starting lines, a rifle across every saddle. The atmosphere was charged with the agony of anticipation – tongues stuck to palates. At last, at precisely 12 noon the starting guns were fired, and the overall scene was one of pandemonium, as a thunderous roar and thick cloud of dust went up. With reins loose, and spurs in flanks, Herbert was off at speed – his hair flying out behind and his moustache – both auburn – sieving the particles of this virgin land now swirling through the hot, noontide air. Annie, his wife, and their boy, William John (Bill), had been left well back. If Herbert had learned one thing in South Africa it was: keep the women and children out of the scene of operations.

Not knowing whether he or his horse was sweating more, each having strained every muscle in a headlong gallop – the word 'run' seemed hardly adequate – he reached a post and staked a claim near Salt Fork River. A day or so later he exchanged this for another nearer that of a friend, some three miles from the site of Wakita which he was to help found. For this town he was appointed the United States Marshal and, in addition, served on its council as well as being the mayor.

This latter claim was duly registered, within a day or so of the run, just over the border at Cameron, Kansas. Seventeen years later, he was to receive confirmatory Letters Patent dated 17 September, 1900 under the hand of the President of the United States, William McKinley, and the seal of the General Land Office, Washington, DC[15]. This land is still held by the family.

William John 'Bill', the boy who kept his mother company while four hooves carried his father like lightning to the site of their new farm was later to have a distinguished career. He served as an agricultural economist in the Federal Department of Agriculture, the United States Department of State and with the United Nations Relief and Rehabilitation Agency (UNRRA).

An early assignment was in Guam where, among other things, he successfully

---

[15] Homestead Certificate 616; Application 2998; Recorded; Oklahoma Vol. 45 p.86.

convinced the local natives that it was not really necessary to tether their chickens.

For several years in the mid forties he served with (UNRRA) in China, helping in the reclamation of land damaged by flooding and the war, as well as training people for the use of agricultural machinery which had been shipped in. His mother used to worry about the Communists, who were becoming powerful in that country at the time. To assuage her fears he assured her that he had a camel tethered at all times at the back door for a quick getaway if necessary. This probably did not console her much, but it is a good example of his sense of humour.

In Taiwan, in addition to his official duties, he took great pleasure in sponsoring 4-H Clubs for the young, and they are strong there to this day. These clubs provide leadership training, and experience in raising show cattle. For his work with the Chinese he was decorated by General Chiang Kai-shek with the Order of the Brilliant Star.

He also worked in South America, and for his work in Bolivia was decorated with the National Order of the Condor of the Andes.

From time to time, his duties brought him to England, when he would visit us. I also stayed with him in Dallas on several occasions during my tours of the States. He used to tell us how in 1951 he called on his father's youngest sister – Annie Elizabeth ('Nancy') Green, aged 84 – for the first time. When he introduced himself, she immediately replied, 'Come in. I've been expecting you.' That is the kind of family the Greens are: sherry decanter always at the ready, with stopper out.

Herbert's younger son, Arthur Eric (who had the unusual nickname of Yenks) represented Grant County – where his property was situated – in the House of Representatives of the State Legislature of Oklahoma (1954-62) in the Democratic interest. At the time, Democrats outnumbered Republicans by 5 to 1 throughout the State, though today (early 2000s) it is about 50/50, and (how times have changed in the South) a Republican Governor is not unknown. He served on the Agriculture and Education Committees, and was appointed Assistant Floor Leader to the Speaker of the House, as well as Liaison between the Speaker and the Governor – a post requiring considerable tact, as the relationship between these two officials was anything but cordial at the time. During the last session of his service he introduced his four young Davis grandsons[16] on the floor of the House, and they had the distinction of being voted Honorary Pages to the House.

Through his marriage with Anna Cates Cissel in 1924 that branch of the family became related to her maternal slave-owning great-grandfather, Richard

---

[16] The children of his daughter, Dr Josephine Anne ('Joanne') Ed. D., by her husband, Ray Lewis Davis: Ray Lewis Davis, Jr. *b*. 14 April, 1953, Eric Ellis Davis, *b*. 20 Jan. 1955, Richard Arthur Davis, *b*. 24 April, 1958 and Derek Vincent Davis, *b*. 5 Oct. 1960.

Creal, Jr. His family owned Sinking Spring farm in Hardin (now Larue Co.), Kentucky where Abraham Lincoln was born. This marriage also brought in a relationship with the celebrated Kentucky Judge, John Cates Creal, who presided from the Bench from 1890-1914.

It was the Judge's son-in-law, Thomas Jefferson Cissel (Anna's father) who brought the family to Kansas and Oklahoma by his taking part in the Cherokee Strip Run of 1893[17].

One of his fellow homesteaders on the Run was, as already noted, Herbert Green. For the latter's son Arthur ('Yenks'), Cissel provided as wife his daughter, Anna.

Descendants of Herbert in the United States still flourish. While all his sisters remained in England, three of them marrying, all his brothers ultimately came to Canada.

The next brother down, as it were, Frederick Bernard Green, settled and farmed at Thorsby, Alberta, where he died in 1961, having also held the appointment of Inspector of Fisheries for the Government of Canada. In addition he was active in local government affairs.

The youngest of these brothers, William James Green, came to live nearby in the provincial capital, Edmonton, where he died in 1950. Both of these Albertan Greens have descendants in Canada.

My grandfather, Alfred Edward Green, the penultimate of this quartet, continued to live mainly in England until after World War I. In 1898 he had married Rose Elizabeth, daughter of Alfred Hanson, Jr and granddaughter of Alfred Hanson, Sr. These two Yorkshiremen were Civil Engineers who spent their entire lives building railways in England, at a time when such work had all the glamour that space travel has today. Alfred Senior's greatest work was the London North Eastern Railway (LNER) line from London (Euston) to Edinburgh. My grandparents had three children: my mother, Edna Hanson Magdalen, and her brothers, Claude Alfred John and Malcolm Edward, who lived with their parents on their property at Wealdstone, Middlesex.

My grandfather was appointed to be a Justice of the Peace for that County, and had as one of his friends and colleagues on the bench, Sir W S Gilbert, the dramatist, humorist and librettist celebrated for his collaboration with Arthur Sullivan. Also fully qualified as a barrister, Gilbert apparently larded the advice he gave to his fellow JPs with the wit of *The Mikado* and the like.

In accord with civic duty Alfred Edward also served in local government and was Chairman of the Urban District Council of Wealdstone (equivalent of a Mayor, in Canada).

---

[17] I am particularly indebted to my cousin, Dr Jo Anne Davis, who has, most generously, made available to me her extensive monograph, entitled *The Cissel-Creal Family Connection to Abraham Lincoln*, 2002 which she produced for distribution within the family. It is the result of much research in Kentucky by herself, her cousin, Mary Kay Creal Hurt, Janet Coulter and Donna Luna.

My grandfather, while keeping his property in Wealdstone, moved, on the advice of his doctors, in 1914 to Folkestone in Kent, as he was threatened with tuberculosis. It was felt that the bracing sea air of the south coast would be beneficial. It was while living there with his family that my father met and married my mother.

Following my parents move to Duncan, upon my father's demobilization from the Canadian Army Medical Corps, at the end of World War I, my grandparents – like so many English over the years – brought their two sons to live there as well in 1921.

As my grandparents lived very close to us, I think I was in their house about as much as I was in ours. They never seemed to mind my popping in to see them. We would discuss all manner of topics, and as a special treat they would bring out of their library such glorious publications as *The Illustrated London News* editions for the Coronations of King Edward VII and King George V. These were filled with illustrations – some sepia, others black and white – and with fully coloured pictures which were reproductions of paintings especially commissioned for the occasion, genealogical charts, articles explaining the ceremonial of the coronation, its significance and the like. We would spend hours poring over these, and so my interest in history, monarchy, the constitution and so forth was stimulated and deepened. Such sessions were an education in themselves. My grandfather also had a great interest in classical Greek history and the attractive, and at times amusing, way in which he presented this knowledge was another avenue my young mind wanted to explore. Then, in lighter vein, he would tell stories of his life as the time he was up in London in the early 1900s on business. Having finished this for the day on one occasion, and with time to kill before taking the trains home, he went to a theatre, which at the time was on the corner of the Strand and Aldwych, where he saw a production of *Swan Lake*. When he got home he told his family, 'There was a young girl dancing. She was superb. I'm sure she will go far. She had a Russian sounding name. It was Anna, and then something like, Pav-lo-va'(!)

Alfred Edward was the type of person who would listen to someone explain how the three angles of a triangle make 180° and indicate conviction but before acting on this knowledge would ask, 'But what does the other side have to say?' He and Aquinas were one in holding that *virtu stat media*. Life to him was one long game of cricket, whether on or off the pitch; he always played according to the rules. His worst possible condemnation of an action would be summed up in the observation, 'That simply isn't cricket.'

He was a Free Mason for almost 60 years, having first joined the Royal Standard Lodge in London in 1909 (he died in 1968). Upon his arrival in Duncan he transferred to Temple Lodge No.33, of which he was elected Worshipful Master in 1927. Three years later the Grand Master of British Columbia and the Yukon appointed him Grand Steward, and in 1959 he was presented with the Fifty Year Jewel. Bearing in mind these impeccable credentials as a Mason it was, nevertheless, typical of his own general attitude to life that when once in Duncan at a Masonic meeting he was taxed over the number of Catholics with whom he associated, he replied, 'Such are either my relations or my friends, and I have no intention of deserting either relations or friends' – and that was that. It will be seen in Chapter IV how when my brother, Peter, was to celebrate one of the most important events for a newly ordained Roman Catholic priest, that is to say the celebration of his first High Mass, and having neither father nor mother, let alone a brother to help arrange matters because of a war, it was his Masonic grandfather and Anglican grandmother who immediately buckled to and organized everything.

Alfred Edward was tall, thin, good looking and topped with a full head of wavy hair to the end of his days. He had the perfect cricket figure, appropriate for one devoted to that game.

Our grandmother, Rose Elizabeth, had inherited from her Yorkshire ancestors that North Country directness. She spoke her mind and did not suffer fools gladly. On the other hand she could be extremely kind and thoughtful. In addition to her interest in history, she had a considerable knowledge of antiques as well as a fine collection of them. So she and I would discuss this subject at length. She and her husband had, when in England, acquired a number of paintings by contemporary artists, all of which had been exhibited at the Royal Academy, and her observations on these increased my appreciation of that form of art. To her religion was a rather private matter, but hers was firmly Anglican. Notwithstanding, she got on extremely well with her equally firm Catholic son-in-law, my father, probably because each knew where the other stood. They also shared the same sense of humour.

Rose Elizabeth was a large, not a fat, but definitely a large woman, with a handsome, rather than beautiful, face. She dressed well and because of her figure always remembered, wisely, that the lines of her clothes must be vertical and never horizontal. Her day clothes were tailor made, preferably by a man. When *en grande toilette*, in the evenings, she was usually to be seen in black satin – dull side up – and floor-length. Over this, covering bare arms and a discreet but definite *décolletage,* would be black lace – no frills – but close fitting. The overall effect was impressive.

For relaxation, there was nothing both my grandparents enjoyed more than a good game of bridge.

From all I have said about my grandparents, it is not hard to see why I became extremely fond of them, and remained so.

We have already considered my mother in some detail, and will have more to say about her, anon. Accordingly, let us pass to her two brothers: Claude Alfred John Green (*b.* 1904) and Malcolm Edward Green (*b.* 1911). The former is usually referred to as Claude A Green. At the time of writing this, he was a widower, rising 97 years of age and continued to pass the (now obligatory) annual driving test for people over 80. We exchanged letters frequently: his typing was better than mine. With an extremely active life in local affairs, his greatest monument is, undoubtedly, the Cowichan District Hospital. He was the vigorous and untiring chairman of the committee which brought this into being. Devoted to cricket, as was his father, he has also been a leading Free Mason. After serving in various high appointments in that Order he was installed as Grand Master of British Columbia and the Yukon in 1957. As already noted, he married Edna Frances Castley in 1928, and by her had two children: Claude Rodney Austin Green (b. 1932, d. 1995) and Sylvia Joy Green (b. 1934).

Claude Rodney Austin – Rodney to the family and Claude to everyone else – had a distinguished career as an officer of the Royal Canadian Mounted Police over a period of 27 years, with various postings in the Province of Alberta. Like his father he was a Free Mason of the highest rank, joining the Order in 1958. A quarter of a century later, in 1984, his father was invited to attend his installation in Calgary as Grand Master of Alberta – an event which, I understand, is considered unique in Canadian Masonic history. In 1955 he married Jean Carolyn Henderson (who predeceased him in 1992) and by her had three children (for details see the genealogical chart, p. 45). He married, secondly, Eileen Rose Stiles (née Wempe) in 1994.

His sister, Sylvia Joy Green, BA(UBC) and M.LbySc. (Washington), in 1956 married Ronald Ian Cheffins, BA, LLB(UBC), LLM(Yale) etc (divorced 1978) and they had three children. In 1994 she married Glenn Murray Dyer.

The younger brother of my mother was Malcolm Edward Green (b.1911) – in fact so much younger that he was more like an elder brother to Peter and me. He became an architectural expositor. In 1935 he married Louise Stannard Rumsby and they had two children. She pre-deceased him in 1969.

The genes of this family appear to carry with them the ability to organize and administer. Such are seen recurring again and again in the descendants of John Green Senior – the straw plait entrepreneur – of Tring, Herts. These include my grandfather and his brothers, and their descendants, along with Mother, my uncles and my brother, Peter. I, too, enjoy organization and administration. As to how successful I am, well that is for others to say. But if I came upon a scene and found, 'everywhere, careless confusion, charming disarray'[18], that to me would be a vision of hell.

---

[18] Mickiewicz, Adam. *Pan Tadeusz*, trans. Kenneth Mackenzie. The Polish Cultural Foundation, London, 1964 p.4.

Genealogical descent of
Green
of Tring, Hertfordshire,
British Columbia, Alberta and Oklahoma[19]

John Green, Sr. *Bpt*. 3 Jan. 1808 at   =   Elizabeth Taylor *m*. 9 Nov. 1829
Wendover, co. Bucks. Straw Plait   at Tring Parish Church. *d*. 18 April
Manufacturer. Deacon of the New   1874 aged 65 at Tring.
Mill Baptist Church, Tring co. Herts,
1842-58. *d*. 29 June 1880
Aged 72 buried at new Mill.

John Green, Jr of The White House,   =   Emma, *dau*. of James Gower,
Tring. afsd Straw Plait Manufacturer.   Manufacturer of Cloth. *m*. 6 Aug,
b. 10 Sept. 1833. Precentor of the   1856 at New Mill afsd. *d*. 29 August
Akeman Street Baptist Church, Tring,   1915 aged 72.
1861-85.
d. 11 March, 1923 at Tring.

I   Alice Emily Green. *b*. 30 July 1857. *m*. 13 Aug. 1878 both at Tring afsd
      William Bligh. *d*. 28 Dec. 1933 at Chipperfield co. Herts.

                                   =
                                   *

II   Clara Ellen Green. *b*. 10 Dec 1859. *m*. 2 July 1885 both at Tring afsd
      Alfred Ernest Randall. *d*. 6 Nov. 1924 at St Albans co. Herts.

                                   =
                                   *

III   Herbert John Green. *b*. 1 Jan. 1861 at Tring afsd. Fought in the Zulu
      War, 1879. Took part in the last Land Run in U.S.A., Cherokee Outlet,
      16 Sept. 1893. Mayor of Wakita, Oklahoma, etc. *m*. 3 May 1888 at
      Ellsworth, Kansas, Annie, dau. of John Nikodem (*d*. 17 Nov. 1949 at
      Enid, Oklahoma). *d*. 5 June 1950 at Enid afsd.

                              H | A
                          See following page
J   E
See following pages

---

[19] CAR: Surrey 21/166 and 269

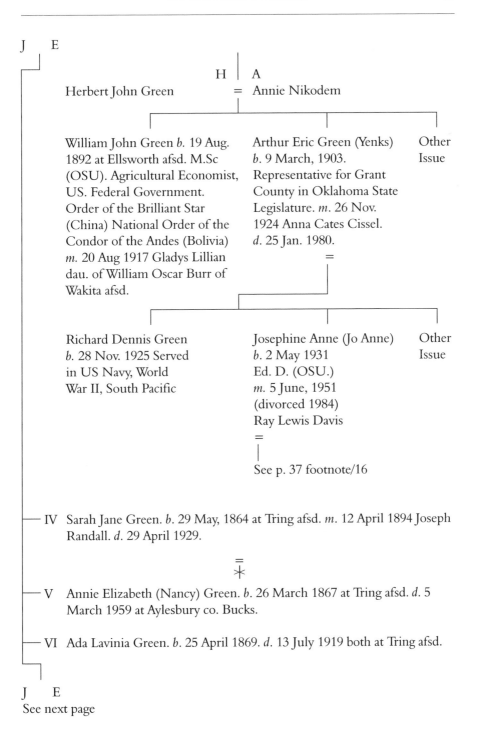

J   E

H │ A

Herbert John Green   =   Annie Nikodem

William John Green *b.* 19 Aug. 1892 at Ellsworth afsd. M.Sc (OSU). Agricultural Economist, US. Federal Government. Order of the Brilliant Star (China) National Order of the Condor of the Andes (Bolivia) *m.* 20 Aug 1917 Gladys Lillian dau. of William Oscar Burr of Wakita afsd.

Arthur Eric Green (Yenks) *b.* 9 March, 1903. Representative for Grant County in Oklahoma State Legislature. *m.* 26 Nov. 1924 Anna Cates Cissel. *d.* 25 Jan. 1980.

=

Other Issue

Richard Dennis Green *b.* 28 Nov. 1925 Served in US Navy, World War II, South Pacific

Josephine Anne (Jo Anne) *b.* 2 May 1931 Ed. D. (OSU.) *m.* 5 June, 1951 (divorced 1984) Ray Lewis Davis

=

See p. 37 footnote/16

Other Issue

IV Sarah Jane Green. *b.* 29 May, 1864 at Tring afsd. *m.* 12 April 1894 Joseph Randall. *d.* 29 April 1929.

=
✳

V Annie Elizabeth (Nancy) Green. *b.* 26 March 1867 at Tring afsd. *d.* 5 March 1959 at Aylesbury co. Bucks.

VI Ada Lavinia Green. *b.* 25 April 1869. *d.* 13 July 1919 both at Tring afsd.

J   E
See next page

J   E

VII   Frederick Bernard Green *b.* 29 Feb. 1872 at Tring *afsd.* Inspector of Fisheries for Government of Canada, 1905-12. Councillor for Municipal District of Bigstone, Alberta 1918-28.
m.(1) 16 April 1893 at Ellsworth afsd. Eva Rachel Russell (*d.*13 June, 1913 at Bonnie Glen, Alberta) *m.*(2) 28 April 1915 Cema Constance Littlewood.
(1) = (2) =
*   *

IX   William James Green. *b.* 6 Sept. 1877. *m.* 17 April, 1900 Jessica Elizabeth Hambley, both at Tring *afsd. d.* 19 Aug. 1950 at Edmonton, Alberta.
=
*

VIII   Alfred Edward Green. *b.* 9 July 1874. *m.* 26 Dec. 1898 both at Tring *afsd.*, Rose Elizabeth dau. of Alfred Hanson, Jr. son of Alfred Hanson, Sr. Civil Engineers (the latter builder of L.N.E.R. Euston, London to Edinburgh) (she *d.*19 Nov. 1957 at Duncan, British Columbia). In the Commission of the Peace for co. Middlesex, Chairman of the Wealdstone District Council, 1912-14. Coroner within and for the Province of British Columbia, 1938-57. *d.*11 April 1968 at Duncan.

=

A   R

Edna Hanson Magdalen Green. *b.* 12 Nov. 1899 at Wealdstone afsd. (and see Święcicki Swan genealogical descent on p. 71)

Claude Alfred John Green. *b.* 11 March, 1904 at Wealdstone afsd. Grand Master of the Grand Lodge of British Columbia and the Yukon 1957. Chairman, Cowichan District Hospital Board from 1959 (and Chairman of Planning Committee) – Hospital opened 1966.
m. 25 July, 1928 at Victoria, British Columbia, Edna Frances dau. of Elias Castley, of Duncan afsd. (*d.* 22 Nov. 1999 at Duncan afsd). He d. 7th Sept 2003 at Victoria afsd.

=

A   R

C   E

See following page

C   E

A   R

Claude Rodney Austin Green. *b.* 12 June 1931 at Duncan afsd. Officer in RCMP, 27 years. *m.*(1) 29 Oct. 1955 at Lethbridge, Alberta, Jean Carolyn Henderson (*d.* 1992). Grand Master of the Grand Lodge of Alberta, 1984. *d.* 12 June 1995.

=

Barbara Lynn Green. *b.* 21 March 1958 at Medicine Hat, Alberta.

Lyle Rodney John Green *b.* 25 Nov. 1960 at Tofield, Alberta.

m.(2) 14 May, 1994 Eileen Rose Stiles (née Wempe).

Malcolm Edward Green *b.*12 June 1911 at Wealdstone afsd. Architectural Expositer. *m.*(1) 4 dec. 1935 Louise Stanard Rumsby (*d.* 5 Sept. 1969)

=

John Edward Green *b.* 14 Oct. 1940 at Duncan afsd.

Anne Elizabeth Green *b.* 2 July 1943 at Duncan afsd.

m.(2) 12 June 1970 Myrl (widow of Richard Herman Blaxall) at Nanaimo, British Columbia.
He died 17 May 2002.

Sylvia Joy Green, BA(UBC) M Lib. Sc.(Washington) *b.* 28 Dec. 1934 at Duncan afsd.
m.(1) 25 Aug. 1956 (divorced 18 Jan.1978) Ronald Ian Cheffins, BA and LLB(UBC), LLM(Yale) etc.

=

S   R
See following page

S   R

Brian Robert Cheffins, BA, LLB(UV), LLM(Cantab) S.J., Berwin Professor of Corporate Law, Univ. of Cambridge. *b.* 21 Jan 1961 at Montreal, Québec. *m* 10 October 1992 at Birmingham, Joanna Hilary Thurstans

=

Hannah Victoria Cheffins *b.* 24 May 1998 at Cambridge

Lucy Sylvia Cheffins *b.* 9 Feb. 2002 at Cambridge

Ian Michael Cheffins *b.* 13 Oct. 1959 at Monreal afsd. *m.* 13 June, 1992 at Teresina, Piaui, Brazil Dináurea Reis e Silva

Jonathan James Muir Cheffins. *b.* 30 June 1970 at Victoria, British Columbia.

Sylvia Joy Green *b.* 28 Dec. 1934 (*vide ut supra*) *m.*(2) 30 July 1994 Glenn Murray Dyer.

Design for engraving on metal, by a Herald-Painter of the College of Arms,
showing the tinctures indicated by a system of hatching (lines at various angles,
dots and so on) known as Petra Sancta. Photography by Peter Norris.

The Armorial Bearings
of
Green
of Tring co. Hertford, England
and
of Duncan, Vancouver Island, British Columbia, Canada.

Arms: *Vert a Cross triparted and fretted between in the 1st and 4th quarters a Rose and in*
the 2nd and 3rd quarters a Pine cone Or all within a Bordure Erminois.
(That is to say, on a green background, a gold Cross consisting of three
vertical and three horizontal pieces fretted at the centre, the arms so
formed reaching right to the edge of the design. In the upper left and

lower right quarters, a gold rose, and in the other two a pine cone also gold; the whole design contained within a gold border peppered with stylized black ermine tails. The background colour is an obvious pun on the family name. The fretted cross alludes to their connection with straw plaiting. The rose refers to the English origins of the family, and that it should be coloured gold makes a somewhat unusual charge in heraldry. The pine cone alludes to the other branches of the family located abroad, particularly in northern climes. The border is rendered in one of the several variations of stylized heraldic ermine and so recalls the several judicial offices held within the family.)

Crest: *With a Wreath of the Colours, On a Mount Vert a Stag at gaze proper charged on the shoulder with a Clarion Or and resting the dexter fore-hoof on a Torteau.*
(That is to say, with a wreath of two pieces of material twisted so as to show gold and green alternately – the Livery Colours of the family; rising therefrom a green, grassy mound upon which stands a stag, in its natural colours, and looking at the viewer. On its shoulder is a gold clarion. It rests its right, fore hoof on a red disc. As the family was long resident in the county of Hertfordshire so the stag which occurs in the Arms of that county. The clarion (an early type of organ) refers to certain musical connections of the family. The red circular object beneath the stag's hoof reminiscent of a cricket ball, alludes to the devotion of the family to that game).

Motto: *Integritate* ('By integrity')[20]

---

[20] CAR Gts 116/26

CHAPTER III

Szlachta-Literati-Catholic – or more concisely: Stemma Polonicum Mei Patris.

'LITHUANIA? Now that's not Europe is it?' mused the village post mistress aloud as she read the address on a letter I had given her to weigh. She is the dearest, kindest woman but, like many Anglo-Saxons, she is heiress to an old attitude noted by Edmund Burke that Lithuania 'might be considered as a country in the moon.'

Poor Lithuania! Recently French scientists have declared it the centre of Europe. Strange, perhaps. But remember that Iceland is also in Europe, which obviously shifts the axis from Paris, Strasbourg, Bern or some other place that likes to think itself the hub. Yet again, many seem to have forgotten, if ever they knew (for universal, compulsory education during the past century or so has not quite achieved that degree of knowledge among all levels of society that some had hoped for) – they have forgotten that Lithuania was once the largest state in Europe. It stretched from the Baltic to the Black Sea, and from a few miles short of Moscow westwards to the Polish border.

Granted, the area today called Lithuania is the vestigial remnant of this once vast empire, being more or less coterminous with the borders of the Duchy of Samogitia. It is here that my paternal family spent the greater part of the 400 or so years of its recorded history. Accordingly, it may be as well to recall a few background details of this area: *terre de nos aïeux*, to apply a well-known phrase[1].

Present-day Lithuania is the largest of the three Baltic States. From north on the gulf of Finland – to south – on the border of Poland – they are: Estonia, Latvia and Lithuania. To the east is Russia – lovely Easter Eggs; to the west the Baltic Sea – beautiful Amber, and all that.

Mile for mile, Lithuania is a fraction smaller than Scotland (more or less 25,000 as against 30,000 square miles). Topographically, it is more like Prince Edward Island or East Anglia: gently undulating countryside with woods. In population it is slightly larger than Southern Ireland (3,700,000 as against 3½ million). Like Ireland, it consists of a core native population with additions, originally from outside, but resident within the country for centuries.

Hotly disputed by scholars, Lithuanians may not be a Slavic people, and

---

[1] From the opening words of the original version of the Canadian National Anthem 'O, Canada, terre de nos aïeux…

49

linguistically they may be close to Sanscrit. What is certain, however, is that their language is quite different from their neighbours': Russians, Byelorussians and Poles. For example, 'thank you' in Lithuanian is 'achu' (conveniently pronounced as if you have a bad cold) whereas in Polish one says, 'dziekuje' pronounced 'dzhshn-koojeh' – and so on.

Historical Background

Not long before the Conqueror invaded England, Lithuania – a barbarous land of heath, river, lake, marsh and limitless forest – starts to be mentioned in Christian chronicles (1009). Along with those lands that came to be known as East Prussia, Latvia and Estonia, it was still pagan. The whole area thus attracted the attentions of, among others, German crusaders: the Knights of the Sword and, more particularly, the Teutonic Order[2]. Although founded in the East (1187), the latter order really came into its own on this Baltic seaboard, where it set about converting the local pagans to Christianity with all the histrionic yet brutal efficiency of which the Germans are capable.

By the Golden Bull of Rimini of 1223 from the Emperor they became sovereign and created the *Ordenstaat* (the State of the Order) stretching from East Prussia along the coast right up to Estonia.

The 12th and 13th centuries, in particular, saw great military activity by these crusaders. Frequently, they were joined by men from further west anxious to acquire military experience – who rather regarded the area as some do today the grouse moors at certain times of the year. The twenty-year-old Sir Geoffrey Scrope – brother of a future Archbishop of York – fell fighting, in 1362[3], at the side of the Order's Hochmeister, Winrich von Kniprode. Scrope was buried in the cathedral at Königsberg where his comrades placed his Arms – the celebrated: *Azure, a Bend Or* (blue shield with a gold band from upper left to lower right) – in a window. My wife's family had some connection with the order: an uncle (X18), the future Henry IV (when Earl of Derby[4]) paid two visits to the order when out fighting, as did Chaucer's knight in the *Canterbury Tales*:

	In translation
A Knyght ther was,	There was a Knight,
and that a worthy man,/	a most distinguished man,/
That fro the tyme that	Who from the day on
he first bigan/	which he first began/
To riden out, he	To ride abroad had

[2] Their full name was, The Teutonic Knights of St Mary's Hospital in Jerusalem. Their religious habit (uniform) comprised a large white cloak with a black cross on the left shoulder, which latter ultimately inspired the Decoration of the Iron Cross of Prussia and so of Germany.
[3] *Burke's Landed Gentry*, Burke's Peerage Ltd; London, 1965 p.623.
[4] Vide Appendix I.

Loved chivalrie,	followed chivalry,
Trouthe and honour,	Truth, honour,
Fredom and curteisie,	generosity and courtesy.
…	…
And therto hadde he	And ridden into battle,
riden, no man ferre,/	no man more,/
As wel in cristendom	As well to Christian
As in hethenesse,	as to heathen places,
…	…
Ful ofte tyme he hadde	He often sat at table
the bord bigonne/	in the chair/
Aboven alle nacions	Of honour, above all
in Pruce;/	nations, when in Prussia;[5]/
In Lettow hadde he	In Lithuania he had
reysed and in Ruce	ridden, and Russia

It is not recorded if any of my Lithuanian ancestors came face to face with these terrific fighters, but if they did I am sure they gave as good as they got! Undoubtedly, the Lithuanians did not take kindly to these lethal attentions, and under their leader Mindaugas (d.1263) they united to form the Grand Duchy of Lithuania. He put his entire domain on a military footing. Every able-bodied man was trained to raid and fight. Equipment captured from the crusaders was used, and Mongol-style tactics, learned from the invasions led by such as the grandson of Genghis Khan, Batu the Splendid and the like, in 1237, were employed.

Whereas the Teutonic Order was able to pick off one by one the disunited Livonians (modern Estonians and Latvians) and *Prusiskai* (Prussians), the unity of the Grand Duchy proved impossible to break[6]. Contemporaneous with Mindaugas, Robert de Sorbonne, chaplain to St Louis IX, founded in the University of Paris the college that bears his name, and the better part of Lincoln Cathedral (not so far from where this is being written) was built. From this period onwards stems a record of great pride for the Lithuanians: when the combatants have been equally matched in numbers, they have never been beaten.

In the next and 14th century – when much of Europe mourned the death of Dante[7] and Clare College, Cambridge was emerging[8], the Grand Duke Gediminas reigned over Lithuania (1316-41). He proved to be a brilliant military commander, conquering extensive territories to the east and south and so

[5] The area until World War II called East Prussia.

[6] For further details about the Teutonic Order and Lithuania, *vide* Seward, Desmond. *The Monks of War. The Military Religious Orders.* The Folio Society, London, 2001.

[7] 14 September, 1321.

[8] 1326 – among colleges of the University of Cambridge second only to my own, (Peterhouse) in age.

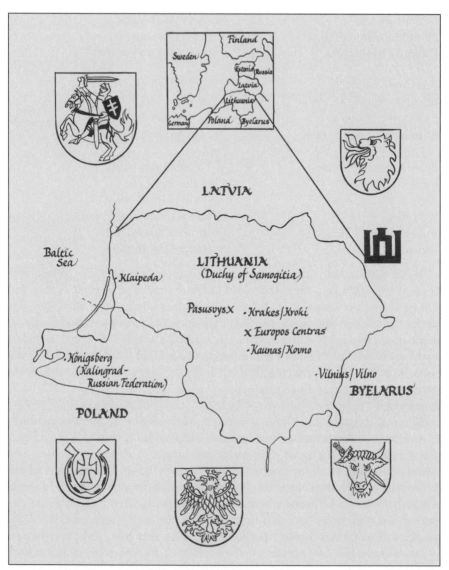

Map of Lithuania, post 1918, in relation to the other Baltic States. The arms are: upper left, Lithuania (Vytis in Lithuanian, Pogon in Polish 'pursuit'); upper right, the herb Zadora (of the Author's grand-maternal family); lower left, the herb Jastrzębiec (Sparrow Hawk – arms of the Author's male-line ancestors); lower centre, Poland (Orzel Bialy – White Eagle); lower right, the herb, Pomian – European buffalo, arms of the Author's great grand-maternal family. About half way down on the right is the historic, runic-like device known as the 'Towers of Gediminas'. For Lithuanians, this has the same national significance as the Thistle for Scots, the Maple Leaf for Canadians, and so on.

creating the vast empire referred to earlier on. Notwithstanding, the formation of this large state – perhaps all the more because of it – Lithuania continued to be plagued on its western borders by the repeated incursions of the Teutonic Order.

To put a stop to this once and for all an ally was needed. Poland, the immediate neighbour to the west – also vexed by these Knights – was the obvious choice. Accordingly when Richard II (1377-99) reigned in England, a marriage was arranged between the Grand Duke of Lithuania, Jagełło, and the Queen of Poland, Jadwiga[9].

Among the diplomatic questions raised by such a union, two concerned the Queen personally. First of all Jagełło and his people were still pagans. This question was resolved when, despite the treatment meted out to his country by the Catholic crusaders, the Grand Duke decided to be baptized a Catholic – mercifully, theology and politics are not always synonymous! From this point on one notes the gradual conversion of Lithuania to Christianity: the last country in Europe to be converted. Before this they had been Animists, investing all creation, especially trees, with a spiritual dimension – just like the Dravidians I came across, high up in the Nilgiri Hills, when serving in the Indian Army[10].

The second problem for the Queen was much more delicate. Rumour had it, not discouraged, for obvious reasons, by the Teutonic Order that her intended husband was, like a badger, covered with hair from head to foot and, as if that was not enough for the young lady to contend with, that his genitalia were larger than those of a stallion's. Jadwiga, only 16 years of age at the time (equivalent, probably, to late 20s in terms of modern development) was quite willing to follow the advice of her councillors and do her duty in this diplomatic marriage. Nevertheless, if these tales were true the prospect was daunting, duty or no duty.

How to discover the truth was, obviously, a problem, but she had to know. Accordingly, a favourite young knight of hers, Zawisza of Oleśnica was despatched to Jagełło's court to investigate. How was the young man to accomplish his task on behalf of his tall young Queen? (She was about 6 feet tall – unusual at that time).

Fortunately, a solution presented itself, as the Grand Duke was in the habit of taking a bath daily in the presence of his courtiers. So the Polish emissary joined this Baltic version of the French *levée*, and was able to report his findings to his mistress: the Grand Duke's body hair was in fact much less than the average man of his acquaintance, and, by the same token, his genitalia appeared to be somewhat smaller.

Doubtless, the young Queen was much relieved. Jagełło undertook the long journey to the Polish capital, then situated in the far south of the country at

---

[9] Interestingly enough, crowned as *Rex* not *Regina Poloniae*. There was a logic about that, just as we refer to a female Mayor or Prime Minister as such and not Mayoress or Prime Ministeress.

[10] Their conversion to Christianity is much helped by the fact that they have an acute appreciation of the spirit, of the soul.

Krakow. He was baptized, taking the name of Władisław (Ladislas) II Jagello, and three days later on 18 February, 1386, he married Jadwiga. Thus came about the Jagellonian dynasty for Poland and Lithuania which lasted until 1573.

Within a quarter of a century of this marriage, the Lithuanians and their Polish allies mounted a joint force, and at the battle called: Zalgiris by the Lithuanians; Grunwald by the Poles and Tannenberg by the Germans – it seems that everything has several names in this part of the world! – the allies inflicted a crushing defeat on the Teutonic Order, which never again proved a serious threat to either Lithuania or Poland. The battle was one of the largest and longest of the Middle Ages; it was also one of the bloodiest. The Grand Master, Ulrich von Jungingen, and all the order's officers, save one, were killed. For the Poles and the Lithuanians it was all highly satisfactory; for the order it was a mortal blow. And as the Lithuanians were now Catholics, its very *raison d' être* had ceased.

In the history of a nation, frequently there are one or two battles which are crucial in its historical development, and this one was so for the two allies.

Indeed, the word Zalgiris is so branded into the Lithuanian consciousness that today they call their best football club, 'Zalgiris' – rather as we might name one of our sports clubs 'Agincourt United', 'Plains of Abraham Maple Leaves' or 'Waterloo Wanderers.'

First, as with England and Scotland under the Stuarts, under the Jagellonians the union between Lithuania and Poland was personal. Later, in 1569 (the Elizabethan period for my English ancestors) by the Treaty of Lublin, the two countries united, to form what was termed The Most Serene Commonwealth – with Poland referred to as The Crown, and Lithuania as the Grand Duchy. Further, so as to accommodate the Lithuanians, the capital of the new alliance was moved from Krakow northwards to a small town on the Vistula called Warsaw. From then on, that is where the joint *Sejm* (pronounced 'same' – the Parliament) met, in the Royal Castle. This arrangement lasted until 1795 when, by the 3rd Partition of The Most Serene Commonwealth, Lithuania was annexed by the Russian Empire.

Following the Treaty of Lublin, movement within the Commonwealth became quite usual, with Lithuanians, such as the Radziwiłłs and the Sapiehas, taking part in Polish affairs. Similarly, Poles moved eastwards, as with my family of Święcicki – the subject of this chapter – going in about 1590 to that part of the Grand Duchy which today we would identify as Lithuania (see a genealogical chart for this family at the end of this chapter p. 67ff).

Intermarriage naturally took place, so there was a very considerable mixture of the two nationalities. In such cases, the Poles usually kept their names in the Polish form, as with Święcicki. Upon occasion, a Lithuanian family would Polonize its name as with Besierkierski – that of my great-grandmother, Isabella, who brought the family into the British Empire. Yet again some families kept a more Lithuanian form, as with Dowgiałło[11] – that of Sylveria (wife of Paul), my grandmother. The family of the actor, Sir John Gielgud, is another that kept its Lithuanian form – being easy for the Anglo-Saxons to pronounce.

Just as the then advanced governmental methods of Norman administration were introduced into England (a process which had started under King Edward the Confessor, prior to the Norman Conquest of 1066), so with Poland being a much more advanced state, Polish ways of doing things were gradually adopted in Lithuania following the marriage of Jagełło and Jadwiga.

The upper echelons of administration and society became, to a great extent, Polonized. This process is characterized by the fact that, at just about the time my office of Garter Principal King of Arms[12] was founded, the Boyars (Lithuanian nobles) were by the Treaty of Horodło, 1413, adopted into the Polish heraldic clan system.

As a result of this one has, for example, the Radziwiłłs henceforth bearing the *Herb* (arms known as) *Trąby*[13], and yet again, our own Dowgiałłos bearing the herb Zadora[14].

As a result of this whole process of Lithuania and Poland coming together, the position of the Poles in the Grand Duchy has been and still is rather like that of the Anglo-Irish in Ireland: at times advantageous, at others, not[15]. The difference, however, is that the assimilation was *not* the result of conquest – Lithuania and Poland came together in a voluntary union.

Yet again, in that part of the world if enquiring the nationality of a person, 'What are you?', one of Polish descent will answer, 'I'm a Pole, a Lithuanian-Pole' – with the emphasis on the noun. This attitude is well-illustrated by an instance during the visit of the Holy Father to Lithuania in 1993, a few days after the final Russian withdrawal from the country, when he addressed a large group of Poles whose families had lived in Lithuania for hundreds of years. His opening words were, 'Lithuanians, of Polish descent...' and in so doing gave grave offence!

However, just as they say that the best English is to be heard on the streets of Dublin, so probably the most distinguished contemporary writer in the Polish language is a Lithuanian-Pole, Czesław Mełosz, the Nobel Prize winner.

But to get back to the Święcickis: the family is of the *noblesse héréditaire sans titre,* in Polish, *Szlachta*. Literally, that translates as 'nobility', but is better rendered as 'gentry', as it embraced both those who possessed the vast, seemingly limitless estates and the owners, at the other end of the spectrum, of farms of

---

[11] Dowgiałło is the Polonized form of the original Lithuanian: Daugela

[12] 1415

[13] Three bugle horns conjoined as a 'Y' at the mouth piece.

[14] The lion's head with flames coming from its mouth.

[15] By the outbreak of World War II those of Polish descent in Lithuania constitued 18% of the population.

modest size. The Święcickis came from Wielkopolska (Greater Poland) to the west of Warsaw around Gniezno (the Polish Canterbury). Their name derives from their estate there of Święcice.

In Poland, hereditary family names started about 200 years after they were first used in England, that is to say in the 14th century, and the initial, usual form then was as for our family, de Święcice. By the 16th century, the nobiliary designation had become a suffix of 'cki' or 'ski' and so, Swiecicki (which also means, of Święcice)[16].

As a member of the *Szlachta*, the family identifies its status by bearing arms, and in this case they belong to the *Herb*, Jastrzębiec (a pun on the crest, which is a Sparrowhawk[17]). They were also senatorial, with a seat in the *Sejm*, which met in the Royal Castle in Warsaw.

The first recorded member of the family in Lithuania is Nicholas Alexander Święcicki, Honorary Steward of the King's Household and an Elector of the Vasa King John Kasimir in 1648. John Kasimir was the man who had to contend with the almost all-engulfing Swedish invasion of the country seven years later. Nicholas had a property at Zabide near Nowogródek where, a century and a half later, was born the greatest poet of the Polish language, Adam Mickiewicz, author of the celebrated epic poem *Pan Tadeusz*.

Nicholas's great-grandson, Joseph, was lieutenant-governor of Padlachia during the reign of the Elector of Saxony who became King of Poland in 1697 as Augustus II. How fortunate that gubernatorial responsibilities require only the upholding of constitutional and legal rights and duties, and do not enjoin the imitation of one's master's personal characteristics for

> The twenty-seven-year old Augustus was nothing if not picturesque. Universally known as Augustus the Strong and described by one of his subjects as 'half bull, half cock', he could break horseshoes with one hand, shoot with incredible accuracy, drink almost anyone under the table, and fornicate on a scale which would be hardly believable if he had not left regiments of bastards to prove it. He was not a stupid man, and he intended to turn the Commonwealth into a centralized monarchical state.[18]

To achieve this ambition he allied himself with Peter the Great against Charles XII of Sweden – an alliance that did not work out either to the King's or Poland's

---

[16] Should the family name not be: name of estate + 'cki' or 'ski', but rather the name of a town + suffix, as with Krakowski, then that would identify a *bourgeois* family usually of the Hebrew Faith.

[17] The Polish heraldic system is unlike all others in that it is a 'clan' system in which two or more apparently unrelated male-line families may bear identical Arms. For further details see, Swan, Sir Conrad. KCVO, Garter Principal King of Arms, 'Arma Poloniae – a consideration of some aspects of the Polish heraldic experience' being the 1991 Constance Egan Lecture delivered upon the invitation of The Heraldry Society. *The Coat of Arms*, Spring, 1995 pp 2-14 and Summer, 1995, pp 46-57.

[18] Zamoyski, Adam. *The Polish Way*. John Murray Ltd., London, 1987 p.208.

advantage. Allowing oneself to be embraced by that particular bear usually ends in more than a broken rib. This embroilment moved events forward towards the final debacle at the end of the 18th century, culminating in the Partitions of the Serene Commonwealth:

> It was a Carnival of knavery,
> Soon followed by a Lent of slavery.[19]

Fortunately, our Joseph died in 1710 well before the final humiliation.

That experience was the lot of his grandson, Andrew Ignatius who, along with his fellow countrymen, suddenly found himself a subject of the Tsar following the annexation by Russia of his part of Lithuania – as the result of the third and final partition of Poland-Lithuania in 1795.

Although continuing to live where they had for a couple of centuries, Andrew and his family gradually found that the legal system was changing. One aspect of this was that, in accordance with the imperial Russian system everyone was registered as belonging to one of the five official 'Estates': Noble, Merchant, Burgher, Peasant, Cleric[20]. Each of these notionally established the legal and social status of the holder. As a result, sixteen years after the annexation, Andrew had the *szlachta* status of himself and his descendants recognized by the Russian authorities with their matriculation as *Nobles héréditaire sans titre* of the Russian Empire, Book I of the Nobles Register[21].

This was completed in the year of that fantastic comet known as the Great Comet of 1811[22] which blazed across the night skies, and was seen as far afield from Europe as South Africa and America[23].

> Today the eyes and thoughts of all were turned
> To a new portent recently discerned.
> This was a comet of first size and worth
> That rising in the west flew to the north.
>
> …
>
> Each night the Lithuanians with fear
> Beheld the heavenly prodigy appear.
>
> …

---

[19] Mickiewicz, Adam. *Pan Tadeusz*. The Polish Cultural Foundation, London, 1964 p.13.

[20] Fitzlyon, Kyril and Browing, Tatiana, *Before the Revolution*. Allen Lane, London, 1977 pp. 25-26.

[21] Records of the Department of Heraldry; formerly at St Petersburg, now housed with the main Archival Administration under the Council of Ministers, Moscow. (The reference for our Święcicki entries is 1202 ff)

[22] C/1811 F1 (Great Comet) first seen 25 March 1811 *vide,* Kronk, Gary W: Cosmetography 'Discovery' (18 March 25) soon to be published by Cambridge University Press.

[23] Ibid. 'Observations'.

And just as King Sobieski, John the Third[24]
Was mounting, so his chancellor averred –

…

'See what goes on aloft!' the King exclaimed,
They looked, and saw above their heads a comet,
Advancing like the army of Mahomet.

…

'Amen' replied the Judge. 'I take your word
As omen of another John the Third.
There is a hero in the west today;
The comet brings him here to us, I pray !'[25]

Naturally, the Russians gave the comet a different interpretation. The Judge
was referring here to the advance of Napoleon upon Moscow (1812). The route
of the march of the Grande Armée was very near, though not actually over, our
property, by way of Kovno and Vilno (modern Kaunas and Vilnius). All the way
it was feted by the local population, from greatest lord to humblest peasant; their
liberators were passing by and so:

The Lithuanian horse [the Arms of Grand Duchy] will neigh again,
The boar of Zmudz [the Arms of the coast of Lithuania] shall roar.[26]

It was a heady moment; good to be alive.

The politically significant element of the country, the *szlachta,* sought every
means to persuade the emperor and his army to free them from the Russian
yoke, and in this the Święcickis naturally joined with fervour. The most
generous hospitality was extended to the French.

It so happened that one of the recipients of this liberal dispensing of vodka –
the Lithuanian variety of that delicious drink is excellent – and other tokens of
hospitality was a very young staff officer of Napoleon, Sous Lieutenant Armand
Swanton[27]. When in Vilnius, Napoleon set up his headquarters on Daukanto
Square in the residence of the former Russian Governor General. It was in this
palace of classical design that Armand attended to his military duties – used the
immaculate white marble grand staircase and trod its magnificent parquet floors,
so characteristic of that part of the world. Subsequently, Armand reached
Moscow with his commander-in-chief and, what is more remarkable, survived

---

[24] King John Sobieski completely crushed the Turkish army at the battle of Vienna, 1683 (referred to
here) and so saved Europe from Islam – Poland's most splendid achievement in history.

[25] Mickiewicz *op cit*. pp 166-169.

[26] *Ibid*. p.135.

[27] The French-born son of a 'Flight of Geese' Anglo-Irish family. Such were those who, because the
Penal Legislation against Catholics prevented their having a military career at home, went abroad in
droves and upon occasion formed whole regiments. Armand's father, Colonel Jacques Swanton,
commanded the Berwick Brigade under Louis XVI and was *Chevalier de l'Ordre de St Louis.*

the Retreat with all its horrors. Having arrived home in France he fell in love with a married lady – how typical, many an Anglo-Saxon might say! Being virtuous, she agreed to their being friends – but nothing more. In the end, her husband did the decent thing and died. So, at a mature age, she and Armand were married – *quel denouement romantique, n'est-ce-pas? Vive l'amour, vive la vertu de tous les deux!*

That is not the end of the story. Just short of a century and a half after Armand had been feted by the Polish-Lithuanian gentry, such as Andrew Ignatius Święcicki, Armand's niece (X3 through his sister, Louise, who married the artist Hilaire Belloc, [the 'French Lawrence']) that is to say, the Lady Hilda Northcote[28], was to marry in 1957 the grandson (X3 of Andrew Ignatius): the author of this book[29].

Almost half a century after that happy event, I followed in Armand's footsteps, as it were, in Vilnius when, on 16 February, 2003, I mounted the grand staircase and walked on the parquet flooring he had known in his work-place – by then the Presidential Palace – to be invested by His Excellency Valdas Adamkus, President of the Republic of Lithuania, with the Cross of a Knight of the Order of the Grand Duke Gediminas[30].

One of the properties of Armand's host, my great-great-great grandfather, Andrew Ignatius was the Manor of Pasusvys (pronounced: Pa-soo-sa-vis) in the Parish of Kroki (modern Krakes) near Kovno (modern Kaunas), and nearer still to that point recently adjudged by French geographers as the centre of Europe, upon which stands a simple granite slab inscribed, *Eurupos Centras*. Pasusvys means 'near/by' the river Susve, in much the same way as one finds in Suffolk, Stoke-by-Nayland, for example[31].

Krakes has, among other reasons, a place in the history of Lithuania in that it was its Parish Priest, Mikalojus Dauksa, who wrote the first book published in Lithuanian in the Grand Duchy (1595).

The property was owned later by Andrew's son, Julian Constantine Andrew who in 1848 – that fateful year of revolutions throughout Europe – married at St John's University Church, Vilnius, Isabella Paulina Bisieriskierska of the *Herb, Pomian*[32].

During the Autumn of that year, when the preparations for the wedding were well advanced[33], Chopin was in Scotland enjoying the hospitality of Lord

---

[28] See Appendix III. The descendants and connections of Dr. Joseph Priestly, FRS the 'Father of English Chemistry'.

[29] See genealogical chart at the end of this Chapter.

[30] Pursuant to Decree No. 1806 dated 14 June 2002 by the President of the Republic of Lithuania.

[31] Of which the church tower can be seen from the window of our drawing room at Boxford.

[32] The head of a Bison transfixed with a sword.

[33] The wedding took place on 20 Oct. 1848.

Torpichen at his Midlothian home[34] – let us hope he had frequent opportunities to appreciate drams of the restorative beverage of that country!

All of this was in the middle of that period of Polish history when guns were not proving effective in the restoration of Polish independence[35].

It fell to artists of different disciplines to impress upon the consciousness of the world – especially those about the diplomatic tables where the fate of nations is decided – that Poland, though removed from the map of Europe by acquisitive neighbours, still existed in spirit and showed its muscle by various insurrections during this period.

Chopin's works were 'like cannons hidden beneath the flowers' as Schuman put it[36]. One has only to listen to his Polonaises to sense their grandeur and declamatory rebelliousness.

Poland's latter-day answer to James Northcote, RA[37], that is to say Jan Matejk (1838-93), was painting those heroic, enormous canvasses of great events in Polish history – some an inspiration, others a warning.

Adam Mickiewkz (1798-1855) – as recently pointed out, the greatest of nineteenth century Polish poets, and a profound admirer of Byron's individualism and spirit of revolt – reminded everyone, in such works as his masterpiece, *Pan Tadeuz*, of the civilized and humane life of the Polish-Lithuanian countryside often as epitomized by that of the szlachta and their dependants on their estates, such as Pasusvys.

In addition to the diplomatic/political implications of their works, they also aimed at nourishing the psyche of the Polish people. The goal was, in fact, not a matter of art for art's sake. That Mickiewkz could even go so far as to urge Chopin to write an opera(!) is a superb example of the thrust of all this artistic endeavour of the nineteenth century.

Dąbrowski's March[38], sung by his Polish Legionnaires fighting for Napoleon in Italy since 1797, which begins with its defiant, stirring proclamation: 'Poland's

---

[34] *Korespondencja Frydryka Chopin* ed. B.E. Sydow, Warsaw, 1955 Vol. I. letter to Auguste Franchomme II/VIII/1848 p. 255.

[35] Various Polish insurrections took place: 1794, then efforts during the Napoleonic Wars, followed by revolts in 1831, 1848, 1863 and 1905.

[36] *Neue Zeitschrift Für Muzik*, No. 33, 1836.

[37] 1796-1831. Famous for his large historical paintings, such as 'The entry of William of Orange into Exeter.' A story in my wife's family of Northcote runs as follows: When their fellow Devonian, Northcote, was a young, struggling artist: 'he was not related.' However, upon his becoming famous and a Royal Academician then it was: 'of course he must be'(!). James did not hold this against them; became a good friend, and left them some of his works. Alas, so far, no relationship has been established. In England, certain names are particularly to be found in certain counties; and this is so with Northcote and Devon.

[38] General Henryk Dąbrowski formed the first of the Polish Legions in Milan (1797). The original text of the 'Song of the Polish Legions in Italy' – as the anthem was originally called – was by Józef Wybicki (Dąbrowski's close associate) and the music was by Prince Michal Kleofas Oginski.

not dead as long as we live...' immediately captured the imagination of the soldiers and émigrés as well as the country's population.

Banned by the Tsarist and Prussian governments in 1815 (after Napoleon's defeat) and again in 1860, it lived on, in numerous textual variants depending upon the patriotic, socio-political purposes it served, into the 20th century[39].

No wonder it became the Polish National Anthem once independence was regained following World War I[40].

But mid-nineteenth century life in Poland – Lithuania was not all a matter of the contemplation of Poland's messianic role, nor patriotic inspiration through musical, graphic or poetic masterpieces.

More down to earth, it is somewhat amusing to recall that in a village near Pasusvys, there was a hard-working and efficient Jewish shopkeeper, one Ephraim Sieff by name (until recently almost all commerce in the country was conducted by those of the Hebrew Faith): from Ephraim descended Israel Moses, Lord Sieff, of Marks and Spencer fame[41]. Did the Święcicki account help his family on its way to being represented in every large town in Britain?!

The emigrant Ephraim – to Manchester first – was born in that portentous year 1863 – the year of the Great Insurrection of the Poles and Lithuanians which all but succeeded. This alarmed the government in St Petersburg to such an extent that draconian measures were introduced: all education to be in Russian; no publications in either Polish or Lithuanian; all ecclesiastical recordings, even of non-Orthodox churches, to be in the Cyrillic script, and so on. A period of frustration set in, all the more for the Święcicki family who had been active in the insurrection: it is always unwise to be on the losing side in a rebellion, *n'est ce pas?*

Eventually our great-grandmother, Isabella, decided to leave the country and take her five sons and two daughters abroad. She sold Pasusvys to her Zaborski cousins (whose descendants, having survived the Communist regime, still live in Lithuania)[42]. In two journeys, Isabella took her family, by way of

---

[39] As in the uprisings against the Russians (1830 & 1863); during the 'Spring of the Nations' (1848); as the hymn of the students' union (Zwiazek Burszów, 1816-30). In wartime versions 'Dabrowski' is replaced by various military leaders including: Pilsudski (as leader of the Polish Legion, 1914) and Sikorski (C-in-C Polish Armed Forces, World War II).

[40] From 10 Nov. 1917 onwards Marshal Jósef Pilsudski organized the re-birth of independent Poland and on 10 Feb. 1918 the first sovereign session of the Polish Sejm (Parliament) began, following the re-establishment of independence.

[41] Created (Life Peer) 16 January, 1966, Baron Sieff, of Brampton in the Royal County of Berkshire – *vide, Burke's Peerage*. Burke's Peerage Ltd., London, 1967 pp. 2288-2289.

[42] The name is now spelt Zaborskis. Most Lithuanian names end in an 'S'. In view of the strong nationalism in the country at present our cousins have wisely added a final 'S' so as not to be regarded as 'un-Lithuanian' in the sense of 'un-American' – essential when making one's living there!

Hamburg[43] to England; crossed to Halifax, Nova Scotia; after that through Canada to Southern Ontario and across to Detroit; from there through the United States by train (as the railway across Canada had not been completed yet) and so to San Francisco. From there the journey was by boat northwards to their final destination, a place then called Granville and from 1886, Vancouver. These journeys were completed by 1884, two years before the first trans-Canada railway reached the Pacific. According to some, this early arrival of the family in the province of British Columbia gives it a status analogous to that of a pre-Conquest family in England!

One might well ask, why did Isabella choose distant, all but inaccessible British Columbia as her goal? There are two reasons for this. First, she wanted her family to be as far as possible from any area where the writ of the Russian government ran, and the most westerly Canadian Province qualified ideally on that count. It is just as well, however, that she did not decide to go there a few years before, or she would have found that she had placed them almost cheek by jowl with the Russians once again by being next to their colony in North America, Alaska[44].

Second, the construction of the Canadian Pacific Railway (CPR) played its part. This monumental undertaking attracted great attention in the Russian Empire as the building of the Trans-Siberian Railway was very much *sur le tapis*. As the problems being faced and solved by the CPR were similar, to those that would confront the building of their railway to the extreme Orient[45], a flood of newspaper articles poured from the press. These also spoke of an expected economic boom in the area of what is now Vancouver once the CPR was completed to that point – a possibility not lost on the ever practical and courageous Isabella.

She brought with her the proceeds of the sale of Pasusvys in gold Roubles – 'everyone understands gold' was her comment, with that characteristic dash of angostura bitters in the gin of Polish humour. It was enough to buy a farm for each of the sons, and provide a dowry for the two daughters. The family even brought some of their servants with them, though that was an investment that did not produce the desired return. However, the journey must have been a great education for these peasant girls, and if they found good husbands in their new land, well, that was a positive aspect to be considered!

---

[43] SSA. New Series II. HPS. to EHS. 18 May, 1947 from The 94 British Military Hospital, Hamburg, BAOR. 'my mother and father passed through Hamburg, on their way to the new World. Mother… as she looked at the vast expanse of this big city, over the rail of her ship, little did she realize that her still unborn son [father of the author] would one day be a gynaecologist here in one of the biggest Military Hospitals of the British Army. I often think this as I cross and recross, by car, the bridges of the Elbe at Hamburg.'

[44] Russia sold Alaska to the United States in 1867.

[45] The Trans-Siberian Railway was built at the end of the 19th century.

Finally, in 1895 Isabella's eventful life came to a close, but not without one final characteristic adventure: she became the first white woman to be buried in the Red Indian churchyard at Mission, British Columbia – now the site of a Benedictine monastery founded from Fort Augustus, Scotland.

The family thus established itself in the British Empire and, in addition to making available the site for the Holy Rosary Cathedral in Vancouver, has, among others, produced a general; a Justice of the Supreme Court; a Papal Knight; an Oblate Missioner to the Red Indians[46]; a Good Shepherd Sister[47]; a university Vice-Chancellor and a Garter Principal King of Arms.

Prior to the epic emigration of the family, Isabella's eldest son, Paul Constantine had married Sylveria, of the distinguished and historic Lithuanian family of Dowgiałło. They had as their first child born in Canada, Henry Peter, my father, born in Vancouver in 1892[48]. Educated at St Louis' College, New Westminster, as a young man he tried his vocation to the Catholic priesthood with the Oblates of Mary Immaculate, of which Order his elder brother, Anthony, was already a member. As he used to joke later, 'I couldn't get *les girls* out of my head!' Wisely he and his Religious Superior decided that, as with St Thomas More, the celibate priesthood was not for him. Some years later, Mother, when in Rome, arranged to call on that Superior – by then the Superior General of the Order – so as to let him know how his sometime charge had fared. Upon being brought up to date he replied, 'I knew he would make a good husband and father. He was a generous young man.' After the monastery, Father's qualifying in medicine, marriage, service in World War I and subsequent medical practice at Duncan and the Cowichan Valley on Vancouver Island in British Columbia have already been discussed in some detail.

It will also be recalled from Chapter II that I was very close to my maternal grandparents. But what was the position *vis-à-vis* my father's parents?

Unfortunately, I never knew my paternal grandmother, Sylveria, as she died five months before I was born.

My grandfather, Paul Constantine, was alive when I arrived, but died a fortnight before my 5th birthday in 1929. During those five years he lived on the mainland at New Westminster, and to get there the journey by car and ferry from our house took the best part of five hours, at that time: while we did visit

---

[46] Anthony John. All of his work was in the Rockies where he did much of the visiting of his flock on horseback.

[47] An Order that looks after delinquent girls. The nun in question, Lydia Rita Delphine (in religion Sr Mary St Stanislaus) on the night before entering the convent called each of her own sisters separately into her room and gave her a beauty secret!

[48] It is significant of their rather grand attitude as far as governments were concerned that although his parents had my father baptized at an early age they did not condescend to register his birth with the Civil Registrar of Births, Marriages and Deaths at about the same time. This omission was not discovered until my father was about to be commissioned into the Canadian Army during World War I and he did not 'exist' officially until the matter was then put right at the age of 25!

him from time to time one could not exactly dash over for lunch and be back for tea.

Notwithstanding, I soon learned that Sylveria had been a woman of great character. Even my mother was somewhat in awe of her – and that required some doing! Further, she was a woman of firm religious faith.

In addition, she was extremely artistic. To take one example, she could embroider, in silk on linen, a bouquet of coloured flowers with such fineness that one could not tell the obverse from the reverse. We still have examples of this exquisite work in the family[49].

She was also fully conscious of the obligations incumbent upon anyone who bears a name of historic significance, as she did: that of the Lithuanian boyar family of Dowgiałło which, as already seen, ante-dated the Treaty of Horodlo, 1413.

Turning to my paternal grandfather, Paul Constantine, I have vivid recollections of sitting on his knee while he talked with me, during our visits from Duncan to New Westminster to be with him.

He had had an eventful life, and could remember well taking part in the Great Insurrection of 1863 against the Russians; he was 13 at the time. And then the aftermath following its suppression: at school having to learn and write everything in Russian – could there be anything more galling for a Pole – especially a Lithuanian-Pole for such have always considered themselves much more truly Polish than those living on the banks of the Vistula! However, he ultimately had his revenge, so to speak, as in time he went to St Petersburg and graduated MA in Philosophy from 'their' university.

In a sense, he was something of a Renaissance man, for quite apart from his intellectual abilities he was extremely adept with his hands and loved new experiences. For example, he was able to turn a piece of wood into an object of elegant furniture – some pieces of which we inherited.

Yet again, it was typical of him that when the Klondike Gold Rush broke out in 1896 he could not resist the thrill of going up, 'just to see what it was like!' After a short visit he was happy to return to the comparative civilization of the Fraser Valley, and the joys of *le foyer de sa famille* where Sylveria presided with the 14 year old Anthony – later the Oblate Missioner – and my father aged 5; my uncle, Alphonse, was the product of the happy reunion.

My grandfather too, was a man of solid religious convictions, and joined with the rest of the family in making available the site of the Holy Rosary Cathedral, Vancouver, as previously mentioned.

One of the great joys both he and my grandmother shared was living to see Poland restored as an independent state at the end of World War I.

---

[49] Artistic skill was inherited by her daughter, Ann, who received the Governor-General's Gold Medal for her ability as an organist.

To achieve this, the more or less simultaneous collapse of no less than three great empires was necessary. That such would take place must have been almost beyond the wildest dreams of most Poles during their experience of one and a quarter centuries of partition; but in the end that is precisely what happened.

The fact that, Marshal Józef Pilsudski[50], should bring this about was an added matter of satisfaction for their patriotic hearts he, like they, being of a Polish family long associated with Lithuania..

I would much like to have known more of them both, yet such was not to be.

But one important aspect of all this has not yet been touched upon. It is as old as Methuselah. This concerns the problems caused when a person has a name from a language area different from that where he lives. The usual solution is to make it easier for the host area to pronounce the name. We find records of this problem as far back, at least, as the exilic and postexilic periods of Babylon, when local names were adopted by Jewish parents for their children, such as with Sheshbazzar and Zerubbabel the future royal governors[51].

Sometimes the spelling is kept the same but the pronunciation is varied, as with the classic case of the French name, Cholmondeley which is pronounced in English as 'Chumley', or the Irish name McMahon, in French as 'Muck-ma-harn', and so on.

If different scripts are used between the two areas, this usually causes little difficulty as the name will be rendered phonetically in the 'host area' as, for example,

Трубецкой is rendered as Trubstskoy for us or, *vice versa,* Barclay de Tolly as Барклаи-де-Толли for the Russians.

The real problem comes, however, when the two languages concerned have the same alphabet but use identical letters for different sounds, (not to mention other complications), as with a Slavic language using the Roman alphabet for a name such as Święcicki.

Even for the local Indians, Chinese and Sikhs the language in common for everyone in the Cowichan Valley where my father had his practice, was English. As none was – understandably – adept with Slavonic pronunciation they found Święcicki daunting. While it is quite simple when you know how, confronted by an acute accent over the 'S' and a cedilla beneath the 'e' most of Father's patients would have asked: where does one start? Such a predicament is obviously not encouraging to those needing medical help. Confidence, not apprehension, is what one must encourage in a patient. Accordingly, my father adopted in 1919[52]a rough Anglo-Saxon approximation of the first syllable of his hereditary family

---

[50] *b.* 1867 (at Vilno) d. 1935.

[51] Lee, Howard Clark; Rogerson, John; Meyers, Eric M. and Sandarini, Anthony J. *The Cambridge Companion to the Bible.* Cambridge University Press, 1977 pp.148-155.

[52] Recorded by executing a Deed Poll dated 20th December, 1919.

name, and so became: Swan. By this name, Henry Peter's family has been known ever since.

In so many ways it was a great pity as our old name had been part of the history of two countries for several hundred years. However, one must conduct oneself in the face of existing reality, not as one would have it be.

The King whom my father had served so loyally in World War I had also realized this imperative, and some few months before my father had executed his Deed Poll, George V had issued a proclamation[53] declaring that henceforth the name of his family would be Windsor, and renouncing all German honorifics.

This quintessence of a tweedy British, huntin', shootin' and fishin' Norfolk squire, faced with the tide of Germanophobia which was sweeping through so many of his subjects, as their brothers, sons, sweethearts and husbands were slaughtered on the fields of France, considered it necessary to defuse the situation as far as the monarchy was concerned. Change was definitely in the air at this time.

Other members of the British Royal Family followed suit, as did the Battenbergs, becoming Mountbatten – a name to which I was to become not indifferent, as will be seen in Chapter VI dealing with my India days.

---

[53] 17 July, 1917.

Outline Pedigree of the family of Święcicki otherwise Swan[54]

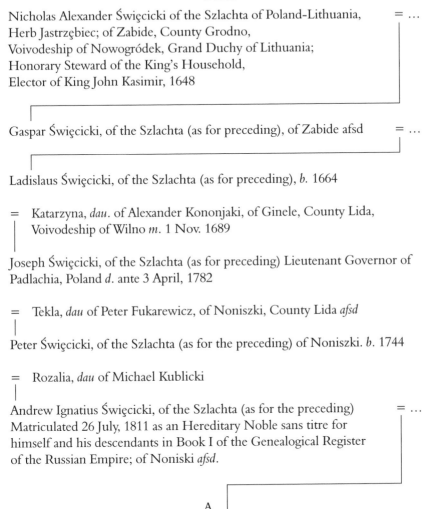

Nicholas Alexander Święcicki of the Szlachta of Poland-Lithuania,   = ...
Herb Jastrzębiec; of Zabide, County Grodno,
Voivodeship of Nowogródek, Grand Duchy of Lithuania;
Honorary Steward of the King's Household,
Elector of King John Kasimir, 1648

Gaspar Święcicki, of the Szlachta (as for preceding), of Zabide afsd   = ...

Ladislaus Święcicki, of the Szlachta (as for preceding), *b.* 1664

=   Katarzyna, *dau.* of Alexander Kononjaki, of Ginele, County Lida,
    Voivodeship of Wilno *m.* 1 Nov. 1689

Joseph Święcicki, of the Szlachta (as for preceding) Lieutenant Governor of
Padlachia, Poland *d.* ante 3 April, 1782

=   Tekla, *dau* of Peter Fukarewicz, of Noniszki, County Lida *afsd*

Peter Święcicki, of the Szlachta (as for the preceding) of Noniszki. *b.* 1744

=   Rozalia, *dau* of Michael Kublicki

Andrew Ignatius Święcicki, of the Szlachta (as for the preceding)   = ...
Matriculated 26 July, 1811 as an Hereditary Noble sans titre for
himself and his descendants in Book I of the Genealogical Register
of the Russian Empire; of Noniski *afsd*.

A   ...

---

54 For full details of this pedigree *vide* 1) concerning the initial and subsequent Matriculations as Hereditary Nobles sans titre of the Russian Empire, Book I in Records of the Department of Heraldry formerly at St Petersburg now housed with the Main Archival Administration under the Council of Ministers, Moscow (reference for the Święcicki entries: No 1202 etc); 2) concerning the Official Registration of the entire pedigree in the College of Arms, London, consult CAR: Norfolk XCIII. 145-149 and XCIV. 244; A to R 3, 8-9.

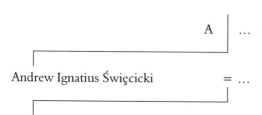

A   ...

Andrew Ignatius Święcicki   = ...

Julian Constantine Andrew Święcicki of the Szlachta and hereditary Noble
both as for the preceding (confirmed in the latter status 20 Sept 1826);
of the Manor House, Pasusvys, Parish of Kroki, and of Novomsyl both Province
of Kovno, and of Vilna living 12 Dec 1870 aged 53

=   Isabella Paulina Besierkierska *m.* 20 Oct. 1848 at the University Church of
    St. John, Vilna. Completed two journeys, by 1884, taking her family to
    British Columbia where she died 16 May 1895 and buried in the Oblate
    Mission at Mission in that Province.

— 1S Paul Constantine Święcicki *b.* 22 Dec. 1850 (of whom more later)

— 2S Joseph Stanisław Święcicki/Svenceski* *b.* 12 April 1858 of the Szlachta
      and Hereditary Noble both as for his father Julian Constantine Andrew
      Święcicki
      = Constance Ann Mieunska *m.* 1 July 1892

      5 sons and 3 daus.

— 1D Eleanor Margaret *b.* 21 Feb 1857 of the Szlachta and Hereditary Noble
      both as for preceding
      = Francis Joseph Wojtkiewicz/Voitkevic *m.* 28 Jan. 1879

      3 sons and 3 daus.

— 3S Adam Julian Constantine Święcicki/Swencisky* *b.* 1 Jan 1863 of the
      Szlachta and Hereditary Noble both as for the preceding
      = Michalina Wojszwillowie *m.* 7 Aug. 1893

J   I   A   M
See following page   See following page

---

*It will be noted how there was no agreement between the brothers as how to render, phonetically,
their family name for the ease of their English-speaking neighbours. This is an example of the typical
extreme individualism characteristic of many Poles. It reminds one of the saying among Poles: When
there are two Poles in the room, there's one too many!

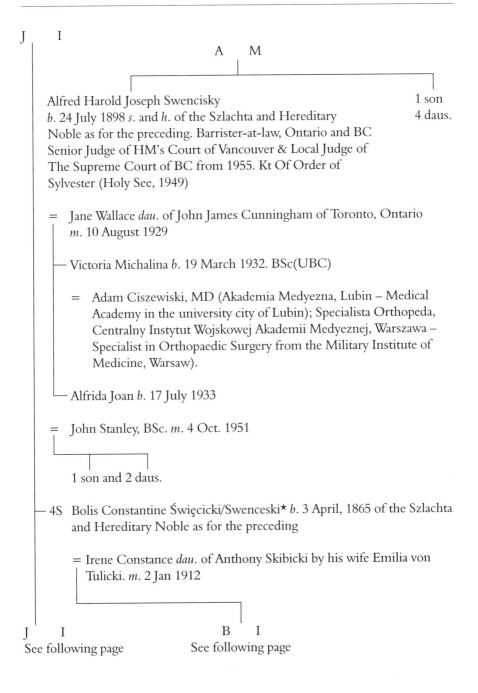

J   I

A   M

Alfred Harold Joseph Swencisky   1 son
b. 24 July 1898 *s*. and *h*. of the Szlachta and Hereditary   4 daus.
Noble as for the preceding. Barrister-at-law, Ontario and BC
Senior Judge of HM's Court of Vancouver & Local Judge of
The Supreme Court of BC from 1955. Kt Of Order of
Sylvester (Holy See, 1949)

=   Jane Wallace *dau*. of John James Cunningham of Toronto, Ontario
    m. 10 August 1929

— Victoria Michalina *b*. 19 March 1932. BSc(UBC)

   =   Adam Ciszewiski, MD (Akademia Medyezna, Lubin – Medical
      Academy in the university city of Lubin); Specialista Orthopeda,
      Centralny Instytut Wojskowej Akademii Medyeznej, Warszawa –
      Specialist in Orthopaedic Surgery from the Military Institute of
      Medicine, Warsaw).

— Alfrida Joan *b*. 17 July 1933

=   John Stanley, BSc. *m*. 4 Oct. 1951

1 son and 2 daus.

— 4S   Bolis Constantine Święcicki/Swenceski★ *b*. 3 April, 1865 of the Szlachta
     and Hereditary Noble as for the preceding

   = Irene Constance *dau*. of Anthony Skibicki by his wife Emilia von
     Tulicki. *m*. 2 Jan 1912

J   I   B   I
See following page   See following page

J   I   B   I

Alexander Bolis Swenceski. *b*. 13 Oct. 1913 *s*. and *h*. of the   1 son
Szlachta and Hereditary Noble both as for the preceding.   1 dau
Brigadier General U.S. Marine Corps (from 1955).
Commissioned 2nd Lieut. Served in World War II & Korean
War. Silver Star; Legion of Merit with combat 'V'; Presidential
Citation and Purple Heart (all U.S.A.); Order of the Cloud
and Banner (China); Presidential Unit Citation (Korea) *d.s.p*
22 Nov. 1959.

= Ruth May Merrit *m*. 20 Aug. 1940 (*d*. 2 May 1965)

— 2D Veronica Susanne. *b*. 25 Aug. 1871. Of the Szlachta and Hereditary
Noble both as for preceding.

= Dolphis Laneuville *m*. 28 April 1892

2 sons and 6 daus.

— 5S Anthony Michael Święcicki/Swencisky* *b*. 10 Sept. 1860 of the Szlachta
and Hereditary Noble both as for preceding

= Joanna Angelina Uscich *m*. 6 Aug. 1893

2 sons and 6 daus.

— 1S Paul Constantine Święcicki, (see above) *b*. 22 Dec. 1850 at Pasusvys *afsd*.
s. and *h*. Of the Szlachta and Hereditary Noble as for his father Julian
Constantine Andrew Święcicki. Of Novomsyl and Rosten all *afsd*., and
subsequently of New Westminster, British Columbia. MA Univ. of St
Petersburg *d*. 16 April 1929 at New Westminster.

= Sylveria, *b*. 22 May 1860 *dau*. of Jan Guvaszkiewicz Dowgałło by his
wife Paulina Dowgałło of Chekiski Castle. *m*. 10 January 1880 at
Univ. Church of St John afsd. *d*. 21 Dec. 1923 at New Westminster
afsd

P   S
See following page

P   S

— 1S Anthony John Święcicki/Swenceski. *b*. 7 Feb 1883 at Pasuvys *afsd. s.* and
      h. Of the Szlachta and Hereditary Noble as for his father. Oblate Father,
      ordained priest 1912. Missioner to the Indians in the Rocky Mountains.
      d. 12 Feb 1956.

— 2S Henry Peter Święcicki *b*. 6 Dec. 1892 (of whom more later)

— 3S Alphonse Święcicki *b*. 22 Nov. 1896. Of the Szlachta and Hereditary
      Noble as for his father. (Assumed by Deed Poll 20 Dec. 1919 name of
      Swan). DDS (McGill) *d.s.p.*

— 1D Ann *b*. 25 July 1900 *m*. 14 Feb. 1931 Donald McCarthy

— 2S Henry Peter Święcicki *b*. 6 Sept. 1892 at Vancouver, B.C. Of the
      Szlachta and Hereditary Noble as for his father. MD, CM(McGill),
      LMCC, LRCOG, LM(Rotunda). Major RCAMC & RAMC etc.
      (Assumed by Deed Poll 20 Dec. 1919 name of Swan)
      d. 23 Nov. 1963 at Colchester, Essex.

      = Edna Hanson Magdalen *b*. 12 Nov. 1899 at Wealdstone, Middx., *dau*.
        of Alfred Edward Green, J.P. (see pedigree of Green at end of chapter
        II) Cross of Honour Pro Ecclesia et Pontifice (1979) *m*. 8 Sept 1917
        at Folkestone, Kent. *d*. 10 Nov. 1988 at Boxford House, Suffolk.

      —1S Rev. Peter Julian Michael Swan, *b*. 21 May 1919 at Folkestone
           afsd. Of the Szlachta and Hereditary Noble as for his father.
           Member of the Congregation of St. Basil. Ordained Priest
           18 Dec. 1943 at Toronto. BA, MA, PhD(Toronto), LLD(Honoris
           causa) Assumption University of Windsor (2002), DD (Honoris
           causa) University of St. Michael's College (2003); Registrar
           1949-61, Academic Vice-President 1958-61 Assumption College
           subsequently Assumption Univ. of Windsor; Sixth President and
           Superior, St. Thomas More College, Univ. of Saskatchewan,
           1961-77; Vice-Pres. 1977-78, President & Vice-Chancellor, Univ.
           of St. Michael's College, Toronto; 1978-84; Dean, St. Joseph's
           College, Univ. of Alberta, 1985-91. Chaplain, SMO of Malta.

H   E
See following page

H   E

└─ 2S   Sir Conrad Marshall John Fisher Swan, KCVO (1994) LVO (1978)
CVO (1986) KGCN (2003)
b. 13 May 1924 at Duncan, B.C. Of the Szlachta and Hereditary Noble
as for preceding. Served World War II (Capt. Madras Regt, I.A.) BA &
MA(UWO) PhD(Cantab). Lecturer 1955-57 Assistant Prof. of History,
1957-60, University Beadle 1957-60, Assumption Univ. of Windsor.
Rouge Dragon Pursuivant of Arms, 1962-68, York Herald of Arms,
1968-92, Garter Principal King of Arms, 1992-95, College of Arms. Kt
of Honour & Devotion, SMO of Malta 1979

= The Lady Hilda Susan Mary Northcote SS StJ *b*. 23 July 1937 at City
of Westminster, *yr. dau*. of Henry 3rd Earl of Iddesleigh & 10th Bart.
m. 28 Dec. 1957 Rep. For Boxford on Cosford RDC 1971-73;
Suffolk County Chairman, Riding for the Disabled Assoc. 1983-92;
President, St John Ambulance of County of Suffolk, 1989-95. Dame
of Honour & Devotion, SMO of Malta. *k*. 4 Dec. 1995 by 'hit and
run' driver at Boxford, Suffolk. (And see royal Descent, Appendix I
descent from Joseph Priestly, FRS, Appendix III)

├─ 1D   (Mary) Elizabeth Magdalen Swan *b*. 5 Aug 1959 at Pynes, Devon.
Of the Szlachta and Hereditary Noble as for her father. *m*. 6 June
1981 Graduate Nurse St Bartholomew's Hospital, London

= Roger Peter le Strange Herring *s*. of Peter William le Strange
Herring, CBE, Colonel in the Army. Provost Marshal U.K. Land
Forces. *Educ*. At Haileybury.

Alice Elizabeth le Strange Herring *b*. 23 Nov. 1985	John Roger le Strange Herring *b*. 11 March 1987
Thomas Peter le Strange Herring *b*. 15 May 1990	Rafe Henry le Strange Herring *b*. 1 Oct. 1991

C   H
See following page

C   H

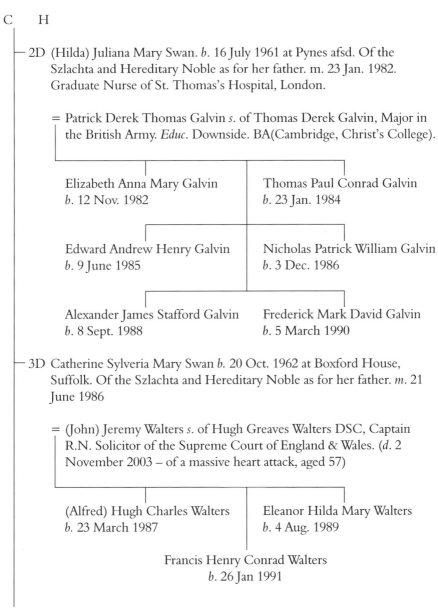

2D (Hilda) Juliana Mary Swan. *b.* 16 July 1961 at Pynes afsd. Of the Szlachta and Hereditary Noble as for her father. m. 23 Jan. 1982. Graduate Nurse of St. Thomas's Hospital, London.

= Patrick Derek Thomas Galvin *s.* of Thomas Derek Galvin, Major in the British Army. *Educ.* Downside. BA(Cambridge, Christ's College).

Elizabeth Anna Mary Galvin
b. 12 Nov. 1982

Thomas Paul Conrad Galvin
b. 23 Jan. 1984

Edward Andrew Henry Galvin
b. 9 June 1985

Nicholas Patrick William Galvin
b. 3 Dec. 1986

Alexander James Stafford Galvin
b. 8 Sept. 1988

Frederick Mark David Galvin
b. 5 March 1990

3D Catherine Sylveria Mary Swan *b.* 20 Oct. 1962 at Boxford House, Suffolk. Of the Szlachta and Hereditary Noble as for her father. *m.* 21 June 1986

= (John) Jeremy Walters *s.* of Hugh Greaves Walters DSC, Captain R.N. Solicitor of the Supreme Court of England & Wales. (*d.* 2 November 2003 – of a massive heart attack, aged 57)

(Alfred) Hugh Charles Walters
b. 23 March 1987

Eleanor Hilda Mary Walters
b. 4 Aug. 1989

Francis Henry Conrad Walters
b. 26 Jan 1991

C   H

See following page

C   H

— 1S Andrew Conrad Henry Joseph Swan. *b*. 29 Jan. 1964 at Boxford House
      afsd. s. and *h*. Of the Szlachta and Hereditary Noble as for his father.
      Educ. Downside. B.Sc.(Hons) Liverpool Univ. A.C.A.

      = Fenella Jane Rogers *m*. 17 June 1989. *dau*. of Air Chief Marshal Sir
        John Rogers, KCB, CBE.

      Isabelle Frances Anna Swan   Amelia Elizabeth Mary Swan
      b. 30 June, 1992   *b*. 9 May 1994
      Of the Szlachta and Hereditary   Of the Szlachta and Hereditary
      Noble as for her father.   Noble as for her father.

      Alexandra Hilda Catherine Swan   Cecily Victoria Helena Swan
      b. 15 July 1996   *b*. 7 March 2000
      Of the Szlachta and Hereditary   Of the Szlachta and Hereditary
      Noble as for her father.   Noble as for her father.

— 4D Anastasia Cecilia Mary Swan *b*. 25 July 1966 at Boxford House *afsd*. Of
      the Szlachta and Hereditary Noble as for her father. Graduate Nurse of
      St. Mary's Hospital, Paddington, London. *m*. 2 September, 1984.

      = His Honour Peter Galbraith Mark Hatvany, Deputy District Judge
        (England & Wales) from 27 June 2001. Baron Hatvany de Hatvan, of
        the Kingdom of Hungary (hereditary to all male-line descendants)
        Patent of creation dated 23 Oct. 1908 (*Liber Regii* Vol. LXXII p.266) *s*.
        of Baron Paul Imre Hatvany de Hatvan.

      Alexander Imre Hatvany   Alicia Mary Hatvany
      b. 11 March 1991. A Baron of   *b*. 10 Jan. 1993. A Baroness
      the Kingdom of Hungary.   of the Kingdom of Hungary.

                    Benedict Xavier Hatvany
                    b. 22 July 1994. A Baron
                    of the Kingdom of Hungary.

The Armorial Bearings
of Swan
of Duncan, Vancouver Island, British Columbia, Canada
And
of Boxford House, Suffolk, England.

De heraldica Polonica – a note on Polish heraldry before considering Arms of the family.

In most countries that follow the Western European tradition in heraldry, armorial designs are almost invariably described by blazons (technical descriptions). Nevertheless, there are a few designs where a blazon is unnecessary as the design is known by a single word or short phrase as with *France ancient* which signifies: a blue background and thereon an indeterminate number of gold fleurs-de-lys, and treated as if cut from a piece of wallpaper bearing a design throughout.

The situation in Polish heraldry is the exact reverse. In this system, almost all Coats of Arms (*Herbs* in Polish) are identified by a simple name.

Accordingly, in the case of the Święcicki Swans the *Herb* is *Jastrzębiec* (which means, Sparrow Hawk). These Arms are found borne since 1386.

A further characteristic of Polish heraldry is the fact that two or more apparently unrelated male-line families can bear the same Arms (*Herb*). As a result this tradition has been described as a clan system in some rather distant ways analogous to the Scottish system.

The Polish arrangements can arise in one of two ways. As already explained in this chapter, when hereditary family names began to be used in that country in the 14th century – some 200 years after Western Europe – a person/family would be known as 'of a particular place/property' as in our case, de Święcice ('of [the estate of] Święcice). By the 16th century, the nobiliary description had become a suffix of ' cki' or 'ski' and so Święcicki (which once again means, 'of Święcice').

Yet again, if a male-line family owned several estates then one could have one branch being known as 'of this estate' and another 'of that estate' and so on. The result follows that despite being of the same male-line they have different family names.

On the other hand, upon occasion, a family (alien in blood) was 'adopted' into an heraldic clan and so would henceforth bear the *Herb* of the 'adopting' family though unrelated in blood.

Just as today a Regimental Officer will refer to his 'brother-Officer' so those who share the same *Herb* will say, my *'brat herbowy'*, that is to say my 'Arms-brother' – brother in Arms, if you like, in a Polish, heraldic sense.

The classical example of this followed the Treaty of Horodlo (1413) when 48 Polish heraldic *gentes* (not separate families) 'adopted' a corresponding number of

Lithuanian Boyars (nobles) as brothers in chivalry and bestowed on them their Arms. *Eo ipso* the Boyars were recognized as members of the Polish Szlackta. Thus my grandmother's family of Dowgiałło henceforth bore the *Herb, Zadora*: a lion's head, the mouth belching forth flames – little wonder none crossed Grandmama with impunity! Similarly, the Lithuanian family of Sir John Gielgud, the actor, became entitled to bear the *Herb, Dzialasza* (an eight-pointed star to the viewer's left and an eagle's wing to the right) and so on[55].

Now, passing from this brief survey of the Polish heraldic system, let us consider the general position of Arms which come to be borne within an heraldic jurisdiction different to that within which they originated.

In such cases, according to the Laws of Arms, in order to bear the original Arms with due authority they need to be brought onto the registers of the heraldic jurisdiction of one's new domicile.

As a result, in my family's case, it was but appropriate that a Justice of the Supreme Court of British Columbia – my father's first cousin, Alfred – should in 1966[56] petition the Earl Marshal for a patent confirming the ancestral Arms of our family, not only to himself and his descendants but also to all the other male-line descendants of his grandfather, Julian Constantine Andrew Święcicki of Pasusvys in the Parish of Kroki (currently Krakes) whose five sons and two daughters had all come to Canada in the 19th century, as detailed earlier in this chapter.

With the Earl Marshal acceding to this petition and his warrant[57] having been issued to Garter, Clarenceux and Norroy & Ulster Kings of Arms they, accordingly exercised the Royal Prerogative and issued a Patent of Confirmation dated 17 January, 1967. Pursuant to that patent my father, my brother, Peter, I – and so my descendants – all became authorized to bear within Her Majesty's Realms and Territories the ancestral Arms.

Now, by the heraldic traditions of the British Crown particular Arms pertain to a particular male-line. Accordingly, if the *Herb, Jastrzębiec* was confirmed *simpliciter* to us that would exclude every other *brat herbowy* ('Arms-brother' of ours, in the Polish sense, as recently described) who might come to live within the Queen's realms, and desire to bear his ancestral Arms with due authority by obtaining a patent of confirmation. Accordingly, in order to preserve the design of the ancestral Arms *in toto* – but in such a way as not subsequently to exclude an 'Arms-brother' from the same exercise, a bordure was added (see below) so that a similar path could be followed with different bordures for him and so for any others in the same position.

---

[55] For further details concerning the Polish heraldic system *vide*, Swan, Sir Conrad. 'Arma Poloniae' *The Coat of Arms,* N.S. Vol. XI No. 169 Spring 1995 pp 2-14 and No. 170 Summer 1995 pp 46-57.

[56] This was the correct procedure at this time. The Canadian Heraldic Authority was not established for a further 22 years.

[57] Dated 9 Jan. 1967.

Thus we arrive finally at the

Armorial Bearings of Swan

Photography by Peter Norris.

Arms.   *Azure, a Cross formy within a Horseshoe heels upwards Or* (which is the *Herb, Jastrzębiec*, that is to say: upon a blue background a gold Cross with arms of equal length and gradually widening towards the extremities, within a gold horseshoe, heels upward).

a Bordure compony counter-compony Or and Gules (That is to say, a border of brick-like design of two layers, the segments alternately gold and red. This was the technical addition so as to, 1) preserve the design of the *Herb Jastrzębiec simpliciter* while 2) making the total design particular to us and so obtain the laws of Arms of the British Crown.).

Crest: *With a Wreath of the Colours* (That is to say, material of the two colours twisted into a wreath showing gold and blue alternately, being the livery colours of the family).

Rising from a Szlachta coronet proper a Sparrow Hawk wings elevated and addorsed Gules grasping in the dexter claws a Cross patty within a Horseshoe Gold – (That is to say, a coronet upon its rim four strawberry leaves all gold (and in the centre of each leaf a pearl (three leaves manifest) and four pearls (two manifest); rising from the coronet a Sparrowhawk, its wings elevated and back to back, all red; grasping in its right claws a gold cross patty ie. A cross with limbs of equal length, splayed and with straight ends).

Mantled Gules lined Argent (That is to say, the customary *parasolesque* material, which floats out from the base of the Crest on either side of the helm, is red lined silver/white – in honour of St George).

Motto: Nunquam cedamus ('never surrender')[58]

In addition, there are two Badges granted to me. The first commemorates the first time that a herald carried out duties in tabard south of the equator. This was during the Queen's Silver Jubilee of Australia in 1977.

Badges (1) *A Cross of Malta Azure dimidiating a Rose Argent barbed and seeded proper.* (That is to say, an eight-pointed blue cross and a white rose each cut in half vertically and jointed with the cross to the viewer's left and the rose to the right. The Crest of the State of Queensland includes a blue Maltese Cross, and as it was in Brisbane, the State capital, where the duty *tabardé* was carried out by myself[59], then York Herald of Arms – whose official badge includes a white rose – these two heraldic devices were conjoined in this way to form a badge)[60].

Upon the death of the last of the Jagellonian dynasty in 1572, Poland became an elective monarchy. Each member of the Szlachta – from the grandest to the most humble – had the duty, privilege and right of electing the king. So each was, like Richard Nevill, Earl of Warwick, of English history a 'Kingmaker'. Yet unlike Warwick, what is more, upon going to the Election Field at Wola, just outside Warsaw, each was conscious that as only members of the Szlachta, or of a ruling foreign house could be candidates for the throne, so each carried a crown in his haversack, so to speak.

To commemorate our family's participation in this constitutional process, the following badge was granted in 1992 to me and my descendants:

Badge (2) *A Hurt charged with the Bolelas Chrolry Crown proper all within an Annulet tasseled outwards to dexter and sinister in fess Gold.* (That is to say, on a blue circular disc, a representation of the Crown used in Polish coronations, known as the Boleslaw Chrolry Crown [rather as one would say, 'A St Edwards's Crown' in respect of British coronations] all as it existed originally [the Prussians broke it up(!) at the Partition]; the total outer edge of the blue disc edged gold and with two tassels, also gold, one pointing outwards to left and the other towards the right of the viewer. The whole design gives the idea of looking into an open haversack [which could be closed by pulling the tassels] containing a crown).[61]

---

[58] CAR: Gts 130/67 and 159/241.

[59] Described in detail in chapter IX.

[60] CAR Gts 142/239.

[61] CAR. Gts 159/241.

CHAPTER IV

The Coronation of the Last King-Emperor
And
School 6,000 Miles from Home

MY SCHOOLING IN Duncan had started at a kindergarten which I much enjoyed. Then came Queen Margaret's, which I have already mentioned.

At the age of ten I moved not far away from that school up Gibbins Road to Mr R. E. Honour's boys school – the formal name was the Duncan Grammar School. It is difficult to understand why it was so called by this Englishman, as it was not a Grammar School in the English sense . It was neither endowed – being wholly privately owned and fee-paying – nor was it a place staffed with teachers of serious academic qualifications who helped their pupils achieve high scholastic attainments.

Only one of the three Staff had a degree – the most junior teacher, Mr Jack Parker, BA, of the University of British Columbia. There was also a part-time instructor in manual training (carpentry) and the Matron, Miss Rice. The greatest treat for the boys was to be invited to accompany her in her electric car for a ride down to Duncan. The experience was rather like riding on the upper deck of a London bus; one got an almost aerial view of every house and garden as one proceeded on one's way, absolutely silently.

Despite being called a grammar school, it did not cater for the sons of the local shop keepers, but rather for those of the gentry. As a result of the social make-up of the Cowichan Valley already discussed in some detail (see Chap I), the school found itself surrounded by a large number of potential pupils.

It was run on British lines: forms not grades, student prefects and compulsory games. We had a smart uniform: mainly black with a blazer.

The Headmaster tended to be somewhat unconventional, but such never bothers the gentry. However, some of his attitudes could cause problems. For example, as far as he was concerned daylight saving time did not exist. Everything was run according to the sun. Obviously, parents delivering their boys to school in the mornings and collecting them after school had to have their wits about them when everywhere else in Canada was on daylight saving time.

While neither the Headmaster nor R.G.L. Parker had academic degrees, they were not without pedagogical skills in the subjects they taught, and to the levels of which they were capable. They were examples of the fact that teachers are born rather then made; a BA does not – as some seem to think – automatically confer competence in the classroom.

My form master was the young lone academician of the establishment, Mr Jack Parker (no relation of R.G.L.). My first lessons each morning were with him. I must have been his despair for every day, as part of our homework, we were given ten to fifteen words to learn by heart and spell correctly next morning. I could not even manage to read until I was about 10 years old, and spelling has never been my strong point – even now – so there was going to be trouble.

If you got any wrong – and I always did – then you stood before the class, held out your hands and were struck with three rulers held together. There was a certain stinging elasticity in such an instrument – once for each wrong word, on alternate hands, depending upon the number of mistakes. After a while I was able to control myself to the extent of showing no reaction. The stiff upper lip has many advantages. Among them is that of frustrating 'the other side's' attempt to see if he is even making an impression, as well as the avoidance of that nauseating subjective indulgence, self-pity.

Though doubtless failing in political correctness at this present juncture of history, I have never been against corporal punishment *in se*, even as a child. Later I came to understand that it may, upon occasion, be necessary, as man is not pure intellect and reason; that is the kernel of its justification.

But to return to Mr Jack Parker, I fear that my attitude to my form master was one of pretending that he did not exist. Of course, I knew he did, but doubtless felt that if I ignored him as much as possible, then he would not really impinge on my life. Naturally, I fully appreciated that I had to be perfectly polite when doing so. Both my parents and the headmaster would have required nothing less, and quite rightly so, as the basis of politeness for the Christian is, surely, the acknowledgement that Christ died for the other person – be he ne'er so revolting – as well as for oneself.

Young Parker was the only Catholic on the Staff. It was ironic that with the remainder – all Protestants – I got on extremely well, liked them, enjoyed their lessons and laughed at their jokes (always tactful on the part of a subordinate). The Head taught me history, and I could not get enough of his lessons. Sometimes, he would tell me about the history of Tring in Hertfordshire from which he and – as explained earlier – some of my maternal ancestors came. So there was an added bond between us.

R.G.L. Parker started me off on English literature, which has become more and more of a joy as the years pass along.

Nevertheless, the truth is that I was what one could describe as a 'late developer'. On the other hand, I was described as 'good with his hands' – usually a euphemism of sheer despair when uttered by a parent though, mercifully, its import did not dawn upon me until later in life. There must, nevertheless, have been something positive in this description; I attained excellent results in the examinations in drawing held locally by the Royal Academy of Art (of London), which gave my father the opportunity to praise me volubly – he was always a good psychologist. This ability to draw has always given me great pleasure, and proved most useful when later on I became a herald.

That was all very well, but the desire of my parents for something along more practical lines while still at Honour's school caused my enrolment in the manual training (carpentry) class. The instructor was excellent. He taught me how to hold a hammer and bring its full weight onto a nail, not wasting an ounce of energy. I have long had reason to be grateful to that man when pitting my wits against animals, filled with cunning, getting into fields where they should not be: some 4" nails, a few whacks with the hammer and a good piece of 2x4 timber usually foxes them as far as the fence is concerned – until the next time, of course.

Among the most vivid memories of my last few months at Duncan Grammar School is being acutely conscious that I was living in a period of high historic drama. Mr Honour had all of us sit down and listen to the Abdication Broadcast by the erstwhile King Edward VIII. I can still see the very serious look on the headmaster's face. When I got home after the broadcast, 'that American woman', as my mother referred to Mrs Simpson, was definitely *persona non grata*. That the King should desert his duty, and use the verb 'quit' when so doing, was for my elders beyond belief.

The Spring Term of 1937 was my last at Honour's School[1], as we had to get to London for the Coronation on 12 May of that year. So we scurried around, getting the right clothes and packing. To my bedroom, and all my household gods therein, I said *au revoir*.

Finally, we crossed over from The Island and took the 'Dominion' CPR train from Vancouver at 7.15 in the evening bound for Toronto. The journey was some 2700 miles – further than from London to Moscow, as the crow flies, more like London to Tehran. All things being equal, and passing through the Rockies – an unforgettable sight – the journey was scheduled to take eighty-one hours: three and a bit days and four nights.

Train travel at that time was efficient – even if one got stuck in a snowdrift, (which we did not on that occasion). We have lost something civilized and pleasurable with its passing as the usual mode of land travel over long distances.

Ultimately, and dead on time, we arrived in Toronto at 7.30 in the morning to be greeted by my brother, Peter, who was attending St Michael's College in the

---

[1] The school closed down some years later. Its site is now occupied by the Cowichan District Hospital with the foundation of which, as will be recalled, my maternal uncle, Claude A. Green, had so much to do.

University there. He was just rising eighteen years of age and was one year off taking his BA degree. I may have been precocious in history; Peter was precocious in almost absolutely everything. It must have been agony to have a 'slow developer' for a brother. Nevertheless, as a man of the world, like all university undergraduates, he welcomed us with open arms.

Then on to Montreal to stay with my paternal uncle, Phonse, who had graduated from McGill. Phonse practised dentistry in West Mount where he lived with his extremely vivacious *Québecoise* wife, Belva, who was great fun. Finally, on 24 April we sailed from Montreal on the RMS *Alaunia,* a Cunarder, for England.

A further eleven days of travel followed, flavoured with all the delights of ship-board life. Our progress was gradual and there was no such thing as jet-leg on arrival. En route we stopped at Quebec City, Plymouth, Le Havre and finally Tilbury.

That voyage in 1937 was the first of twenty times I crossed the Atlantic by ship; I cannot remember how many times it has been by air since then. Finally, the white cliffs of Dover were in sight on the port side as we passed Folkestone, where my parents were married during World War I. Then Dover itself with, high up, its castle and the pharos – the Roman lighthouse still beside it after nineteen hundred years or so. Calais was over on the starboard side, clearly visible; it would not be long before Hitler would be standing there looking across the Channel, envisaging an invasion, and settling down in Buckingham Palace. We, though, knew nothing of that as our ship went on round North Foreland and so on into the Thames and to Tilbury, very close to London, where we disembarked.

By way of the capital, we made straight for my mother's paternal cousin, Arthur Bligh, and his wife, Alice, who lived in Bedfordshire some fifty miles slightly North West of London in a village called Toddington. As they were to be my legal guardians while I was at school in England, they became an important part of my life, and were very kind to me. Their house was crammed with antiques, which made it the sort of place I liked to stay. Their only child, a son, had tragically died very young of tetanus.

So here I was in England. Polite society, its customs and norms were all those among which I had been brought up. From that point of view, going from Cowichan Valley to Bedfordshire in 1937 was, in a way, not all that different from going from the Isle of Wight to the mainland: in each case one was moving within the same social milieu.

At that time, and certainly back to the 1870s, when ones friends in Cowichan said, 'I'm going *home* for a visit' that meant one thing, and only one thing: Britain. Though all this is now a matter of history such was the existential, psychological experience one had in the years before World War II in that valley; and so it was mine.

Having placed our heavy luggage with the Blighs, Mother and I returned to London and awaited the coronation, due in two days' time.

★   ★   ★

12 May 1937 – a Wednesday – was a dry, bright day, – and just right for enjoying the great event which was about to take place. The actual ceremony was to be in that originally Benedictine foundation, Westminster Abbey[2], the scene of the coronation of thirty-nine sovereigns since that of William the Conqueror on Christmas Day, 1066.

Almost nine hundred years later this ceremony was to be broadcast for the first time ever. Millions upon millions throughout the world tuned in to listen no matter the time of day it was for them: 'awaked about 4a.m., by the sound of heraldic trumpets trying to lift the roof' as one in the Cowichan Valley was to put it – actually my brother Peter's exhibition dancing partner, Muriel Jarvis, sixteen years old at the time; with every 'old spartan radio cranked up to full volume'.[3] Possibly Spain 'in the hour of its own martyrdom'[4] was one of the few places in the world otherwise occupied.[5]

Stands had been built, where possible, all along the route to and from the abbey and we, fortunately, had excellent seats in one of these on Constitution Hill. It forms the north boundary of the Palace gardens. We had our back to the garden wall, and overlooked the road, into Green Park and beyond. We were near the Victoria Memorial end of the road so that all the comings and goings to and from the Palace were clearly visible.

From 8.40a.m., there was continual movement. Nine minutes later, came three glass coaches each drawn by a pair of bay horses; all accompanied by a captain's escort of the Life Guards. In the second were two sisters-in-law of the King. One was the Scottish Duchess of Gloucester (born the Lady Alice Montagu-Douglas-Scott, daughter of the 7th Duke of Buccleuch). She was the wife of Henry, Duke of Gloucester. I was to have much to do with her when some years later I became the Genealogist of the Order of the Bath,[6] and she was the first Dame Grand Cross of that Order. Upon suitable occasions, such as Christmas, birthdays and so on I, along with the other officers of the Order, would send greetings to her husband in his capacity as Great Master of the Order. By the time I became the Genealogist, the Duke had become seriously

---

[2] The Benedictines restored to Westminster Abbey by Mary Tudor (out of her own pocket) were driven from the Abbey, upon the accession of her half-sister, Elizabeth I, by the religious policy of Elizabeth and her government. After a period of exile on the Continent, the community is now at Ampleforth Abbey, Yorkshire, where they conduct one of Britain's Public Schools.

[3] Ackinclose, Muriel Jarvis. *Between Tzouhalem and Prevost*. Priority Printing Ltd., Duncan, B.C., 2000 p.74.

[4] *The Illustrated London News*, 15 May, 1937 p. 851

[5] The Spanish Civil War was on at the time.

[6] 1972

incapacitated, and was to remain so for the rest of his life. As a result, such greetings were sent by way of his Duchess. On one such occasion, she thanked us for our thoughtfulness, and said she would present these to the Great Master when a suitable opportunity presented itself but, as she put it 'possibly I should mention that he has not spoken to me for the past two years' – no wonder we all loved Princess Alice, (as she has long been known familiarly) so much.

The other sister-in-law of the King in the same carriage as the Duchess of Gloucester was the extremely beautiful Duchess of Kent (Princess Marina, daughter of Prince Nicholas of Greece by his wife the Grand Duchess Helen Vladimirovna of Russia), first cousin of Prince Philip, Duke of Edinburgh, and wife of Prince George, Duke of Kent. Within five years of the coronation she was to be widowed when her husband was killed on active service in World War II. At the time of this carriage journey she and her husband had a son, rising two years of age, Prince Edward George, now the Duke of Kent. In 1961 he married Katherine, daughter of Colonel Sir William Worsley, Bt, a direct descendant of Oliver Cromwell.[7] Several years later she completed part of a spiritual aeneid by coming into full communion with the Apostolic See in 1994[8], but as she and the Duke were already married, the fact of her now being a Catholic did not debar him the line of succession to the throne pursuant to the Act of Settlement of 1701. However, their son, George, Earl of St Andrews, is so barred by his marriage (1988) to the Torontonian Catholic, born Sylvana Tomaselli. The 'Greek Chorus' that I echo more than once in this book, *dans la généalogie on ne jamais dit jamais* does appear extremely apposite in the history of this family.

A series of cars from the palace headed for the abbey as did the carriage procession of Prime Ministers, including that of the Senior Dominion bearing the Right Honourable W.L. Mackenzie King, with an escort of the Royal Canadian Mounted Police looking splendid in their red tunics. On went further carriages with equally distinguished personages.

Finally, the King and Queen left the palace at about 10.30a.m., in the magnificent gold state coach. As it was built in 1762 its suspension has no springs, simply leather straps, so it must proceed at a slow pace unless the occupants are to have a somewhat nauseous experience. On the other hand the advantage of all this is that it affords spectators an admirable view of those inside.

Behind the state coach rode the King's four personal *Aides de Camp*: who included his uncle, the Earl of Athlone (Queen Mary's brother) who would

---

[7] The author is indebted to his confrère in the Order of Malta and Founder of the Institute of Heraldic and Genealogical Studies, Cecil R. Humphery-Smith, Esq., OBE, FSA, for much help over this descent, and *vide* Wayden, John. *The House of Cromwell and the Story of Dunkirk*. Eliot Stock, London, 1891 p.106ff; Burke, John and John Bernard *Extinct and Dormant Baronetcies of England, Irleland and Scotland*. John Russell Smith, London, 1884 p.456, and *Burkes Peerage and Baronetage*. Burkes Peerage (Genealogical Books Ltd) 1999 Vol. 2 pp 1068 and 1069.
[8] 14 Jan 1994.

Henry, 3rd Earl of Iddesleigh, 10th Baronet, and his wife, Elizabeth, Countess of Iddesleigh
in their robes for the coronation of King George VI and Queen Elizabeth (12 May 1937)
with in utero, *the future wife of the Author, the Lady Hilda Northcote.*

serve as Governor-General of Canada during World War II; and his second
cousin, then Lord Louis Mountbatten (later Earl Mountbatten of Burma), whose
implementation of policy as the last Viceroy of India was to have an important
influence on my future career in the Indian Army (see following chapter).

Once the King and Queen had arrived at the abbey the coronation service
began.

At the moment St Edward's crown was placed on the King's head we almost
jumped out of our seats as the Royal Horse Artillery – a mechanized unit for the
first time – fired a royal salute of 41 guns using 3.7 Howitzers. This took place
right next to us on the other side of the palace . We could smell the cordite and
see the smoke rising; it was terrific, just like so much incense. It was all most
arresting: none could be ignorant that we had crowned a King.

Fortunately, those explosions did not cause a premature confinement of

Elizabeth, Countess of Iddesleigh, who was in the abbey at the time. She was there accompanying her husband, Henry, 3rd Earl and 10th Baronet, along with the other peers and peeresses. He was the grandson of Sir Stafford Northcote, 8th Baronet and 1st Earl of Iddesleigh who, as Governor of the Hudson's Bay Company, persuaded the company to arrange for its territories to be transferred to the new Dominion Government and so doubled the size of Canada at the time.[9] As Lady Iddesleigh was enceinte, her coronation robes had been let out just a little, 'to allow'. Two months later she was safely delivered of The Lady Hilda Susan Mary Northcote, my future wife. Some 20 years later we were married, and she would joke about, 'When I was in the Abbey at the Coronation!'

Her mother tended to be a little absent-minded. As a result, her three older children were somewhat nervous when she went to the Abbey. Their apprehension arose from the fact that because of the great length of the service, the peers and peeresses would take small 'picnics' in their coronets. These were carried upside down into the Abbey, and held in that position for much of the service. The red velvet, ermine-edged caps inside the metal circlet of the coronets formed ideal 'hampers'. Minute sandwiches, Ovaltine tablets and the like comprised the relief against hunger, and could be popped into the mouth discreetly. So far so good, but at the moment the sovereign is crowned all the peers and peeresses turn their coronets right way up and put them on their heads. The Northcote children feared that at that moment there would be a cascade of 'picnic' all over their mother. All was well: Lady Iddesleigh had transferred what was left of the 'picnic' – not much – into her handbag. She was not descended (3 greats) from Dr Joseph Priestly, FRS, the 'father of English Chemistry' (see Appendix III) and Isolator of Oxygen, for nothing where manual dexterity was required.

After the service, a huge procession made its way from the abbey on a long route through London, back to the palace, so that as many as possible would be able to see and cheer their newly anointed and crowned King and Queen. Many infantry regiments, from every part of the Commonwealth and Empire (some 53 detachments in all) as well as from the United Kingdom, were introduced into the return procession. The result was a magnificent and impressive cavalcade of the Empire. As history transpired, it was to be the last of its kind.

In this return procession, one was able to greet Queen Mary – the first of our royal ladies to have visited Canada, which she did with the future King George V in 1901 on their return journey from his opening the Commonwealth Parliament of Australia.[10] In her collection of jewellery Queen Mary had a splendid spray of Maple Leaves carried out in diamonds, a reminder of her visit,

[9] For further details Vide, Swan, Sir Conrad. *The Northcote Millennium Commonplace Book.* Heraldic Enterprises, Boxford House, Suffolk, 2000 chapter VII

[10] The details of this visit were kindly communicated to the author by Oliver Everett, Esq., C.V.O., Assistant Keeper of the Royal Archives, Windsor Castle, by his letter of 15th February 2001.

and this she would wear on other appropriate occasions, as we shall see later. In her glass coach during this return procession she had with her the two young Princesses: Elizabeth (aged just eleven) – now our Queen happily reigning – and her sister, Margaret (six and a half). They wore their appropriate coronets as children of a sovereign: crosses[11] alternating with fleurs-de-lis set on a rim, all gilded. Whereas the usual female custom is to wear very small coronets perched on the crown of the head, it was obviously considered wiser, in this instance, to have something guaranteed not to fall off, so the Princesses had the male version of coronets, that is worn over the forehead and back of the head. Twenty-five years later, after the elder of the two had become Queen, I was to begin more than 30 years of service in her Household in that department known as the College of Arms.

As the state coach came clearly into view, one could see the jewels of the imperial state crown worn by the King whom, as the last King Emperor, I was to start to serve seven years later, in the Indian Army. Seated beside him was his Scottish consort, Queen Elizabeth (later Queen Elizabeth the Queen Mother). She was wearing a crown especially made for this occasion which included, among its jewels, the celebrated *Koh-I-Noor* ('mountain of light') diamond. Three months before, the King had made her the first Grand Master of the Royal Victorian Order within which I was to be enrolled some forty years later.

The roar of cheers grew louder and louder as the coach drew nearer. On the one hand it was an appropriate acknowledgement of our undoubted monarch. On the other hand, however, it was something more. It was a salute to one who had been forced to take up onerous duties in the most unfortunate circumstances, but that was not all. Everyone knew that he had a bad stammer which he was doing his best to overcome (and which he did eventually): the British always love the under-dog.

The 29-year-old man who had been ultimately responsible for organizing and mounting this whole complicated and great event: Bernard, 16th Duke of Norfolk, Earl Marshal and Hereditary Marshal of England, was nowhere to be seen. After the service in the Abbey he had retired for a well-earned rest – and, one hopes, adequate refreshment – to his London residence. It is by virtue of these offices just mentioned, that the Dukes of Norfolk have the hereditary responsibility for all state occasions. It is among the curiosities of English life that the chief Roman Catholic layman of the country – a descendant of St Philip Howard – should have the duty of arranging the coronation of the Supreme Governor of the Church of England. Twenty-seven years after this particular coronation, as we shall see later, this same Earl Marshal was to nominate me to the sovereign to be a member of the Royal Household as Rouge Dragon Pursuivant of Arms.

---

[11] Technically described as 'crosses patty': square in shape.

Soon after the state coach had passed our stand, it swung in through the main gates of Buckingham Palace. It was not long before all of us – and there were literally thousands – swarmed in front of the Palace and stood calling in a great and rhythmic chant: 'We want the King! We want the King!'. Soon the French windows onto the balcony opened and the King and the Queen came out to wave and acknowledge our salutes. In front of them, and just tall enough to see over the stone edge of the balcony, were the two little princesses. How wise their elders had been over the type of coronets they were to have – by now Princess Margaret's was anything but horizontal to the ground. Queen Mary, that personification of royalty, was a step or two to the rear – if anyone knew protocol she did – and giving support and keeping an eye on the little princesses. Having stood and acknowledged the cheers and salutes of the crowd – which was not just around the Victoria Memorial, but stretched as far as the royal eye could see from the balcony right down the Mall to Admiralty Arch – for about half an hour, they went back inside, for an evening of official functions within the Palace ahead of them.

Certainly Mother and I were exhausted from the excitement of it all so we made our way back to our hotel in order to get ready for a good dinner. Nevertheless, it had been a day of days, and it was great to be alive. Now proper victuals were much appreciated after a long day on sandwiches and hot drinks from refreshment counters under the stands.

After the excitements of the coronation – and my thirteenth Birthday on the day after (13 May) – my mother and I set out to visit different relations and friends in various parts of England. In this we were joined by my brother, Peter, after the end of his academic year at Toronto. Armed with a list of schools provided by the academic agents, Gabbitas Thring, we called upon each nearest to the place where we happened to be staying at the time, one after the other. In addition to being Catholic, it was obviously preferable if the one selected was in the south-east as my future guardians, the Blighs, lived in that part of England.

In the end, St George's College, Woburn Park, Weybridge (a public school in the English sense) was chosen. Located in Surrey to the West of London, about 20 miles up the Thames not far from Windsor Castle, and some 40 miles almost due South of my guardians, it was conveniently situated.

All in all, St George's was a good choice. I settled in quickly and have remained in touch ever since – though I must admit that I am not one of those classic Old Boys who seem to spend almost their entire time visiting again and again the haunts of 'the halcyon days of their youth'.

St George's was, and still is, conducted by the Congregation of St Joseph, usually referred to as Josephites (or irreverently by the boys as 'holy Joes').

On the appointed first day of the Autumn '37 term, I went with Mother by train from London to Addlestone, a station close to the school. We walked up the long tree-lined drive towards the College buildings. I felt somewhat apprehensive; after all, I was to be there – whatever 'there' would turn out to be like – for months on end, with my parents some 6,000 miles away. Granted, the Blighs were up in Bedfordshire but, undoubtedly kind though they were, they were not ones for going any distance by car unless I happened to be *in extremis*. So, half-way up the drive I stopped and asked Mother if I could give her my good-bye kiss there, as I was not sure how the other boys would react if I did so in front of them. In fact, I need not have worried; it turned out to be a most humane establishment. The foreign boys would kiss their entire family and any other connections who happened to be around. Nevertheless, upon arrival at the front door I noticed inscribed above in stone, *AUT DISCE AUT DISCEDE.*[12]

As at Honour's school, in addition to a uniform, we had forms, student prefects – appointed by the school authorities – and compulsory games. Plus the usual academic curriculum – half days on Wednesdays and Saturdays and no work on Sundays – there were debating, scientific and other societies. Theatricals, both straight plays produced by the masters and reviews mounted by the students, were features of the school. Also once a year, a professional company of actors came and produced the Shakespearean play that the senior boys were studying for their university entrance examinations that year. The whole school comprised the audience and these productions proved to be a wholly new experience; they whetted my appetite for Shakespeare.

There was Mass which we attended every day and twice on Sundays (the daily Low Mass early in the morning and a sung High Mass at about 11a.m.). A choir made up of the boys provided the music in chapel, though the whole school would often join in, not simply with such well-known hymns as 'Faith of Our Fathers', but also with the Mass itself if the musical setting was one they knew such as *Missa de Angelis* – raising the roof in the process – doubtless on the basis of *quis cantat bis laudat*[13].

We all learned how to serve both High and Low Mass in Latin, as it was all Tridentine Rite at the time. Some were specially proficient at swinging the thurible in ways that defied Newton – while, naturally, maintaining at all times a solemn demeanour appropriate to the holy offices of which they were a part. When one of my grandsons, many years later, said, 'Yes, I'm the bloke with the smokey handbag,' I knew exactly what he meant. On the Feast of Corpus Christi[14] there would be an enormous procession through the grounds with benediction at several altars especially erected for this occasion. The most senior boys would take it in turn to carry the canopy over the priest carrying the monstrance, and in the path of this part of the procession rhododendron flowers were strewn. Woburn Park had a magnificent collection of this shrub and, with the soil there just right, they grew into small trees. The whole occasion was

---

12 'Learn or leave' – the boys rendered it as, 'Work or get out'.
13 He who sings [once], prays twice.
14 The Thursday after Trinity Sunday, at the time.

impressive and inspiring, so that many people from the surrounding area would come and join in. It was an expression of pre-Vatican II devotion at its most magnificent.

The Josephite Congregation had been founded at the end of the Napoleonic Wars in Belgium in 1817. By the time I arrived at St George's, the Josephites there had long been completely English. The head of the school throughout the whole of my time was the redoubtable Fr George Kean, CJ, – possibly the ugliest man, in a bulldog sort of way, that I have ever known – but also one of the kindest. He was also a big man, and looked even bigger when he wore the Josephite habit: a black cassock with a broad waistband which finished in tails that flew out behind. Technically, he was the religious superior of the house and was known as the President. In addition to looking after the religious community he set the general tone, received the parents, recruited the boys, and administered everything about the school (except the academic side, for which there was a Prefect of Studies). Further, it was the President's duty to administer punishment with the cane, if necessary – 'Take your trousers down, bend over those library steps and receive six of the best.' There was no nonsense about Fr George.

Fr. George was always most considerate to me. As an example, he noted how during my first year at the school that whereas parents or friends came to visit and take out other boys, few came to visit me. Accordingly, from time to time he would collect me up of an afternoon, and off we would drive to visit some place that interested me. The first lessons I had on pre-Reformation ecclesiastical architecture were from him: I devoured these sweeps of history avidly.

The sports consisted of rugby football in the Autumn or Christmas term, grass hockey in the Easter term and cricket, tennis and swimming in the Summer. There were gymnastics throughout the year, and it was at this that I became really proficient. There was also a farm on the property – about 100 acres – and if that sort of work appealed then we were detailed to go off and help the Lay Brother and others who ran the farm. As a treat we could drive the tractor. There were also ferrets which we would put down the rabbit warrens to keep down the numbers of Mopsy, Flopsy and Cotton Tail – engaging to look at but incredibly destructive if they put their minds to it.

The three Houses – groupings of students, not buildings – into which the school was divided were Southcote, Kilmorey (mine) and Petre, which were the names of some previous owners of Woburn Park. By having the school divided up in this way one had ready-made teams for academic and sporting competitions.

The history of the property went back to being part of the lands of the nearby Chertsey Abbey, founded in a.d. 666. With the Reformation it went the way of all monastic land and was distributed by Henry VIII into lay hands only too willing to receive it. By the nineteenth century, the owner was a member of a recusant

Catholic family: the Rt Rev. Mgr the Honble William Petre (later 13th Baron Petre)[15] – an educationalist ahead of his time, who even considered the students of his school should have a degree of self government. The property was finally taken over by the Josephites in 1884.

So for anyone with an historical bent the place was full of interest and possible avenues of research. On the other hand, one had to keep one's eye on one's day-to-day academic work and behaviour. Marks were given for each and these were indicated by weekly cards as follows:

Pink = 90% Very good
Green = 80% Good
Buff = 70% Moderate (in practice unsatisfactory)
White = 50% Bad.

Three consecutive buff cards or one white made one liable for a whacking.

Yet, if by half-term one had had consecutive good cards, mostly pink, then one was one of the *Bene Merenti*.[16] On a specified weekday, while the others continued with their lessons, those who had been so awarded could go out to Weybridge, take in a show at the Odeon (the local picture theatre), and have tea out. That, however, was not all, for – joy of joys – during the study period that evening, while everyone else sweated it out preparing lessons for next day, one sat at one's desk in the Study Hall and did as one wished: read a book, wrote letters, sat and thought, provided one was quiet. It was sheer bliss!

For the Christmas term, 1938, I needed a new uniform: a Marlborough Suit, which consisted of striped long trousers with black jacket and waistcoat (could there be anything smarter?, I wondered). The reason was, I was now fourteen, and so moving up from the junior school, the White House, to the senior one, the Red House (built of bricks, hence its name). For the first year, though, one would be known as a member of Pink House. This was simply an organizational concept, not a separate building.

Members of one such house were not permitted to speak to members of the other two. This was partly for purposes of discipline, and also part of a regime to guard against unnatural practices between the boys – a situation that can become a pest in boys' schools, and is not confined to those in England.

A further part of the discipline to the same end was the rule that at all times, all boys were in fact supervised, and not permitted to wander off at will. During class time there was, obviously, the teacher – lay or clerical – who was in charge of his group; at all other times, whether during recreation, meals, sports, study periods or when in the dormitories there was always a person on duty in charge of the boys. The arrangement was usually one master for the White House, and

---

[15] *Burkes Peerage and Baronetage*, 1999 Vol. II p. 2240.
[16] 'Well deserving'.

one for the Pink and Red Houses combined. If one needed to be temporarily absent from such a group; because of a dental appointment in Weybridge, work on the school farm and so on, one got permission from the master in charge. The aim was that at all times each boy was accounted for.

It sounds oppressive; in fact it was not. One was kept so busy one did not have time to consider the matter. Finally, there was the principle: *wash well but do it modestly; no nudity in public* – baths in cubicles were provided; there were no open showers as at many schools. All of this was within an atmosphere of objective morality. As a result of this overall regime, I never during the whole of my time at St George's, saw, heard of – even so much as a whisper – any unnatural practice between boys. So even if one might have adopted other prudential methods aimed at a similar goal, one had to give the Josephites full credit for achieving this highly desirable situation. Having had, I understand, what might be termed, hair-raising experiences at their main school in Belgium – Melle, that country's Eton – this could well have encouraged the Josephite approach to the subject at St George's.

In view of the *no nudity in public* principle, one can imagine the reaction of the school authorities – led by Fr George – when it was found out that three of the VI Formers (most senior boys) had gone, without permission (that was bad enough in itself) to a more or less secluded section of the nearby Thames (yet by a public footpath), and had spent some time swimming in the buff. Had they been guilty of taking part in a multiple rape, the reaction could not have been worse. Immediate expulsion was expected. The only time in my life that I ever experienced such an atmosphere of impending Nemesis was later on in the Indian Army when I had to attend the cashiering of an officer before the whole battalion. The badges of rank were literally ripped off his shoulders. The Georgian miscreants were only saved from being expelled forthwith by the fact that they were in the middle of their university entrance examinations. Physically the VI Formers were undoubtedly men, mentally one doubts if they had reached the age of discretion. There was nothing basically wrong in swimming in the nude, but they had completely ignored the location – silly young men.

There was an interesting group at the College. Many were the sons of those in the Colonial or Indian Civil Service, or in the professions or commerce overseas and so had lived abroad. These included the Lucie-Smiths, sons of Sir John Lucie-Smith, Puisne Judge of Trinidad; they were very much in evidence at the College into the thirties. Also from that colony was my contemporary and friend, Michael Pocock. His mother's family, French nobles by the name of Valleton de Boissière, having escaped from the Terror arrived in Trinidad in 1790; seven years before the British.

From nearer home was another friend, Bernard Rossiter. His was an old milling family from Paignton in Devon. He already had a Josephite uncle at St George's, Fr Cuthbert Rossiter, the long-time Bursar of the College. He was down-to-earth; there was no nonsense about him. He forcibly reminded me of the soldier turned priest in Mickiewicz's *Pan Tadeusz:*

> He seemed a soldier not alone in look
> But in his voice and every step he took.
> At Mass where're he turned about and said,
> 'The Lord be with you' with his arms outstretched,
> His turn was with a single motion made,
> As if he were a soldier on parade.
> He read the phrases of the liturgy
> Like the commander of a company.
> The boys who served the Mass remarked these tricks[17]

...as we did with Fr Cuthbert's. Bernard, became a Josephite as Fr Aidan.

There were just two from the Old Dominions, Terence McGuire, from New Zealand and myself. But there were a number from the Continent and from South America. One of these boys was an Austrian who had been got out of his country by his parents at the time of the 1938 *Anschluss*, after which he was looked after by an English family who even paid his fees. He was a pleasant, blond, typical Austrian boy and not without a sense of humour, and he settled in well. I was told, however, by one of the masters who taught him English Literature that no matter the subject set for an English essay, this boy always somehow brought in the horrors of the Nazis – little wonder.

Several of the Josephites were not without genealogical interest. Fr George Kean's parents were intimate friends of Alfred Bernhard Nobel, the founder of the Nobel Peace Prize. Fr Hugh Ryan, a brilliant academician – one felt that no catgut could have been stretched tighter on a violin than he – his father was the personal Medical Officer to Field Marshal the Lord Kitchener during World War I. The now Fr Francis Owen – a debonair young scholastic at the College when I was there, and now of the religious community of St George's with seniority *ne plus ultra* – his father had the fascinating appointment of Senior Resident[18] and Assistant to the white Raja of Sarawak.

Then there was the future Fr Kemble Bryant, a Scholastic when I was at St George's and so plain Mr Kemble then. We got on well, as we had gymnastics in common, at which he was first-class. He descended collaterally through his mother from a characteristically English saint, the Seminary Priest, John Kemble[19], who was a victim of the Titus Oates Plot, being executed in 1679 in his 81st year – a great age at that time. When the Under-Sheriff came to bring

---

[17] Mickiewicz, Adam. *Pan Tadeusz*. Trans by Kenneth Mackenzie. The Polish Cultural Foundation, London, 1964 p.28

[18] In the British Empire, a Resident was an official with diplomatic character. For more on this *vide* Chapter V on India.

[19] One of the Forty English Martyrs canonised by Pope Paul VI on 25 October, 1970

him to the scaffold, he asked time to say his prayers, smoke a pipe of tobacco and drink a cup of sack[20]: a typical example of English sang froid. One can relate to such a saint.

Sometimes the saint's collateral, Mr Kemble, would come of an evening to the bank of washbasins in the Red House dormitory to brush his teeth. He and all others at those basins would be wearing pyjama bottoms and slippers, only. If I happened to come and fill a vacant space next to him, there would be much laughter in our juxtaposition. Kemble was like an Apollo of the Belvedere: muscle and hair in all the right places, no exaggeration, just as it all should be. And there was I, a skeleton covered in cling-foil; even I could see how risible the comparison was, and we would all have a good laugh.

The Summer Term of '38 was well under way, and I had survived almost a whole academic year at St George's, and had enjoyed it. On the other hand I was also looking forward to returning to the Cowichan Valley for the summer holidays that year, as had been settled before I left for the coronation. Then one day Fr George sent for me and told me my parents had asked him to let me know that instead of my going out to the West Coast, they and my brother would be coming to England instead. This was a rather bitter-sweet message, but I much looked forward to being with my family once again, wherever it was.

Apparently, one of my father's patients had a daughter who had married a doctor, and this patient had bought my father's practice for his son-in-law. The possibility of selling practices, though common in Britain, was almost unheard of in Western Canada at the time. Nevertheless, an adequate price had been agreed upon, and my father wanted to do some postgraduate work in gynaecology and obstetrics in Britain.

So in August that year Mother and Peter sailed on the Norwegian freighter, the SS *Tranger*, from Seattle for Europe by way of the Panama Canal – a popular six-week voyage at the time. My father went straight across to England, and all four of us met up just in time for the Munich crisis in September.

In a letter to his grandparents in Duncan, Peter described the atmosphere of the period:

'They had dug trenches in the park [Kensington Gardens and Hyde Park] for refuge in air-raids. We certainly had a scare last week. It looked hopeless on Wednesday and there was gloom everywhere. We got our gas masks, and were preparing for the worst when it all blew over. They certainly were prepared – they had plans all ready for evacuation, rations, defence etc. The radio had nothing on but instructions to this outfit and that. It must have scared Hitler off![21]'

---

[20] A dry South West European white wine, especially sherry.

[21] SSA New Series III: P.S., to Mr and Mrs A.E. Green. No date but from internal evidence written early October, 1938. The envelope bears the Duncan, BC, postal frank for 15 October, 1938.

The family took a flat in a new block close to Kensington Gardens in London. Peter's presence had been required by our father for about a year upon being told by him that when he graduated (June 1938) he wished to enter the priesthood with the Congregation of St Basil who, as mentioned before, conducted St Michael's College. As Peter was only nineteen at the time, and although the Superior General of the Basilians was, naturally, anxious to recruit this promising young man, our father (at that time still legally responsible for his offspring until they were twentyone) said, 'Good, in time, but not till after spending a year or so in a completely different atmosphere', so as to see if Peter really had a vocation to the priesthood. As will be recalled, my father had, many years before, tried his own vocation, and thus knew what he was doing.

So that is how matters continued from late 1938 through into the next year: the parents and Peter in London and myself at St George's during term-time, but back with them for each holiday.

After some days in Edinburgh in early July '39, Peter drove down, passing through Tweedsmuir – 'it's no wonder Buchan ran away from it – very desolate'.[22] On the 15th of that month he sailed on the SS *Carinthia* from Liverpool for New York, from which he went up to Toronto in order to enter the Basilian Novitiate.

At that time I was confined to the infirmary: the only time I was while at St George's. The reason was mumps, with complications so severe that I could only lie flat on my back – any other position was agony for the delicate masculine area. In fact, things were so bad the school doctor said that I would be sterile. Naturally, I was depressed. My father cheered me up by saying, 'Remember, whatever any doctor says, it is only an opinion – it may be a very learned opinion – but is simply, in the final analysis, an opinion.' In view of the fact that, subsequently – as the father of five marvellous children (to say nothing of the twenty grandchildren who came along later) one wonders, if this is sterility, what would be fecundity? So in this regard I incline, gratefully, to the 'old man's' view.

Peter had only been gone six weeks when the Germans invaded Poland. Accordingly, on 3 September Chamberlain announced over the radio that unless the Third Reich immediately withdrew, Britain and Germany would be at war. My parents and I listened to this broadcast together, and as we were staying near Cambridge at the time, we went for a walk that afternoon along the Backs, as that part of the river that runs near the rear of some of the colleges is called. We did not talk a great deal, but as we crunched the gravel of the paths under our heels we realized that the hitherto idyllic situations of so many of our lives – symbolized by this civilized picture of disciplined horticulture, the product of Southcote, Capability Brown and other landscape artists, through which we were sauntering – were soon to be shattered. Yet despite this expectation I do recall, as

---

22 *Ibid*. Same to same, 15 July 1939.

we walked through the grounds of St John's, remarking that I would like to study at this university. Under the impending circumstances we all wondered when that could be. Twelve years later, I did, but not at St John's, rather at Peterhouse, the then mecca of historians and the oldest Cambridge college (founded 1284).

'Back on the farm' at St George's we prepared for war. We dug trenches near the Red House where we would take shelter during air raids. While our clothes remained upstairs in the dormitories, we brought our beds down to the ground floor, as that was considered safer. It was a case of sleeping cheek by jowl. Much of the park was dug up for crops. Such was part of a national effort which, in the end, was so successful that as much as half the total amount of food needed by the population of Britain was produced by utilizing every piece of ground available – even Hyde Park was dug up. The result was that convoys of ships had more room to bring materials vital to the war effort back to Britain. As for getting that other half of the food from overseas, it was not long before one of our recent Old Georgians – as one-time students at St George's are called – by the name of Hugh Owen[23], entered the Merchant Navy and was bringing food on the United Kingdom-New Zealand run, dodging Nazi U-Boats and Japanese submarines much of the way.

Early in December Mr Vincent Massey, Canadian High Commissioner in London (later Governor-General of Canada) brought together a number of persons interested in founding a Service club for the Canadian Forces on leave in London. There had been a Beaver Hut on the Strand serving the same purpose during the first World War. One of those who helped with these moves by the High Commissioner was my mother. The old London County Council building was obtained for such a club. It could not have been more centrally located, being in Spring Gardens just inside Admiralty Arch, at the end of The Mall leading to the Palace, and so next to Trafalgar Square. In February 1940 it opened its doors as the Beaver Club for Canadian and Allied Forces. My mother was the Joint Supervisor of the Voluntary Staff. She served as such, in a completely voluntary capacity, seven days a week, fifty-two weeks a year for the next six years and a day until it closed its doors on 19 February, 1946. EHS did not do things by halves. Her *alter ego*, as it were, as Joint Supervisor was Mrs Charles Cambie (born a Nordheimer, of Toronto). They made an ideal pair. During my early holidays from St George's, before I joined the army, I used to help at the Beaver Club frequently.

Three months after the opening of the Club, the evacuation of Dunkirk took place (27 May–4 June 1940). On the day after it concluded, Churchill, now Prime Minister, snarled defiance at the Hun with his famous speech of June 4 in the House of Commons:

---

[23] Hugh Adrian Owen who left St George's in 1941, younger brother of the Rev. D. Antony Francis Owen, C.J., to whom reference has already been made.

We shall not flag or fail…
We shall defend our island, whatever the cost may be.
We shall fight on the beaches…
we shall fight in the fields and in the streets…
we shall fight in the hills;
we shall never surrender…
[the struggle will go on]

until, in God's good time, the new world, with all its power and might, steps forth to the rescue and liberation of the old.

Cheeky young devil that I was, I soon knew the speech by heart, and used to delight in reciting it, imitating Churchill's marvellous, gravely voice. At the time, a clutch of Channel-drenched soldiers, not enough cartridges to go round, and Churchill's rhetoric was about all we had. Yet his wonderful command of the language, the clear purpose of a statesman – not just the mouthings of a politician – and trust in God's providence – made us all determined not to give in, but to see the thing through to victory.

Immediately, after Dunkirk an urgent appeal went out from the Royal Army Medical Corps for doctors. Without hesitation my father volunteered, and service in that Corps was to be his life for practically the next decade.

Another two months and the vital Battle of Britain (8 August–6 October 1940) was fought out, and the hammering of the London Blitz followed immediately (up to 31 October).

At the beginning of the Blitz, I had been down at Tenby in Pembrokeshire – the extreme south western tip of Wales, where there are palm trees in the churchyards as the climate there is so mild. I stayed there during part of my summer holidays as my father was stationed nearby. The soldiers used to open up the barbed wire on the beach so that we could have a swim. All beaches throughout Britain were so fortified, bearing in mind how some of our ancestors, the Angles and Saxons, had invaded England across such sandy entrances. Well, that was all very well and good for our ancestors but we had no intention of allowing the Nazis – coarse *canaille* – to be ancestors of future generations here!

When one night I returned to London from that holiday, the Jerries (as we called the Germans) were at it in a big way. The taxi driver who agreed to try and get me home told me to lie down on the floor in case a bomb shattered the cab windows. As we rounded Marble Arch it was like daylight, and I thought we were about to meet a stick of bombs. I need not have worried. I can say that now, but at the time I was very worried and prayed hard. In the end we arrived safely on Queensway, opposite Kensington Gardens, and so to our flat at Queen's Court. The taxi driver refused a tip! 'We're all in it together, young sir' – that summed up the 'Blitz' spirit that one found throughout the length and breadth of the country.

The Battle of Britain and the Blitz certainly brightened the skies over St George's in no uncertain terms. The trenches we had dug came in for real use. As we were marshalled during a raid from the classrooms to the trenches Johnny Ryan – as we students irreverently called Fr Hugh Ryan – used to jump about saying, 'No panic, chaps! No panic, chaps!'. He was a grand man, and we all liked him, but I did wonder, at times, if I should have slipped him a sedative.

Several bombs fell on Woburn Park though, fortunately, none on the school buildings or personnel. Nevertheless, many of our windows were shattered by the firing of the anti-aircraft batteries located nearby on the Meadowlands. When rockets started to be sent over by the Germans a V2 fell close to the north-east corner of the property, causing serious damage.

Every evening, sitting at our places in the Study Hall of the Red House, the senior students of the Pink and Red Houses, would listen to the BBC evening news on the radio at 9p.m., preceded by the reassuring booming of Big Ben. 1940 and '41 were particularly grim years, our forces being ignominiously pushed off the Continent with our Allies. There was also the loss of the pride of the Royal Navy: HMSs *Hood, Prince of Wales* and *Repulse*; our surrender of Hong Kong and, for our own family in particular, the nightmare of the annexation of Lithuania by the Soviet Union – Poland had been occupied by 'the two thieves' since '39. However, in June '41 Germany attacked its erstwhile ally, Russia, and that brought us an ally worth having. Not that there was anything to choose between Nazism and Communism – each as vile as the other – nevertheless, when someone fights your enemy he is your ally. At the end of that year, Japan attacked Pearl Harbour and that, too, brought – this time – a welcome ally to our side though for some time yet the Germans made all the running.

The essential victory of the Battle of Britain and the fortitude exhibited by the country during the Blitz were shots in the arm – and the anthem of every ally played one after the other, before the BBC evening news at 9p.m., helped to jolly things up. Fortunately, we were not required to stand to attention throughout, though we would have done so willingly; we were so grateful for all their help, and proud of their gallantry.

During those grim days, it is significant that the only ecclesiastic, without exception, who used to be asked to put heart into the country over the BBC was the old and physically frail – but mentally completely alert – Cardinal Arthur Hinsley, Archbishop of Westminster. Though in many ways different from Churchill, there were similarities: he had a most distinctive voice, was craggy of appearance and was a man for the hour. And he was widely respected. Hinsley was a great favourite with my parents, and when they celebrated the silver jubilee of their marriage in 1942 he sent round his assistant, Bishop Myers, with a special blessing and signed photograph – the Cardinal could not come himself, as he was living in the country. We had had a Mass celebrated for the occasion round the corner from our flat at the Spanish Convent opposite Kensington

Gardens, and then came back with the guests for a reception, when the Bishop arrived. Naturally, we offered him some champagne – of the little we had procured from somewhere – and then a piece of the silver wedding cake. This had been made by the baker in exactly the same way all wedding cakes at that time were. It was all white and decorated outside but when it came time to cut it, one lifted this all off like the lid of a tureen; it was made entirely of cardboard and paper – sugar being all too scarce.

Fairly early on in the war we started to learn of casualties among Old Georgians serving in the forces. Nevertheless, there was one experience of extreme poignancy and immediacy for the whole of us at St. George's. This concerned a day-boy who lived locally. One day he came to school, as usual. When it came time to go home, he had neither home nor parents to go to – a bomb had destroyed both. The family were Protestants, so the funeral was held at a local Anglican church. In support of their fellow Georgian, aged about fifteen, and rare as this was at the time (long before Vatican II, be it remembered) the entire school, led by the Josephites, turned up *en masse*. The last time so many Catholics, clerical as well as lay, could have been at that church would have been 23 June, 1559 – the day before the Anglican Settlement of Religion came into effect[24].

The boy was now an orphan with few relations. As if that was not bad enough, we were all cut to the quick as we stood there round a *single* coffin: sufficient for his parents few bones as they were committed to Christian burial. The stiff upper lip did not survive for long, and there was not a dry eye throughout the obsequies. It was said that when the 'rugger buggers' of the school sent their handkerchiefs to the laundry that week all were shot through with holes caused by the force with which they had blown their noses during the service. Doubtless, this was apocryphal, but it does give an idea of how much the boys took this tragedy to heart and their orphaned fellow Georgian to their manly chests – be they ne'er so broad or narrow.

It was, fortunately, by no means all sadness. As the war got under way one learned of this and that OG, who had won a decoration for bravery. Naturally, we all rejoiced on such occasions.

Nevertheless, I think that the greatest thrill we received was when one who had only left St George's a few weeks before was awarded the George Medal for outstanding bravery: Derick Baynham. The occasion, on 28 August 1941, was when a Polish bomber crashed into the sea about a mile off Anglesey, that island at the north-west corner of Wales. It was during a south-west gale. Baynham and a friend managed to reach the plane in a small dinghy, and to get the sole survivor off the sinking craft. Their dinghy was overturned, but they managed to cling on to it for about four hours. A volunteer lifeboat on its way to the rescue

---

[24] Pursuant to I Eliz. c. 2 which became operative on the Feast of St John the Baptist, 24 June, 1559.

upturned and all eleven crew were drowned. Baynham and his friend were awarded the George Medal and the Silver Medal of the RNLI (Royal National Life-boat Institution). General Władysław Sikorski, the Polish Commander-in-Chief and Prime Minister awarded each a Citation of Bravery, as well as a solid silver cigarette case engraved with his signature – Poles understand the grand gesture.

A few weeks after this rescue, Baynham paid St George's a visit. It was one of those wonderful September days one often gets in England, with everything still green and the sun soft and golden. We crowded round him on the grass of the playing field near the tennis courts, and pressed for a stroke-by-stroke, and gulp-by-gulp description of his extraordinary exploit in the worst possible marine conditions; eventually he obliged – not without his characteristic sense of humour[25].

To us at the time his action was as thrilling as it was sobering. It demonstrated that even of us – at much the same age as he was – great courage could be demanded; it also asked, were we capable of rising to such occasions?

The academic terms rolled on with rugger balls, grass hockey balls, cricket balls and bombs bouncing about the place. During the Summer Term, 1942, and now in the Upper Vth, I sat one of the school leaving and university entrance examinations available at the time: the School Certificate of the Conjoint Board of Oxford and Cambridge. How I did will be gathered from the following chapter.

---

[25] Soon he started on a distinguished life-time military career which included a period in France on SOE assignment as a wireless operator and saboteur agent. He rose to be a brigadier.

CHAPTER V

And so to War with Leg O'Muttons and Madrassi Sepoys

I HAD STOOD AROUND naked for an hour and a half. At the end of all this I was told, 'Mr Swan, go home and put your body on. When you have done that, then come back and see us again.' The examining doctor of the Canadian Ministry of Defence surgery on The Haymarket in London, where all this took place, did not say that in an unkind way. I think to him it was simply a statement of fact.

Granted, I was no Atlas. As already mentioned I had had congenital rheumatic fever in childhood. However, with the careful attention of a medical father matters had improved immeasurably. I was really quite good at gymnastics, which I much enjoyed, and according to my schoolfellows, had a grip like steel. Riding had been a pleasure for years and I could put a horse over a hedge – I wondered if that doctor could do the same? Further, I was now rising nineteen years of age and wanted to volunteer for active war service in one of the Canadian Armed Forces – hence my seeking out and attending this medical examination.

At the outcome I was not simply crest-fallen: the whole escutcheon had been torn from the wall for me. What was to have been the beginning of a worthy endeavour – after all, all my friends were joining up (it was the Summer of 1943) and I wanted to do the same – now threatened to be an experience of soul-destroying frustration.

As I walked slowly down the staircase towards the front door onto the Haymarket, I gradually came to feel that there were two immediate alternatives: once out on the street, I could either turn left, take the bus home and finish off some of that Veuve Cliquot I knew was in the fridge or I could turn right, walk up to the top of the street, go into one of the many public houses round Piccadilly Circus, get drunk, then wander over to Leicester Square and Soho – just a short distance further to the right – and pick up one of those girls who hung around there with one intention.

Whatever I was going to do, I had to cross Haymarket, which took some time, as the traffic roars down at great speed towards Trafalgar Square. I began to think, well, yes, nothing can stop me going up to a pub and then Soho if I decide to do so. Yet, quite apart from it being absolutely wrong, especially the Soho aspect – it would be against one of the two promises I had made myself when I was fourteen.

One had been that I would not smoke until I was eighteen. I suppose I thought smoking was a manly thing to do, and as I had a father who was definitely all man, and he smoked sixty a day, one thing just followed another, naturally. However, he had advised me that smoking was undoubtedly bad for my health when growing up, hence my resolve. I had kept it but now that I was nineteen I had been smoking Abdullah no. 11 for about a year. The aroma of the Turkish tobacco was marvellous.

As for the second decision made at the same time, it concerned sex. By fourteen I was fully aware of my potential in this regard, yet also quite precocious in my general attitudes. I realized that either I would become like those jellyfish one saw in Maple Bay and Mill Bay, on Vancouver Island, simply going whichever way the tides or currents took them or I was to be the boss, as I put it to myself. I had the idea of 'the boss' as one in command from my father, who would use that phrase to describe such a situation. He was definitely the boss in our family. Even at that age I wanted eventually to marry, and it seemed to me that if I could not control myself over sex before marriage then that was hardly a preparation for fidelity towards one woman in marriage.

Also, when coming to this decision I recalled something that our French-Canadian cricketing Pastor at Duncan, Fr Latour, had said to me once: 'Man is the only living being in existence capable of chastity, as it depends upon free will'. He also said it would be tough, but with prayer and the sacraments it was possible. So at the time of deciding over tobacco, sex was lined up as well for attention. It had, indeed, been tough. For one thing, Polish blood is anything but hormone-free, and my ancestral dose of that is particularly strong. But, so far, by God's grace, I had kept to my resolve.

Notwithstanding, I was distraught. I needed some sort of release for all my pent up emotions – I was not sure what I wanted, but I wanted something, desperately.

So with such thoughts going through my mind, and feelings running through my whole being, I gradually wended my way through the Haymarket traffic, and started to walk along Charles II Street towards Lower Regent Street where I could either turn right to the pub and so on, or, on the same street take the bus home. The traffic on Lower Regent, though one-way (as on The Haymarket) went in the opposite direction, and so towards Hyde Park, Kensington Gardens and our flat at Queen's Court. Walking along, I thought, 'Christ almighty, have mercy on me. Mary, Mother of God, get cracking on my behalf – both of you PLEASE – I'm in a terrible fix.'

By now I had reached Lower Regent Street. After some hesitation, I dodged the traffic and took refuge on the raised pavement beneath Florence Nightingale's statue – did I need a lamp! – then crossed over to the Italian Bank side, turned right and walked on, appropriately enough, up towards the Office of the Agent General for British Columbia. The no.12 stop was just outside. A bus drew up as soon as I did. For a moment I hesitated, letting two women get on the bus. It was now or never: was it to be the pub and a poke or Queen's Court and Clicquot? I watched the finger of the conductress move up towards the bell. In an instant I leapt onto the rear platform. It was like jumping with the springboard in a gymnasium. Such a sensation at a bus stop was novel.

There were few people on the lower deck, so I chose a place at the front where I could be alone for the half hour or so's run to my stop. It was reassuring that every window – as on all buses at the time – was covered with a closely woven blast proof netting. I felt that no one outside could peer in on my misery.

The conductress came along to take my fare. She was probably a grandmother, and had one of those figures that would have been the despair of Yves St Laurent encased in a uniform from which hung about her all manner of impedimenta: ticket machine, money satchel and so on. She was one of those motherly, Cockney women, and when she gave me my ticket and saw in my face a combination of rage and misery, she looked at me in a way that said, 'Now love, it'll all be all right in the end.' At that particular moment, I would not have been inclined to believe her, but I could have kissed her.

Finally, I got home. My parents were out, which was, probably, a good thing under the circumstances, but they soon returned. I told them I had failed the examination but said I preferred not to discuss it further just then; they respected my wishes. So we finished off the Veuve Clicquot.

Some days before, I had arranged to meet a good friend of mine from St George's, R.C. ('Bob') Loadsman. After the war I was to be the Best Man at his wedding with Mary – that was the sort of relationship we had. So within a few days of the disaster on The Haymarket off I went to see him. Bob had continued on at St George's, whereas at the end of the previous academic year (July '42) I had left, having taken my Schools Certificate Examination of the Conjoint Board of Oxford and Cambridge – one of several possible school-leaving examinations of the time.

At that meeting with Bob I discovered that while I was absent, so to speak, the India Office – that department of the United Kingdom government then ultimately responsible for India – had 'discovered' St George's in its search for potential officers for the Indian Army. Apparently, the Brigadier in contact with St George's liked the Georgian product: 'just the right type' he said – whatever that meant. Bob had signed up and was soon to go off to the army. I wondered if this was the answer to my ambition to get into the fray, plus travel, adventure and – a great attraction to me – the chance to visit a place of almost infinite history. So I got the Brigadier's name from Bob, and set about tracking him down in the corridors of the India Office.

Eventually I located him and called by appointment. I more or less said, 'I'm a Georgian – what about me?' So in no time at all the Brigadier arranged for me to appear before a Selection Board, consisting of himself and two others. As directed, I presented myself in an old brick building in a back street very near the present Queen Elizabeth Conference Centre, opposite the West door of Westminster Abbey. The Board explained the whole scheme, and pointed out that, if I wished, it could lead to a lifetime career in the Indian Army, which appealed to me. Naturally, they had questions to ask, and these led to my telling them of the good number of retired Indian Army Officers and members of the Indian Civil Service in Cowichan, along with the lumbering community of Sikhs who included my turban guru – all of which much interested them.

The Board told me there and then that if I passed the medical, which they would arrange, I was accepted. I passed and was in.

The next step was to take the Oath of Allegiance and be taken onto the roll of the Queen's Royal Regiment (of the British Army) from which, all things being equal, I would be commissioned into the Indian Army. Following notification, I presented myself at an office in London on the appointed day and time. It turned out that a civil servant was to administer the oath. There were about four to be sworn in before me and several afterwards. Prior to administering the oath, the civil servant filled in a form, asking: full name, religion, date of birth, full names of parents and their address or addresses. When it came to my turn, and I answered his question as to my date of birth with: 13 May 1924, he stopped writing and said, 'But you should have joined up a year ago. You've broken the law. We must see about this.' I replied that I had not broken the law of the United Kingdom as I was a Canadian National, resident in England for the sole purpose of education, and that according to United Kingdom National Service regulations I was therefore exempt from conscription – and that, notwithstanding, I now wished to volunteer for war service. 'Volunteer!' he barked, '*You* can't volunteer! You'll be a *conscript* – after the police have dealt with you.'

Obviously, we were heading for choppy waters. So I tried to calm matters with a vague and somewhat laboured pun by saying that my situation *vis-à-vis* his usual work was perhaps one of a *rara avis* – he did not get it; obviously went to a very dull school. Rather than waste his time the more, and that of all those behind me – as well as my own – I suggested, with respect, that he consult his superiors immediately. I went on to say that I felt I had to be absolutely honest: if I were prevented from taking the Oath and being enrolled in the Queen's Royal Regiment, our family solicitor would immediately contact directly not simply the Ministers of State for War, but also for India, as well as the Canadian High Commission – which would involve the Foreign and Commonwealth Office.

One could see his eyes narrowing at this firmness by a young man. Probably he was thinking to himself: These public school boys think they run the Empire. Well, of course, when we had one, we did. Anyway, he hesitated for a moment.

Something must have told him that he had better be careful, for he picked up the telephone and explained matters briefly to someone at the other end. Then a long listening took place, after which he put the telephone down, and without saying a word simply proceeded to complete my form. Thereupon he gave me a copy of the Douai Bible[1] together with a card on which was the text of the Oath. In so doing he said, 'State your full name after "I" and then read the rest'. Which I then proceeded to do.

Upon completing that, I handed him the card and Bible whereupon he observed, 'Well you know what to do now' – which I did: leave and proceed as previously instructed. There was no handshake, as for the others; I did not worry. I was IN!

The Queen's Royal Regiment, of which I was now a member, was rather appropriate for those destined for the Indian Army, as the lady in whose honour it had been named had brought with her, as part of her dowry, Bombay. She was Queen Catherine of Braganza, who became the wife of Charles II in 1662. Her badge, which became that of her regiment, was the *Agnus Dei,* usually represented as a lamb. As a result of this badge, members of other regiments, with that highly developed and amusing sense of humour of the British Army, frequently referred to us as 'Leg O'Muttons' – it was given and taken all in good part. We wore our badge with pride and recalled its 300 or so years of service to the Crown.

What I had been told to do after taking the Oath was to attend at the School of Oriental and African Studies in the University of London.[2] A special course had been arranged by the India Office to give those prospective officers of the Indian Army who could attend, an introduction to the history, culture and religions of India, as well as preparatory tuition in the *lingua franca* of the Indian Armed Forces: Urdu. I attended daily next to the British Museum in Bloomsbury, at the Senate House of the University.

The course went on for several weeks and I enjoyed it enormously. The lecturers were excellent, and enthused us for the delights to come in India. Our tutor in Urdu was the Imam of the London Mosque. His smart suits, wing collars and elegant ties had something of the Parisian chic about them. He was the very opposite of what one imagined the average Mullah would be like, but then he had been the Imam of the Paris Mosque.

With that course concluded, thirty-two of us – we were to form a complete platoon of potential officers – converged on the barracks at Maidstone, Kent, in order to start some real soldiering. The day was 18 November, 1943. Over the door was inscribed 'Balaclava'. One wondered if it was a good omen: an inconclusive battle some 90 years before which included the Charge of the Light

---

[1] An English translation by William, Cardinal Allen and other exiled English Catholic scholars. The last part of its publication was in 1610. The King James Authorized version was published a year later.
[2] SSA. New Series, Misc. II: C.S. to R.E.G. 23 Oct. 1943.

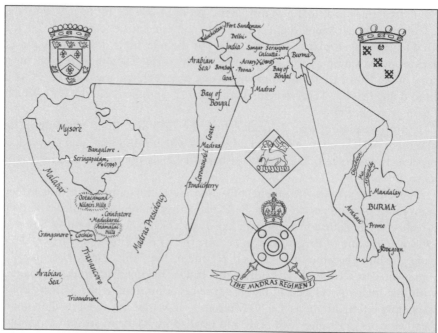

Map of India and Burma, with places referred to in the text, indicated. The armorial details are: upper left, the arms of Field Marshal the Viscount Wavell, Viceroy of India, 1943-47 (the Author's time on the subcontinent): upper right, the Lord Northcote, Governor of Bombay, 1900-03, Governor-General of Australia, 1903-08 (great-uncle of the Author's wife), the badges: upper, the Queen's Royal Regiment (upon a diamond-shaped background, indicating Officer Cadet); lower, the Madras Regiment.

Brigade – gallant in the extreme but to what purpose? But there was no time to consider the regiment's history; we all lined up for the Quartermaster Sergeant to issue us with our uniform:

> Anklets, web, 1pr.
> Boots, ankle, leather, 1pr.
> Jackets, KD (khaki drill) 1
> And so on and so on

until we were all kitted out with a complete uniform. When put on, I was definitely 'No. 6101156 Swan, C.M.J.F. Private of no 4 Platoon, 'A' Company 63 PTW,' and I had an official Soldier's Service Book (Army Book 611 [Part 1]) to prove it.

Now we had to learn not only to be, but also to behave as, disciplined soldiers. Much drill on the parade ground smartened us up. 'Get that salute right:' the NCO would bark out. Folded fore and aft caps were to be worn at an angle over the right eye – and so on. No wonder we were confined to barracks for a couple of weeks, – just as well.

We were up early and kept busy all day[3] with 'parades' (duties) of various kinds. TEWTs (Tactical Exercises Without Troops) were fun. Grouped around a model of countryside raised from the ground, we discussed how best to get from points A to B, or attack point C, and use the countryside in doing so. If one wanted artillery fire onto a particular point, a junior NCO. would let some cigarette-smoke up through a hole in the model (under which he crouched) to simulate the explosion of shells!

Route marches in full kit (weighing some 80lbs) were endless. During these, as soon as the hourly break was announced by the NCO with 'Fall out!' there was a rush to the nearest hedge, wall or gate, then down on one's back and up with the feet as high as possible. The resultant draining of the blood worked wonders for the next part of the march. This was announced by the NCO with: 'Right, get fell in you lot – what a shower you all are', usually with a smile, I must admit. Then off we would go, singing 'She'll be coming round the mountain' or some other suitable rhythmic piece. These definitely helped the marching though the librettos were not always those one would sing when visiting one's nun aunt!

Cross-country runs were another form of toning up, sometimes without rifles, sometimes with. So our days were kept busy and there was no time for mischief. We fell asleep quickly – despite our bedclothes. The blankets (no such things as sheets) were, I was sure, made of some coarse horsehair – certainly nothing like the hair of any mount I ever had. As the under-blanket beneath the sleeper was all there was between me and the mattress, I used to spread a clean handkerchief where I laid my head to prevent being woken up in the night when I turned over and my cheek was 'grated' by the horsehair.

The room in which we slept was the one and only room in which we lived. There was, in fact, no privacy except in the lavatories. This presented me with something of a dilemma on the very first night. Time for bed had been announced by the Lance Corporal who slept in the room with us, and we were getting into our pyjamas (non-issue but permitted). I had been accustomed to kneel down by my bed and say my prayers before getting in, but no one was doing that. What should I do? I was not scared, but I was shy. I thought to myself: well, St Louis[4] used to pray, and he was a good soldier, so down I went on my knees. Everyone was well on the way to bed now and once in, stayed there. Granted, it was only a matter of the sign of the Cross, a quick examination of conscience, quick act of contrition and firm purpose of amendment, then an Our Father, Hail Mary for my parents, my brother, Peter, and all those in the

---

[3] SSA. New Series, Misc. II: C.S. to R.E.G. 18 Nov. 1943 – training from 6.15AM to 5.30 PM Free until bed at 10.15PM (but much cleaning of kit even then).

[4] Louis IX, King of France, 1226-70 – Crusader.

room, whom I hoped would soon be my friends. Finally, the sign of the Cross and an almighty leap into bed. The lights were soon out and that was that. The next night everyone – except one – was on his knees before going to bed, and so it continued for the rest of our time at Maidstone. The one who did not offer up orisons said he was an atheist. I was not with him in a fox-hole (where I never found an atheist) so cannot say how devoted he was to the Supreme Negative.

While I was at Maidstone, beginning to learn how to be an officer, my brother, Peter, was thousands of miles away in Toronto, in the last stages of *his* commissioning process, so to speak, preparing to be ordained a Catholic priest, as he was on 19 December, 1943[5].

Thus began for Peter a brilliant career between this and that university. He was to become the Canadian representative on IFCU (International Federation of Catholic Universities) which required more flying, and much enjoyment therefrom. Perhaps the multiple peregrinations of our great-grandmother, Isabella, between the Baltic and Pacific Coasts some sixty years before had passed something on through the genes.

Having fitted in that family gusset, as it were, let us return to my passage through Maidstone. There was no let-up all week, but on Saturday afternoons and Sundays we were free, and could get permission to stay out for a night if we wished. Those who could went off to friends nearby. Mine were Sir Garrard and Lady Tyrwhitt-Drake, of Cobtree Manor (the location of 'Dingly Dale' of Pickwick Papers), just outside Maidstone. They were cousins of some friends of ours in Victoria, one of whom, Montague William Tyrwhitt-Drake, had been a Justice of the Supreme Court of British Columbia.[6] When staying at Cobtree Manor, one frequently woke in the morning to the roar of lions being fed, as they had a private zoo[7].

Our Platoon had the usual ration of Officers and NCOs. The relationship between them and us was always correct and, in some cases, friendly. There was, however, a certain Sergeant Dunkeld, who took us for some parades and duties. At the age of twenty-one, and a Lance Sergeant, he had survived Dunkirk. It seemed this gave him certain ideas about himself. He combined great rudeness with bullying. We put up with it at the time – but remembered. Accordingly, very near the end of our time at Maidstone, and having already demonstrated to our officers that we too were 'officer material', we decided to observe a symbolic ceremony. The Cadets cornered Dunkeld and de-bagged him; thereupon, using dubbin as paint, they aimed it with great accuracy at his testicular region.

A month or so after our arrival at Maidstone it was Christmas. Following the age-old tradition of the army, we stayed in bed in our barrack-room dormitory on

---

[5] SSA. New Series. Misc. II: description of the ceremony: an extract of a letter from a witness written to Capt. P.R. Gilman, 9th Can. Inf. Brgde, RCASC.

[6] Burkes Landed Gentry, 1925, p. 519.

[7] SSA. New Series. Misc.II. C.S. to, R.E.G. 15 Jan. 1944.

Christmas morning while our officers served us with tea in large mugs. We thought that was grand, but it was not the last of such attentions from on high. This followed at the main meal of the day, at noon, when, supervised by the Commanding Officer of the Barracks, no less, – a lieutenant colonel – all the officers under his command served us our food before they had theirs. It was on the old Army principle that, 'men eat first, officers last'; of course, such an order of precedence does ensure uninterrupted enjoyment of the officers' pre-prandials.

We were free after that 'dinner', as they always called the mid-day meal, so I spent the remainder of the day at Cobtree Manor.[8] Preparations for an elegant supper were in full swing when I arrived. The Staff had the day off, so Lady T.-D. was busy making something, and I asked if I could help. To this she replied, 'Oh, Conrad, make me a Manhattan – you'll find the things for it in the cabinet.' I was floored; I had never made a cocktail in my life. So I replied, 'Lady Tyrwhitt-Drake, in my home occasionally we have punch for the winter parties and my father makes that. Otherwise we take our liquor straight, so you'll have to tell me how.' We all laughed. Ever after, they referred to me as 'the man who takes his liquor straight'.

Seven days later, New Year's Day, 1944, saw the whole Platoon say farewell to Maidstone as we moved about eight miles away to the pre-OCTU (Officer Cadets' Training Unit) at Wrotham Camp – a desolate spot in the middle of a wood on the top of an escarpment. The fact that a mediaeval Pilgrim's Way ran along its top towards Canterbury failed to enthuse my historically attuned soul.

Unpromising though all of this was, we were now Cadets and, were accordingly identified by having a lozenge-shaped piece of white plastic placed behind the regimental badge on our uniform berets, as well as white flashes on our shoulders. When off duty we were even allowed to wear a shirt and tie, both khaki.

Our Officers and NCOs were a completely new group, the former from Indian Regiments – the Rajputana Rifles, and the 11th Sikhs, so we really started to feel that we were getting towards our goal. The same type of physical training as at Maidstone continued – but everything was at the double! There were also most interesting lectures and discussions of Indian matters.

There was an American Air Force base nearby. We often saw their bombers coming back from raids – some limping along. When the Luftwaffe returned the call, usually at night, our ack-ack was intense, and from time to time one would hear small splinters from our shells falling on the metal roof of one's Nissan hut. When that was going on one did not venture out to the loo; it helped to have a bladder like steel.

There was a Catholic chapel in the camp and Mass was well attended. Afterwards most of us trooped across the road to a public house where we drank

---

[8] SSA. New Series IV: C.S. to E.H.S. Boxing Day 1943.

rum and ginger wine; I was starting to take a leaf out of Lady T-D's book in mixing my own drinks.

We were at Wrotham for about two months, at the end of which (12 February, 1944) we went on embarkation leave for two weeks[9]. We then reported to the Assembly centre in the Grand Central Hotel in Marylebone, London, which had been commandeered by the War Office for this purpose; it was anything but the Ritz. Leaving London in an Air Raid we went by train to Liverpool to board the S S *Otranto*, previously the flag ship of the Orient Line but very much converted for troop-carrying purposes. We set sail on 29 March, 1944.

The food was disgusting, and as we soon ran into very heavy weather many were sick. During that part of the journey the only reasonable situation was achieved in one's hammock at night when the rolling of the ship[10] was not so obvious. The showers were hot salt water – not such a good idea – but the special soap, though it looked and smelt as if made for some cart horse, did help.

Dodging the Nazi submarines we made our way south, and as we steamed along the cost of Portugal we were amazed, after our four years of blackout, to see all the villages ablaze with light at night[11].

When we reached Malta we moored off shore in the Grand Harbour. An announcement came over the tannoy system: 'Cadet CMJF Swan to report to the OC Troops', which he did. The OC told me that I was to report to GHQ, Malta and that the admiral's pinnace would take me ashore. So off I went and having arrived at the quayside was met by a young Subaltern from GHQ, who took me to the office of the editor of *The Times of Malta* and leader of the Progressive Constitutional Party, the Honble Mabel Strickland.

As soon as I arrived at that office, I knew that the wire I had sent off just before leaving England had arrived, and that Miss Strickland had used her not inconsiderable influence. I did not know her personally, but was very friendly with her sister, the Honble Mrs Henrietta Bower, her husband, Cmdr Robert Bower, MP, their son Paul (my age) and his sisters. For long periods during the early part of the war, I had spent holidays at their home, Sizergh Castle, Westmorland (now Cumbria). The castle was the Strickland's ancestral home. It was from there that Sir Thomas Strickland had set out to carry the banner of St George at Agincourt.

One of Paul's sisters, Marianna, was at the time staying with her aunt in Malta. The Stricklands were an old English Recusant Catholic family but were also part Maltese; the father of the Honbles Mabel and Henrietta, Lord Strickland, 6th Count della Catena in the Island of Malta, had been the Chief Minister of Malta.

---

[9] SSA. New Series. Misc. II: C.S. to R.E.G. 15 Jan. 1944.
[10] SSA New Series IV-4: C.S. to parents, undated. Written on board S.S. *Otranto* before reaching Malta. Address given as Grindlap & Co., Ltd., Bombay.
[11] *Ibid.*

So having landed safely, I was whisked off to Miss Strickland's home, Villa Parisio. This was my base for the next two days of sight-seeing under the guidance of Marianna,[12] and I thoroughly enjoyed domesticity again after the conditions on board, including the luxury of a bath, alone and not in hot sea water.

Once back on the ship I discovered that I was the only one of the thousand or so passengers who had been allowed ashore – not even the OC Troops – so I had to be extremely discreet.

Leaving Malta and by the usual route of Suez, the Red Sea and the Indian Ocean, we arrived at Bombay, where we found several ships up on dry land as the result of the biggest munitions' explosion of the war. The journey from Liverpool to Bombay took just a full month: remarkably quick, considering the detours we had taken.

Bearing in mind our original patron it was appropriate that members of the Queen's Royal Regiment should disembark at that part of her dowry, the 'Gateway of India', Bombay. Right there on the quayside there was a permanent gateway built in the Indian style in basalt in 1924. It was here that, in peace time at least, viceroys were welcomed upon their arrival. For us the Viceroy of the day was Field Marshal the Viscount Wavell: gallant soldier, poet and gentleman. Thus we could say, All's right with the world: God's in his heaven and Wavell's in Delhi; our experiences in the latter quarter later on were to challenge this assertion with his successor.

There were two main military academies in India to which cadets could go for their final training before commissioning: Dehra Dun (the equivalent of Kingston and Sandhurst) almost due north of Delhi, about one hundred miles, and half way to Simla, the summer capital. On the other hand there was Bangalore (the largest in the British Empire) which was opened for the war, in the South of India, in the extremely advanced Native State of Mysore, about five hundred miles from Bombay as the crow – or in India possibly one should say, the Kite Hawk – flies. It was a healthy spot, about three thousand feet up (but not the Silicon Valley it is to-day). We were allocated Bangalore, and so set off by train for three days in 3rd Class carriages sleeping on the floor in considerable discomfort. At last this was over when we took up our quarters at the OTS (Officers Training School) which was in the country just outside the Bangalore cantonment.

Our quarters were commodious: two cadets to each large room. These rooms doubled as bedroom and study. There were a number of such rooms in one bungalow so that the door for each opened immediately onto the pathway outside. The interior walls of the room stopped short of the roof: helping

---

[12] She married Major General Gilbert, 2nd Viscount Monckton of Brenchley, son and heir of Sir Walter Monckton, 1st Viscount, the lawyer to Edward VIII at the time of the abdication, and much involved on behalf of the Indian Princes running up to Indian Independence in 1947.

ventilation – and the broadcasting of some fascinating conversations! Each of the two typical beds in India comprised a wooden frame over which strips of webbing were stretched and woven. On top of this was a blanket, and over that, a sheet; no mattress. There was a pillow and pillowcase. At the bottom of the bed a sheet and blanket to pull over one were folded but rarely used. Then suspended (either from a thin wooden frame, or from the ceiling) a mosquito net which one made sure was always tucked beneath the under blanket and sheet, except when getting into and out of bed.

When so doing the latter in the morning one always shook one's slippers to remove any scorpion (or other uninvited guests) before slipping them on! Ablutions were in other buildings nearby with lavatories in both European and Indian style.

Four of us shared a bearer (native servant). It was bliss not to have to clean one's boots and equipment, nor tidy one's own quarters.[13] Early on, I was dressing one morning and had just got into my smart regulation khaki shorts. While adjusting my shirt, I felt my bearer's hand go up my shorts and over my right buttock. I was just about to strike him into the middle of next month when there was a sudden jerk of my shirt into position. I spared him the blow. It was a good lesson not to jump to conclusions too quickly.

Cadets were paid monthly forty Rupees (about £4 = about $8 in 1944; possibly x 20 in value to-day)[14]. They had the privilege of censoring their own letters, and indicated this by signing the front of the envelope. This was to help lift the burden of the official censors.[15]

The Mess, for all meals and social activities, was one of those large white buildings with thick walls, typical in India. Most are examples of classical or Georgian, British architecture. Columns are profuse, ranged into aisles on either side of a long, rectangular central room. Such rooms helped to keep out the sun while allowing as much circulation of air as possible.

The training was basically the same as at Maidstone and Wrotham though 'modified for India.' This phrase, often to be found in official forms and manuals, used to make us laugh, and we frequently applied it as a joke. However, in southern India – we were about 13° off the Equator – it was not a matter of the cold and the snow we had to contend with, but the blistering heat or the all-pervading moisture of the monsoon.

Our battle-training was realistic, with live ammunition. And later on in the course, during the monsoon, when the *nullahs* were full we had to swim across them. We had these exercises by day and by night; in the continual shower of the

---

[13] SSA New Series IV C.S. to E.H.S. 2 May 1944.

[14] *Ibid* 14 May 1944.

[15] *Ibid* 2 May 1944. On the envelope, in addition to the name of addressee, one wrote, upper left 'Air Mail', upper right 'Forces Mail' and then at lower left one signed one's name and added one's number – first cadet and later commission number.

monsoon and in the tinder dry of the other months. In the latter, everything appears to heave and shimmer before one's eyes, so one had to take very careful aim on the rifle range in order to get the 2oz of lead into the target.

One of several occupations at Bangalore was learning Urdu and passing the necessary examinations in this *lingua franca* of the Services. As there are about 250 different languages in India, all as different as Russian is from English, or Italian from Icelandic, as well as a diversity of completely different scripts (English being known by a tiny minority) it was obviously essential to have a common tongue in which to communicate with one's men. After all, if one wanted them to follow and capture that particular hill, and they wandered off in another direction, it could be embarrassing. The result was that as soon as a recruit entered the Indian Army, even if he was illiterate – as most were – he is made literate in *Urdu,* and everything thereafter was conducted in that language. Oddly enough, the word order of a sentence is as for Latin: subject first, verb at the end with the object in the middle. In connection with these lessons, we had a Sepoy to talk to once a week. He would pretend that he had a request or had overstayed his leave, and we would have to sort it out with him. They were a good group of men, from a Punjabi Regiment who wore 'turbans like Queen Mary's hats only a little more "chic"'.[16]

The Indian Army was, in fact, very keen on languages. It made it attractive to learn them by reimbursing one's expenses on the *munchi* (teacher) after one passed the examination in question – and also by raising one's pay. Upon becoming proficient in the language of a bordering country, Delhi would send one documents and newspapers in the language in question and ask that translations be made.

Mess life was good and we all started to develop a taste for curry. As one would expect, it was excellent. The alcohol was adequate. It was usually either beer (which goes well with curry) or spirits. The latter could be somewhat coarse (they were almost always local products), but there was alcohol lurking somewhere at the bottom of the glass.

'The opening of the "second front" [in June] caused quite a stir... the first news we had was over the German radio shortly before the British announced it.'[17] What were we doing listening to the Nazi news?

I had arrived in India with a fistful of letters of introduction to army personnel, civilians, bishops, nurses, rajahs, teachers and so on. Being anxious to start to find out about India from as many different angles as possible, I pressed these into service early on. The local official known as the British Resident, (the representative of the British Governor-General of India at the Court of an Indian ruler, in this case the Maharaja of Mysore, within whose domain all of us were

---

[16] SSA new Series IV: C.S. to E.H.S. from Bangalore 25 June 1944.
[17] SSA New Series IV: C.S. to E.H.S. from Bangalore 11 June 1944.

residing), lived conveniently for me in Cubbon Park, Bangalore. He was a Lieutenant Colonel Fraser, and proved a mine of information about the Native Princes, their history, role and position in India.[18]

The Native South Indian Bishop of Bangalore, the Right Reverend Thomas Pothacamury, welcomed me whenever I called and gave me some penetrating insights into Hinduism.[19] Brigadier Basil Trappes-Lomax, MC, of HQ, Southern Army, was most hospitable. He was able to supply me with much information on the role of the British in India from the point of view of a senior army officer who had resided in the country for some time. He was a member of an old English recusant family,[20] which gave a certain sharpness to his comments on the position of Indian Christians. At the time, these numbered about the same as the total population of Canada. Curiously enough, some years later, when I entered the Royal Household, in that department known as the College of Arms, I became a colleague of his brother, Michael, who was then Somerset Herald of Arms.[21]

Though friendly with all our group, when not on duty one naturally tended to associate with those whom one had most in common. My off-duty friends included AC ('Tony') Buckingham who, upon being commissioned, went to the 12th Frontier Force Regiment; S.R.O'R ('Rex') Shearburn, 9th Gurkha Rifles; Alan Burnett, 10th Baluch Regiment; David Wade, 2nd Gurkha Rifles, and K.P. Murphy, 4th Gurkha Rifles and later the 2nd Karen Rifles. We have all kept in touch ever since.

Of these, the one I had most to do with from Maidstone to Bangalore was Kevin (Patrick) Murphy.[22] We had both entered St George's College together in the autumn of 1937. His family were in business in China, though I doubt if he ever saw them again.

Though we were both in the same Form, we were not in the same House. He was a devoted sportsman, a 'rugger bugger', as the term went. I was certainly anything but that, though a gymnast. So at school we paid little attention to each other. However, from the time we met up again at Maidstone barracks we

---

[18] *Ibid.*

[19] SSA New Series IV: C.S. to E.H.S. from Bangalore 29 May 1944.

[20] For details on the family, *vide Burke's Landed Gentry*, Burke's Peerage Ltd, London, 1965, 118th Edition, Vol. I pp. 453–456.

[21] Soon after my joining my regiment, Brigadier Trappes-Lomax – quite unbeknown to me – wrote on 4 December, 1944 to my mother – though he did not know her – saying, 'A line to tell you that I have recently seen your boy. He looked very well and was in good heart. The authorities of the Officers Training School tell me he did very well there and it is a compliment that he should have been posted to the Madras Regiment... [as]... it has been found necessary ... to strengthen the officers. Your son has been picked with that object in view.' It was only when researching for this book that I came across this letter. It was kind of the Brigadier to have taken the trouble to write. I am glad that the decision of my superiors coincided with my preference. SSA: New Series, IV Misc.

[22] I understand his later colleagues insisted upon calling him by the abbreviation of his second name, Pat, he being Irish.

became good friends and used to go about together fairly frequently. I felt, also, that if ever we got into a fight, while I would defend his back, he would certainly defend mine – as the best Irish do if they are one's friend. He was a good all-rounder, and an exemplary Catholic.

We would go off to Mass together, and at Bangalore would, sometimes – about once a month on a Saturday – jump on our bicycles (the usual form of transport for the cadets) and go to the large Catholic church in the cantonment for confession.[23] Thence to the club for a slap-up dinner, and after a film, back to our quarters at the OTS All of this was finished before midnight and we had had a terrific time – what innocence!

About halfway through the course in Bangalore, one was asked which regiment one would like to join and, if at all possible, one's preference was granted. I decided on the Madras Regiment, for the historical reason that it is the oldest regiment in the Indian Army.[24] In the face of a fierce French threat, the regiment was raised by a 23-year-old former clerk of the East India Company then in its army: Colonel Robert Clive – 'Clive of India' – Commander-in-Chief of the Army in India (1755-60). The regiment fought at several of the great battles of the country: Arcot, 1752; Seringapatam, 1799; and Assay, 1803. At the last named it was commanded by Sir Arthur Wellesley, later Duke of Wellington, who said of the battle: 'Our troops behaved admirably. Our Sepoys astonished me'[25] – and Wellington did not prostitute his compliments. In the suppression of the Indian Mutiny, 1857-60, the loyalty and determination of the Madras Regiment was of vital importance.

Finally, on 18 November 1944, the great day arrived, and in a splendid ceremony, in the best military tradition, we received the Commission of the King-Emperor, substituted pips for the white flashes on our shoulders, and wore, for the first time, a peaked cap, each with his appropriate regimental badge.[26] I had become 2nd Lieutenant C.M.J.F. Swan, Madras Regiment,[27] the second person in my male-line family to have the honour of holding a commission of the Crown. [28]

Joining Leave then followed. I spent mine in Delhi – lovely at that time of

[23] The church was known as St Patrick's – though actually dedicated to the Immaculate Conception. This was due to the fact that some years before the Connaught Rifles had been stationed there and had built onto the church a chapel dedicated to St Patrick so that the name stuck – trust the Irish! SSA New Series IV: C.S. to E.H.S. from Bangalore, 7 May 1944.

[24] Dodwell, H.H. *The Cambridge History of India,* New Delhi, Vol. V, pp 156-161

Mervyn Davies, A. *Clive of Plassey*. London, 1939 p.43.

Newell, H.A. *Madras, the Birth-Place of British India*. Madras, 1919 pp27-29

Watney, John. *Clive of India*. 1974 p.30.

[25] Wilson, J.J. History of the Madras Army. Madras, 1883 Vol III p. 109.

[26] SSA New Series IV: C.S. to E.H.S. from Bangalore 19 November, 1944.

[27] GHQ (India) No. 0983/3 MS4B dated 22-12-44.

[28] My father was the first.

year with sunny but not hot days and refreshingly cold nights. I stayed at the Cecil Hotel in Old Delhi (run by a Swiss family called Hory, to whom I had an introduction. They also ran Wild Flower Hall, Simla) During the day I visited Mrs Prince and her husband, then Colonel, (2/6 Gurkha Rifles) later Major General H.A. Prince, CBE, who showed me around. She was a family friend, the former Betty Bapty, of Victoria, BC, daughter of Lieutenant Colonel Walter Bapty.[29] He was a local *Aide de Camp* of the Governor General.

There was much to be seen in both Old and New Delhi. In the former, the Lal Khela – the Red Fort – was a monument to the Mogul Empire with exquisitely inlaid marble in its state rooms.[30] It was from the river side of this building that George V and Queen Mary – as Emperor and Empress of India, adorned in all their magnificent regalia – appeared to the general public during the Delhi Durbar in 1911. This occasion was attended by no less than 562 Maharajas, Rajas and other Indian Princes to whom the King-Emperor announced – a closely guarded secret up to that moment – that the Capital was to be moved from Calcutta to Delhi. At this, as I was told by one present, the taking in of breath was distinctly audible, for it was an old saying that the moving of the Capital to Delhi had always been in the past the first step towards doom.

New Delhi was magnificent: an Imperial Capital designed throughout by that master of architects, Sir Edwin Lutyens. To me it was all so perfect that it could have done with a 'rent a crowd' of revolutionaries to give it a little character (soon, of course, to be thoroughly driven out by the Bengal Lancers or similar worthies).

The delights of the two Delhis – historical and constitutional feasts for me – came to an end, and Burma beckoned. It took some time to get to 268 Brigade of the Indian Army, of which the 4th Battalion of the Madras Regiment formed part, with Lieutenant Colonel ACL Dredge Commanding. My good friend Major SD Clarke was the Officer Commanding C Company – a welcome situation for me. At this point in my career I had just become, through my being commissioned, one of an armed Force which had expanded from a pre-war complement of one hundred and sixty thousand to two million, four hundred thousand, every one a volunteer. About ninety-five percent of these were in the Indian Army; the remainder in the relatively small Indian Navy and Air Force. There was no question of conscription. We could not have enforced it. British rule in India was a classic case of rule by consent.

By January, 1945 the 4th Battalion had got to Tongon and so to Kyaunggon on the Mu River – a tributary of the Irawaddy before the Chindwin empties into the former – not far from Mandalay, which is as near dead centre of Burma as can

---

[29] who fought in the Boer War and upon returning to Canada on his 17th Birthday, then graduated as M.D., from the first medical class of the University of Western Ontario – of which I am also an alumnus.

[30] SSA New Series IV: C.S to E.H.S, 26 November, 1944

be. The Indian and British Armies were at last gaining the upper hand, although the Japanese were in no mood to show the white flag. There was no question of a rout by us, and it was necessary to fight all the way. The role of the 4th Battalion, as matters turned out, was to press on down the centre of Burma, once it had got near the Irawaddy, and so in the general direction of Rangoon, by way of Swebo, Sagaing, Myinguan and Prome – and countless little villages en route.

The moves round Kyaunggon and the Mu River were carried on with the help of mules.[31] The Japanese visiting cards were often grenades released from a discharger cup, which we found particularly unwelcome. We returned the compliment with vigour. Fighting in Burma was *sui generis*: every bush could camouflage the enemy, and similarly every tree support one of their snipers.

On the other hand we had good transport for our gear. There were bullocks – the traditional animals for pulling carts in the whole of India and Burma (where in my day, at least, they had the right of way); there were also six elephants under command – wonderfully patient animals of enormous strength. On the other hand, security measures had to be tightened up as Japanese had been found roaming the countryside in Burmese dress. At Thetseingyi – a small village about 50 miles from Mandalay – they had four-inch mortars and several 75mm guns, which made our life rather uncomfortable. In addition they caused a tragedy. One of their shells passed through the narrow entrance of a pagoda and exploded in the small room inside which was the Officers' mess. Mercifully, the servants – by some miracle – escaped with their lives, but the décor of this room was completely changed, with the exploded tins of jam and bacon plastered all over the walls, and tragedy of tragedies: the whisky and beer was no more!

★   ★   ★

When I went down soon afterwards with dysentery and suspected pleurisy everyone joked that this was because the disaster had been such a shock to my system. Accordingly, after some five weeks I was evacuated and sent for recuperation to our Madras Regimental Centre, which meant going down to the extreme south of India to the Madras Presidency.[32] The centre was situated at Madukarai (which means, 'The Place of Honey') near Coimbatore in the Polgot Gap that leads from the Presidency to the West Coast and so to Malabar, Cochin and Travancore.

Thanks to the excellence of the Indian Medical Service, it was not too long before I was feeling and looking much better. There was the distinct possibility of getting back into action again. While I was thinking along these lines one day, the Commandant, Colonel A.L. Collingwood sent for me. He said he wanted me to go to Saugor to be trained as an Instructor in Small Arms.

---

[31] These were temporally 'de-ee-awed' by our clever vets so as not to give the game away to the enemy, who had a habit of turning up uninvited.

[32] A province of British India now called Tamil Nadu.

Officers (King's Commissioned, Viceroy's Commissioned and Non-Commissioned) of the Madras Regiment, Indian Army, taken at the Regimental Centre, Madukaria, Madras Presidency. 29 October, 1945. The Author is seated fourth from the right.

'But Sir, the 4th Battalion?'

'Mr Swan, in the Army one learns to obey even if one thinks otherwise' and indicated that this was the end of the interview. Whereupon, I gave him a salute, turned about and walked towards the door of his office. When I was almost there, the commandant said: 'Conrad, come here and sit down; take your cap off.' I obeyed. He observed that he admired my spirit, but that there were three things he wanted me to know: first, that the MO had told him that I was not as recovered as I imagined; second, that as the longest-serving Battalion in Burma, the 4th was about to be withdrawn, and third, that my going to Saugor, and getting a good qualification would serve the Regiment best of all.

'Sir, I now go willingly, and shall do my very best.'

'See you at lunch, Conrad, and over a beer.' Such an avuncular approach, typical of the best senior officers, was all that was necessary to put me in the right frame of mind. It was in accordance with the old military principle of, 'Always tell your men the reason why.' So off I went.

Saugor was in the Central Provinces near the border of Rajputana[33] and the city of Bhopal.[34] Ballistics had always interested me, and I thoroughly enjoyed the course, doubly so, as I discovered an ability to teach which has proved

---

[33] A group of Native States now mostly part of Rajasthan.
[34] Capital of the Indian State of that name.

extremely satisfying ever since. My GHQ grading for the course was 'QI'.[35] Mental note on receipt of said 'QI, that's good, it will mean a strawberry not a raspberry from the CO!'.[36]

Having qualified, I returned to the Regimental Centre and was put in charge of Weapon Training with a Staff of twenty-one.[37] The main work of the Centre was turning the new recruits into soldiers. They came not only from the Madras Presidency, but also from the Native States of Cochin and Travancore, and the surrounding areas. They were mainly Tamils, Telagus and Malayalis – with their three languages. Physically, they have high cheek bones, pointed noses, straight black hair. The Tamils tend to be very dark, almost black. They are country people, generally farmers. In religion they are mostly Hindus, but with a large number of Christians and a few Muslims. Madrassi is the generic term for the people of this area. They are intelligent, cheerful and with a great sense of humour. They are all born actors, and the Regimental theatricals had one in stitches (they had me off to a tee!). A good number are literate (unusual in India). They are loyal to superiors, colleagues and subordinates. They have a good deal of common sense, admire leadership and react well to good management. They do not pick fights but if they have to fight they do so with vigour and, as Wellington attested, want to see it through to victory. One might say that the Madrassi is the nearest thing east of Suez to the citizen soldier of the West.[38]

The greatest compliment a Sepoy could pay a white Officer was to say, '*Major Sahib, Mam-Bap hai*' – that is to say, 'The Major Sahib is Mother-Father to me/us', i.e., he leads and looks after me/us well.

When a native recruit first joins the regiment, it is akin to stepping into an entirely new world. First, he has to change his manner of dress. In Southern India before entry the Hindu and Christian will wear, as a minimum, a piece of straight material wound round the lower part of the body to form a jock-strap, and this they continue to wear in the army as what we would call underclothes. In general, they are extremely modest. Accordingly, when I took my Sepoys on a route march and let them have a swim in a tank (as an artificial lake is called in India), they would automatically keep on their minimum underclothes just referred to, and I would have to swim in my underpants. After a few minutes standing around once out of the water, everything would dry off and so there was no problem. If one appeared naked in public in India one loses caste and is regarded as no better than a prostitute. (British regiments in that country had to be particularly careful over this. All this goes to show that it is always wise for an Imperial power to be aware of local customs and the reasons behind them.).

---

[35] SSA New Series IV C.S. to E.H.S. 18 March, 1945. 'QI' = very good.
[36] *Ibid.*
[37] *Ibid* 18 March 1945.
[38] SSA new Series IV C.S. to E.H.S. 7 January 1945.

Getting back to the average South Indian's wardrobe, in addition to the jock-strap he might have a turban of sorts. For some that is all. Then, if they can afford it, various other very thin clothes.

Coming into the Army, the young man – unless he is a Muslim – must learn to wear trousers; but even those of the Muslims are more baggy than those that soldiers wear. This must require getting used to, not forgetting the complications when wishing to answer the calls of nature. Then there are woollen socks to be worn for the first time, and boots, which always require much breaking in and polishing. The blouse or jacket is much less open and free compared with the *banyan* (civilian shirt-like garb). Lastly, the ordinary headgear is different from that to which he is used. So it is all quite a change.

Then, as mentioned before, he must learn Urdu and train in all other ways so as to be an efficient soldier. To this end, my contribution was, in the main, and naturally in view of my extra training, that of teaching each man to handle the weapons on which his life might depend.

At this point I detail, in the form of a diary, life at the Regimental Centre over three days. Every event mentioned occurred while I was there, and every person cited, was at or visited the Centre during my time there. The timings are typical. For convenience' sake, I shall compress them all into a period of three consecutive days.

Friday 05.30hrs: My bearer, Anthony, brought a cup of very sweet tea and some biscuits called *chotta hazari* – meaning 'small breakfast'. Placing these on a small table he slipped them under the mosquito net of my bed.

Got up. Said the Morning Offering,[39] shaved, got dressed: shorts, – no shirt – boots, socks, woollen leggings, puttees, cap.

06.15hrs: Joined the platoon of recruits, already fallen in by the Havildar (Sergeant) and marched them for about twenty minutes to the rifle range. I demonstrated how to aim and get the bullet into the bull's eye. They practised for about an hour, by which time the men's breakfast had arrived so had them fall out and eat it.

In the meantime, Anthony arrived along with my Subaltern assistant's bearer with our breakfasts in a series of metal boxes fitted together, one above the other, for carrying. The bearers spread two *durries* (rush mats) on the ground and placed the food on one of them, while my assistant and I sat, cross-legged, on the other and demolished our breakfast; the eggs and bacon were cold, but not to worry as the coffee was hot!

08.00hrs: Got the men back on the range and continued for another hour. When finished we carried out the inevitable drill of collecting up all the spent cartridges lest they find their way into unfriendly hands.[40]

---

[39] A short Catholic prayer said upon getting up in the morning, offering up all prayers, work, joys and sufferings of the day for Christ's intentions in the Holy Mass.
[40] SSA New Series IV: C.S. to Parents, 11 February, 1945.

Then marched them back to the Regimental Centre; let them have 10 minutes for a 'pee'; then showed them how to clean their guns; inspected them and had them put their guns in the Guard Room. Handed the men over to the Havildar for gym until 12.00, while I helped the Company Commander to inspect the men's lines. As this was the period (April–June) running up to the monsoon, made sure no Sepoy had hanged himself. That is the time they tend to if they are going to do it – tedious of them. As the sun by this time of day is tyrannical, the bearers produce the officers' shirts. The men have a shower after their gym.

12.00hrs: Supervised the men's lunch – the main meal of the day – curry and mountains of rice (the latter all flaky and in no sense 'nanny's rice pudding'!).

12.45hrs: Handed the men over to the Havildar. The major and I went off to join our brother officers in the Mess for lunch. Had a glass of beer with a light lunch. Collected my letters from my pigeonhole in the Ante Room of the Mess.

14.00hrs: To the office for some administration. By now the temperature is high so the men have a quiet time in the barracks. At this time of year, after a while, as my bare arms move backwards and forwards over the papers on the desk, they get a line of dirt on them from the fine sand blown about by the monsoon winds.

16.00hrs: Went for a ride with my Sikh brother-officer and good equestrian, Grewal Singh. The men played hockey with bare feet – as they wished – on the ground baked cement-hard by the sun. On my return, watched the match for a while.

18.00hrs: The men broke off and returned to their barracks for showers. Rode to the stables and handed my horse to the *cise*[41] who told me his wife had just had a baby boy – gave him my warmest congratulations (he and she had been trying for some time, so all v. satisfactory). I did not refer to her as according to local ideas that would have been bad form as it might put the evil eye on her. Gave him a little something for celebrating the event. Had my bath. Wrote letters and called on one of my brother officers who shares the bungalow with me and others.

19.00hrs: Changed into trousers, jacket with patch pockets and polished brown shoes (Anthony does these well).

19.30hrs: Walked over to the mess and had a whisky before going in to eat, as and when I and the others wish. It is only on a Mess Night – about once a fortnight when we have local guests – that we all go in together, led by the Colonel taking in the guests. Anthony waits on me as the other bearers do for their Sahibs.[42] The bearers look very smart: white trousers, with frock coat with high collar and with wide kamarband[43] of the Regimental Colours; white turban

[41] Stable boy.
[42] A term of respect among Indians somewhat equivalent to Sir/Lord/Master. In conversation it is added after the person's name so that I was Swan Sahib.
[43] Becomes cummerbund in English.

with thinner band of the same Colours worn at an angle to which is pinned the Regimental Badge. Following the usual custom, all the bearers were barefooted as sandals are only worn out of doors so as not to bring any dirt inside. Sat in the Ante Mess after dinner and read the *Times of India* and *Country Life* and chatted to other officers. Had coffee.

22.00hrs: Decided to go back to my quarters so I walked to the doorway of the Ante Room and just before leaving turned towards the most senior officer who happened to be present, came to attention and said, 'Good night, Sir,' to which he replied, 'Good night, Swan – sleep well.' That is the custom for all officers of the regiment upon leaving the Mess for the last time during the day. I fell in with another officer as he left and we discussed tomorrow's visit by the governor as we walked to our quarters.

The Sepoys were just coming out of a film show and making for their barracks. They had been at it since 19.00hrs. Unless a film is about three hours in length – usually some great epic – the Indian feels he has been cheated! The film industry in India is second only to Hollywood, and as Bombay is the centre it is called 'Bolliwood'.

22.25hrs: By now had changed into a pair of shorts (nothing more) which serve as night wear because of the heat. Having finished my night devotions, got onto my bed and ensured the mosquito net was well tucked-in – have no intention of getting malaria. Soon asleep on the verandah – I always sleep outside because of the heat.

Saturday 05.30hrs: The getting up procedure the same as on each weekday morning.

06.15hrs: This time wearing a jacket with patch pockets, went up to discuss and confirm with my Havildar the programme we shall lay on for the visit of the Governor of Madras, His Excellency Sir Arthur Hope, GCIE,[44] who was bringing with him Field Marshal Sir Claude Auchinleck, GCB, Commander-in-Chief, India.[45] HE has been very helpful over the regiment (a Coldstreamer himself) so we wanted to put on a good show. The regiment is very much a focus of his attention.

08.00hrs: To the Mess for breakfast.

08.40hrs: Back to the men's lines. Checked that all those things had been done that should have been done, but would very likely not have been done but for a visit such as this – one of the advantages of a general's inspection!

10.30hrs: HE, and C-in-C, arrived in an open car. HE, in pearl grey frock

---

[44] Governor of Madras, 1940-46. He was a collateral Hope of the Marquesses of Linlithgow – a family of Newman's Second Spring converts to Catholicism. Sir Arthur succeeded his father as 2nd Lord Rankeillor, 1949. He was the original Bubbles in Siegfried Sassoon's *The Memoirs of a Fox Hunting Man*.

[45] 1943-47. Each visited the Madras Regimental Centre while I was there but separately. For the convenience of this imaginary diary I have concertinered the visits.

coat wearing the star of a GCIE, and a Topee; the FM, in military uniform. FM much impressed, apparently, by the smartness of the ceremonial parade by the men. Both he and HE inspected the shooting range (one of my pigeons), the physical education of the recruits, the men's quarters and my other responsibility, The Boys' Company of which I am the Officer Commanding[46] – a species of headmaster with a khaki mortarboard.

H.E. was very anxious for the C-in-C to see this, and asked me to fill him in. This I did, briefly, pointing out that it was regimental tradition to provide a secondary education for the sons of men of the regiment who had lost their lives on duty.

The C-in-C showed great interest in the whole programme of the Boys' Company, and asked if I found it a strain being in charge of Small Arms instruction as well as looking after the boys. Not really, I explained, as I had excellent help for both duties. We then went on to the Sick Bay

13.00hrs: HE, FM and officers to the Officers' Mess for luncheon. Our Colonel made a speech afterwards thanking both for their interest. HE responded and invited the C-in-C to address the officers of 'his'(!) regiment. The FM spoke well and brought us up to date on the general situation in SEAC[47] and how matters were moving against the Japanese.

14.30hrs: Both HE and FM departed for other visits in the Presidency. As they left, F.M. stood in the rear of the open car and gave that type of salute, to right and left, which is more of a broad wave of the hand and arm than how the sergeant taught us according to King's Regulations. The entire Centre lined the route of departure and cheered the two very distinguished visitors on their way.

Later I asked some of the recruits what they made of the visit and they told me they were thrilled actually to have seen the two great sahibs in the flesh. I then asked: 'And what was the Field Marshal Sahib doing as he stood in the car when he left?' I expected the reply: 'Saluting, acknowledging the cheers, Sahib' – but what I got was: 'Calling down the blessing of God upon us, Sahib' Oh, you Europeans, both 'poor clods of earth and men nobly born,'[48] when will you understand the soul of India?

16.30hrs: Received the officers' wives who lived in the Centre for some shooting on the rifle range. The wives took it in turns, two at a time, to do the shooting. It was arranged that as soon as a memsahib[49] settled herself prone on the ground, ready to take up a rifle, a Naik (Corporal), who had been stationed

---

[46] Soon after returning to the Regimental Centre after qualifying as an Instructor in Small Arms I was appointed to this additional post which I thoroughly enjoyed.

[47] South East Asia Command which included India, Burma and contiguous areas.

[48] Psalm XLVIII:3 This incident just related actually took place when Auchinleck visited the Regimental Centre.

[49] The feminine equivalent of Sahib used for European women. The word is a combination of 'mem' for Madam and Sahib.

by the memsahib for the purpose, deftly flicked a travelling rug in the air so that it landed on the memsahib covering her from waist to ankles, thus preventing the wind blowing up her skirt and causing any embarrassment. When she had finished shooting, the Naik pulled the rug away – but from her heels. Everything went off without a hitch – and the men were much impressed with the memsahibs' accuracy!

18.30rs Back to my quarters to change for an early dinner, as some of us had decided to drive into Coimbatore – the nearest town, seven miles away – for a film. Told Anthony to go home and spend the night with his family.

22.05hrs: Arrived back at the Centre and after changing for bed, and a prayer or two, was on my bed with mosquito net well tucked in by 22.25hrs. To cool off a little, as I lay there I poured half a glass of water on my chest – it evaporated before it reached the sheet beneath me.

Sunday 07.00hrs: Got up. Made a cup of coffee, as Anthony would not be back until later. He had laid out my clothes before he left. Got dressed and went to 08.15hrs Mass in the Centre – in 'The Old Beer Canteen'(!) – said by Fr J.S. Arulswamy, our civilian chaplain and the headmaster of the diocesan St Joseph's Industrial School (furniture) in Coimbatore.[50] Got to know him well. The general form over accommodation in the Regimental chapel was the same as all over India: the locals – in this case the Sepoys – sat cross-legged on rush matting – as they preferred, while at the side chairs were provided for the Europeans.

Breakfast: fresh mangoes, bacon, eggs, toast, marmalade and coffee; then read *The Times of India* in the Ante Room for a while.

11.00hrs: Went to the Guard Room where the havildar and about a dozen men waited for me. Yesterday, I told the havildar that if anyone wanted to go out and walk across the countryside I would be happy to take them at 11a.m. The Sepoys are not permitted to leave the Centre except with an Officer. So set off down to the farms nearby. The men were much interested to see how the locals do things, being farmers themselves.

Walked out into the broad valley with hills rising in the distance on either side. Those behind the Centre, the Nilgiris, quite high, those in front of us the Anamalais, lower.

Stopped at a farm-well for animals. These 'wells' are in fact small square ponds, yet quite deep enough for swimming. So the men stripped off, dived in, swam around and generally messed about, but always wearing the jock-strap already mentioned. The havildar and I sat at the side and put the world to rights.

The scene was idyllic. Farmland stretched away to the other side of the Polgot Gap: a patchwork of paddies as well as fields of different crops, like chillies on small bushes, and peanuts looking, above ground, like a crop of clover, all growing well. Some bullocks ploughed to one side, and on another water

---

[50] The seat of a diocese.

buffaloes were being brought in for milking. The occasional palm tree rose up from the fertile soil – some doing so with a curve that defied Newton. Over there stood a temple arch, and nearby a Banyan tree with its aerial roots growing down into the soil to form additional trunks. Not far from this almost architectural feature was the silhouette of three peasant women walking one in front of the other. Each carried a brass pot of water on her head – nestling on a small rag cushion for comfort – and steadied by the right hand. On the left hip a child was cradled by the other arm. All walked with a carriage that would do a Western catwalk credit. To one side, and nearer to us, the orange blossoms of a *Flame of the Forest* tree helped set off this domestic scene.

There in front of the havildar and me the sepoys were enjoying themselves in a relaxed and innocent manner. When they had had enough, they got out of the well and sat around talking while they dried off in the bright sun. When they were dressed we set off on a circular route towards the Centre – but not before a Kingfisher, in a flash of turquoise, flicked over the now deserted well.

On the way, we stopped at one of the farms and I asked if they had enough coconuts for all of us. They had, and after I paid the farmer he picked up the right number, all in their green outer covering, and deftly sliced off the top of each with one blow of his long, heavy knife so that we could drink the milk – very refreshing.

In this and other parts of India they make a toddy by cutting off the forming coconuts and collecting the juice into a jar. It ferments quickly and makes a wickedly strong drink, similar to arrack. Simple, easy and cheap to make, it is the liquor of the poorest and they get roaring drunk on it. The Congress Party went to the extreme of demanding prohibition[51] – like good socialists, they want to nanny everyone. So I did not ask the farmer if he had any toddy, but simply to open up the shells when dry, so that we could eat the white meat as we walked back to the Regimental Centre by way of a sugar cane field.

12.00hrs: Got back to the men's lines where I supervised their lunch and then went off to mine.

13.00hrs: Lunch in the Mess, served by Anthony back from his family.

15.00hrs: Attended a debate arranged by a company commander on a favourite topic that was guaranteed to get the men really worked up: 'Marriages for love or arranged marriages?' This is always sure-fire, with excellent arguments coming from each side – neither giving way. Had to conclude the proceedings, with them still arguing as they left the hall.

---

[51] When prohibition was threatened, I observed (SSA. New Series V: C.S. to E.H.S. 11 Aug. 1946) '... we have little to worry about as the Europeans are registered as addicts which entitles us to draw a good ration!! Rather amusing, don't you think, to find in my autobiography 'how I registered as an alcoholic addict in '46!!' By October '46 it had been introduced (*Ibid.* same to same 6 Oct. 1946) and by 13th of that month I reported that prohibition 'is raging (outside the Military Area – Deo Gratias)' (*Ibid.* same to same 13 Oct. 1946).

16.30hrs: Cheered a soccer match between A and D Companies – also played in bare feet!

18.30hrs: to my quarters for a bath and to change for the mess. The bathroom in India has a smooth cement floor, with one section, about a quarter, cut off by a small raised wall about one brick high. There is a hole at one corner of this cut-off area. It runs two or three feet directly down onto the garden, taking the bath water away when the tub is tipped up on the floor. Anthony had arranged with the Sweeper[52] in the usual way to heat up some water and put it in the bath, which he had done. I undressed and got into the bath – a tin affair so small one has to leave one's legs outside and only bring them in when one stands up in the bath to wash them. Everything was going well: Anthony had come in and scrubbed my back, and had left to lay out my clothes. I was humming away as I finished off washing my hair. Then, all of a sudden – through eyes half-filled with shampoo – I saw a cobra, with hood inflated, rising up at the end of the tub, two feet away. It was more or less between my legs. I let out an almighty yell that filled the bungalow and beyond, and with one great splash was out of the bath and bathroom crying out, 'Cobra, cobra – come and *get it!*' Anthony and the sweeper, the mali[53] and a host of other servants from various bungalows rushed in brandishing sticks. Into the bathroom they piled and had a great time attacking the snake, which fought back with sudden lunges here and there. In the end, numbers won and five foot cobra, hanging limply over one of the carried sticks, was brought into the bedroom for me to inspect. The throng then walked out, calling to other servants of the various bungalows to come and see what they had missed.

'In India, the annual figures for man-killing by snakes are as uniform, as regular and as forecastable as are the tiger average and the suicide average,' as Mark Twain had it,[54] and I was grateful not to have become a statistic. After such an experience one feels a particular gratitude to St George, for, in addition to his being the Patron Saint of England and of several distinguished Orders of Chivalry, in India he is Patron also of those plagued by serpentine attentions. No time for musing, though, as it was already getting late and I had yet to dress for dinner. Anthony was ready to pour me into my clothes. I got to the Mess in time for one whisky before the few officers who were in that night went in to the dining room together and sat at the main table.

After dinner, went to have a drink with the VCOs and NCOs. The former, Viceroy Commissioned Officers, are men who after twenty or so years of impeccable service, many as NCOs, are given a commission by the Viceroy. The rank is peculiar to the Indian Army and is one of the greatest prestige. There are

---

[52] The one who cleans away the night-earth and performs other such menial tasks.
[53] The gardener.
[54] Twain, Mark. *The Complete Works of Mark Twain. Following the Equator.* New York, Harper and Brotes, 1925 Vol. 2, p, 226. There are about 20,000 deaths by snake bite per year in India.

three ranks: jemedar, subedar and subedar major. They wear miniature pips on their shoulders – as worn by King's Commissioned Officers of some British regiments – and are entitled to a salute by all ranks below them. They act as advisers to the officers holding the King-Emperor's commission on all matters of an Indian nature: religious customs, food regulations and so on. One always listens very carefully to what the VCO has to say, especially as he knows the men through and through. The officer always addresses the VCO as Sahib: 'No, Jemedar Sahib', 'Yes, Subedar Major Sahib.' They are the salt of the earth, and an enormous help to the British officers.

From time to time the VCOs and NCOs invite us to their mess for a convivial evening, and this was one of them. They are always most generous with their hospitality. My own Jemedar, Louis Sequira – an excellent and most efficient man – helped to do the honours. As his name suggests, he was of Goanese extraction but despite his name completely Indian. It was the custom in Goa for Indian converts to Christianity to adopt the family name of their godfather at baptism.[55]

During the evening there is singing, and I join in with such songs as *Chal Chal Re nua Jawan* ('March on, March on Young Soldier'. – an Urdu song). It's all very pleasant and civilized.

22.30hrs: Back to my quarters, and after a prayer or two, to bed with lights out by 23.00hrs ready for to-morrow, Monday, and its parades.

[55] SSA New Series IV C.S., to E.H.S. 7 October, 1945.

CHAPTER VI

Sub-continental Explorations by Swan Sahib and Other Regimental Matters

NORTH

'ONE SIMPLY MUST serve on the Frontier. It's terribly pukka[1] – don't you know – and looks very well on one's military record.' So spoke the accepted wisdom of the Indian Army Officer.

So, in October 1946 I was off like a flash to Fort Sandeman[2] in Baluchistan on the borders of Afghanistan. Next year, with the division of the sub-continent into India and Pakistan[3] Baluchistan became a province of the latter. I was posted there for a short assignment to do with small arms.

The journey, first by broad and then narrow gauge railway, deposited me not so far from Kandahar at Fort Sandeman: eight days after leaving the Regimental Centre in the far south[4].

My journey time was about right, what with all the changing and waiting for connections. Meals were quite amusing. A couple of hours in advance one wired to a station ahead for breakfast, lunch or dinner to be prepared. Except for breakfast, I always asked for curry. That way one was bound to get something good. As we got further and further north the curries got cooler and cooler. Upon arrival at a station, the child beggars, five or six years old, would soon note the first class carriages. They would rush and station themselves outside these and, more or less naked, start to chant a rhythmic chorus: 'No Mama, no Papa, no Mama no Papa', slapping their bare tummies in time with the libretto. One had to give them something. Whereupon they dashed off to the non-existent 'Mama,' or someone else who played the Fagin role.

As the trains were civilian ones, the Indians disgorged themselves upon arrival at the station: from inside the carriages, from the outside where they had been hanging on, and from the roof where they had been sitting. It seemed as if the world and his wife were on every station. A further thing one noticed as one got further north, and so more and more into Muslim territory, was the

---

[1] From the Hindi meaning 'firm' but extended to mean 'good', 'suitable', 'proper', 'as it should be' and so generally approved as with the phrase 'He's a pukka Sahib'.
[2] Now called Zob.
[3] 15 August 1947
[4] SSA. New Series C.S. to E.H.S. 30 Oct. 1946.

apparent absence of women. They were present, all right, but, as often as not, observing strict *purdah*. They looked like lampshades or tea cosies, covered head to foot by their *burka*, which had a small piece of crochet at eye level for them to see out of.

When the first class passengers got out of their carriages on arriving at a station they went into a tiled, and so relatively cool restaurant, sat down and ate what had been ordered over the wire. That was the only time one met passengers from the other compartments as, for security reasons, there were no corridors joining them. So if one struck up agreeable acquaintances one invited them into one's compartment for the part of the journey up to the next stop – or *vice versa*. In the restaurant the *punkah* would be moving slowly back and forth causing a slight breeze, making the room less stuffy. The movement of its beam was caused by a cord pulled through a hole in the wall by the *punkah-wallah* in the next room or on the verandah. If he was experienced in all this he would lie down on the cool stone floor, attach the cord to one of his big toes and simply bend his knee and stretch his leg to get the mechanism moving. After about forty minutes, the bell on the engine would announce the imminent departure of the train and we all climbed back up into our compartments. The *punka-wallah* could snooze until the next train arrived.

The reason for the presence of the battalion on the North West Frontier was to show the flag there, so to speak. Further, we were to keep our eyes and ears open in case Russia was up to her old habit of stirring that cauldron of trouble, Afghanistan.

As background to all this there was, up and down the North West Frontier – 'the Frontier' as we usually called it – an odd state of intermittent hostility between ourselves and the lawless tribes by whom we were surrounded. As far as they were concerned they lived in a species of national park from which they emerged to carry out some outrage and then retire knowing that nothing very terrible would happen.

The relationship between them and us was something not quite war but more of a game. This was played – fought – in accordance with certain understood rules. Granted it was a rough game – some of us, and some of them got killed – nevertheless each side found it exhilarating.

When an engagement was over, everyone went home – rather as in a cricket match one breaks off for tea, expecting a resumption of play later. However, some might advise:

> When you're wounded and left on Afghanistan's plains,
> And the women come out to cut up what remains,
> Jest roll to your rifle and blow out your brains
> An' go to your Gawd like a soldier.
>
> Kipling, 'The Young British Soldier'

Though the solution was morally unsound the predicament was compelling, as the cutting up was castration.

Despite, on the Frontier, being in a land of sun-baked rock and earth at the back of beyond, which I described as the 'outer back door of Empire',[5] our social life at Fort Sandeman was good. The local Political Agent and his wife were most hospitable. In India, Political Agents were, in a sense, deputy governors of their bailiwicks, and the appointment was one of real prestige.

On the Frontier, in addition to entertaining the army officers – if so minded, and they usually were – they also kept in contact with the local tribesmen. One of the ways of doing this was to give, once or twice a year during the less hot seasons, 'garden parties'. For this the Political Agent would first consult the *durbar list*[6] – a list available in each local area of India giving the names of those usually invited to official functions because of their importance in the community. He would then send out the invitations for the early evening party. All manner of food was served, including extremely sweetly-iced cakes in accordance with the tribesmen's taste. Tea, coffee and a range of fruit juices were available – no alcohol, the tribesmen being Muslims to a man.

So on the day a large group of the most villainous-looking men with hawk-like eyes, all smiling and showing off brilliant teeth, would arrive. They would be wearing turbans, very baggy trousers, loose-fitting shirts hanging over the trousers, coats (often sleeveless) and substantial shoes. One or two bandoleers of cartridges were worn as well, and they carried their guns – from which they were never separated. The latter were often up to five feet long. They had been made in some local, clandestine gun-making establishment. With my interest in ballistics and small arms I was able to chat them up in *Urdu* and so try and pull my weight as a guest.

Apart from the Political Agent's lady, plus a daughter if he had one or a female houseguest, there was not a woman in sight – that being the Muslim custom of the area. The Political Agent and his party, including his staff, would mingle with the guests. They could be loquacious, and sometimes one learned something interesting about a rival group, but in general the idea was to make the local tribesmen feel that one knew they were persons of consequence.

Just in case a tribesman had any idea of not behaving like a perfect guest, he was reminded that the Raj[7] was in control: the battalion would station a company of sepoys together with an officer and NCOs on the flat roof of the Political Agent's residence. They were spread out in lines along the edge of the roof,

---

[5] SSA New Series V C.S. to E.H.S. 13 Oct. 1946.

[6] Durbar – from the Hindi and ultimately Persian originally meaning a court or levee held by a Native Prince or British Governor, and so with the Delhi Durbar of 1911 held by the King-Emperor and Queen-Empress – King George V and Queen Mary. It came also to mean a grand party of an official character.

[7] The British officials.

facing all points of the compass. They stood at ease, but with their rifles, butt on the roof with muzzle between the thumb and forefinger, ready to be brought up to the shoulder in a flash upon the first command. It was extremely rare that such had to be given, but the mere presence of sepoys in that position of readiness conveyed the right message. It did nothing to dampen the enjoyment of the proceedings.

In January 1947 the local Treasury Officer – an Afghan in the Indian Service – held a dinner party at his home for the new District Superintendent of Police. Anyone who was anybody locally was invited: all Indians except for a Subaltern, called Morgan and myself. Presenting ourselves at the appointed hour we were refreshed with whisky and the like (despite it being a Muslim household!). Upon entering the dining room one held out one's hands over a silver bowl while a servant poured rose-water over them from an elaborate silver ewer shaped like a grand and large coffee pot. A towel was produced by another servant, and having dried one's hands, the appropriate place at table was indicated. We would then be served the most delicious curry – much cooler here than back in the South – which we ate with our fingers. The pre-prandial procedure over hand washing was repeated after the dinner.

The host was present and looked after his guests with great attention. He never sat and ate with us. This was the height of local good manners. We would be told that his wife and the other women of the house had prepared the meal. Accordingly, from time to time one said in a loud voice how delicious the food was, and this was greeted with loud titters from behind a screen where our hostess and her helpers – enveloped in complete darkness themselves – watched over our every mouthful. Sometimes the very small sons and daughters were brought in to be introduced. One then said in a loud voice, 'To be sure, how ugly [so and so] is, praise be to God.' At that, there would be more appreciative titters from behind the screen and our host would smile approvingly because by phrasing our observations in that way they all knew we thought the child good-looking but had averted the evil eye.[8]

If the weather was fine on a Saturday or Sunday, one could have a walk to one of the nearby burial mounds of one of Alexander the Great's men who did not make it back to Greece in the fourth century BC.

So to those with interests like mine, such expeditions were fascinating.

Towards the end of my time there, winter was upon us and it was very cold, complete with snow. One advantage of having Madrassis in the snow is that one cannot lose them: their marvellous, dark faces show up so well. On one occasion, I went outside and found a sepoy stuffing a bottle with snow. When I asked him the reason, his answer was, 'Well, Sahib, I'm going to send it back to my parents in the Madras Presidency. They have never seen this stuff before'.

---

[8] SSA. New Series V. C.S. to E.H.S. 19 Jan. 1947 describes the dinner.

The time soon came for me to return to the Regimental Centre at Madukarai, and so I said my goodbyes. It had been a great experience in a totally different part of India. For me the only bore was the lack of opportunity to go to Mass. On one occasion when a travelling Dutch Franciscan arrived – clothed in his habit – we were fortunate enough to have him perform his sacred offices. He was making his rounds from his friary in Quetta, the centre of a parish six times the size of Britain! The area was almost entirely Muslim – fanatical at times, remember the Taliban[9] – with an occasional parishioner here and there, but there were no conversions from Islam. He told me that the tribesmen showed great respect for his habit. It was all rather *à la* Charles Foucauld and possibly, as for the latter, they would all turn up in force at this friar's funeral.

My return journey was a mirror image of my proceeding North. I arrived back at Madukarai most anxious to see if both the small arms training and the Boys' Company could possibly have got on without me. The truth is, they had done so very well – good for my humility.

SOUTH

In the Madras Regiment I had the honour to command sepoys whose ancestors were Christians when mine – at least the British ones[10] – were running around as woad painted pagans. Generally these sepoys were referred to (though not by themselves) as St Thomas Christians and came from the Malabar coast of South Western India, mainly in the Native States of Travancore and Cochin. The Thomas referred to here is Doubting Thomas, St Thomas the Apostle.

There were colonies of Jews up and down the coast in the first century and probably one at Cranganore when, we are told, St Thomas arrived in AD 52. These would have been viewed as suitable groups among whom first to introduce the gospel; such was the practice of the other Apostles when moving out from the Holy Land to evangelize the Mediterranean. The first converts in India were Brahmins, and to convert a Brahmin is like converting a Jew: very difficult. It happens at times in ones and twos, but in large numbers, rarely – except in Apostolic times.

They were first called Nazrani (the followers of the Man of Nazareth), and even to this day are so described in all legal documents and family histories. They claim that the reason for this is that their ancestors were baptized in the name of Jesus of Nazareth before believers were called Christians for the first time (of which we learn from the Acts of the Apostles).[11]

---

[9] Among those responsible for the destruction in 2001 of the rock-face carvings of Buddha – works of great archaeological importance – in Afghanistan.

[10] As will be recalled from Chapter III my Lithuanian ancestors were pagans for much longer, until the conversion of Jagiełło, Grand Duke of Lithuania in 1386.

[11] Acts XI:26

The tomb of St Thomas is in the Cathedral at Mylapore – now a part of Madras – the existence of which was known to our King Alfred the Great.[12]

These Christians of the Malabar Coast are the indigenous Christian church in India. According to the firm tradition, St Thomas landed on the island of Malankara opposite the port of Cranganore. The first converts adopted the East Syrian (Syro-Chaldean) rite and so the name of the rite of these Christians: Syro-Malankara.

With such a history behind so many of my sepoys, I obviously needed to get to know this group further, and who better to approach with such an aim than The Most Reverend Mar Ivanios, Archbishop of Trivandrium and Metropolitan of the Syro-Malankara Rite in union with Rome, to whom I had an introduction. His Grace most kindly invited me to come and stay, so off I set by train from Coimbatore, first almost due west to the Arabian Sea and then south along the coast, for the relatively short journey to the capital of Travancore, Trivandrum, and so for ten days' leave in February 1947.

Having arrived at Trivandrum, I first had to call on His Highness the Maharaja of Travancore in order to present my humble duty. He turned out to be a young man, and an extremely observant Hindu, little contaminated by Western materialism. His name, styles and titles give one strongly the flavour of Princely India:

**Colonel His Highness Sri Padmanabha Dasa Vanchi Pala
Sri Chithira Thirunal Sir Bala Rama Varma
Kulasekhara Kiritapathi Manney Sultan Maharaja Raja
Ramaraja Bahadur Shamsher Jang, GCSI, GCIE, D.LITT,
Maharaja of Travancore.**

From the palace the route lay to Archbishop's House. Mar Ivanios turned out to be a tall, thin, distinguished man, every inch a Brahmin. Following the age-old custom he wore a cassock and instead of a cerise skull cap, as for a Latin bishop, a black cap which covered all his hair. This was embroidered with a series of small white Crosses.

The Archbishop had arranged for me to stay nearby. Upon arrival, I was shown to my room on the first floor: large and airy with venetian blind-like shutters which hung from the top of the window frame. There was a mass of coconut palms just outside my windows, and as I dozed off at night I was conscious of the rustle of frond against frond in the evening breeze. In the

---

[12] The first alleged Englishman to have visited India was Sighelmus around A.D. 883 (*vide Anglo-Saxon Chronicles*, An,DCC, LXXXIII: DCCC, LXXXXIV). Perhaps he was the one sent to the tomb of St Thomas with Alfred's gifts. The first undoubted Englishman to have gone to India is Fr Thomas Stephens, S.J., of Oxford University. He went to Goa in 1579 and worked on the missions until his death there 1619. His reports to his father stimulated, to some degree, the interest in trade with India at the end of Elizabeth's reign and so to the founding of the East India Company, 1600.

morning, my alarm was, at times, an Indian cockatoo, or the less mellifluous squabbling of crows in those palms.

I would attend the Archbishop's Mass in the early morning. It intrigued me that while part was in the local vernacular, Malayalam, and part, for historical reasons, in Syrian, the actual words of consecration were in Aramaic – the usual language of Our Lord. Long before the reforms of Vatican II, it was at these Masses that for the first time I received Communion under both kinds.

After Mass, we had breakfast together: mangoes or other fruit or both, toast, jam and coffee. Then out we were driven into the country to visit this church, that school, the other institution. The countryside of Travancore could not be in greater contrast to that of Baluchistan, for example. In this southern state, it was a picture of the lush and the verdant with a profusion of inland water-ways.

There was the odd church, temple or mosque here and there, and likewise the odd shop and post office, but villages did not really exist. This well spread-out tradition reflected a relatively peaceful history.

As we travelled from one area to another, when it was the right time of day, we would be invited to join our local host or hosts in their curry. I enjoyed these simple meals, but not without feeling rather like Louis XIV at Versailles, in that every door, and every window of the room in which we ate, was crammed with the faces of the locals who wanted to be near their Father in God. Possibly, they also wanted see if the Sahib knew how to eat properly with his right hand. They were far too polite to pass any comment; they just stared in silence.

The archbishop's old chauffeur-driven car passed over interminable bridges crossing the ever-present inland waterways, or through avenues of coconut palms. From time to time our discussions, as we were driven along, were interrupted by blasts from a trumpet made out of a conch or Indian Chank shell: symbolic of Hinduism. They are sounded to celebrate some joyful occasion[13].

Yet again, if we were driving past a mosque, the Imam could be calling the faithful to prayer. I am always edified by the number of Muslims who answer the call of the Imam at the specified moments of the day for prayer, get on with developing their relationship with God, and forget, just for a moment, the pursuit of the almighty dollar, pound, rupee or whatever it is.

One of the things that Christians do have in common with Muslims is the practice of breaking off for a moment or so, during the day, to remember that we are contingent beings. In this regard, if during these drives through Travancore we went past a Latin Rite church at 6a.m., 12 noon or 6p.m., the Angelus bell

---

[13] When I was in India the relationship between Hindus and Christians was generally quite good. There was, however, a tiny cloud on the horizon then over this relationship in the form of the RSS (Rashtriya Swayamsevak Sangh) an extreme Hindu group, relatively small in the 1940s. It now numbers 4.5 million active members, and they are demanding a Chinese-style National Catholic Church. They are regarded as the parent of the BJP (Bharatiya Janata Party) the major party in the present 2000 Indian Government.

would ring and remind us that, *Angelus Domini nuntiavit Mariae…* (The angel of the Lord declared unto Mary…).

Conversation flowed between us. At times we would discuss the problems resulting from the mistaken view of the Portuguese in the sixteenth century that the indigenous Christians of South-western India were Nestorians. At other, the Archbishop explained how descent in the princely and noble families of Travancore was matrilineal. Yet again, sometimes, as we drove along, we would both fall silent for a few moments. My mind would be buzzing with much new and utterly fascinating knowledge. It would be at such a juncture that the archbishop might turn and ask some such question as, 'Captain, what do you think Hamlet really meant when he said…..?' At which I would think to myself: 'Gad, sir, what a question to ask a chap mentally halfway round the globe, and more up the Khyber Pass than wandering around the ramparts of Elsinore!' I would then do my best to give an intelligent answer. Before becoming a priest, my utterly charming, civilized and generous host had been a Lecturer in English Literature at the University of Madras.[14]

EAST

From the Madras Regimental Centre, if one proceeded in a north-easterly direction one arrived at the City of Madras, about five hundred and fifty miles away on the Coromandel Coast facing the Indian Ocean. I was there fairly frequently on duty and would put up at an officers' hostel, an old mansion called Mackay's Gardens, run on behalf of the government of India, by an Italian Army Officer who wore his full Italian military uniform in accordance with our regulations. Following the fall of Mussolini in 1943, Italy became a 'co-belligerent', as the description went. I suppose our masters simply could not stomach, 'ally'. However, the Italian captain in question was as efficient as he was obliging. The situation always rather amused me.

The name Madras is a contraction of Madraspatnam, the fishing village where the East India Company built Fort St George and established a trading post in 1639-40. For many years it was the hub of the English presence on the sub-continent, with Fort St George as the administrative centre.

One of the early Governors of Madras who, as a fellow North American, particularly interested me was the Bostonian, Elihu Yale,[15] who occupied that appointment, 1687-92. The famous American university was named in his honour, he having been a generous benefactor.

Some two hundred and twenty years later (1964) as Rouge Dragon Pursuivant of Arms, I had the honour of being invited to deliver the Woodward Lecture at Yale, and was delighted to discover that the university had an officer of arms of

---

[14] SSA New Series V C.S. to E.H.S. 28 Feb.1947 and 12 March, 1947 – descriptions of the visit.
[15] Born, Boston, Mass. 1649.

its own: Yale Pursuivant. His staff of office proudly displayed a representation of the heraldic monster known as a Yale – a species of antelope with horns that swivel.

In Governor Yale's day, and for many years thereafter, there was a brisk trade between the New England Colonies and Madras. One of the curious products exported all the way by ship from New England was ice. Cut from frozen lakes during the winter, packed on board in sawdust to prevent melting, having arrived at Madras it was unloaded into the ice-house on the water front there. This was a large, thick-walled, windowless building, and I recall giving it close inspection. The ice was kept there until sold to cool the spirituous drinks or fevered brows of the Company servants – or of anyone else who wanted to buy it. Once free of ice, the ships were filled with spices, cloth and other oriental products for shipping back round the Cape of Good Hope, on up through the South and then North Atlantic and eventually to Boston and other New England ports.

Among all the churches of Madras, the most famous, and a focus of great pilgrimage, was, and is naturally, the Latin Rite Catholic Cathedral of San Thome in Mylapore which contains the tomb of St Thomas the Apostle. Our King Alfred the Great sent gifts to this tomb.

His place of martyrdom is St Thomas' Mount which can be reached by rickshaw in about half an hour from the cathedral. The climb up is by means of stone steps, and the ascent is so steep one feels upon reaching the top that a strong gin and tonic would not go amiss.

On the first occasion that I clambered up those steps – as there was not a drop of Gordon's in sight – I sat down on a rock and looked over the edge into the fields on the sides of the mount. Beneath me a large herd of India's ubiquitous suppliers of traction and givers of milk, the water buffalo, grazed. They were typical of those large, heavy, ponderous, almost elephant-skinned animals with their curious back-curving horns that look as if they ought to be the frame of some giant lyre. They had that contented, bovine, knowing look as if they had seen it all before.

I looked at them and thought to myself somewhat along the following lines:

Yes, you were here with the original Dravidians, those animists – some of whom still live, as did their ancestors thousands of years ago, high up in the Nilgiris – quite untouched by the advent of the Hindus. Then St Thomas could well have seen you and patted your broad, great rumps – that is before he was finished off with a lance on this very hill.

After him came the Moguls whose baggage you very likely carried. If one looks carefully, one can see that they have included you in some of those exquisite miniatures for which these invaders are so justly famous. The next group to arrive were the Portuguese, who set up the capital of their great Eastern empire at Goa on the other coast. When they brought back from China the body of St Francis Xavier you could well have pulled the hearse of that great *puja*[16] man to his last resting place in Old Goa.

A little further down that coast at Cochin, the Dutch came for a while. Right over on the other, our side in Bengal, close to Calcutta, the Danes were there for a short time at Seranpore (which they called Fredericksnagar after their king). My Baptist ancestors, the Greens, knew all about this enclave and how, in view of the then anti-missionary policy of the East India Company, it made possible in the late seventeen-hundreds the introduction of the Baptist Mission to India by the redoubtable William Carey. Early on in his time there one of his sons died of dysentery and Mrs Carey slowly went mad.

Notwithstanding, over a period of thirty years the Seranpore Mission produced translations of the entire Bible in six languages, and of the New Testament in twenty-three. Bearing in mind the acute privations, most unpromising conditions and terrible experiences had by Carey and so many other missionaries, one can only conclude that they must have loved Our Blessed Lord a very great deal.

During the eighteenth century, the French and the English were all over the place. The Madras Regiment came into its own. It was the time of Seringapatam (1799) and Assaye (1803); of Clive and of Wellington. You were pulling the guns of both armies here, there and everywhere as they fought to the death in pursuit of what might be termed their 'mountain of light', or as the Moguls said in Persian, *Kohinoor*.

In the end the French seemed to evaporate under the relentless sun, and had to be content with a little colony south of here at Pondicherry. This proved a great convenience for us, as when we wish to say something uncomplimentary about the Eurasians we can say, 'All very Pondicherry French, if you know what I mean'. So all you buffaloes have seen a great deal, and all the newcomers are still very much here save for the two starting with 'D'. How much longer will they all be here? Ah, you are too polite to hazard a guess.

I remember reciting to myself a chronology of Indian history *vis à vis* foreigners, but I cannot quite remember how my reverie ended. Probably it was something like this: 'Well good milking ladies, I'm off to pay my respects to a very great Rani in heaven with some *puja* – we call them *Aves* – all in this little barrel-shaped chapel built in the sixteenth century by the Portuguese on the top of this mount, and dedicated to Our Lady of Expectation.'

I wondered what the Portuguese had in mind when they gave the Mother of God this anticipatory brief.

---

[16] Puja = prayer.

WEST

The momentous passage to India of Francis Xavier started from Lisbon in April 1541 and ended at Goa in May, 1542.

Old Goa he entered was so magnificent there was a Portuguese saying: *Quem viu Goa, excusa de ver Lisboa* – he who has seen Goa need not see Lisbon. It must have appeared as if it would last one thousand years. However, two blockades by the Dutch in the seventeenth century, plus a huge epidemic decimated the population. Further diseases, especially cholera, reduced the population from two hundred thousand in 1695 to under two thousand in 1775. Finally the seat of government was moved, ultimately, to Panjim, five miles down the Mondovi River.

The old capital was gradually deserted, so that when I was there it reminded one of so many photographs of Aztec ruins in the *National Geographic Magazine*: overgrown buildings, trees growing up where they were not intended, creepers everywhere, the odd pye-dog wandering around and considering me the intruder. One shared with Graham Greene the desolation and the silence.

Yet there are still some gems there, including the Bom Jesu, with its splendid Renaissance Baroque façade. A silver reliquary there contains what is left of Xavier's body. Enthusiastic piety and a desire for first-class relics has somewhat reduced its total size. It is said that one pious woman bit off one of his toes when the body was undergoing a periodic exposition for the veneration of the faithful. Lest an Anglo-Saxon feels a little superior to all this – and I cannot say that it is exactly my cup of tea – let me ask what is the attitude of even the agnostics among them towards the Unknown Soldier and his tomb? And quite right, I would say?

The Cathedral – the largest church in Asia – is pure Renaissance and a splendid building. In fact this and the Bom Jesu are, undoubtedly, two of the world's greatest religious buildings. It is interesting that from the point of view of pure architecture, the major European additions to the buildings of the first rank in India are the Portuguese Renaissance and Baroque along with the British neo-classical.

The Chapel of Our Lady of the Rosary is exquisitely situated on the Holy Hill. It is an excellent example of Manueline architecture where the decorative elements reflect the great marine tradition of Portugal.

Behind this chapel is the Royal Chapel of St Anthony, built when Xavier was there. This Anthony is – by the non-Portuguese – usually called St Anthony of Padua as he happened to die, aged 36, in that city and so the Padovians fell heir to the body of this very popular saint. But he is really St Anthony of Lisbon, where he became a Canon Regular. It was later that he joined the Franciscans in whose grey-brown habit he is usually depicted. He was a very great expert on Sacred Scripture, so much so that when in 1946, in declaring him a Doctor of the Church, Pius XII described him as *Doctor Evangelicus*. In addition to his great scholarship, he has always been highly esteemed by the laity in general as a sure-fire saint for getting things done. His intercession is invoked when one wants to find a lost article. The poor ask for his help. He is the patron of lovers and married people.

So with all due deference to his scholarly reputation, when I paid my respects to St Anthony in the Royal Chapel, while I neither had a lady friend nor was married at the time, I calculated that as he was concerned with those two conditions he must know what made lovers happy, and so what made for good spouses. Accordingly I asked him to put in a good word for me in finding a wife – he did, a blissful creature; but more of her later.

As mentioned before, from an early age I wanted to get married. Nevertheless, India in wartime was an arid desert for a young white looking for a wife unless he was stationed in one of the large cities where there could just possibly be some female service personnel. The 'fishing fleet' was definitely in dry dock back in England. All the other white women in India were either nuns or wives of brother officers – both off limits obviously.

This is not to say that some more or less discreet, clandestine affairs did not go on, during the hot season in the Hill Stations – such as Simla, Wellington, Ootacumund (always called Ooty) – between unattached, young, white, Indian Army bucks on leave and other men's wives whose husbands were sweating it out down on the plains. While the young wives frequently exhibited considerable virtue, some of fifteen or more years' marriage pursued the reverse, and were amused by the lack of finesse of their transient bedfellows, yet delighted in the firm muscularity of their physically fit bodies. Technically natural though such intercourse was, there was something nauseating about it, particularly when the female seducers – that is all they were – bragged about it in the club. On the other hand, how could a young man want to make love to a woman old enough to be his mother, except out of sheer carnality?

Lest I give the impression that white female society in the Hills was generally nymphomaniac, that was not so. Most of the wives there bore their separation from their husbands with fortitude and set a good example. In this connection I wrote to my parents:

Today [3 September, 1945] I received a most amusing letter from Betty Prince[17] who is up in the hills now and being madly domestic. Beans, carrots, onions, beets, lettuce, cucumber, marrow, radishes and potatoes ('I have a whole hillside of spuds and gold bantam corn'!) together with chickens, a lamb, jams and pickles are among or are in fact the list of her home produce.[18]

---

[17] It will be recalled that she and her husband, Col. H.A. Prince, had been very kind to me during my commissioning leave in Dehli.

[18] SSA New Series IV C.S. to E.H.S. 3 September, 1945.

These women were frequently extremely active, promoting such good causes as medical centres for poor Indians, the Red Cross and the like. Quite a number had the unusual – for India – responsibility of looking after their children of eight or more years of age, for if they had children from 1934 onwards they could not, because of the war, be sent to England for schooling aged seven as was usual in peace time. So when I was in India there were white children about of ten and more years of age. This was a boon for the few private schools in the Hills, and doubtless the children enjoyed a much freer life in India, even if they had to make do with a mongoose rather than a ferret as a pet.

Of course, if one took a leaf out of the Indian's book one could have copied the format of one of the sheets of marriage advertisements which occur in every newspaper in India. Mine could have read something like this:

> WANTED by young, white,
> armigerous army officer, well-educated,
> not married before, Catholic, young,
> armigerous, well-educated, Catholic,
> virgin. Apply...
>
> But really...!

Doubtless, after the war all this would change so my word with the good saint on that occasion in the Royal Chapel was all rather like taking out an insurance policy with a reliable, experienced broker. And it paid off handsomely.

My visit to Goa in September 1946 was facilitated by an introduction to the Archbishop of Goa and Daman,[19] and Patriarch of the East Indies,[20] The Most Reverend D. Jose da Costa Nunes. I needed a passport, so obtained a British India one from Delhi, and a visa, which I received upon application to the local Honorary Portuguese Consul – a Goanese priest, Fr Alberto Lopes; who doubled up his sacristy with his consular office. The locked cupboard that contained his chalice accommodated his official seal. *En route*, I collected the passport, duly stamped with the visa, from Fr Lopes at Bangalore where he greeted me 'in white cassock, velvet hat and cheroot in hand'(!)[21] Interestingly enough, our oldest ally did not require that I wear civilian clothes when in its territory, so I went about everywhere in my Madras Regimental uniform and the locals could not have been more welcoming – a British Officer was *rara avis* in Goa.

My arrival in Panjim, the capital, was by train. My host sent his car for my

---

[19] Goa was established by Rome as a Diocese in 1553 with jurisdiction from south Africa to Japan. In 1557 it was elevated to be an Archdiocese.

[20] In 1570 the Archbishop of Goa and Daman was recognized as Patriarch of the East Indies.

[21] SSA. New Series V. C.S. to E.H.S. 30 Sept. 1946.

convenience: a pre-World War I Silver Ghost Rolls Royce. It was a conveyance of considerable style, made the more impressive by its antiquity.

The Archbishop received me almost immediately in his drawing-room – one of those large rooms one found so often in India with the outside walls nothing but windows, every one open and with Venetian blind-type shutters lowered on the sunny side. The humid air of the coast circulated through the room freely. The Secretary presented me and, as all this took place before Vatican II, when my host offered me his hand I immediately started to go down on one knee in order to kiss his ring, as was then the correct form. (Further, one gained an indulgence by doing so, and for a one like myself this was most attractive: every day off purgatory was a bonus!). As I started to kneel, the Archbishop immediately lifted me up saying: 'Oh, please, please,' but not before I had kissed his ring. In so doing I noticed that it was a fine sapphire surrounded by diamonds. As I rose, encouraged by my host, my eyes noticed that his double-barred pectoral cross as a Patriarch was *en suite*. I thought to myself, 'The sort of prelate I understand'! He did, in fact, become a Cardinal in Rome later – all very suitable.

It was just before lunch, and as I had been travelling a long way before arriving I asked if I might wash my hands. His Grace pointed to an open door and said: 'Just go through my bedroom there to the far side where there is a door into the bathroom'. So I did as he indicated, on the way glancing at his bed. It consisted of an old iron bedstead with wooden planks in place of a mattress; there was a pillow at the head and a blanket folded at the foot. The Archbishop was, obviously, one of those old-fashioned prelates who believed in a good show for the laity – his white cassock, purple edged and buttoned, sapphire and diamond ring and cross – and some penance for himself: an expression of religion I revere.

Having returned to the drawing room, my host asked if he could give me something to drink before lunch and said: 'I fear I have no whisky, and I do appreciate that for you British, what is life without whisky? However, I do have some excellent Portuguese brandy.' So I asked for that and hoped it would be a small one, as it was midday in hot India and *before* luncheon. It was obvious to me that we were going to get on like a house on fire, especially as my bed was not wooden planks.

So the visit started as it would continue. His Grace would fill me in with various details both historical and current. Many of these I have already included in the text. In respect of others, he would face me in the right direction, so I was able to find the answers.

I would go off to visit this and that site, frequently only returning for the evening meal. What I saw and thought, and what I did in this enchanting and historic enclave I have already described.

On one occasion I remarked to him that I had noticed a smart corvette of the Portuguese navy in the Mandosi, to which he replied: 'Yes, here for colonial purposes, don't you know'. He and I obviously thought along the same lines. No wonder my visit to Goa was such a resounding success.

I made sure I kissed his ring before I left![22]

★   ★   ★

At all times the necessary military routine of the Regimental Centre went on with training – for which I had special responsibilities as the Training Officer, for the entire Battalion since June, '46. There were also my duties as OC Boys' Company.

Correspondence with my family continued, with letters coming, sometimes, in batches directly from my parents in England. From my brother, Peter, in Toronto, and my grandparents in British Columbia they came by way of Brazil and then across to Africa and so to India. My old Headmistress, Miss Nora Denny, of Queen Margaret's School, Duncan would also correspond. It was characteristic of her thoughtfulness. My parents kept me supplied with reading material, both periodicals and books.

While in India I was able to indulge a passion, inherited from my father, for Persian carpets so that by the time I left the country I had acquired about two dozen interesting examples, including *Shistan, Shiraz, Turkh, Bokhara* and so on. Some contain a *Kirmarsh*[23] and, in later life, all have been a constant reminder of my Indian experience.

For a weekend, once a month, we would take it in turns so that some of us could go to Ooty[24] five thousand feet up and about fifty miles away: one of the main Hill Stations in South India. There we would stay at Ratan Tata Home[25] (an officers' leave hostel). We would wear tweeds, flannels, suits; walk or ride on the Ooty Downs – could be anywhere on the South Downs in Sussex. 'The great thing about Ooty is that grass grows without being asked'.[26] Then back to Ratan Tata and after dinner, and possibly a show, to bed under blankets – 'what fun to have a fire flickering in the grate'. It was a time of relaxation in a climate we considered normal.[27]

From time to time, several of us would band together and give a dinner party in our quarters. There was no problem over male guests but finding enough available females was another matter. One, from the local hospital, seven miles away in Coimbatore was, oddly enough, from Saskatchewan. I think she, Betty Prince of Delhi and the Hills – already mentioned – and I must have been the only Canadians in India.

---

[22] *Ibid.* – a description of the entire visit.
[23] A mistake made on purpose to attest that only God is perfect.
[24] Ootacumund.
[25] The Hill Station residence of Sir Ratan Tata of a well-known Parsee family of coal, steel and airline interests which was placed by the family at the disposal of officers.
[26] SSA New Series V C.S. to E.H.S. 2 May 1946
[27] *Ibid.*

At fairly regular intervals I would entertain my two staffs to a Bara Khana –
literally 'big meal', but the phrase is used to signify a dinner to which one is
invited. One of these of May '45 was mounted as follows:

Bara Khana
For the
Weapons Training Staff
Madras Regt'l Centre
5 May, 1945

Bill of Fare

Throughout	**First Course**
Beer	Fruit, cakes
Brandy	Gelebe (cake-like form of barley sugar resembling a
Soft Drinks	fancy pretzel)
	Hot 'sweet meat'

Main Course
Mutton Pillow with rice, Raisins, nuts
Mutton in gravy
Side dish of milk (curd)
Onions and black seeds (to scent)

With the pudding	**Last Course**
Cigarettes	Poisom – 'The Food of the Brahmins'(vermicelli
Speeches	and Raisins)[28]

The order of the dishes was in accordance with local custom. In keeping with
this, the meal was eaten off a piece of washed plantain (banana) leaf measuring
about fifteen by twelve inches placed before each guest. The advantage of this is
that after the meal these are thrown away, so that only the serving-dishes and
glasses need be washed.

> The meal was eaten with the right hand, and those of high breeding only
> dirty the lower parts up to about the first knuckle, the others got in among
> the food and soiled even their palms. As I have become quite proficient at
> this type of eating I can hold my own with the former![29]

I reported to my parents. The left hand is not used for eating, as it is reserved
for helping with the natural functions of the body, so the whole custom may be
regarded as a traditional form of prophylaxis.

Such bara khanas with the weapon training staff were particularly enjoyable.

---

[28] SSA new Series IV C.S. to E.H.S. 6 May, 1945.
[29] *Ibid.*

Although it was a military unit and I was in command, we constituted very much a team. I think this was partly the result of my having all the staff into my office about once a month, sitting them round a table and discussing the programme for the next four weeks. We were all proud of the way we turned farm lads into efficient, disciplined soldiers. This was achieved by continual co-operation between all of us. The staff were an excellent group of men and I was fortunate to have them.

The day before that particular Bara Khana, that is to say on 4 May 1945, the German Forces in North West Germany, Denmark and Holland had surrendered.[30] The war in the West was really all over except for the final unconditional surrender of all the Forces of the Third Reich on 7 May. The official VE Day celebrations in the capital of the Presidency took place five days later on 13 May, I and others of the regiment attending. The city was *en fete* with flags and parades; there was a solemn *Te Deum* and benediction in the cathedral attended by the Governor, Sir Arthur Hope. The various other churches held services of thanksgiving.

Everyone looked forward to the speedy end of the War 'this time next year',[31] although we knew very well that reinforcements could not be expected from Europe for some months yet. However, when writing to my parents I observed:

> If the campaigns are as brilliant as this recent capture of Rangoon (obviously accomplished before the break of the monsoon) all should go well with us. This whole Burma campaign has been marvellously conducted, that is after we were thoroughly thrashed out of the country and then decided to learn how to fight in the jungle. Any nation who could learn a totally new type of warfare from scratch, and then beat an experienced enemy in such a short time is truly great; who said the British were decadent!?[32]

This 13 May was for another reason 'without a doubt the most memorable day',[33] as it happened to be my twenty-first Birthday. My parents had sent me a gold signet ring bearing our family crest – heaven only knows where they got the gold from in wartime Britain, but I didn't ask. There was also a handsome cheque.

Despite what everyone in India expected – '18 months was the usual estimate'[34] – the war with Japan came to an end within three months of the surrender of the Third Reich. That for Japan followed on 14 August, 1945.

The cessation of hostilities was duly celebrated with two days' holiday in the

---

[30]The surrender was received on behalf of the Allies on Luneberg Heath by Field Marshal Sir Bernard Montgomery – first cousin of the author's future father-in-law, the Earl of Iddesleigh. Their mothers were sisters.

[31] SSA new Series IV C.S. to E.H.S. 13 May 1945.

[32] *Ibid.*

[33] *Ibid.*

[34] SSA New Series IV C.S. to E.H.S. 19 August, 1945.

Regimental Centre. On one of these there were various sports, during which 'one of the events was musical chairs at which the officers had to perform to the great delight of the sepoys! There were one or two more strenuous items for the sahibs also!'[35]

One was, of course, eternally grateful: we had won at last and could look forward to peace. My family was doubly grateful that unlike so many in Eastern Europe – in Poland and Lithuania in particular – we of our family had not been subjected, as peace dawned, to the crushing embrace of the Russian Bear.

Now that the war with Japan was over, there was some 'mopping up' to be done. This concerned, in particular, the so-called Indian National Army (INA), which had been formed to fight against us and with the Japanese. In the main they were recruited from Indian Army Other Ranks being held as prisoners of war and being treated abominably. As often as not they surrendered as soon as they got near to our troops in Burma, so glad were they to be away from the Japanese. The policy of the Government of India was to return these men to their homes, nothing more being said, in view of the conditions of their recruitment.

However, there were also a number of former Indian Army officers who had become officers of the INA. For these the situation was, quite other. The Government's policy, even during the War, was to release very quietly and without fuss any officer of the armed forces who said that he could no longer serve with a clear conscience due to his Congress sympathies. In spite of this some, having been captured by the Japanese, joined the INA; some even shot their fellow Indian prisoners of war if they would not join.

As a result, trials of INA officers were held in the *Lal Quela* (The Red Fort – Delhi's Tower of London) from November '45 to January '46. For this, the Orderly Officer on duty was an Old Georgian friend of mine, William Eldridge, who had been commissioned in the Gurkhas.[36] The Congress Party made a terrific political issue of it, demanding that all should be released. This despite their having expelled members of their own party for disobeying Congress rules at about the time of the Red Fort Trials. What was sauce for the goose was not sauce for the gander.[37]

Two months later, in January '46, the trials concluded and all were let off and simply cashiered. 'Is a contract and an oath nothing?...It's weakness, not clemency. I wonder what the forty thousand of the sixty thousand prisoners of war who remained loyal think of this?,[38] I groaned.

Next month, in February, I was fortunate to have 28 days' leave in the United Kingdom. The journey both ways was by a 'belsen flying boat' as I dubbed them.[39]

---

[35] *Ibid.*
[36] SSA New Series V C.S. to E.H.S. 30 Oct. 1946.
[37] SSA new Series IV C.S. to E.H.S. 25 Nov. 1945.
[38] SSA. New Series IV C.S. to E.H.S., 6 Jan. 1946.
[39] SSA New Series V C.S. to E.H.S. 15 July 1946.

Conditions aboard were most primitive: wooden seats and straps to hold us in, but that was the least of my worries. In England I was able to attend the farewell party for the closing of the Beaver Club. As mentioned before, this was a club for the Canadian and Allied Forces in London. For the total six years and one day of its existence, as mentioned before, my mother had been the Joint Supervisor of the voluntary staff with Mrs Charles Cambie. It had been a great achievement, quite apart from having to cope with bomb damage and keeping the peace among a large group of female voluntary staff. The party was graced by Queen Mary, as regal as ever despite her eighty odd years. She wore a wonderful ensemble of purple velvet with a diamond spray of Maple Leaves at her shoulder – most appropriate being, as already noted, the first lady of the royal family to have been in Canada.[40] The servicemen much appreciated her coming. When she finally took her leave one of the soldiers noticed that she had not quite finished her doughnut. So when the Queen was safely through the door he pocketed the remains of the doughnut 'to show the folks back home in Canada.'

But where did all this leave me? Did I have a possible life career in the Indian Army? From about 1942 onwards there had been a general feeling that after the War India should be granted independence. Exactly when was not specified. During my discussions and interviews with the India Office in early 1943 the whole attitude of the officials was that life-time careers for white officers in the Army of British India were assumed. If India Office personnel were not conscious at that time of impending precipitous changes immediately after the War who would be?

Churchill, the Prime Minister, was somewhat hesitant over the whole idea of independence. Nevertheless, he agreed that the Lord Privy Seal in the coalition government, Sir Stafford Cripps, an austere socialist, should visit India and work out a basis on which independence could be granted. His mission foundered, but Cripps committed the British Government to a policy of complete independence. The Congress Party was not satisfied with jam tomorrow, but the British were not prepared to hand over with the Japanese at the very gate of India, indeed with a foot over the threshold.

So the Congress Party embarked on a policy of civil disobedience. Its leaders, such as Gandhi and Nehru, had to be imprisoned – even if the British idea of prison in Gandhi's case was the Aga Khan's palace at Poona. Some of the more radical members of the Congress had willingly collaborated with the enemy, such as Suba Chandra Bose, who broadcast on behalf of the Nazis from Germany. Later he was taken – in great secrecy – by submarine to Japan, where he organized the (INA). He died in Japan before the end of the War, which spared us the trouble of shooting him.

In general, this was the background towards the end of my time in India. Wavell, the Viceroy, honest man and without guile that he was, was no more

[40] See chapter IV p 86.

successful than Cripps in reconciling the irreconcilable: the Congress Party and the Muslim League.

A federation was advocated by Britain that would include the area of British India, the Native States and the strongly Muslim areas. However, as time went on, the Muslim League became more and more determined to have a completely separate state, even if in two parts at either side of India. This was to be known as Pakistan. When a Cabinet Mission came to India in March '46 to press for a federation, the country was more divided than ever. In a recent election Congress had swept the board in the Hindu areas, the League in the Muslim. Polarization was complete.

In July of the same year there was a general election in the United Kingdom. Despite Churchill having been, without a doubt, *the* great leader during the war, the Labour Party, led by Clement Attlee, won an enormous majority in the House of Commons. Three days later my reaction was: 'We have noted the election results. Being a Canadian, the only comment I have to pass is that I am glad it is not my country in which such a party got into power'.[41]

The new socialist Government was determined to press ahead with the rapid withdrawal of the British from India. Wavell, a man of experience, considered that something like fifteen years would be needed for this if bloodshed was to be avoided. This would not do, and he had to go. Mountbatten was appointed as viceroy in his stead. Being the person he was – with many undoubted virtues, though humility was not among them – he was sure he could arrange a swift handover. Appalling massacres at the time of partition resulted. Fortunately, I had left India before they occurred.

In the meantime, the Muslim League had called for its followers to observe 16 August 1946 as a 'Direct Action Day' in protest against what they considered Congress intransigence. In Calcutta the 'action' became a massacre, with 5,000 killed and 15,000 injured in the city and suburbs. When the news got out, the conflagration spread to Bihar and beyond. The 1st Battalion of the Madras Regiment was sent to suppress the riots. It was stationed in Calcutta and Bihar from November '46 to March '47. The soldiers conducted themselves with great distinction and impartiality both in dealing with the riots and protecting refugees. In this connection the GO C-in-C, Eastern Command, Lieutenant General Sir Francis Tucker, observed: 'There is no doubt that the resolute action of Col. Venning and his Madras Regiment's soldiers saved the situation in the whole of this area'.[42] There are shades here of the Madrassis to the rescue at the time of the Mutiny; nor can I forget the compliment to the training received of late under my direction, at the Regimental Centre.

With these events happening in India and England waking up to the peacetime policies of the newly elected Labour Government, it became clear that we had

[41] SSA New Series IV C..S. to E.H.S. 29 July 1945
[42] Tucker, Lt. Gen. Sir Francis. GCIE, CB, DSO, OBE. *While Memory Lasts*. London, 1950 pp 187-88.

reached the end of a chapter in our history. Of course, a new one was about to begin. Nehru invited British officers to stay on, as he fully realized that the Armed Forces of India could not be officered entirely by Indians overnight. But I felt it was time to leave when my brother officers asked: 'Do you have to go?' rather than waiting until they asked, 'Why doesn't he go?' I had already discussed the position with my father in April '46.[43] If I went soon, still only in my early twenties, I could easily train for another career.

So, it was with regret, that I retired from the Indian Army, received government tickets back to Duncan, British Columbia, and in Bombay on 26th March, 1947 boarded a Cunard White Star ship, the *SS George*. Two days later, at 2 o'clock in the afternoon, we were on our way, bound for Liverpool.[44]

It is a privilege to have lived in India; to have come to know a people of such rich, diverse culture and history, a people capable of such character and loyalty; to have had the opportunity to contribute – even if in a very small way – to the great development by the British of that remarkably seductive land. Like so many returning from India, I left behind a little piece of my heart. I hope it may be said of my time there, in the words inscribed on the tomb of Henry Lawrence in the Residency garden at Lucknow: 'He tried to do his duty.'

As the boat moved out into the Arabian Sea, I recalled the old saying: 'The best view in India is Bombay from the back of a boat'. But that was not my reaction. In fact I felt, 'no better than a pelican out in the desert, an old owl on some ruined building.'[45] What I had set out to accomplish – a life-time career in the Army of British India – had come to naught.

On the other hand, I was not yet twenty-three years of age, and my life still lay before me: new and other things, wonderful things, could yet be done. So instead of desponding my thoughts soon turned to that beautiful piece in Ramayana, one of the two great epic poems of Hindu literature, where Valmiki paints this picture:

> And white foam – clouds and silver spray
> Were wildly tossed on high,
> Like swans that urge their homeward way
> Across the autumn sky.[46]

Certainly it was the autumn of my Indian sojourn; yet at home it was already spring. So for this particular Swan, sailing away from the sub-continent, the ozone of new opportunities was strong in the nostrils.

---

[43] SSA New Series II H.P.S. to E.H.S. 21 April 1946.

[44] SSA New Series V. C.S. to E.H.S. 30 March, 1947. India was granted Independence some 3 months later by 10&11 Geo. VI c. 30 Indian Inndependence Act, 1947 to which Royal Assent was given 18 July 1947.

[45] Psalm C1.7.

[46] Monier Williams, Boden Professor of Sanskrit, University of Oxford.. *Indian Wisdom or Examples of the Religious, Philosophical and Ethical doctrines of the Hindus*. Wm H. Allen & Co, London 1875 p304.

CHAPTER VII

At 23 a relic of the Raj, and so from the Maidans of Hindustan to the Fields of Academe

THE SEA VOYAGE back from India, – 'very much a powder keg at present'[1], as I put it in a letter written on board – was pleasant enough. I was in an eight-berth cabin; many officers had to put up with hammocks on troop decks. The fact that my old friend of Maidstone and Bangalore days, Tony Buckingham, was ship's adjutant was not unhelpful.

By 8 April we had arrived at Malta. As on the first voyage to India, my Strickland/Bower friends were able to arrange that I got ashore for a short time – once again, the only onward passenger allowed to do this. Spent a few very pleasant hours at Miss Strickland's new villa with Mariana Bower and her brother, Paul. Had to be back by noon, when the ship moved out of the Grand Harbour to the sound of the church bells of Valetta ringing *The Angelus*[2].

Finally, greeted by the Liver Birds, we docked in Liverpool on Monday, 14 April 1947, some 17 days after having left Bombay. So began three months' leave on full pay[3].

Father had got leave to join me from Germany, where he was serving in the BAOR We were social; took in some plays such as *Cyrano de Bergerac* at the Old Vic with Ralph Richardson playing the lead; called on various relations and friends, but invited them out to meals as rationing was 'remorseless'[4].

Before leaving India, I had made up my mind that I had to go to a university and get a qualification[5]. As a result, the main topic of discussion between Father and me was my future. Enquiries were made at the Canadian High Commission as to university courses and possibility of government grants.

As the United Kingdom financial regulations were severe, there were all manner of hoops to be jumped through before I could get permission for the money transferred from India to my account with Grindlays Bank in London, to be sent to Canada. But in the end it was received.[6]

---

[1] SSA. New Series V. C.S. to E.H.S. 30 March 1947.
[2] *Ibid.* same to same 13 April, 1947.
[3] *Ibid.* same to same 16 March 1947.
[4] *Ibid.* same to same 20 April, 1947.
[5] *Ibid.* same to same 10 Feb. 1947.
[6] *Ibid.* same to same 21 June, 1947.

Yet again, one had to harry the Ministry of Transport over my passage and ticket to British Columbia. Finally, that too was forthcoming. In the meantime, my father had to return to Germany at the end of his leave. To fill in the time while waiting for my boat, I was fortunate enough to be able to take some drawing lessons from Newbury A. Trent, an established Chelsea artist. That tuition – or 'counsel of Trent' – came in very handy when, some years later, I became a herald.

Then, at last, on 26 June I boarded in Manchester the SS *Manchester Port* and sailed down the Manchester Ship Canal to the Mersey. Apparently, the water of the canal is so foul it de-barnacles a ship's bottom without further ado, so any boat that can squeeze into that waterway gets that service, gratis! The ship was comfortable. It accommodated 12 passengers and as much luggage as they wanted, being a cargo vessel. After a crossing of 11 days, by way of the Belle Isle Strait between Newfoundland and Labrador, we disembarked at Montreal[7].

Once landed, the journey was straight down to Windsor, Ontario, for a week's visit to my brother, who was teaching there at Assumption College, then an affiliate of the University of Western Ontario. Upon our meeting, I reported to our parents, 'Peter and I are mutually staggered with the great change in each of us – adolescence to maturity in one hop is rather great to take in at one go'[8].

From there, my ticket took me on by train out to the West Coast, and so to my grandfather Green's place at Duncan on Vancouver Island, where my mother had been staying for the past year since the close of the Beaver Club in London. Wives were not yet allowed to join their husbands stationed with BAOR – much to the frustration of E.H.S! It was, of course, a very happy reunion, and most pleasant to catch up with other relations and friends after such a long separation amid so many adventures.

During this return to where I had started life, because of the intervening experiences, one appreciated it all the more. Here I first had the psychological experience of *ego sum*. While Anatole France's wretched little dog thought *it* was 'the centre of *the* universe', I came to realize that I was the centre of mine and must – one day – account for my stewardship of it. Such stemmed from the Faith first developed in Cowichan, not forgetting what my relationship with all the other 'universes' must be, in short an objective morality.

Similarly, I first had that Homeric appreciation of how the 'rosey fingered dawn appears in her beauty'[9] – for us say, over Mill Bay where we spent our summers. When the sun appeared there, that very same sun – some 10 hours before – had given life to the grass over the graves of my ancestors by both Święce and Pasusvys. Continuing on its dutiful course through the heavens it had – some 8 hours before – performed that same office for those sepulchred at

[7] Ibid. same to same 6 July, 1947
[8] Ibid. same to same 11 July, 1947.
[9] *Iliad* book 9.

the New Mill, by Tring, in Hertfordshire. That is, before it finally appeared over the Strait of Georgia to our great satisfaction.

If one starts life here, amid those masters of totemic art, those Gentlemen Emigrants, those Chinese and those Sikhs in the Cowichan Valley – where I played in the wood, swam in Maple Bay, and climbed Mount Tzouhalem – could there have been a better place to do so?

With such a beginning to life, surely one then 'exults like some great runner who sees the track before him'[10]. In those far away ancestral tombs and here in this valley was that granatic origin of my corporeal dust.

Peter joined us on the coast for a few weeks. I still had not made up my mind what to do. 'Take a BA', he wisely suggested. 'With your credits from the University of London, it'll take you 2 years. That'll give you 2 years to think and decide.'

Accordingly, early in September we both went back to Windsor. I enrolled there through Assumption College as an undergraduate of the University of Western Ontario.

To me this city was a curious and, at first glance, an unprepossessing place. It lies on the north bank of a river with one of the largest cities in the United States, Detroit, opposite. Windsor is located – oddly enough – to the south because of a twist in the water system of the Great Lakes. Detroit sprawls there, an elephantine monument to materialistic vulgarity, with Windsor a (rather large) proverbial mouse. It is a wonder the place is not completely suffocated. The general character of Windsor was not helped, in my opinion, by being 'the Auto Capital of the British Empire'.

Getting on the packed bus at about 5p.m. in the afternoon, one would encounter a shift just out from the factories: all sat with ashen faces, staring to the front like zombies. Each had been giving 3 twists to No. 10 bolt – or whatever his soul-destroying work had been – for the previous 8 hours. It was a wonder they did not all rise up and join some mad political party. No wonder the Trade Unions had them in a vice-like grip.

However, if one scratched the surface one found a remarkable history for Windsor, going back to the days of New France when the area was called *L'Assomption d'étroit*[11]. The adjectival part of that name grew into the monstrous Detroit – characteristically losing an accent on the way. The nounal part was somehow transmogrified to Windsor. It is said that some neighbours from across the river would come over and ask, in all seriousness, 'Where's the castle?'; fortunately, even if Anglicized, the noun was retained in the title of the local university college.

---

[10] Psalm XVIII.6

[11] For some aspects of its history *vide,* Swan, C.M.J.F. 'The Roots of a University' *Canadian Georgraphical Journal*, Dec. 1956. Vol. LVII. No. 6 p. 204 ff.

As is so often the case in places of which one might at first be tempted to despair, I discovered some civilized, some educated persons, and upon occasion, as a bonus, these characteristics combined. I had the good fortune to make a number of extremely agreeable friends in Windsor and the surrounding area – and even (low be it spoken) in Detroit! – and they were most hospitable. Yet again, in a city that has at one end an institution of higher learning, acting as a beacon, reminding man of the intellectual and spiritual heights to which he can aspire, and at the other a whisky distillery (Hiram Walker's), surely there is hope of salvation!

About half of the undergraduates, when I was there, were ex-servicemen – or 'Veterans' as we were called – both Canadians and Americans, and among this convivial throng, I enjoyed myself immensely.

Our Dean, the Reverend E.C. LeBel, CSB, CD, MA, once told me that towards the end of the war there had been a meeting of university Deans from across Canada. One of the most pressing questions raised was – in substance – What are we going to do when the rude, crude soldiery who have been whoring and boozing over half the globe come onto our campuses and mingle with our fine, young men straight from High School?

As history recorded, Fr LeBel pointed out, the so-called 'rude, crude soldiery' were to be found living in garrets, writing their university essays on all-purpose tables beneath canopies of drying nappies, their wives doing their best to keep the babies quiet while Daddy studied! Those just out of High School, on the other hand, caused mayhem, doing what they thought the Veterans got up to at university.

Although I had already started at Assumption as an undergraduate it still had not been decided by the Department of Veterans' Affairs (DVA) whether, because I had not served in the Canadian Armed Forces, I qualified for a grant. Fortunately, the local Member of Parliament, the Honble Paul Martin, was in the Federal Cabinet[12] and had been, at one time, on the faculty of Assumption. The problem was put to him, and with that 'voice at court' matters were swiftly settled: it was decided that any Canadian who had served in any of the Forces of the Crown was eligible for a university grant.

The Bachelor of Arts course I took was a general one with several subjects, rather as in Scotland. In my opinion, such an arrangement is a good idea; one has ample time for specialization later. And such a course has a mind-broadening and civilizing influence.

But it must be admitted that, at first, I found it extremely difficult to get back onto the treadmill of continual study. This had been anticipated and acknowledged to my parents in a letter written on my return from India as we neared Port Said when I wrote:

---

[12] At the time he was Minister of National Health and Welfare (1946-57).

I fully realize that it will be a grind, and for the first year, hell, no doubt, trying to get my mind back to studying.[13]

– and how true that was! At the beginning I could not concentrate for more than 20 minutes. But gradually discipline triumphed.

The college was much influenced by the approach to higher education of John Henry Newman. The lecturers, both clerical and lay, were well qualified and some excelled in getting their subjects across.

While speaking of lecturers, I am reminded of an incident which concerned me. One aspect of philosophy is ethics, and I had followed a course in this subject and enjoyed it. The lecturer was keen on his subject and lectured well. After the final examination, the grades were, following the usual custom, posted on a notice board. I studied the list and saw that I had come second. It would have been more pleasant to have come first, but the man who did was a good student, and my grading was certainly respectable. As I walked away from the board, two other undergraduates came up from a different direction to see how they had done; they clearly did not notice me. One said to the other, 'I see that Conrad Swan has come second.' To which, the other replied, 'Well, you wouldn't expect *that* lecturer to make him first. He'd fail his own mother!' My brother had been the lecturer!

One of the other subjects I took was Biology. Upon turning up for the first lecture I was slightly surprised by the preponderance of female undergraduates present. I soon knew why: the lecturer – a recent graduate – studying for a higher degree was a young layman, who was extremely good-looking. He was of Italian descent – of the blond variety. Biology was very popular that year.

Eventually we got to human reproduction, and when we reached the lecture which really got us down to the nitty gritty, I noticed that it was given by the lay head of the Department – an unprepossessing, middle-aged man of extreme dullness!

After India, one was spoilt for choice when it came to women. To me the female 'bobby-soxer' undergraduates seemed somewhat gauche – or was it that I was long in the tooth at 23? Be that as it may, there were many others, more mature and more charming, to be found in such *banlieues* as Walkerville – a pleasant, residential part of Windsor. I felt they deserved their escort to be properly dressed for the balls that seemed endless in Windsor, so I treated myself to a set of tails made by a good local tailor. It was so well made I am still using it to this day when required (as when commanded by the Lord Chamberlain to Buckingham Palace). For a period after we were married, my wife and I house-sat in Walkerville for some friends when they were abroad. When doing so, we used to go to Mass at the local church. The parish priest was a Monsignor, who much amused us on one occasion by saying, 'When I reached

<hr />

[13] SSA. New Series V: C.S. to E.H.S. 30 March 1947.

the age of reason – several years after ordination' – one could not but warm to such a man.

On the campus life was full of every sort of activity. In addition to the lectures, there were all manner of clubs, sporting groups and theatrical activities. My brother was much in demand for the production of the latter. After successfully mounting one of these, he immediately fell sick with pneumonia and was taken to the local hospital called *Hôtel Dieu* – an echo from New France days. Though there were some French-speaking people in the area of Windsor, it was largely Anglophone. Some of the latter spoke a language they called English and seemed to delight in assassinating anything that was French; they called the hospital 'Hotel Do'! When I first called to see my brother there, the receptionist said, 'Oh, Mr Swan, we are particularly worried about Fr Swan. He hardly says a word!' To which I replied: 'Sister. When my brother starts inconsequential banter, immediately call the priest, the doctor and me in that order.'

When I called next time, I found him sitting up in bed between a pair of the most adorable, new born piccaninny twins. The hospital chaplain had produced them and was in the process of photographing this unlikely trilogy. Obviously, Peter was getting better.

During the total of four years I was at Assumption, my Christmas holidays were spent on the upper reaches of the Mississippi – where it flows between cliffs – at St Paul, Minnesota, with old friends, Mr and Mrs David Daly. He was a civil engineer who had worked on such famous projects as the Bolder Dam. His hobby was the American Civil War and he would keep me enthralled recounting its progress and aftermath in the Deep South. He was about 80 when I stayed at his house and, in his youth, had known many who had fought in and experienced that terrible war. These included some Southerners who, for the rest of their lives after the war – including an old Catholic priest – utterly refused to take the Oath of Allegiance to the Union.

For the Easter holidays – a few days either side of Easter Sunday – I would stay in Windsor. This gave me the opportunity of attending the Holy Week liturgy in the Assumption parish church. On special occasions it doubled as the college 'chapel', as it was located on the campus.

Some of my summer holidays were spent in Canada in Quebec City at Laval – the oldest French university outside of France – others were with my parents in Germany. By that time, wives were permitted to join their husbands serving in BAOR.

After two years at Assumption, I graduated Bachelor of Arts *summa cum laude* – cannot think how I achieved that but then, in life, one must be humble and simply accept such situations! So on the appointed day up I went to London, for the graduation ceremony in the grounds of the University of Western Ontario. This surely must be among the most beautiful campuses in Canada.

As an initiation into the discipline and methods of original research I decided that I would continue on at Assumption and take a Master of Arts degree in Philosophy, a subject in which it was particularly strong.. My thesis was entitled, *The Concept of Being in Contemporary Existentialism with Particular Reference to Jean-Paul Sartre.*

Existentialism's success, at the time I wrote my thesis, was phenomenal. It was led by such atheists, among others, as Gabriel Marcel, author of *Être et Avoir*[14], Jean-Paul Sartre – *L' Être et le néant*[15] and Simone de Beauvoir – *Le sang des autres*[16]. De Beauvoir was the ethicist of the movement and also Sartre's mistress – *oh, la, la, les Français!* Well, at least they did not label her with the present-day euphemism, his 'partner', as if all they did in bed together was to play bridge!

One of the fascinating paradoxes of this movement which called itself 'existentialist', was that it had its beginnings in the doctrines of Soren Kierkegaard – author of *Either/Or*[17] and many other works. He was an ardent Christian. Yet despite this and other paradoxes that mark off the history of existentialism from that of other philosophies adhering, more or less, either to a Christian theology or a materialist atheism, it is possible I believe, to disengage a common core of principles that may be called 'existentialist' whether this core is the centre of an atheist or a Christian philosophy. In so doing, my intention was not to polemicize. Rather it was to give an objective exposition of the concept of being as found in existentialist philosophy. In accordance with this purpose, I compared and contrasted, wherever it appeared desirable to do so, the existentialist notion of being with that of Aristotle and Aquinas.

In the course of all this, I must admit that, from time to time, I did wonder very quietly to myself what the reaction of some of my former colonels would have been had I told them that such men as Sartre could write works entitled *Les Mouches*[18] and *La nausée*[19](!!). Probably, it would have been 'Gad, Sir! What regiment did the fella belong to?', and I would have agreed.

The MA took a further two years, and I graduated with that degree in 1951, concluding my time at Windsor *in statu pupillari*. It had been a singular experience, and one I particularly valued. After India, the sensation of life there had been astringent: rather like using surgical spirit as after-shave lotion, following a very close shave with a good razor.

Towards the end of my BA course and throughout the MA researches my goal

---

[14] Gallimard,Paris, 1935.
[15] Gallimard Paris, 1945.
[16] Gallimard,Paris, 1945
[17] Vol. I translated by D.F. Swenson and Lilian M. Swenson. Vol. II translated by Walter Lowrie. O.U.P 1944.
[18] Gallimard, 1944.
[19] Gallimard, 1942.

had been to take a doctorate in history. To this end, when in England during the summer holidays of 1950, I applied to both Cambridge and St Andrew's and was accepted by both. This posed a dilemma: for various reasons, each had its attractions. Finally, upon the advice of a friend, the Preces of the Pontifical Institute of Mediaeval Studies[20] in Toronto – the future Cardinal George Flahiff, CSB, CC – I decided on the former, where I enrolled as a Research Pensioner at Peterhouse – the oldest of the Cambridge colleges (1284) and still the smallest. It was then the mecca of historians, boasting Postain, Butterfield, Dom David Knowles and other luminaries, as Fellows.

So in the Michaelmas Term, 1951, I settled into my rooms in the Old Court up the Sex staircase – no, not that you would, but others might misinterpret that description. It was so called as it also led up to the students' common room, the Sexcentenary Club (inevitably called the Sex Club by the undergraduates – and hence the naming of the staircase). The 'club' had been founded in 1884 upon the six hundredth anniversary of the founding of the college.

My doctoral thesis was on: *The Introduction of the Elizabethan Settlement of Religion into the Universities of Oxford and Cambridge with particular reference to the Roman Catholics, 1558-1603*. At least, that was the official, academic title; the gist of my research was to find out how they got rid of us! My tutor was a Fellow of Peterhouse, the Reverend Brian Wormald, the expert on Clarendon. He was in the middle of being converted to Rome, so these promised to be interesting times.

The custom was to live in college for the first year. That ensured one would have an opportunity to get to know a good number of one's fellow Petreans, as we were called. After that, one lived out in lodgings throughout the town for the remainder of one's time at Cambridge. The evening meal only – called 'hall' – would be taken in college. I had no objection to moving out of college at the end of the first year as my rooms, in winter at least, had been bitterly cold: the water froze in the jug on the washstand. Fortunately, I found comfortable quarters opposite Jesus College. As a result if a car pulled up near me as I walked around Cambridge, and a young face asked, 'Where's Jesus?' I did not automatically assume he was some earnest evangelical, but directed him to the college near my lodgings.

In these were both a bedroom and a sitting room in which I had breakfast and lunch – provided by my landlady – and where I studied when not in the University Library or the myriad archival repositories and record offices not only in Cambridge, but also in various parts of England and on the Continent (where English colleges had been founded by Catholics because of the penal legislation of the Elizabethan government).

---

[20] The only Pontifical Institute outside of Rome. It is conducted by the Basilian Fathers in the grounds of the University of St Michael's College, Toronto.

This work produced the evidence of a contest between two sets of people: one determined to preserve the religion of their ancestors, going back to St Augustine of Canterbury and in union with the Apostolic See – the Catholics – and the other equally bent on introducing a new religious dispensation, albeit as inclusive as possible – the Anglicans. The resistance of certain colleges to the changes; the pace at which each university was marshalled towards governmental policy; the exit of men from each university and their founding colleges abroad to continue the fight back in England – were all investigated.

Some went further afield, to Goa, for example, as with the Oxonian Jesuit, Thomas Stevens, the premier translator of the Bible into an Asian language. Yet again, there was that Fellow of Exeter College, John Hawlet[21] who went north to my ancestral Lithuania and joined the faculty of the University of Vilno (now Vilnius) – the 'Cambridge' of the Most Serene Commonwealth; the 'Oxford' being the Jagellonian at Krakow (some four and a quarter centuries later I was to lecture at both).

The sum total of my research revealed that the generally accepted picture we have today of this period is quite different from that as seen by those at Oxford and Cambridge during the reign of Elizabeth. It was a fascinating period to have been able to study in real depth.

There were about a dozen Research Pensioners at Peterhouse doing doctorates when I was there. My father used to tease me about the description asking, 'This pensioner business, who pays whom?!' My fellow Pensioners were doing theses on a variety of subjects, but mostly historical.

I was soon struck at Cambridge by the fact that, in contrast to Assumption, there was an almost universal, pathological reticence to predicate anything of anything. I thought to myself, 'How fortunate for the mathematicians that they had not succumbed to that academic complaint or they would have been up the creek.' Yet again mercifully, when the time came to decide whether or not to fight the Nazis, it was not left to the local academics, or we could well have been studying at Peterhoff rather than Peterhouse by the time I got there. Fortunately, not all academics were so taciturn, as witness the late Enoch Powell: Trinity College, Cambridge; youngest brigadier in the British Army in World War II; notorious later for his 'rivers of blood' speech[22].

In hall we Research Pensioners used to sit at one table – near the fire (!). We took it in turns to buy two bottles of wine for dinner which we then shared. It was drunk out of wonderful old, heavy, solid silver beakers engraved with the arms of the college. The food at Peterhouse was good. A former Petrean had

---

[21] Foster, Joseph. *Alumni Oxoniense,* Vol. II, Parker & Co., Oxford, 1897 p. 757.

[22] Made at Birmingham, 1968 on the subject of immigration. The quotation was based on the Sibyl's prophesy in Book VI of the *Aeneid*. He first quoted it in Latin and then, as an aid to those not versed in Virgil, did so in translation – his 'fatal decision was not to be pedantic and leave it in Latin', as he said later.

endowed the Buttery (the kitchen) – presumably, in his day, the food was not *cordon bleu.*

For reason of this benefaction, members of other colleges always liked being invited to dine at with us. I hope that the sparkle of our conversation was an added attraction!

The post-graduate students got on well together, and I made friendships among them which have lasted ever since. These included: Dr Ian Macpherson, Fellow of Gonville and Caius College, Cambridge; the late Reverend F. X. Martin, OSA, Professor of History at University College, Dublin – the one who led the people of that city in the preservation of its Danish antiquities – and Dr Richard Bakemeier, the cancer specialist at the University of Colorado. There was also a temporary Fellow at Peterhouse, Dr D.B.C. Taylor, who was very much one of us. He later became the Vice-Chancellor of the Victoria University of Wellington, New Zealand.

Our period up at Cambridge was during the tenure of Monsigneur A.N. Gilbey as chaplain to the Catholic undergraduates. He was a Gilbey of Gilbey's Gin; had a Spanish mother; was quintessentially English and was, probably, the best-mannered man I have ever known. As a result, this remarkable man had a great influence, not simply among his 'flock', but throughout the university. As he was chaplain for 100 terms, and kept up with Cantabrigians long after they had left the university – marrying them, baptizing their children, and burying them, if necessary – he became something of a national figure. He was also a most apostolic person, and if an undergraduate wanted to know more about the Catholic Faith, he gave him absolutely individual instruction.

However, when some of us 'dyed-in-the-wool Catholics', as the phrase goes – all doctoral candidates – asked him if he would brush up our understanding of the Faith, he invited us en masse – about eight of us – to Fisher House (the chaplaincy) once a week, after hall, for three terms. With a decanter of port circulating, he took questions and answers from the then well-known Penny Catechism, as it was called, a simple statement of Roman Catholic tenets. He then delivered a brilliant exposition on each of them. We, each with our own experience and expertise in a particular subject of research, would enquire, challenge, and contribute in a positive way. The result was a mini Gregoriana on the banks of the Cam. The Monsignor's exposition was later published as *We Believe*[23].

When he died in 1998 aged 96 his requiem in the Brompton Oratory – one of London's largest churches – was packed from door to altar. As one of the newspaper articles remarked, 'Mayfair was on its knees.'

Work on a doctorate is a relentless grind: it is said that about 75% of those

---

[23] The Rt Rev. Mgr A.N. Gilbey. *We Believe*. Progress Press Co. Ltd., Valetta, Malta, 1983; 3rd edition: Bellew Publishing Co. Ltd 1994.

who embark towards the degree do not complete the course. I used to find I needed a complete break from time to time. It so happened that one of these required recreational periods coincided with my mother, in her capacity as the National President of the Catholic Women's League of England and Wales, having to go on a tour of the South West: Devon, Cornwall, and the like. So I offered to be her chauffeur, and that is how I came to meet my future wife, Lady Hilda Northcote – but more about that later.

By 1955 the thesis was completed, the *viva voce* endured. The doctorate followed in due course. The diploma had to be posted to me as I could not attend at the Senate House, Cambridge, to receive it in person; by the time of that convocation I was back at Assumption.

While I had been away, it had severed its links with the University of Western Ontario and had (in 1953) received degree-granting powers from the Ontario Legislature. Then after another three years, while I was there, it changed its name to 'the Assumption University of Windsor'. My position on the faculty was that of Lecturer in History and also Lecturer in Political Science. It seems to be well known in universities that when you are supremely qualified in, shall we say, Icelandic philology, you are not allowed to concentrate on that, but are asked to lecture in geography, or some other improbable subject. So it fell to my lot to lecture in political science. Nonetheless, I enjoyed it, having an academic interest in the subject – acquired when I was in India noting the antics of Gandhi, Nehru, Jinnah *et alii*, (not forgetting Mountbatten). In my first lecture each year in political science, I would tell the undergraduates to go away and read Marx's *Das Kapital* (the Bolshevik bear was still uncomfortably active at the time), and also *Burke's Reflections on the French Revolution* (an excellent antidote to starry-eyed liberalism). Once they had done that, I said, we could start talking. They soon found out where I stood!

One of my students was a Baptist Minister. He was, a very decent fellow, but had he been a horse I would have recited his pedigree as: by backwoods liberalism out of egalitarianism. He used to say, 'Until you've taken a course by Dr Swan, you haven't lived' – I put the best construction on that! As to my history course, that was concerned with England. The undergraduates continued to be an interesting mixture of Canadians and Americans, though all the Veterans had vanished by then.

From 1957-61, the year I finally left Assumption, my rank was Assistant Professor of History, and I was also the University Beadle, which required me to parade before the Chancellor and carry the mace.

This latter duty made me a participant in what was undoubtedly the most significant event that took place during my time on the faculty: the ceremonial affiliation of Canterbury College with the Assumption University of Windsor in 1957.

This was an extraordinary act of ecumenism since it was the first, and so far, the only affiliation of an Anglican college with a Catholic university, and occurred well before Vatican II[24].

It was most interesting to note that the enquiries made by the Vatican as to the nature of this affiliation – in the person of Cardinal Cardinali, regarded by many at the subsequent Vatican Council as an arch-reactionary – were obviously couched in such a way as to encourage answers which could be approved – and so they were.

I had been writing a certain amount when on the faculty, and this ultimately led to enquiries from Britain as to the possibility of my being available to join the Royal Household there in that department known as the College of Arms – apparently some Commonwealth representation was considered desirable. Such an appointment obviously held great attraction. If I accepted, I would be not only the first Canadian, but also the first herald appointed not from the British Isles since Roger de Machado, apparently a Portuguese, in *c.* April 1483[25]. So, and not without a degree of regret, in 1961 I resigned from the faculty of Assumption University of Windsor; packed up and moved to England – with my wife, Hilda, our first-born baby, Elizabeth, and 17 cases of household goods.

As our ship had an Italian crew, we could leave Elizabeth with the bursar when we went to dinner; he and his staff spoiled her terribly, but she has turned out to be a marvellous daughter (and has kindly typed up this manuscript). The cabin porter was a young man from Naples, efficient and obliging. He told us his wife, whom he had recently married, was beautiful and called Maria.

Upon returning to our cabin each night, I noticed that the bed was always well turned down. My blue silk pyjamas had been laid out neatly, side by side, yet rigidly. On the other side of the bed, Hilda's black georgette nightie – a silhouette against the white under-sheet – had been arranged like an hourglass. The bodice was all puckered up; the hip area invitingly broad – how that young cabin porter must have missed his Maria di Napoli!

---

[24] Swan, Rev. Dr P.J.M. *Peter Swan's Memoirs*. St Michael's College, Toronto, 2001 p.35. The author was the Registrar of the university at the time and had taken a leading part in the discussions between the Rt Rev. George Luxton, Bishop of Huron (on behalf of the Anglicans) and the Rt. Rev. J. C. Cody, Bishop of London, Chancellor of the university.

[25] Leicester Herald *c.* April, 1483; he finished up as Clarenceux King of Arms in 1493.

Edna Hanson Magdalen, Mrs H.P. Swan. Decorated by Pope John-Paul II with the Cross of Honour pro Ecclesia et Pontifice *for her charitable work particularly in respect of Concentration Camp victims. Shown here in an evening gown she had made in Paris, 1925. Mother of the Author.   SSA.*

Major General Cosmo A.R. Nevill, CB, CBE, DSO: The College of Arms and St Benet's Church (red brick) with St Paul's Cathedral in the background, prior to the completion of the City of London School (1986) between them and the River Thames.   SSA.

Garter (the Author, standing on the right in tabard) about to conduct the Introduction Ceremony of the Lord Menuhin (second from the left) into the House of Lords, with his Supporters (extreme left) the Lord Armstrong of Ilminster, sometime Secretary of the Cabinet, and the Lord Jacobovits, Emeritus Rabbi of the United Hebrew Congregation of Great Britain and the Commonwealth. 20 July 1993. Courtesy of Universal Pictorial Press & Agency Ltd.

Insignia of a Companion of the Order of Canada. Created by H.M. The Queen of Canada, 21 March 1967. Courtesy of Rideau Hall.

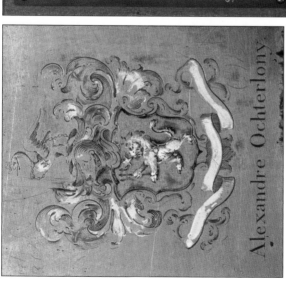

'Triple firsts!' Left, the first American herald: Alexander Ochterlony, Blanch Lyon Pursuivant of Arms, born at Boston, 1764, step-son of Sir Isaac Heard Garter Principal King of Arms; centre: the first Prime Minister of Canada, the Rt. Hon. Sir John A. Macdonald, GCB. 1867-73 & 1878-91; right: the first Canadian herald, the Author, York Herald of Arms as Genealogist of the Order of the Bath – plates in the chapel of the Order, Henry VII's, Westminster Abbey. Courtesy of the Dean and Chapter of Westminster.

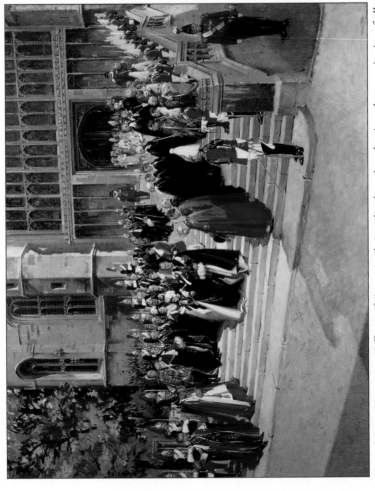

Standing towards the foot of the steps are two Officers of Arms (each in tabard, and at the time the most junior of all the heralds) left to the viewer, and wearing glasses: Rodney Dennys, OBE, Rouge Croix Pursuivant of Arms and right to the viewer, the Author, Rouge Dragon Pursuivant of Arms – the most junior. Terence Cunio: Departure following the Order of the Garter Service, St. George's Chapel, Windsor, 15 June, 1964. The Royal Collection, ©Her Majesty Queen Elizabeth II.

The National Flag of Canada established by H.M. The Queen of Canada by Royal Proclamation, 1965, which also brought into being a new term in blazonry: a Canadian Pale.   SSA.

In Canada primus. *The first occasion that an Officer of Arms carried out duties in Canada, attending upon the Lieutenant Governor of Ontario when he presented a Patent of Arms to the University of St Michael's College, Toronto, 29 November, 1980. Extreme left, the Vice-Chancellor of the University, the Rev. Dr P.J.M. Swan, CSB, PhD, brother of the Author on extreme right wearing Herald's Royal Household uniform; between them, left, their mother, Mrs Edna H. Swan, and centre right, their aunt-by-marriage, Mrs Edna F. Green. SSA.*

HRH Princess Anne, Patron of the Riding for the Disabled Association, with the Lady Hilda Swan, Suffolk County Chairman, RDA, and children making a Presentation to the Princess. Hadleigh, Suffolk, 3 June 1985. SSA.

The Quincentenary of the foundation of the College of Arms, 2 March 1984. Seated: left to right, (all Officers of Arms-in-Ordinary unless otherwise specified): D.B.H. Chesshyre (Chester); J.P.B. Brooke-Little, CVO (Norroy & Ulster); Miles, 17th Duke of Norfolk, KG, Earl Marshal; Sir Colin Cole, KCVO (Garter); Sir Anthony Wagner, KCB, KCVO (Clarenceux); the Author (York); T.D. Mathew (Windsor). Second row: T.D. McCarthy (Bluemantle); P.L. Dickinson (Rouge Dragon); P. Ll. Gwynne-Jones (Lancaster); M. Maclagan (Richmond); T. Woodcock (Somerset); P.B. Spurrier (Portcullis); H.E. Paston-Bedingfield (Rouge Croix). Third row: (all Offices of Arms Extraordinary): R.O. Dennys, CVO, OBE (Arundel); Sir Walter Verco, KCVO (Surrey); G.D. Squibb, MVO (Norfolk); Francis Jones, CVO (Wales); F.S. Andrus, MVO (Beaumont); Dr. J. Martin Robinson (Fitzalan). Credit: 'Veryan'.

Left: The Author, York Herald, Senior Herald-in-Waiting and Registrar, greets The Queen; J.P.B. Brooke-Little, Norroy and Ulster King of Arms, greets the Duke of Edinburgh; Garter Cole supervises the occasion – all under the 'security eye' of Mr Peter Marshall, QPM, Commissioner of Police for the City of London.

Right: 'Edinburgh quizzical; York indicative'. Photographs taken by Garter Cole's well-known portrait painter son, Christopher Cole, by whose courtesy they appear as illustrations. Royal Visit to the College of Arms during its Quincentenary year, 15 November, 1984.

Cum Regina Canada primus in Canada. *The Queen of Canada – for the first time attended there by an Officer of Arms – signs Royal Warrants (in English and French) establishing Crest and Supporters for her pre-existing ensigns of Dominion and Sovereignty of particular purpose in right of British Columbia. Left, the Author, York Herald, and right the Hon. David Crombie, PC, MP, Secretary of State of Canada. Vancouver, 15 October 1987. Ian Lindsay/Vancouver Sun.*

The Author, Garter Principal King of Arms, with Lady Hilda Swan, their daughter, Juliana Galvin and son, Andrew Swan. Taken at Buckingham Palace following Sir Conrad's investiture as a Knight Commander of the Royal Victorian Order. 24 June 1994. Photograph by Charles Green.

A family gathering at Boxford House. Lady Hilda sits third from right; the Author stands behind her. 'Some of our best friends in Suffolk would remark, upon occasion. "Those b...y Swans are trying to populate the county"!   S.S.A.

173

Grand Collar of the Most Distinguished Order of the Nation (Antigua & Barbuda) with sash – each with relevant dependant Badge – and the Star of the Order. (Her Majesty's suite). Insignia designed jointly by HE the Governor General, Sir James Carlisle, GCMG, and Philip Eagleton, Esq., of Worth, Bahamas. The Royal Collection, ©Her Majesty Queen Elizabeth II.

Badges of office of (upper row, left to right) Grand Master, Chancellor and Secretary of the Orders of Chivalry of Antigua & Barbuda with (second row, left and right, respectively) Antigua Herald *and* Barbuda Herald. *Courtesy of the Chancery of Orders and Decorations, Government House, Antigua.*

CHAPTER VIII

From the Banks of the Detroit to the Strands of the Thames: Rouge Dragon Pursuivant of Arms to Garter Principal King of Arms

'GOOD GOD! A PhD, at the College of Arms, what next?!' So said that peppery Irishman, the Honble Sir George Bellew[1] on hearing of my appointment. Ironically, one of the most important influences towards my interest in heraldry had been the same Bellew's article on the heraldry of the 'Black Napoleon', *Henry Christophe, roi de Hayti* (1811-1820) in *The Illustrated London News* of June 1934[2]. Just 10 years old at the time, I was so inspired by it that I laboriously, if crudely, copied out the arms of the king illustrated in the article and kept it ever since. Be the downy head of the dandelion n'er so beautiful, beware when the wind blows – *n'est ce pas*?!

Bellew's remark expressed an attitude to be found among certain groups in the United Kingdom: 'Ah yes, a PhD or DPhil. (Oxon) is our export degree, don't you know.' Be that as it may, I have always noticed that those who make such comments have never submitted themselves to the laborious discipline of original research towards a thesis; writing it up, and defending the result in a *viva voce* – all 'in course', as the phrase goes. As for the good Sir George, he was nonetheless a man of exquisite taste in many ways. A gallant Squadron Leader in the RAFVR, (despatches and all that) during World War II; he had, nevertheless, come down from Oxford without any degree at all. So much for his opinion on post-graduate degrees.

On the other hand, his successor – and reigning Garter at the time – was quite different in his attitude towards scholarship and its outward, academic signs: Sir Anthony Wagner, KCVO, MA(Oxon) and a DLitt, no less. Granted, his doctorate was not received in course, nevertheless, it was a well-deserved academic accolade in recognition of his masterly writings, especially in the field of historical genealogy. This was awarded before he became Garter and until he was

---

[1] The recently retired Garter Principal King of Arms Portcullis Pursuivant, 1922; Somerset Herald, 1926; Garter Principal King of Arms, 1950-61.

[2] Bellew, G.R. 'Strange Heraldry for a Nego Aristocracy: The 'Register of Arms' of King Henry Christophe's Haitian Court. *The Illustrated London News*, 16 June, 1934 pp.964-965. This was based upon the *Armorial Général du Royaume de Hayti*, a holding of the College of Arms.

knighted he was proud to be addressed at all times as 'Dr Wagner'. So one may form some idea of his attitude when Dr Swan joined the College – the first PhD in all its history of half a millennium.

This I did by virtue of Letters Patent dated 10 December, 1962[3], issued under the Great Seal of the Realm by Her Majesty The Queen with the 'name style title liberty and pre-eminence' of Rouge Dragon[4] Pursuivant of Arms, being the fiftieth holder since the creation of that office in 1485[5] by the Welsh Henry VII.

Prior to the issue of this patent, several hoops had to be jumped through. One of these was an interview with the Earl Marshal. This is the man who has the duty of nomination in respect of Officers of Arms for appointment by the Sovereign into the College of Arms. The Earl Marshal in this instance was Bernard, 16th Duke of Norfolk – the one who, aged 29, it will be recalled, organized the coronation of King George VI. Our meeting took place in the Jockey Club on Carlton House Terrace – he was much devoted to the horse. From the point of view of presenting myself, I felt that the interview was my worst ever. However, he must have felt otherwise, as he nominated me.

Another hoop had been a period of working in Garter's chambers in order both to be looked over, and to have the opportunity of seeing the College from the inside. No institution is ever quite the same when experienced from within as it actually is in contrast to being viewed from without.

The antiquity of the College and its labyrinthine ways of almost Byzantine complexity stimulated me. On the other hand, it would appear that 'they' found that I knew how to eat peas with a knife and fork!

My work in the Garter's chambers consisted mainly of indexing and cataloguing the Garter Papers, as they were called: the extensive records of that office.

This gave me an invaluable insight into the workings and character of the College. One soon realized how over hundreds of years the officers had managed to keep the College afloat – if only just at times – so that the accumulation, maintenance and preservation of the incomparable College records, were achieved. Also the upkeep of the fabric of the building – old historic buildings require constant attention – was on the same basis. Furthermore, there is the question of paying the wages of the small ancillary staff of the College itself such as the porters and scriveners (as distinct from the staff of each officer, which is his responsibility alone). All of this had been done, and

---

[3] *The London Gazette*, 11 December, 1962 p. 9648. The original is held SSA. I was the last Officer of Arms-in-Ordinary from whom the 100 guineas joining fee was levied.

[4] The origin of the Red Dragon device of Wales (the Red Dragon of Cadwalader) stems from such a device of the Roman army, the memory of which was carried into the fastnesses of Wales by the original inhabitants of Britain, soon to be England when driven out by the invading Angles, Saxons and Jutes.

[5] 29 October 1485, the eve of the coronation of the king.

is still, without a single penny from the Government. When Agencies – official bodies responsible for their own financing through fees – were set up in the United Kingdom under the then Prime Minister, Mrs Margaret Thatcher, this development was hailed as a master-stroke of modern administration. None seemed to recall that we of the College of Arms had been doing just that for pressing 500 years – and it does work!

The money for all this is raised mainly from fees exigible upon grants of armorial bearings being made by Letters Patent. If a person or institution is deemed by the Earl Marshal worthy of such an exercise of the royal prerogative by the Kings of Arms, a fee is charged to cover the 30 or so 'movements' concerned with the issue of a Patent granting armorial bearings. These range from the initial investigation to ascertain if the Earl Marshal is likely to agree that they may be granted; through the painting and scrivening of the Patent; its recording and final handing over.

Of the fees charged to cover all this, some 85% goes to the College treasury for the maintenance of the official records and the building as already described. The balance of about 15% is returned to the Officer Agent for his time and trouble in all this.

A smaller proportion of the total College income derives from the fees charged for entering genealogies in the College records upon the completion of the process described later. So the entire financing of the College is the result of the efforts of the heralds, and their success over the centuries despite, at times, great difficulties redounds to their eternal honour.

The source of this financing is the professional practice of each herald in matters armorial and genealogical. The 'annuity or annual salary' – to quote from the Patent of Appointment of each officer – laid down as payable from the Privy Purse of the Sovereign is:

For a Pursuivant:	£13.95 (about $Can. 25.00)
For a Herald:	£17.80 (about $Can. 34.00)
For a Provincial King:	£20.25 (about $Can. 40.00)
For a Garter:	£49.07 (about $Can. 95.00)

there has been a pay-pause since the reign of William IV (1830-37)[6]! So it will be appreciated that unless the officer has private means, he must address himself assiduously.

There is, however, a certain equity in all this, in that an officer is only required

---

[6] With £1 in 1830 worth £42.27 in 2000 terms (according to the Bank of England) the annual annuity would have had the following purchasing power at the time:

Pursuivant	c. £590 (about $Can. 1,180) p.a.
Herald	c. £760 (about $Can. 1,520) p.a.
Provincial King	c. £845 (about $Can. 1,790) p.a.
Garter	c. £2,100 (about $Can. 4,200) p.a.

to assist at all state ceremonies, and to carry out his duty periods (called 'Waits' when he is the Officer-in-Waiting), which occur for one week at a time about every 9 weeks (the Kings do not Wait) when the College is at full complement. Otherwise he can, within reason, do as he wishes.

Quite apart from people coming to one privately – because of books or articles written or lectures given – the Waits are the main occasions for generating income for the officers, as during these they receive and handle all callers at the College who do not ask to see a specific officer. Further, they handle all correspondence addressed simply to the College of Arms and not to a specific officer. Once an officer has taken on such an assignment, all work derived therefrom goes into his personal practice.

My work on the Garter Papers made it quite clear to me that, as the result of these arrangements, a considerable rivalry exists between officers. Good humour usually prevailed, but on occasion it degenerated into envy; knives were long and sharp, and feuds were carried on beyond the grave. 'Shades of C.P. Snow's *The Masters*?!' I thought to myself. At the time this portrait of donnish rivalry was still much discussed. Later, during my 33 years at the College I found that things had not really changed that much, and the sin just mentioned, that gives no pleasure to anyone, did venture to surface in the odd corner from time to time. As we are all human and subject to Original Sin, I suppose it is a wonder that it does not break out more often.

The fact that the officers do not mess together, as in a regiment, can cause an isolation which heightens such feelings. Two or three officers will, quite often, strike up real friendships, frequently lunch and dine together, become godfathers to one another's children and so on. But because all 13 are not working together – but in competition, cheek by jowl in the same building, sharing the same records, all under one roof – regimental camaraderie is scarcely nourished. Yet in my fellow heralds I learnt to appreciate their virtues as well as to tolerate lack of the same, hoping that they would in charity return the compliment.

When I had chambers at the College in which one could give lunch and dinner parties, from 1968 onwards, my wife and I would quite frequently entertain other officers and their wives (in rotation for obvious reasons) during the remainder of my 25 years at the College. Yet, there were only two occasions upon which all officers ate together. The first was on 30 March 1967, when we entertained at St James's Palace the Earl Marshal upon the fiftieth anniversary of his succeeding to that office; and second, on 1 October, 1984 when we held a dinner party in the College itself to mark its quincentenary. So none could accuse of us of hedonistic orgies of wining and dining together!

The function of the College of Arms is, basically, threefold: ceremonial, armorial and genealogical. Under the Earl Marshal[7], it is responsible for the

---

[7] The Earl Marshal is not the head of the College of Arms. In academic terms he would be the *Visitor* and is ultimately responsible for discipline.

mounting of all State Occasions in England: coronations, state openings of parliament, state funerals and so on, the members of the College act as his staff officers.

In matters armorial, the College is a double registry: of arms, crests, supporters and badges, whether granted personally by the sovereign, or on the latter's behalf by the Kings of Arms.

Its third and other main function, is as a registry of genealogies. These are researched and prepared by one officer (called the Agent); examined by two other officers (called the Senior and Junior Examiners); appointed by the Chapter (the governing body of the College) against the evidences (Birth, Marriage, Death Certificates, Monumental Inscriptions and so on, all in accordance with the Law of Evidence); and produced by the Agent. When the two Examiners are satisfied that the case has been made then, upon their recommendation, the genealogy is entered in the official records of the College of Arms upon the order of Chapter. All these records are evidence producible in a court of law.

As the records date back for six or more centuries, they comprise an invaluable source of both historical and current information. They are considered to be the oldest and most comprehensive collection of their kind in the world. Their subject matter pertains not only to England but also to all those areas sometime of the British Empire – no matter the name or constitution obtaining in a specific instance today[8].

As to the origins of heralds, they began as umpires at tournaments, those great sporting events of the Middle Ages. The participating contestants were knights. Completely encased in armour, they could only be identified by the devices displayed on their surcoats (hence the term, 'coats of arms') and on their shields and the like. As a result, the heralds had to become familiar with armorial bearings. Further, the tournaments being extremely ceremonious, they became, as it were, professors of ceremony. It is from these two aspects of the tournaments that their future and current functions stem.

At first they appear to have been attached to private individuals as with Lancaster Herald (for whom the earliest reference is 1347), serving the Dukes of Lancaster. Gradually all heralds were brought into the royal household and, finally, in 1484 were incorporated by Richard III as the Corporation of the Kings Heralds and Pursuivants of Arms[9], otherwise known as the College of Arms and sometimes colloquially, as the Heralds College.

---

[8] Other officials and official bodies similar to the College of Arms today are: the Lord Lyon King of Arms of Scotland; the Canadian Heraldic Authority; the Chief Herald of the Republic of Ireland; the *Cronista rey de Armas* (Spain); the Bureau of Heraldry of the Republic of South Africa; the College of Arms of Kenya; – the *Hoge Rad van Adel* (The Netherlands); the *Conseil Héraldique de Belgique;* the *Conseiller Héraldique de l'Etat Danois*; the State Herald of Sweden.

[9] For the text *vide* Squibb, G.D. ed. *Munimenta Heraldica MCCCCLXXXIV to MCMLXXXIV*, The Harleian Society, New Series Vol. 4, London 1985, pp. 14-19.

The complement of the College is 13 in number and comprises:

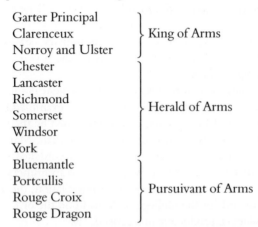

Garter Principal Clarenceux Norroy and Ulster	King of Arms
Chester Lancaster Richmond Somerset Windsor York	Herald of Arms
Bluemantle Portcullis Rouge Croix Rouge Dragon	Pursuivant of Arms

All 13 are Officers of Arms-in-Ordinary, that is to say they are full-time members of the corporation of the College of Arms. From time to time Officers of Arms Extraordinary are appointed for particular purposes because of their expertise, but they are not members of the corporation, though closely associated with it.

It should be understood that the College of Arms is not an academic institution but a *collegium* carrying out official functions as with the College of Cardinals, the American College of Electors and similar bodies.

Needing somewhere to house its, by then, voluminous records, the College was given, by Queen Mary Tudor, Derby House[10]. On a site between St Paul's Cathedral and the River Thames, this was burned down in the Great Fire of 1666 – though, I hasten to add, all the records were saved by being put on a barge and taken up river to Whitehall Palace, from which the heralds functioned while their present building was erected and completed by, on the same site as Derby House, 1688. It was the first purpose-built office block in the City of London[11]. It now faces onto Queen Victoria Street[12].

The building is occupied on the basis of (though at times more) one main room for a pursuivant, two for a herald, three for each of the two provincial Kings (Clarenceux and Norroy & Ulster). As for Garter, he has a whole house, and some, in the past, have had their families living there.

---

[10] *Ibid* pp 20-25.

[11] For details of the building of the present building vide Godfrey, Walter H. assisted by Sir Anthony Wagner, Garter King of Arms. *The College of Arms Monograph*. London Survey Committee, London, 1963 pp 11-19.

[12] In 1867 a street was made from the Embankment up to the Bank of England in order to get the troops there if necessary. This necessitated pulling down some buildings which included the fourth side of the College of Arms, which as a result now faces to the south and so towards the River Thames.

When I was promoted to be York Herald of Arms in 1968[13], my first set comprised the three rooms (including a kitchen) overlooking the courtyard on the main floor. Some dozen years later I had the good fortune to be able to move into what I considered to be the best herald's set of all: three large rooms and a hall on the second floor overlooking the courtyard. There were also kitchen facilities which, combined with the size of the rooms, made entertaining easy.

Upon entering the College of Arms as Rouge Dragon Pursuivant of Arms I was, obviously, the most junior in precedence. Nevertheless I had the good fortune soon to acquire as assistant John Charles Grossesmith George. With his family name and my heraldic title we soon, inevitably, became known as 'George and the Dragon'. Later on I was sorry to lose him, but pleased to have been able to assist in his appointment as Kintyre Pursuivant of Arms at the Lyon Court in Scotland, and ultimately Linlithgow Pursuivant of Arms Extraordinary. Ultimately, he became the only Pursuivant in history, known to me, to have been knighted as he was by Pope John-Paul II (in the Order of St Gregory the Great – Patent of appointment dated 11 June 2002).

Upon my appointment as a Pursuivant in the College, and in accordance with the rising order of precedence, the other **Pursuivants** (equivalent to subalterns and captains in military terms) were:

Rodney Onslow Dennys, Rouge Croix – about whom more later.

John Philip Brooke Brooke-Little, Bluemantle ('Bluebottle' to his friends). He was a *confrère* of mine in the Order of Malta and would become the godfather of our second daughter, Juliana; about him more later.

(Alexander) Colin Cole, Portcullis. Barrister of the Inner Temple; as a captain in the Grenadier Guards he had a distinguished career in World War II (invasion of Europe and so on). When he became Garter Principal King of Arms in 1978 one felt a fresh breeze blowing through the College. Like the good regimental officer that he was, he tried to live in peace and help his brother-officers. A loyal friend and good companion. I was to become the godfather of one of his daughters. We, all four of us, were excellent friends.

The Heralds (equivalent to majors, half and full colonels and brigadiers in military terms. With a lower case 'h' it is a generic term used in respect of any officer of arms; with an upper case, it identifies a specific grade among those officers). Once again, in ascending order of precedence they were:

John George Verco, Chester – the 'commissioned ranker'. He came to the College as a tea-boy; ended up as Norroy & Ulster King of Arms (1971-80) and Knight Commander of the Royal Victorian Order (1981) – all by sheer merit. There was little he did not know about the workings of the College, and the

---

[13] 4 June, 1968. *The London Gazette*, 6 June 1968 p. 6411. The original Letters Patent are held SSA.

heralds! He was full of wisdom, especially if 'according to the book'. A little non-plussed upon the arrival of the ACLiP (Anglo-Canadian Lithuanian-Pole) with a wife of British title – there was nothing in the book about that. However, we soon became good friends. He and his wife, 'Peggy' would from time to time stay with Hilda and me at our Suffolk place. They seemed delighted to be driven round the country lanes in our horse-drawn governess cart.

I am told that to outsiders interested in the College Verco would say, 'Keep an eye on Swan'. What did he mean by that? When I eventually became Garter he could not have been more generous in his delight. During the last five or so years of his life (he died aged 94 in 2001) he was in a residential home in Sussex. Every month we would speak over the telephone, and to the end he was avid for news about the institution he had served so well.

Robin Ian Evelyn Stuart de la Lanne-Mirrlees, Richmond. Captain, R.A. Served in India in World War II. Later was an attaché in our embassy in Tokyo. ADC to King Peter of Yugoslavia; through his mother, a Count (of France). A man of wide ranging experience and interests. In the early days of my practice he was most kind in passing over to me many worthwhile cases which helped it to develop more quickly so that in the end it rivalled that of Garter Wagner. A confrere in the Order of Malta, and a godfather to our son, Andrew, he used to joke with me that as we were so spiritually related at the College through all these godparenthoods, it would take a papal dispensation for any of our children to marry! A rich man, when he retired from the College he went to look after the crofters on his estate on Great Bernera Island, Outer Hebrides.

(Charles) Murray Kennedy St Clair, 8th/17th Baron Sinclair (Scottish creation 1449), York. Major, Coldstream Guards (wounded, despatches World War II). Representative Peer for Scotland. It was said that he had been considered as a possible husband for Princess Margaret, but made a happy marriage elsewhere. Upon his resignation from the College in 1968 to look after his estate in Kirkcudbrightshire, I suceeded him as 39th York Herald of Arms[14].

John Ridell Bromhead Walker, Lancaster.
Lieutenant Colonel, 14th Sikhs, and so the penultimate Indian Army officer at the College, I being the last. Registrar of the College when I joined. Often referred to himself as 'just a simple soldier' but, in fact, a competent administrator. He and I frequently dined together at a nearby Indian restaurant. Our conversation was completely *Koi hai*, and would have bored our other colleagues to death. He was deliciously Protestant: typical middle-of-the-road, no nonsense Anglican, but we got on extremely well and shared the same *Raj* humour. His assistant was a Mrs Margaret Marshall – sometime of the WRNS. She became particularly knowledgeable over regimental colours when helping

---

[14] SSA. Original patent dated 4 June 1968

Lancaster look after this work for the then Garter who, though Inspector of Regimental Colours, had no experience of the Army. She was also *au fait* with every current in the College and an invaluable source of domestic intelligence.

Michael Roger Trappes-Lomax, Somerset.
Major, Scots Guards. Brother of the brigadier mentioned in connection with my time at Bangalore. An expert on the Gothic revival architect, Pugin. A fellow Knight of Malta. If at about 7p.m. one felt the need of a pre-prandial, one would be welcomed into his chambers with a double gin and tonic. However, one had not to mind his habit of sitting around naked, cooling off from a very hot bath. I never heard anyone say anything unkind about him – an achievement at the College!

(Richard) Preston Graham-Vivian, M.C., Windsor.
Lieutenant, KRRC in World War I – wounded, which left him with a permanent limp. A personal friend of Edward VIII. Had that monarch stuck to his duty, Windsor could well have expected other interesting appointments.

The Kings in order of precedence, starting with the two provincial Kings (equivalent to major and lieutenant general in military terms) were:

Aubrey John Toppin, Norroy & Ulster. Captain, 3rd Special Reserve Battalion, Royal Irish Rifles during World War I. Upon walking to take up his first post with the Science & Art Museum, Dublin, on 23 January, 1901 he noticed that all the flags were at half-mast. Enquiring the reason, he learned that the old Queen had died during the night. He was proud to be able to say that he had been appointed to public service under Queen Victoria. An expert on porcelain. He did much to bring the officers and various staff at the College closer together. From time to time, deciding that I could do with some good food, he would invite me to dine at his club, the Athenaeum (the club of which it is perhaps more justly said than of any other that after not moving for a week from your leather armchair in the library, they consider you may be dead!). This club is located at the foot of Lower Regent Street, already referred to in Chapter V. Of the Irish Ascendancy he was an example of its best sort.

Sir John Dunamace Heaton-Armstrong, Clarenceux.
Squadron Leader, RAFVR, World War II. Upon my joining the College he and I shared the entire first floor of the west wing: his chambers occupied three-quarters; mine the rest. With Austrian mother and grandmother, he was the epitome of the Austrian *Adel*. Little wonder, he had been addressed by none other than the Emperor Franz-Josef himself in the second person singular when out with the monarch hunting chamois. He was extremely kind and welcoming to me. When the von Trapp family (of singing fame) escaped from Austria because of the *Anschluss* their first night in London was spent in Sir John's home.

The appointment of a senior herald to a provincial kingship is regarded, frequently, as an opportunity to make provision for retirement: there being no pensions for officers from the College of Arms.

Sir Anthony Richard Wagner, KCVO, Garter (equivalent to a full general in military terms).

As a civilian served in the War Office, 1939-43, and Ministry of Town and Country Planning, 1943-46. At the very apex of genealogical and heraldic writing when I entered the College. One felt that the motto of my natal province might be applied to him: *Splendor sine occasu*[15]. Yet, as at the time of preparations for the investiture of Prince Charles as Prince of Wales at Caernarvon Castle in 1969, one occasionally sympathized with Lord Snowdon, whose patience had been tested to the limit, [when he] said wearily, 'Garter, darling, do try to be more elastic'(!)[16] More about Garter Wagner, later[17].

The Officers of Arms-Extraordinary, in ascending order of precedence, were:

Charles Wilfred Scott-Giles, OBE, FSA Fitzalan Pursuivant of Arms Extraordinary.

A popular, prolific heraldic author of such works as, *The Romance of Heraldry* (1929 & 1940) and *Shakespeare's Heraldry* (1950 & 1971). He illustrated all his books himself. (During World War II, I was to receive a prize while at St George's College. When asked what kind of book I would like, I replied, one on heraldry. At that time, the then recently re-published (1940) edition of *The Romance of Heraldry* was duly obtained. It was a monument to British determination to uphold civilization: the paper used was a cross between cardboard and a very low class lavatory paper, but the text and black and white line drawings were excellent).

George Drewry Squibb, LVO, QC, FSA, FR HistS
Norfolk Herald of Arms Extraordinary.

Chairman of Dorset Quarter Sessions, 1959-71; Junior Counsel to the Crown in Peerage and Baronetcy cases, 1954-56; Historical Adviser in Peerage cases to the Attorney-General from 1956; Earl Marshal's Lieutenant, Accessor and Surigate in the Court of Chivalry, from 1976, etc. Author of *The Law of Arms in England* (1953), *The High Court of Chivalry* (1959) and many other works.

---

[15] 'Splendour without diminishing.'
[16] Obituary for Carl Toms who collaborated with Snowdon on the spectacular setting created within the castle for the investiture: *The Daily Telegraph*, 12 Aug. 1999.
[17] For further details on the heralds of this period vide Chesshyre, Hubert. Chester Herald and Ailes, Adrian, *Heralds of Today*. Van Duren, Gerrards Cross, 1986.

Francis William Steer, DLitt, FSA, FRHistS
Maltravers Herald of Arms Extraordinary.
County Archivist of East and West Sussex, 1953-59, and of West Sussex, 1959-69;
Archivist and Librarian to the Duke of Norfolk from 1956. Prolific writer on
historical subjects and cataloguer.

Dermot Michael MacGregor Morah
Arundel Herald of Arms Extraordinary.
Journalist: Leader-writer for the *Daily Mail*, 1928-31, *The Times*, 1933-61, *The Daily Telegraph*, 1961-67, etc. Writer on history, constitutional law, imperial affairs, heraldry with special reference to coronation and other ceremonial. The office of Arundel was revived especially for him for the 1953 coronation.

Officers of Arms address each other, all *cognoscenti* do, by their titles: "morning, Rouge Croix'; 'Is Clarenceux free at the moment?' and so on; after all, there is only one of each title in the world, so why beat around the bush?
To give some idea of the workings of a herald's practice, I describe below, in diary form, the first and last days of a week's Wait. All the events took place at one time or another. They are concertinaed here for the sake of economy of space.

Monday.
6a.m. Up at Boxford. Fed animals ('Vesuvius' – Hilda's Jersey cow – has not erupted yet with a calf, but from the signs at the business end it should not be long).
Quick breakfast and off the 14 miles to Colchester railway station – said morning prayers as I drove along so as to fit *multum in parvo*. Caught 8.30a.m train; arrived Liverpool Street Station, 9.20a.m.
Fine day so walked (15 minutes) to the College. Arrived in good time for its opening at 10a.m, and for my duty week as the Officer-in-Waiting. Noticed the porter had, as per custom, put up outside the banner of my arms to identify the Waiting Officer.

9.45a.m. Collected my post and also the pile of letters not addressed to a specific officer. Took the Waiting Book; drew a line under the list of entries for the last Wait; wrote 'York. 20-25 May 19…'. Opened the unspecified letters and entered: date received, name of enquirer, and nature of enquiry such as: 'Identification of Crest', 'Genealogical Research' and so on[18].

---

[18] This record was kept up to date so that there was no doubt in future which officer was approached first. As the practice of an officer much depended on those Waits this could be an important point.

The family arms of the Author are shown surrounded by a Herald's silver collar of S's. His official badge as York Herald – the White Rose of York en soleil *– ensigns the design. Original design by Geoffrey Mussett for the Seal of the Author, York Herald of Arms along with male and female matrices for sealing* en placard. *Photography by Peter Norris.   SSA.*

10.05a.m. Back in chambers. My Secretary and the researchers had arrived[19].

Started to dictate on a tape answers to unspecified letters; indicated recommended course of action along with fee, adding that upon receipt of reply I would be pleased to proceed as outlined. At the College all fees are payable in advance.

10.30a.m. The receptionist of the College rings up my secretary to say there is 'a lady with an enquiry'. She is invited up.

When she arrives, she gives the secretary a simple form she has completed: her

---

[19] Secretaries, researchers and any other staff of an officer are entirely his responsibility as to hiring, firing and terms of employment. So in one building there were, usually, no less than 13 completely separate staffs, plus the small College of Arms staff.

name and address and the nature of her enquiry. I stand as she, one Mrs Brown, is shown in; greet her and ask her to be seated. She explains that she has bought three armorial plates on the well-known market in London, Portobello Road.

I study the plates and indicate which are likely to prove worth researching towards identification, and which not. The fee is quoted, and I say this will be confirmed in writing. Mrs Brown pays right away, and a receipt is prepared. As I see her to the door, I indicate how long I anticipate the work will take, and when she might expect the report on the findings.

10.30a.m. Returned to dictating answers to to-day's unspecified letters and answered phone call enquiries.

11.05a.m. Keith Evans, Clerk of the Records, came with several Letters Patent for me to endorse in my capacity as Registrar. Left these, for me to attend to later, with their photocopies from which the actual records of the College are to be scrivened later. He also wanted to discuss two Patents to be prepared in French for Canadian clients. Reminded him to be careful *not* to split a word at the end of a line in the English manner: arabesques can always be used to fill the resultant gaps.

When I came to the College in '62, Evans was a young trainee under William Thomas Lovegrove, the Clerk of the Records – a great artist, as Evans is now. One weekend Lovegrove went home and died before the following Monday. There was much head-shaking at the College. 'What to do? Evans is so young. He's only been here for 10 years.' The then Registrar (Lancaster, Col John Walker) cut the Gordian knot by saying, 'I recommend, we say to Evans: if you do the job of Clerk of the Records to Chapter's satisfaction for 6 months, you're in.' Evans did; and was. (He still holds that position while I write this book).

12.50p.m. Went across to Somerset's (Rodney Dennys's) chambers and said, 'For the love of God, Rodney, have you any sherry? El Vino's'[20] haven't sent round my monthly order yet. After a hard morning I'm dying for a drink before lunch.' He obliges and we discuss some of his plans for the heralds' museum in the Tower of London[21]. He offers me 'the other half' before I return to my set for a smoked salmon sandwich my secretary has brought in, as I am in Waiting and it is preferable not to leave the College during hours.

1.05-2p.m. Try to deal with correspondence over some of my cases.

2p.m. Thomas Woodard and Mrs Margaret Monger – full-time researchers – come in to discuss a case. Tom is one of the leading researchers[22] and was a great

[20] Of Fleet Street, well known wine bar and merchants. When I was at the College, ladies could go and sit at the tables and drink but not stand at the bar – to the great fury of some!
[21] Of which he was Deputy Director and then Director.
[22] When he died he had been at the College of Arms for over 70 years.

help to Garter Wagner in producing the material for his major cases and books. Mrs Monger has been trained by him. I have had the good fortune to secure their services.

2.30p.m. A part-time assistant wants to discuss a case, as she's come up against a 'brick wall' through lack of evidences. We discuss the case and I tell her to write to the client explaining the problem. 'Say the likelihood of any further positive results is remote. Tell the client what is still held on account, and say this sum will be returned unless it is desired to do something else with it at the College.'

3.40p.m. The receptionist rings up to ask if York would like to receive a lady in the Waiting Room. This is a coded message to say that a caller is either crippled or cannot manage the stairs. In my case: four half flights up to my chambers – lifts/elevators were unknown in the late 1600s when the College was built.

So I go down to the room on the ground floor next to the Earl Marshal's Court, which latter is also the entrance hall. The room has dark panelling – behind it are presses for books (the location of the original College records). The carving is in the Grinling Gibbons style but is, in fact, by William Emmett, brother of Morris, the architect of the College. Over the door, leading into the Record Room a shield of the current Garter hangs; shields of all the other present officers continue on round over the panelling. Against the dark woodwork, their bright colours make a wonderful contrast. The room is called the Waiting Room as it is where the Officer-in-Waiting may receive callers if for some reason he does not wish to do so in his own chambers. As it is a passage to the Record Room it is not always convenient, except in instances such as for the present caller, a crippled woman.

It is also used for parties when the officers and staffs get together, as at Christmas. A unique occurrence in this room was when Richmond (Robin de la Lanne-Mirrlees) arranged breakfast for quite a few of us before we took part in the state funeral for Sir Winston Churchill (1965) – of which more later.

The caller's enquiry was easily dealt with.

4p.m. Having helped the caller negotiate the front steps from the College, the porter took down my banner and closed the doors to the public for the day. Like a bank, work continues after closing time. Had a cup of tea at my desk.

5p.m. Having signed the letters for the day, my secretary left. She will be back tomorrow at 9.30a.m., bringing in some tea, and collecting the chambers' milk from the Porter's Lodge on the way up.

Went down to the Record Room to do some work – the first opportunity to do any there during the whole of the day.

6.30p.m. Left the College for the East India Club on St James's Square – not far from Trafalgar Square. Went to have dinner with my old friend Andrew, Count

McMillan (a Portuguese title) and Baron of Cleghorn (a Scottish baronial [manorial] title). Took about half an hour to get there – had to wait some time for a bus by St Paul's Cathedral. Pleasant evening and back at the College for the night by

10p.m. Undressed, said night prayers, read for a while in bed. Lights out at 10.30p.m. – didn't hear anything more than 10.45p.m. struck by the clock on the Cathedral. Woke and heard 2a.m. strike, but soon fell asleep again.

Friday
Up and about at around 7a.m., and after all the usual ceremonials attendant upon first facing the day, was ready for the last of my Wait – until the next some 9 weeks hence.

9a.m. At my desk with a large pile of letters – both those addressed to me, and others to the College in such forms as, 'The Headmaster', 'The Principal', 'The Chief Gunsmith' and so on.

I noticed in my own pile one with familiar handwriting. It was from Gordon Macpherson[23] of Burlington near Toronto, and a fellow British Columbian. He has succeeded to the mantle of Alexander Scott Carter[24] and Alan Beddoe[25] as the doyen of Canadian heraldic artists. He has sent a design for a client who particularly likes his style.

Fred Booth, an artist who works in the College, came down to discuss some work. He is especially good at doing work in a particular style ie in the Victorian style if desired.

Usually the artists who live and work away from the College come in on Thursdays to deliver work and receive new commissions. For some reason most came in to-day.

Frank Berry brought in a three dimensional Crest for my approval as Genealogist of the Order of the Bath. It will be erected over a stall in Henry VII's Chapel, Westminster Abbey.

Geoffrey Musset – the artist whose horses delight even members of the Jockey Club – brought in a Patent on which he had painted a pair as Supporters[26].

Robert Parsons – capable of extremely fine work – brought in a book-plate design.

---

[23] In 2000 was appointed Niagara Herald Extraordinary of the Canadian Heraldic Authority.
[24] The artist of the splendid heraldic display in the Great Hall of Hart House in the University of Toronto.
[25] The books of remembrance in the Peace Tower at Ottawa are among his best known works.
[26] Beasts, birds or human figures that flank a shield of arms and support it. Their possession is considered a great privilege confined to the Sovereign, Princes of the Blood, Peers, Knights Grand Cross, Companions of the Order of Canada, a few persons specifically authorized, and distinguished corporations.

Norman Manwaring – an artist of an original, modern style delivered some work.

There were also some enquiries by phone.

When answering one of the latter I said – having recently been promoted to be a Herald with a capital 'H':

'This is the new York Herald, here.'

The response was a blast that might have broken my eardrum had it not been so tough:

'I don't want a bloody journalist. I want an Officer-of-Arms.'

To this I replied:

'Oh, I should have said, This is the new (lower case 'n') comma York Herald of Arms-in-ordinary to HM The Queen.'

At that the caller seemed to be re-assured and I was able to help him.

After that I deserved the sherry I shared in my room with Somerset (Rodney Dennys) just before my frugal lunch of a couple of smoked salmon sandwiches. El Vino's had at last sent my month's supply of 'medicine' around.

1.30-2.30p.m. The usual selection of lunch-time callers, and then an Australian knight was shown into my room. He had presented to my Secretary his card which she handed on to me. I saw from it that he was the Chief Justice of one of their States.

As soon as I had greeted him and offered him a seat, he said that his great-great grandfather was charged, pursuant to such and such act of parliament; convicted at the assize held at a certain place on such and such a date, and transported to Australia on a ship whose name he gave. He knew where his ancestor came from in England, and asked if genealogical research could be done.

I took down some details. Felt it likely something could be done, especially as he had an unusual name. He gave me a cheque to cover the fee I suggested. I accompanied him down to the entrance of the College and hailed him a taxi.

As I walked up the stairs back to my chambers, I thought what a refreshing contrast that interview had been to what used to happen when an Australian called in Waiting when I first joined the College. Then, within the first five minutes of our conversation it was made plain that the enquirer's emigrant ancestor had been a free-settler. Now as with my new client, all that was simply a matter of history. In *The Ancestor*, the journal of the Victoria Genealogical Society there is a whole section in each issue on convict ancestry. After all, there is a clear distinction between a convict and a criminal – even Christ was put among the former by Pilate's action of handing him over to his accusers.

3.45p.m. Letters arrive for signature. When completed, picked up my briefcase and the Waiting Book. Thanked the staff and went downstairs. Put the book in the Waiting Room for the Officer-in-Waiting next week. Walked to Liverpool Street Station.

4.30p.m. Caught the train for Colchester and so back to Boxford: another week's duty done.

I would soon know if my diagnostic skills *vis-à-vis* 'Vesuvius' would make me a threat to the local vets!

The State Openings of Parliament

The State Opening of Parliament every year – usually in November – requires the heralds' presence: we would rehearse the evening before. The participants looked terribly dull in their pin-stripes, with furled umbrellas or rolled copies of *The Times* or *Telegraph* simulating the sceptres, maces, wands, and swords which would be carried next day when they would all appear in the gorgeous scarlet uniforms of Guards' officers, the navy blue of the Senior Service or *bleu celeste* of the Air Force, or other equally impressive uniforms – all with suitable amounts of gold.

On the actual day of the Opening, dressed in scarlet with much 'scrambled egg' (gold embroidery) on the manly chests of the Kings' and Heralds' Royal Household uniforms, we would be driven in government cars from the College to the Palace of Westminster, arriving about 10a.m.

Each herald was allocated tickets for a pair of guests whom one would greet in the Royal Gallery along with any other people one knew. They were all placed behind brocaded enclosures from which to view the procession of The Queen to and from the Chamber.

After that social interlude off we would go by way of the Princes' Chamber – a room between the Royal Gallery and the Lords' chamber. It would be stiff with ambassadors and high commissioners, among whom one would greet one's friends. I would single out Canada, India, Lithuania and Poland in particular. Foreign and Commonwealth Office officials – such as the First Assistant Marshal of the Diplomatic Corps (S.W.F. Martin, CVO, a friend of long-standing sharing a common interest in Orders and Decorations of which he is one of the leading authorities in this country) – would be busy shepherding the august diplomats into their correct places, according to seniority, in the Chamber[27]. Finally we would arrive at a room where we could be helped into our tabards by the ubiquitous Ede and Ravenscroft people (the well known robe and official uniform tailors of Chancery Lane).

By 10.57a.m. we would have to be back once again in the Princes' Chamber, in which by now the Honourable Corps of Gentlemen at Arms would be formed up. To be a private in that body one must be a brigadier at least.

---

[27] Senior ambassadors in the specially built 'box' on the floor of the House, to the right of the throne; senior high commissioners in the two officials' 'boxes' to each side of the throne; junior ambassadors and *chargés d'affaires* in the gallery above to the right of the throne; junior and acting high commissioners in the gallery above to the left of the throne; with a few 'also rans' in the Royal Gallery.

From there we would have a private procession, *seniores priores*, to the grand staircase and form ourselves up, on either side, in front of the detachment of the Household Cavalry.

Between us passed various dignitaries – the Earl Marshal, Lord Great Chamberlain and Lord Chancellor going down; various Royals, the Kents, the Gloucesters and so on, going up. We would be there for about 20 minutes and, as we were expected to be silent, I could get several decades of a rosary said: no necessity to frighten anyone by flailing about with a set of beads – one has ten fingers and that is quite enough for each decade. So one filled up the time profitably for the good estate of the Guardsmen behind one, those passing up and down the stairs in front and oneself. Of the three sets of Mysteries recommended for consideration when reciting the rosary, the 'Glorious' seemed most appropriate to me. By them one was reminded that the ultimate source of all authority is God – notwithstanding the flattering blandishments of so many politicians when seeking one's vote (an actual say in the matter of who should exercise that divinely granted authority); and on the other hand, magnificent as was the spectacle of which one was a part on such occasions, it was but the palest earnest of the beatific vision one prayed all present would enjoy one day.

Upon the arrival of The Queen, the Earl Marshal would raise his baton – at that sign all heralds turned inwards and about and moved slowly up the stairs and on into the Royal Gallery. When I, as one of the two most junior pursuivants, was leading the procession, I would stop when I got to the enormous paintings of either Nelson dying on the quarter-deck of HMS *Victory* or Wellington meeting Blucher at *Quatre Bras*. When I was at the College (it differs nowadays) arrived at our places, all heralds about-turned and faced the door at the end of the gallery through which The Queen would appear, robed and wearing the Imperial State Crown. At this, trumpeters of the Household Cavalry would sound a salute; Garter would raise his sceptre and everyone in the procession would turn inwards and about and slowly move towards the House of Lords Chamber.

Once there the heralds formed up on to The Queen's left. After a long wait, the House of Commons would arrive – noisily, just to let you know who they are! The Queen would then receive the text of the Speech from the Throne from the Lord Chancellor and would read out the government's proposed programme of legislation for the next year.

At the end, when she said, 'I pray that the blessing of Almighty God may rest upon your counsels', the heralds left the chamber and formed up in the Royal Gallery, ready to lead the procession, The Queen going off into the robing room again and the heralds onto the grand staircase. Her Majesty would soon appear at the top of the stairs, having removed crown and train and donned a white travelling coat. Whereupon the heralds led her down the stairs and out into the Sovereign's Entrance. There, along with the Earl Marshal and the Lord Great

Chamberlain they would see her into her carriage and bow as it moved off. Her homeward journey had started to the cheers of the spectators as she passed on her way.

The heralds would then move informally through the various courtyards of the Palace of Westminster (as the Houses of Parliament are collectively called) – keeping an eye out for equine relics, as the carriages and horses had stood there for an hour or so prior to moving off again. Having reached our robing room we would take off our tabards and refresh ourselves with a glass of wine most thoughtfully made available by Miss Pat Malley of the Crown Office[28] – and much appreciated.

Having been driven back to the College, we changed out of our 'working clothes' back into civilian dress, and got on with the business of the day. This was usually preceded by taking the guests one had for the Opening out to luncheon at one's club.

★   ★   ★

The other two great Ceremonies of State which took place during my time at the College were the funeral of Sir Winston Churchill and the Investiture of the Prince of Wales.

---

[28] Located in the House of Lords, which has the responsibility of issuing documents which pass under the Great Seal of the Realm.

The State Funeral
of
The Right Honourable Sir Winston Leonard Spencer-Churchill
KG, OM, CH
30 January, 1965

The College of Arms is the greatest undertaker in the world, and given a cadaver will give it a marvellous send off.

The last State Funeral for a non-royal before Churchill's had been on 18 November 1852 for the Duke of Wellington: victor of Waterloo and earlier on, as will be recalled, GOC-in-C of my Madras Regiment in his India days. As the Iron Duke's funeral was decided upon after his death, his remains had to be kept on ice for over two months[29] to give time for the necessary preparations – but only just; the workmen who had been preparing the Cathedral had to be pushed out with the opening of the doors at 8 a.m.to admit the congregation on the day of the funeral.

Fortunately, as far as Churchill was concerned the College had some 7 years to arrange matters. It was, I understand, in the spring of 1958 – four years before I joined the College – that Lancaster (Col John Walker) was first asked to look after seating. Soon after I arrived on the scene I was asked to help Lancaster. Probably it was thought that it was the sort of work one could safely entrust to regimental officers: unimaginative and detailed, as many civilians would see it. They could never have foreseen all the human problems we came up against, as with the demand that the American representative be surrounded by his body-guard. They were duly accommodated by the nearest pillar.

There were interminable meetings of 'Hope Not' – the code-name for those planning the obsequies. Fortunately, one was able to consult the family as to preferences, and it was even possible to find out what hymns the great man himself wanted.

In the end, he was gathered to his ancestors on 24 January 1965, and as matters had been well arranged it was possible for the funeral to take place within a week.

Accordingly, at 9.35a.m.on January 30, the coffin was removed by the bearer party of the Brigade of Guards from Westminster Hall, where Churchill's remains had lain in state for some days beforehand. It was placed on a gun-carriage and was covered with, as the general public would say, the 'Union Jack'[30]. His insignia as a Knight Companion of the Most Noble Order of the

---

[29] The Duke died on 14 Sept. 1852.

[30] Technically the Union Badge in banner form and so properly described as the Union Banner or Flag.

The funeral of Sir Winston Spencer-Churchill, KG, OM, CH, St Paul's Cathedral, London, 30 January, 1965. The Earl of Avon, KG, the Earl Attlee, KG, and others leave following the service. The Officers of Arms, on the upper steps, are left to right: A. Colin Cole, Portcullis Pursuivant of Arms, the Author, Rouge Dragon Pursuivant of Arms, C.W. Scott-Giles Fitzalan Pursuivant of Arms Extraordinary, and at lower right, Michael Trappes-Lomax, Somerset Herald of Arms – all wearing mourning sashes.
Credit: The Sunday Times.

Garter was placed thereon. Those who were to accompany the coffin to St Paul's Cathedral formed up in New Palace Yard outside Westminster Hall and, as 'Big Ben' struck 9.45, the Great Procession – as it was officially designated – moved off. It was arranged that 'Big Ben' would not strike for the rest of the day, once the muted pageant had started its solemn measure.

Pulled by a Royal Naval crew, and escorted by a detachment of the Royal Air Force, the coffin made its way along Whitehall, crossed the south eastern corner of Trafalgar Square into the Strand and so to Fleet Street, Ludgate Hill, and up towards St Paul's Cathedral. Minute-guns were fired from St James's Park and the Tower for the duration of the procession. Amid the various service detachments who made up this entourage of the defunct, eight bands helped them both to keep in step and to maintain the solemn mood. The Earl Marshal, in charge of the whole procedure, walked immediately behind the coffin.

Churchill's orders and decorations were carried on cushions; the banner of the Cinque Ports of which he had been the Warden, and the banner of the arms of Spencer-Churchill were borne aloft.

For some two hours before the procession started, we of the heralds concerned with seating had been in the Cathedral. At 10.10a.m.all the heralds moved out onto the front steps. Each wore his tabard and mourning sash of black crepe from left shoulder to right hip. Four of the College carried the 'achievements', as they are called for such funerals: the spurs by York (Lord Sinclair); the crest by Lancaster (Col John Walker); the targe (shield of the arms of Spencer-Churchill) by Somerset (Michael Trappes-Lomax) and the sword by Windsor (Preston Graham-Vivian) – each mounted on a black pole.

The coffin finally arrived at St Paul's and the last minute-gun was silent. The coffin was then lifted off the gun-carriage by the 10-Guardsman bearer party. They slowly mounted the front steps. Though each was obviously very fit, the strain of carrying a lead-lined oak coffin was evident, and Churchill himself had been no featherweight. Having arrived on the outside platform beneath the Corinthian columns by 10.49, the two most junior pursuivants, Rouge Croix (Rodney Dennys) the senior, and Rouge Dragon (myself) the junior, then commenced leading this, the Earl Marshal's, procession into the brightly lit church. Between Rouge Croix and myself – each 6 feet tall – was the diminutive, yet very dignified figure of the junior pursuivant-extraordinary, Fitzalan (Wilfrid Scott-Giles).

So began that long, solemn yet most honourable duty as we made our way up the nave. Then came the Earl Marshal, followed by the 12 pall bearers. Those included the Earl Attlee, KG, Churchill's Deputy in the coalition Government during the war, the Right Honble Harold Macmillan, a former Prime Minister, the Earl Alexander of Tunis, KG, a former Governor General of Canada – and the Earl Mountbatten of Burma, all in front of the coffin. Then followed the family and principal mourners.

When the heralds reached that part of the cathedral immediately beneath the dome, we entered a square open-space which had been formed with chairs and kneelers. In the centre was the bier upon which the coffin was placed; and behind it on a table the orders and decorations, the two banners and the four achievements were all accommodated. The heralds formed the backdrop to this scene, their backs to the choir and high altar, facing to the west and so towards the congregation, who had been helped to their places by Purple Staff Officers – serving officers of the armed forces and distinguished civilians appointed as ushers for the occasion.

Directly in front and facing us, from the other side of the bier, were The Queen and royal family. To the left were the Spencer-Churchill family. To my right, on the north side in the centre of the front row was General Charles de Gaulle next to Jean, Grand Duke of Luxembourg. I wondered what was going through the mind of that rather tiresome Frenchman at our placing him next to a Bourbon[31]. On the same side Hilda had her seat.

As for the Iron Duke's funeral, the service was conducted from within this square and was short: 30 minutes. The Bishop of London and other clerics were present, but it was the Dean of St Paul's and the cathedral clergy who officiated, though the Archbishop of Canterbury gave the blessing at the conclusion.

Appropriate prayers were said. In the Bidding Prayer we were reminded of 'a great man who has rendered memorable service to his country and to the cause of freedom'.

Suitable hymns had been chosen:

'Who would true valour see';

'Mine eyes have seen the glory of the coming of the Lord' – *The Battle Hymn of the Republic* – Churchill's choice. It will be recalled that his mother was an American.

And, finally, 'Fight the good fight'.

There was no panegyric – everyone knew that under God but for Churchill none of us would have been there that day.

After the National Anthem at the end there was a pause, and then the haunting refrain of the Last Post came from the gallery at the far west end of the cathedral. As these notes died away, there was another short pause. Then, from the same place the Reveille burst forth and filled the church with its notes of expectation.

Thereupon Rouge Croix and I went forward and started the exit procession to the strains of

'O God, our help in ages past'

Having arrived at the west door the heralds fanned out down the front steps as the coffin was again placed on the gun-carriage which then moved off to the Tower. From there it was taken on board 'Havengore' – a Port of London Authority vessel – and taken up river to Festival Hall Pier, Waterloo Station, and Bladon Churchyard, Oxfordshire, near Blenheim Palace, Churchill's family home, for private burial. While moving up the Thames there was an RAF fly past and – a completely unrehearsed gesture – all the river-side cranes dipped in salute as the coffin passed.

The heralds' part in this great ceremony was completed out on the steps of the cathedral as we waited to see off The Queen and all the other important participants of this occasion. We were there for about another half an hour. It was raw and cold, so much so that the servicemen had been put into uniform greatcoats. We stood there, both at the beginning and at the end in our black silk stockings. For me the result was frostbitten calves – which let me know all about it when I got into my bath for the next month or so.

---

[31] Grand Duke Jean (succeeded 1964) was the son of the Grand Duchess Charlotte by her husband Prince Felix of Bourbon-Parma.

Private Eye, *Prince of Wales Investiture edition, 20 June 1969 with Heralds on the steps of the College of Arms wearing their four different uniforms. From left to right: A. Colin Cole, Windsor Herald of Arms, J.P.B. Brooke-Little, Richmond Herald of Arms, Francis Jones, Wales Herald of Arms Extraordinary, and the Author, York Herald of Arms.*
Credit: Courtesy of Private Eye *and* Hulton Archive: Getty Images.

The Investiture of the Prince of Wales
Tuesday 1 July, 1969

It was appropriate that a future King of Canada should be invested on Canada Day, July 1, with the symbols of his position as heir apparent to that realm.

As a state ceremony it was, as always, planned and organized by the Earl Marshal[32] with the heralds as his staff officers. While the site for the actual ceremony was to be at Caernarvon Castle – near the north-west tip of Wales – much of the planning took place in London. An outline of the area available was marked out on a lawn of Buckingham Palace, and we did much rehearsing there – with The Queen frequently coming to watch the proceedings.

Upon occasion, we would go up to Caernarvon, to see how Lord Snowdon, Constable of the Castle (and husband of Princess Margaret) was getting on with his arranging the setting for the ceremony which was to be in the open air in the inner wards of the castle there. He, Carl Toms and others along with the College of Arms Herald-Painters created a spectacular setting. The dais of slate – what else in Wales? – was beneath a great fan-shaped, perspex canopy which rose heavenward. Large brightly-coloured heraldic gonfalon hung down against the stone walls of the castle.

This was the backdrop not only of a constitutional act but also a religious ceremony, both surrounded by a feast of music, orchestral as well as choral. The Welsh can do many things well, but when it comes to singing they leave behind in a state of embarrassed hesitance the rest of the United Kingdom.

While the guests assembled in the castle between 11 and 12.30 three civilian bands were to play them into their places. Accompanied by the BBC Welsh orchestra, two choirs sang as the various processions moved on their several ways up through the castle. Fifteen soloists accompanied by choirs and orchestras required three conductors.

In the general planning, the Earl Marshal and the heralds were most fortunate to have the assistance and guidance of the completely bilingual Major Francis Jones, CVO, TD, FSA, Wales Herald of Arms Extraordinary[33] and County Archivist of Carmarthenshire.

Over the period of the investiture I was in charge of accommodation. Most of us, with our wives and staffs, put up at the Bulkeley Arms, Beaumaris, on the Isle of Anglesey overlooking the Menai Strait and so on to mainland Wales. It was a most comfortable hotel in a dramatic setting.

On the day of the investiture, each herald, dressed in Royal Household jacket, overalls (black trousers with gold stripe down the sides) jemimas, (close fitting, unlaced, long black leather boots worn with and under overalls) and tabard,

---

[32] Bernard, 16th Duke of Norfolk.
[33] Since 1963

Tudor hats (cocked hats for the Kings of Arms) together with wands and collars of S's (where appropriate) – plus our wives and staffs – mounted a motor coach marked 'A' and proceeded to the Slate Quay by the castle. There all except the heralds de-bussed and had their midday meal on the spot, prior to making their way into the castle. On the other hand, all the officers-of-arms continued on in the coach to the County Council Offices on Shirehall. This served as the rendezvous from which all those taking an official part in the ceremony proceeded to the castle at the appointed times. The only exception were the royals. They came to the ceremony by way of the premises of Ferodo Ltd., – a private engineering firm which had a railway siding into which the Royal train could run: a convenient starting point for the Royal processions.

Between 11.45 and 12.30 we were served an excellent buffet luncheon in the County Council Offices. Wisely the *Detailed Instructions – Officers of Arms* included the observation, 'There will also be lavatory facilities in the County Council Offices. (You will be on parade virtually from 13.00-16.30).'

After lunch most of the heralds went across the street to the Assembly Yard, formed up and moved off at 1.15p.m. in procession to the castle. It took four to five minutes to get there. They waited in the Earl Marshal's office in the Eagle Tower until required for duty. Through the Water Gate, situated in that building, all entries and exits to the castle were made – with much showing of security passes. While in the Eagle Tower the heralds were able to inspect their Waiting banners, which they had lent for the decoration of its main hall.

Meanwhile, Windsor (Colin Cole), Richmond (John Brooke-Little), Somerset (Rodney Dennys) and myself were to wait behind in the Assembly Yard and lead various officials to their allotted places in the castle. For me the *Instructions* read:

(a) 13.50 hours, <u>York</u> together with a Green Staff Officer will conduct the Sheriffs of the Welsh Counties to their seats behind the dais where he will leave them at 14.00 hours.

So at the appointed hour, Green Staff and I started off with our charges. Everything went well en route as we passed through the Water Gate of Eagle Tower, and then up the whole length of the castle's wards: lower and then upper.

But then as we neared the dais – immediately behind which we were to seat these chief executive officers of the Crown for the counties[34] we saw, to our horror, that by some mistake the seats for our men had been filled with the Welsh members of the House of Commons! (Thought: why is it that those elected to legislative assemblies seem to think that popular mandate permits presumption?!). As we neared the appointed area, Green Staff and I slackened our pace, and started to discuss, out of the corners of our mouths, what to do – walking all the while. We were fully conscious that anything we did or said risked

---

[34] The office of Sheriff in the United Kingdom is one of great distinction and prestige and is held for one year only.

being relayed by the satellite broadcasting of the event to millions of television screens, across the globe. In the end, he and I decided to show our charges into the seats originally allocated for the MPs and hoped that none would be the wiser – except those who had planned everything so meticulously. Fortunately it worked. So with my charges seated, off I went, as instructed, to join the other heralds in the Eagle Tower.

Within minutes of arriving, there was from our roof a magnificent fanfare by the State Trumpeters of the Household Cavalry stationed on the battlements: Prince Charles had arrived; his banner for use in Wales was run up the flagpole on the tower, and his procession to the Chamberlain Tower began. It was 2.40p.m. As he advanced through the 4,000 and more people within the castle they greeted him by singing that anthem, of such haunting melody, with the well-known chorus:

> Among our ancient mountains,
> And from our lovely vales,
> O let the pray'r be echoed,
> 'God bless the Prince of Wales!'

Many sang it in Welsh. Wales Herald Extraordinary (Francis Jones) and Chester Herald (Walter Verco) immediately preceded the Prince in view of his titles of Prince of Wales and Earl of Chester.

At five to three a further fanfare from the Eagle Tower announced the arrival of The Queen. The Prince's banner was struck and the royal banner hoisted on the flagpole. The remaining six heralds fell in immediately before The Queen, and with other officials led her and the Duke of Edinburgh to the dais, whereupon the choirs and guests sang the Welsh National Anthem, 'Hen Wlad Fy Nhadau', followed by 'God Save the Queen'.

We had now arrived at the ceremony of investiture. The Queen directed Garter (Sir Anthony Wagner) to summon the Prince to her presence which he did from the Chamberlain Tower. Whereupon the Prince was preceded by Wales and Chester Heralds and the Lords bearing the insignia: sword, coronet, golden rod and gold ring. Coming towards the dais, Garter delivered the Letters Patent to the Lord Great Chamberlain[35] who presented them to The Queen. She handed these over: the English text to the Secretary of the Home Department[36] and the Welsh text to the Secretary of State for Wales[37]. The Prince, accompanied by the Peers supporting him, approached the throne and knelt on a cushion before his mother The Queen.

The Home Secretary then read out in English, the Letters Patent which were dated 26 July 1958, which had created him Prince of Wales and Earl of Chester.

---

[35] The Marquess of Cholmondeley.

[36] The Right Honble James Callaghan – later Prime Minister.

[37] The Right Honble George Thomas – later Viscount Tonypandy.

Then the Welsh Secretary did the same in Welsh. When he reached the words, which in English are:

> And him Our most dear son Charles... We do... invest with the said Principality and Earldom by girting him with a Sword and putting a Coronet on his head and a Gold Ring on his finger and also delivering a Gold Rod into his hand.

The Queen invested him with the said insignia. Whereupon, placing his hands between those of Her Majesty the Prince declared:

> I Charles, Prince of Wales, do become your liege man of life and limb and of earthly worship, and faith and truth I will bear unto you to live and die against all manner of folks.

The Queen then 'rose up' the Prince of Wales and exchanged with him the Kiss of Fealty.

The Secretaries of State delivered the Letters Patent to The Queen and Her Majesty handed them to the Prince who then proceeded to his throne to the right of the Sovereign.

The Loyal Address of the people of Wales was then delivered to His Royal Highness by Sir Ben Bowen Thomas, President of the University College of Wales, Aberystwyth of which the Prince was an alumnus[38]. To this he replied in Welsh, to the great satisfaction of all for whom that language was their mother-tongue. They also much appreciated the humour with which he seasoned his speech.

The religious service followed. As there is no state church now in Wales it was broadly ecumenical. After a hymn, the Bishop of Bangor of the Church in Wales (The Right Reverend G.O. Williams) read in English from the first letter of Peter[39] enjoining that one should 'Honour all men. Love the brotherhood. Fear God. Honour the King.'

Soon it came the turn of the enormously tall (6'3") Auxiliary Catholic Bishop of Menevia (The Right Reverend Langton Fox) who, in view of the linguistic composition of those present, invited each to recite the Lord's Prayer 'in the language of his choice'. Whereupon Norfolk Herald Extraordinary (Dermot Morah) took him at his word, and in that marvellous, gravelly voice of his boomed out, '*Pater noster, qui es in coelis...*' (!!). Ultimately, the blessing was pronounced in Welsh by the President of the Free Church Council of Wales. It was a case of 'mixed bathing, in at the deep end', as some waggs put it but all done with the greatest reverence.

The final phase of the ceremonies comprised three Presentations of the Prince

---

[38] Prince Charles studied Welsh at this College.
[39] 1 Peter 2:11-17

of Wales by The Queen to the people of Wales with fanfares of trumpets by the Trumpeters of the Royal Military School of Music: at Queen Eleanor's Gate, the King's Gate and finally from the top of the steps facing the Lower Ward of the Castle to the guests assembled there.

With the heralds leading The Queen, the Prince of Wales and the Duke of Edinburgh, the exit procession then moved to the Eagle Tower and a fly-past by the Royal Air Force took place. With a final blast of the trumpets, the royal party then mounted their carriages for The Queen's Procession through the streets of Caernarvon.

Having seen the Commonwealth High Commissioners and the heads of the diplomatic missions into their cars, the heralds with their wives and staffs mounted their coach to be driven to Beaumaris and the Bulkley Arms.

Then, after shedding (with Hilda's help to pull mine off) one's jemimas and other 'working clothes' came the time for a welcome double Scotch. Over an excellent dinner – after a day's work we felt well done – and in a haze of burgundy and cognac we discussed the setting, the ceremony, the music, the perfect weather, and also the bomb let off some distance away by nationalists – *O, tempora, O, mores!* I suppose they must have their little bit of fun.

Introductions of Peers into the House of Lords

The College of Arms has several parliamentary duties. We have already noted the part played by the heralds in the State Openings of Parliament.

Yet again, when a person is to be created a peer, it is Garter who settles the exact form of the title. Each must be unique. The only exception in such cases is when another of the same male-line family is raised to the peerage and desires to bear the now defunct title once borne by a direct or collateral ancestor. The several Lords Russell of Killowen (referred to earlier) are classic examples of exceptions being made of the same male-line family – in these cases they are Life Peers, being Law Lords (members of the House of Lords who sit as the highest Court of Appeal).

A title has two essential parts: the *nomen dignitatis* and the territorial designation. The former is that by which the person is always known as and referred to in conversation; the latter is only used in very formal circumstances such as legal documents. Take, for example, Lord Tweedsmuir, the sometime Governor General of Canada. When he, as John Buchan, was to be raised to the peerage as a baron he chose a place name as his *nomen dignitatis*. Being a Scot, it was Tweedsmuir, a parish in Peeblesshire on the river Tweed; and then as his territorial designation, 'of Elsfield in the County of Oxford' with which he had family connections. So, while his full legal title was John, Baron Tweedsmuir, of Elsfield in the County of Oxford, he would normally be referred to and addressed as, Lord Tweedsmuir, *simpliciter*.

The term 'Lord' is generic and applies to all Barons (always, except in legal documents) and may apply to the next three grades of Viscount, Earl, and Marquess, but never to a Duke. The only time a peerage Barony is referred to as such in general usage is when held by a woman, who is usually referred to as 'Baroness', and so with Baroness Thatcher, the former Prime Minister.

Upon occasion, a person wishes to retain the family name when raised to the peerage. In view that all such titles are required to be unique, this usually means that it is necessary to have the phrase, 'of (a place)' added after the family name in the *nomen dignitatis*, and so with Field Marshal the Lord Alexander of Tunis. In such cases, the family name + of + place name must always be treated as if hyphens joined all three. Accordingly one must say 'Lord Alexander of Tunis' and not simply 'Lord Alexander' – for by so doing one is referring to a peer living *ante* 1739. Of course, in the field marshal's case he, naturally, wished to recall one of the high points of his military career and so 'of Tunis' was most appropriate in getting the title into the correct form.

However, this desire to retain a family name can produce unwieldy results, as with the title of the well-known (and somewhat notorious) author, Jeffrey Archer, who successfully requested that it should be, 'Archer of Weston Super Mare'. In view of the rules for such titles this is, in my opinion, something of a mouthful.

Many people in public life seem to be intent upon retaining their family name. In the case of the Right Honble George Brown – a well-known Labour government minister – the final result was, if I may be permitted to say, slightly ridiculous. Determined to keep 'George Brown', he thought he could be 'Lord George Brown'. In that form, however, it would have meant that he was not a peer at all, but rather the younger son of a Duke or Marquess, who has such a courtesy title for life! Accordingly, in order to satisfy his insistence he had to execute a Deed Poll that henceforth his family name would be George-Brown. In that form the peerage was granted, so that he became known as Lord George-Brown.

When I was Garter, I have to admit, I failed miserably, except in one case, in trying to convince neophyte peers that simple place names for the *nomen dignitatis* would not only be more in accord with tradition but also more practical. The one exception was Sir Robert Leigh-Pemberton, Governor of the Bank of England, who asked if he could be 'Lord Kingsdown'. His great-great uncle, Thomas Pemberton, was created Baron Kingsdown in 1858 but upon his death, unmarried, the peerage expired. As a result of this family connection this second creation was permitted (1993).

Since the passage of the Life Peerage Act, 1958, one has to admit that the selection of peers has been catholic in the extreme. With some, one can anticipate the positive contribution they will make to the House because of their civilized wisdom and wide knowledge. With others, one is really somewhat doubtful. I must confess that in my dealings with some of them I was reminded of the story about Louis XIV and his old nurse. Apparently, she screwed up her courage on one occasion and asked, 'Oh sire, please make my son a gentleman.' To this the king replied, 'Madam, I can make him a Duke; I cannot make him a gentleman'.

Upon Garter certifying that the proposed title is unique, Letters Patent creating the peerage are issued under the Great Seal of the Realm through the Crown Office.

A further duty of Garter is to carry out the formal Introduction of the new peer into the House of Lords. Garter can appoint a herald to be his deputy for this, as I was by Garter Wagner on fairly frequent occasions from early in the sixties.

As a result I knew the drill for such occasions well before I became Garter myself in 1992.

On the day scheduled for the Introduction my moves were as follows: 11.30 change into uniform: scarlet Royal Household jacket; black knee-breeches; black silk stockings (actually tights modified by my taylor for male convenience); regulation gold buckled patent leather shoes. This took 20 minutes. After that: collect typed card displaying: the title of the new peer as a 'crib' when he/she took the oath, as well as the names of the two peers who would be the new peer's Supporters for the information of the Clerks of Parliament.

The government car would come at noon and having arrived at the House of Lords I would make for the Peers' Guest Room (*vere* the bar, but one never refers to it as such!). There one would join the new Peer and his other guests. After a glass of champagne (orange juice when I introduced Lord Soper, the celebrated Methodist divine), on into the Peers' Dining Room (or the Barry Room, downstairs, which I preferred as, in my opinion, it had more atmosphere – one expected Guy Fawkes to come round the corner at any moment – and the kitchen was better!). The luncheon followed.

Conversation would flow along, even if one had to give it a push at times. There were usually other interesting guests present. On one occasion I was Introducing Lord Balogh – economic adviser to the Cabinet under the Labour Prime Minister, Harold Wilson. The table was arranged as so often with Labourites: all the men at one end and the women at the other. My host did me the honour of placing me on his right. While my place-card identified me by my heraldic title, all the others were 'John', 'Harry', 'Mary' and so on: all relations or close friends, I surmised. We started the meal before the one on my right, marked 'Barbara', had arrived. Then a sudden hush enveloped the whole dining room. I turned and saw a vision entering the room: a picture of emerald green Shantung silk with a pile of auburn hair on top. It was Barbara Castle, a leading and formidable member of Wilson's Cabinet. She sat down beside me and I let her be served. After she had had a couple of mouthfuls, I leaned towards her and said, 'Mrs Castle, don't you really feel that it is high time we did away with [dramatic pause of a few seconds] the House of Commons?' Thereafter I was able to get on with my meal and did not need to say another word: la Castle was off! Some time later she was raised to the peerage and used to say, 'Yes, the House of Lords is all right, but don't inhale.'

After the first cup of coffee at the end of the meal, Garter gathers up the new Peer, his two Supporters and Black Rod[40], or his deputy, and takes them all off for a rehearsal, leaving the others to have more coffee until they are ushered into the gallery to view the Introduction ceremony.

On one occasion, a supporter was Lord Jenkins of Hillhead, a sometime Labour Minister in several administrations, and a founder of the Social Democratic Party. He spoke with a slight lisp and had a great appreciation of wine. I had collected up all the others, and turning to him, said:

'Lord Jenkins of Hillhead, shall we now go to the rehearsal?'

To this he replied:

'Oh, I just want to finish off this "qw-uart". I know the "procedure" so I don't need to practise'.

So off the rest of us went, whereupon Black Rod's Deputy (an airman) said:

'Yes, that's what the pilot says just before he crashes.'[41]

From the luncheon table Garter leads his group to the Moses Room[42] (where at other times the Law Lords hear appeals to the House of Lords). There the new Peer and his Supporters put on parliamentary robes and select cocked hats (lady peers wear tricorn hats). Garter's tabard and sceptre were available there when needed.

With the three peers robed, originally I would sit them down and explain the various moves involved in the ceremony of Introduction. In time a video was produced for them to study. Following that, Garter would take the new peer and Supporters into the actual chamber of the House of Lords and, in private, run through the complete ceremony; repeating parts if necessary. With that completed, Garter and the three returned to the Moses room to await being summoned for the actual Introduction. In the meantime, prayers would be said in the House of Lords (the public are not permitted to see their Lordships in this pious exercise). With prayers over, Black Rod would come and lead us from the Moses Room to the Chamber, the order being: Black Rod, Garter, the junior supporter, the new Peer, the senior supporter.

A pair of massive oak doors were opened by the doorkeepers.

One advanced through a low and seemingly confined corridor beneath the Press Gallery – then suddenly into the full height and expanse of the Lords'

---

[40] Actually an officer of the Order of the Garter, but also the messenger of the House of Lords.

[41] SSA. Garter's Diary. 3 Nov. 1993. Black Rod's Deputy was Air Commodore Alan Cury, RAF, Yeoman Usher of Black Rod. As the No. 2 to Black Rod (who was sick at the time) he was acting in his place.

[42] So named from a painting there of Moses handing down the Ten Commandments.

Chamber. After a few steps the Bar of the House was reached, and there at the far end sat the Lord Chancellor (cabinet minister, head of the judiciary of England and Wales, and Speaker of the House of Lords) on the woolsack. One bowed. The obeisance was not to him nor to anyone else in the room, but to the Cloth of Estate. This comprised the Arms of Dominion and Sovereignty above the throne at the furthest point of the chamber beyond the Lord Chancellor (one ignored him).

In this action, one was immediately conscious of being among the living representatives of so much British history, both at home and beyond the seas, both ancient and modern. Among the older titles one could see from Norfolk to Salisbury, from Wellington to Zetland ranged along the red leather of the benches. More recently the scan might have been from Shaugnessy to Sinha, from Mountbatten to Thatcher. One had entered into the constitution of the country, a constitution which had evolved gradually and worked effectively ever since the barons first assembled in Westminster Hall some 700 years earlier. Straightway one felt oneself a part of it (which, as a herald, one was).

The recently created as well as the hereditary legislators, including those from the one-time kingdom of Scotland, were now anxious to acknowledge a new colleague as a peer of the United Kingdom.

None present was elected. As a result each could escape that presumptuous tendency of so many who are, and who seem to imagine themselves given thereby a direct line to the Holy Ghost.

Leaving aside the Law Lords, the Lords Spiritual and the peers created for life, each had attained his place there in the same way as almost all of us acquire the birthright of nationality. An inherited right to it, no matter where we are born, be it in our ancestral country or in some far-off foreign land. When the lioness drops a cub in a stable, that does not make it a horse; the essential factor is heredity.

On the flip side of the hereditary coin is serious duty. While all citizens must obey the laws of the nation and may be called upon to defend it, even to death, the peer of the realm is additionally required to give counsel in the affairs of state. This was required at one's own expense until very recently, when remuneration for expenses incurred in paying for and taking part in proceedings, such as travelling and subsistence costs, was permitted. In addition, peers may claim a modest allowance for each day of attendance at the House of Lords.

Their coming to the House was to say something meaningful and effective in debate or committee, rather than to enhance their image in the eyes of their constituents, as elected representatives are tempted to do.

The House of Lords always boasted that it could produce at least one expert on any subject that might come before it, from farming and medicine to physics and nuclear engineering. Could 'the other place' say the same? If the House once comprised exclusively the landed barons, it has more recently included the barons of industry and engineering.

Those with no party allegiance claim sanctuary on the cross benches. It must also be noted that a peer of whatever creation and allegiance represents him/herself only, and is not the delegate of any organization or other body. As a result, a field marshal, for example, though regarded as gallant by the rest of the House, does not represent the Army as such.

The House of Lords, mostly hereditary, was not perfect. What human institution is? But it could represent interests and concerns from all corners of the kingdom as well as of the Commonwealth. By the very nature of its composition it was, above all, independent. It could say to the government of the day, of whatever hue – 'Yes', 'But' or 'No'. Since the Acts of 1911 and 1949 it is precluded from saying 'Never' – but it can, nevertheless, still delay to allow wiser counsels to prevail.

But enough of these considerations, serious though they are; there was a job to be done. Further, as I am the last person alive to have been a Garter who functioned entirely in the unreformed House of Lords; and as the many hundred year-old ceremony of Introduction has now been simplified (it used to take 15 minutes and now takes 6); and as it does not appear that that ceremony, which I conducted, has ever been set down diagrammatically in print[43], I thought it would be as well to do so before its details are forgotten.

The new and current ceremony was brought about by a resolution of the House on 30 April 1998[44] agreeing to the amended recommendation of the Select Committee on this subject. The first Introduction according to the new and current ceremony was carried out on July 20 following[45].

The previous ceremony, which I conducted, is set out in four sketches which follow, based upon those I entered in my diary as Garter[46]

---

[43] For a good literary description, and from an historical point of view, see Cole, Sir Colin. KCB, KCVO, TD, FSA. 'Introduction of peers into the House of Lords' in *The House of Lords – a thousand years of British tradition*. Smith' Peerage Ltd. London, WIH 6AD (1994).

[44] *House of Lords Journal*, 30 April, 1998 p.775

[45] *Ibid.*, 20 July 1998 p.1998: Lord Clemont-Jones, CBE.

[46] *SSA*. Garter Diary

Plan I

Entrance and Presentation of Patent of Creation and Writ of Summons to the Lord Chancellor.

Each bows[47] to the Cloth of Estate – the royal arms above the throne – upon reaching points 1,2,3 & 4.

From point 4 the new peer goes to point 5, kneels on one knee before the Lord Chancellor to whom he hands his Writ of Summons.

Throughout this action, the Junior Supporter stands out of the way at point 6.

Garter from point 7 hands the symbolic Patent of Creation[48] to the Lord Chancellor.

Black Rod moves to point 8.

Armorial ensigns to the right of the diagram:

Upper – The Badge of the Westminster Parliament – a crowned portcullis.

Middle – The arms of the Dukes of Norfolk who, as Earls Marshal and in that capacity, have been responsible, on behalf of the Sovereign, for heraldry in Canada for some three hundred years down to the establishment of the Canadian Heraldic Authority in 1988.

Lower – The arms of Victor Christian (Cavendish) 9th Duke of Devonshire, KG, Governor General of Canada, 1916-21, who travelled widely throughout the country, was politically helpful, and the soul of constitutional propriety.

Each of the two shields is ensigned by the coronet of rank of a Duke.

---

[47] With the head only; for a man he brings his chin down on to the knot of his tie and up again.

[48] The actual Patent is in a large box in the Moses Room.

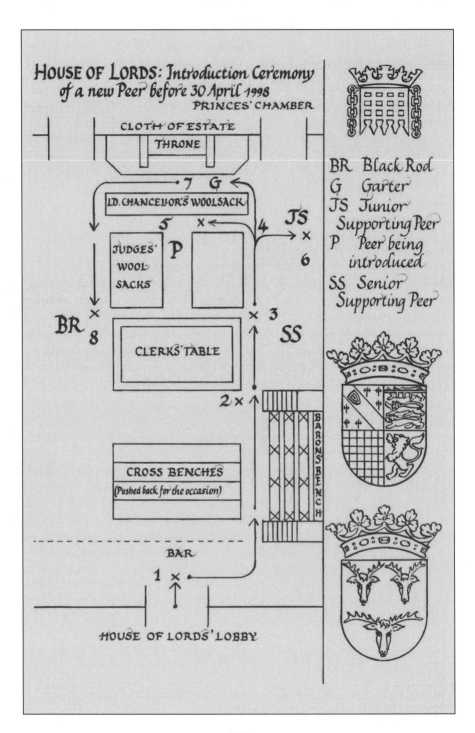

HOUSE OF LORDS: Introduction Ceremony of a new Peer before 30 April 1998

PRINCES' CHAMBER

CLOTH OF ESTATE

THRONE

7 G

LD. CHANCELLOR'S WOOLSACK

5

P

JUDGES' WOOL SACKS

JS

4

6

BR

8

3

SS

CLERKS' TABLE

2

BARONS BENCH

CROSS BENCHES
(Pushed back for the occasion)

BAR

1

HOUSE OF LORDS' LOBBY

BR Black Rod
G   Garter
JS Junior
      Supporting Peer
P   Peer being
      introduced
SS Senior
      Supporting Peer

Plan 2

Reading of Texts of Letters Patent of Creation and of Writ of Summons by a Clerk of Parliament
Taking of Oath (or Affirmation)[49]
Signing of the Roll with Nomen Dignitatis

Having handed the Writ of Summons to the Lord Chancellor, the new peer moves back from point 1 to point 2 at Clerks' table where the four actions above are completed.

Senior Supporter moves from points 3 to 4.

Junior Supporter moves from points 5 to 6.

Garter goes right round to Clerks' table at point 10.

Black Rod moves from points 7 to 8.

Arms to the right of the diagram:

Upper – Henry Charles Keith (Petty – Fitzmaurice) 5th Marquess of Lansdowne, GCMG, Governor General of Canada, 1883-88, during which he had to preside over the turbulent period of the Northwest Rebellion which he did without incident. The coronet above his shield is that of the rank of a Marquess.

Centre – John George (Lampton) 1st Earl of Durham GCB, Governor General of British North America, January–December, 1838, author of the Durham Report which, for the next century, shaped British Colonial policy.

Lower – Stafford Henry (Northcote) 1st Earl of Iddesleigh, 8th Baronet, GCB. As Governor of the Hudsons Bay Company he was instrumental in the conveyance, by the Company, of Ruperts Land (about 50% of the Canadian land mass) ultimately to the new Dominion Government at Ottawa, in 1870; great-grandfather of the Author's wife, the Lady Hilda Northcote.

The coronet above the two lower shields is that of the rank of an Earl.

---

[49] The Oath or Affirmation is usually taken in English but when I introduced the Lords Geraint and Ellis-Thomas (both of the Plaid Cymru Party) they did so in both English and Welsh (SSA. Garter's Diary 27 Oct. 1992).

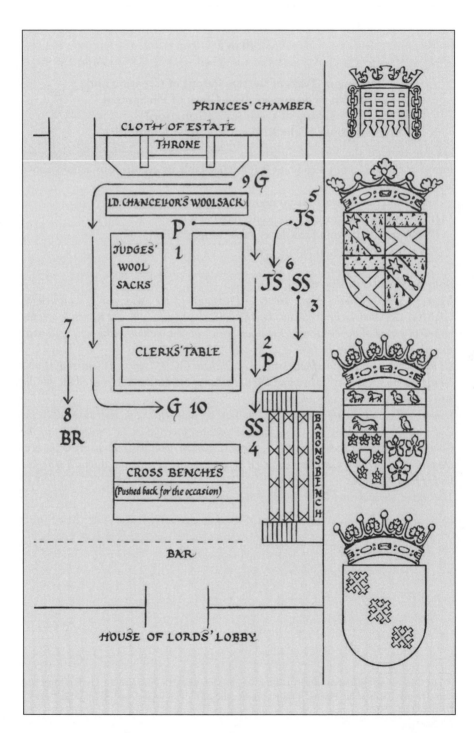

PRINCES' CHAMBER

CLOTH OF ESTATE

THRONE

9 G

LD. CHANCELLOR'S WOOLSACK

5

JS

JUDGES' WOOL SACKS

P 1

JS SS 6

3

7

CLERKS' TABLE

2 P

G 10

8

SS 4

BR

BARONS' BENCH

CROSS BENCHES

(Pushed back for the occasion)

BAR

HOUSE OF LORDS' LOBBY

Plan 3

The Thrice-repeated Obeisance to the Lord Chancellor.

Garter and the three peers bow to the Cloth of Estate at points 4 and 2 – circling the benches of the Cross Benchers[50]. Black Rod leads off this procession, bowing at point 2 and goes to point 3.

With the Senior Supporter leading, the three peers follow Garter and, mounting the gangway steps, go to points 10 (Senior Supporter) 11 (new Peer) and 12 (Junior Supporter) on the Barons' Benches[51] with Garter facing them at point 9.

With the three peers in their places, Garter says to them:

'Sit';

'Put on your hats'[52];

'Rise, take off your hats and bow to the Chancellor'[53];

'Sit'.

This series of commands and actions is repeated twice more. At the end of the third bow[54], Garter (*sotto voce*, reminds the three Peers not to replace their hats on their heads, as done twice before, but to keep their hats at the left shoulder position as upon entering the Chamber) Garter then leads them off down the gangway to Garters left.

[As some of the peers taking part in this ceremony were of mature age, and none too athletic, they would pull on the bench in front of them to help them respond to my command, 'Rise...'. This put a severe strain on that bench, immediately in front of me. To counter this I would place my right knee and press on the seat of the bench being used as a lever. Fortunately, my tabard, plus the back of the next bench down would shield my gymnastic subterfuge from the gaze of their other Lordships!]

Arms to the right of the diagram:

Upper – Charles Stanley (Monck) 4th Viscount Monck, Governor General of British North America, 1861-67 and of Canada, 1867-68; an architect of the Great Coalition devised to achieve Confederation.

Centre – Harold Rupert Leofric George (Alexander) 1st Viscount Alexander of Tunis, KG, Governor General of Canada, 1946-52 in which office he made a strong public impression.

Lower – Richard Bedford (Bennett) 1st and last Viscount Bennett, 11th Prime Minister of Canada, 1930-35, which period coincided with the Great Depression.

The coronet ensigning all three shields is that of rank of a Viscount.

---

[50] Those peers who sit independent of any political party.

[51] Depending upon the degree of the peerage into which a person is admitted he/she is Introduced from the appropriate benches.

[52] Up to this point all three peers have carried their hats in the left hand at shoulder height. Lady peers keep their hats on throughout the Introduction ceremony.

[53] The executive word of command here is 'Chancellor' not 'bow'. The other peers present give marks out of 10 as to how well this is done, privately, of course!

[54] On these three occasions the bows are from the waist.

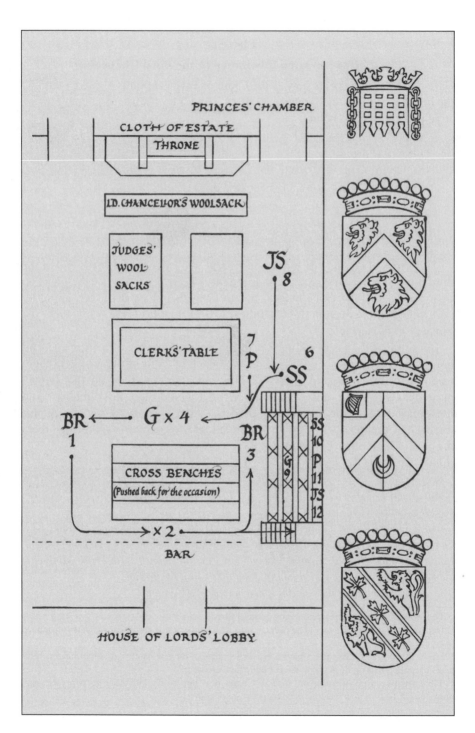

PRINCES' CHAMBER

CLOTH OF ESTATE

THRONE

LD. CHANCELLOR'S WOOLSACK

JUDGES'
WOOL
SACKS

CLERKS' TABLE

JS
8

7
P

6
SS

BR ← ← G × 4 ←

BR
1

BR
3

SS
10
P
11
JS
12

G
9

CROSS BENCHES
(Pushed back for the occasion)

→ × 2 •

BAR

HOUSE OF LORDS' LOBBY

Plan 4

Exeunt

As soon as Garter is in the gangway of stairs, Black Rod moves from point 1 to the exit door into the Princes' Chamber, bowing on the way at points 1 and 2.

Garter, followed by the three peers, does likewise, except that when the newly introduced peer gets near the Lord Chancellor, the Lord Chancellor beckons him/her to shake hands at point 7. At this the whole House says, 'Hear, Hear'.

[When Baroness Bacon was congratulated (1970) at this point by the Lord Chancellor (Lord Hailsham of Saint Marylebone – family name, Hogg) he shook her hand and said, 'Hogg meets Bacon'!]

The new peer then follows the Supporters out into the Princes' Chamber where Garter, Black Rod and others offer congratulations.

All then proceed informally down the side corridor back to the Moses room and take off their robes.

Garter mounts the government car at the House of Lords' Entrance; is driven back to the College; takes off his 'working clothes'; changes into civilian attire and, back at his desk, hears from his secretary what 'horrors' have transpired while he was away: over a cup of tea, he signs the letters of the day.

Arms to the right of the diagram:
Upper – Donald Alexander (Smith) 1st Baron Strathcona and Mount Royal, GCMG; rose through the ranks of the Hudson Bay Company; the Canadian Pacific Railway owed its completion to his financial backing; in the South African War, personally maintained the regiment, Strathcona's Horse.
Centre – Thomas George (Shaughnessy) 1st Baron Shaughnessy, KCVO; had an important career in the Canadian Pacific Railway; following the First War Troubles in Ireland, when it was considered desirable to find a Roman Catholic to be the Lord Lieutenant there, the British Government seriously considered Shaughnessy for this appointment.
Lower – John (Buchan) 1st Baron Tweedsmuir, GCMG, Governor General of Canada, 1935-40 (in which office he died); well-known author; inaugurated the Governor General's Literary Awards, 1937.
All three shields are ensigned by the coronet of rank of a Baron.

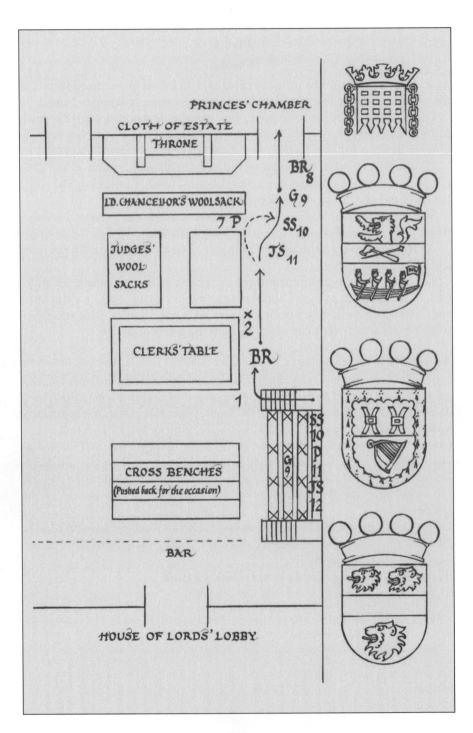

PRINCES' CHAMBER

CLOTH OF ESTATE

THRONE

BR 8

LD. CHANCELLOR'S WOOLSACK

G 9

7 P

SS 10

JUDGES' WOOL SACKS

JS 11

×2

CLERKS' TABLE

BR

1

SS 10

P 11

G 9

JS 12

CROSS BENCHES
(Pushed back for the occasion)

BAR

HOUSE OF LORDS' LOBBY

CHAPTER IX

Tesserae Honoris
et
Vexillum Patriae

Honours Old, Honours New; the National Flag
and the Heraldic Authority of Canada

I. DESIDERANTES MELIOREM PATRIAM[1]

THE TELEPHONE RANG. My secretary – guarding me, as a good amanuensis should – said the prime minister's secretary was on the line and would like to speak with me. I picked up the receiver, expecting the call to be from 10 Downing Street. I was soon relieved to find that it was not a Wilsonian *fonctionnaire* at the other end but Dr J.S. Hodgson, Principal Secretary to the Right Honble Lester B. Pearson, PC, MP Prime Minister of Canada. I had seen in the newspapers that he and other Commonwealth prime ministers were in London for a meeting.[2] That was now over but, before he returned to Ottawa next Friday afternoon, Dr Hodgson said the prime minister would be much obliged if I could call on him at noon that day.

I had no need to reach for my diary to see if I was free, for never, not ever, did I receive or visit on College of Arms business anyone on a Friday unless I was the Officer-in-Waiting. I used to joke that unless both Queen and Pope wanted to see me together on a Friday, this was an inflexible rule.

The reason for this was quite simple: having been at the College all week – both working and sleeping there – from Monday through to Thursday. I then took the 4.30 from Liverpool Street Station out into the wilds of East Anglia. There on Friday, Saturday and Sunday I 'mucked out' and generally did what needs to be done on a fairly extensive property (we were not overrun with estate workers). I tried also to be a good husband to a loving wife whom I loved very much in return, as well as a father to a growing family of five children, ranging in age from 6-year-old Elizabeth, to the youngest, Anastasia, then still at the breast at just two months old.

However, The Queen of Canada's Principal or Prime Minister is not in

---

[1] Motto of the Orders of Canada – They Desired a Better Country. Inspired by Hebrews: 11-16
[2] 6-14 September, 1966

London all that often. I decided to make an exception to my rule. So it was arranged that I would call on Mr Pearson, as requested, at the Dorchester Hotel at 12.10p.m., on Friday 16 September 1966.

As the tube[3] is, under normal circumstances and provided you know the system, the quickest way to get around London, I left the College on that day at about 11.20a.m. I calculated it would take about half an hour to get to the Dorchester, but didn't want to be late. Accordingly, I walked up round the back of the Cathedral and caught the Central Line at St Paul's Underground Station. At Marble Arch, the seventh stop, I would get off, as that was the nearest station to the Dorchester. As the train trundled on through the bowels of London, depositing and taking on passengers at most stops, I wondered to myself: 'Why does he want to see me? Is there some problem with my previous advice? [about which more later]'? No time to mull over that; we had arrived at Marble Arch Station.

It was a lovely autumn day, bright and clear, as I came to the surface and started to walk down Park Lane.

I soon arrived at the Dorchester, and, turning left, was at the porter's desk announcing myself for room 705.[4] No sooner had Dr Hodgson received me, and shown me in, than Mr Pearson came through the door from the adjoining room. After being presented, we got down to discussing the possible establishment of an honour for Canadians that might be called the Order of Canada.

It was odd I hadn't thought of this as I came along on the Underground, as some six months before in April, on the way to Duncan for one of my occasional visits to my aged maternal grandfather, I had called on my good friend Colonel John R. Matheson, MP, Parliamentary Secretary to the Prime Minister. He was then in hospital in Ottawa: gallant service in World War II took its toll from time to time, and this was one of them. As I sat by his bed, he had outlined to me the proposal he had made on 14 April 1966 to Mr Pearson, of a Canadian Order. He had reported on our meeting to the Prime Minister, and said that he had been heartened by my 'entire enthusiasm in all details suggested' and my conviction 'that the Canadian Order would receive immediate international recognition and respect'.[5]

As Pearson and I discussed this idea, both were fully aware of the fact that excellent though it might be, his Liberal Party was caught in a cleft stick of its own making. This was the result of its enthusiastic adhesion to a Resolution of the House of Commons, passed soon after World War I, whereby titles, orders and decorations were not to be recommended by the Prime Minister to the King

---

[3] The London Underground.

[4] NAC: MG26 N8 Vol 6. File: Pearson, L.B. Appointment Book, July-December, 1966 re Friday, 16 September, 1966.

[5] NAC: M26N4 File 001.42 File title General-Canada-Recognition for services to-Order of Canada: John R. Matheson, M.P. to Rt. Hon. L.B. Pearson, PC, MP, Prime Minister, 29 April, 1966.

for bestowal.[6] This had been rigorously followed by successive Liberal administrations.

On the other hand there had been a letup in this official policy when R.B. Bennett was prime minister (1930-35). As a Conservative he took the view, with logic, that the Resolution was simply that, a resolution, and not a statute. Accordingly he once again recommended Canadians for honorific recognition, with the result that such persons as Sir Frederick Banting – the principal discoverer of insulin – Sir Ernest McMillan – internationally acclaimed conductor of symphonic and choral music – and Sir Charles Roberts – poet and at his death in 1943 regarded as Canada's leading man of letters – all three received the dignity of Knight Bachelor. Soon after Bennett ceased to be prime minister he was himself raised to the peerage as a viscount.

With the return of Liberals to federal office in 1935, the self-denying ordnance was once more *de rigueur* until the outbreak of World War II, when honours which did not carry a title, (such as knighthoods) were conferred once again, such as CB, CBE, OBE, and MBE. With the end of the war, strict adhesion to the Resolution of 1919 was once again enforced.

This anti-honorific stance became almost a shibboleth of a real Liberal and was put forward by them as the only attitude for a true Canadian. The indulgence granted during the years of World War II was, in view of this basic position of the party, illogical, but excellence in war made its own demands. The overall result was that for some forty years – more than a whole generation – this attitude to honorifics had been the position of the dominant political force in federal affairs.

Notwithstanding, Pearson fully realized that Canada had come of age, and had entered upon the international stage as a completely sovereign nation, acknowledged as such. It needed to be able to recognize excellence and identify gratitude in the traditional, graceful way of awarding an honour to the well-deserving.

With all this obviously in mind, Mr Pearson admitted to me that while he considered the establishment of some form of honours system highly desirable. 'To be honest' he continued, 'I shrink from the prospect of having to present a bill to this end before Parliament.' One could well imagine not only the potential dismay of some of his own party at such a move by their leader, but also the gleeful ridicule that the Progressive Conservatives would heap upon him and the Liberals in general.

This observation revealed that even the highest echelons of government had completely forgotten how Orders of the Crown traditionally came into being. So when he then looked at me, as much as to say: 'Your reactions to that,

---

[6] 22 May, 1919. *Debates, House of Commons. Dominion of Canada*, Session 1919, Volume III, 2nd Session, 13th Parliament, 9-10 George V, 1919, pp. 2698-2749.

please,' I replied that, as Prime Minister, it was entirely up to him – doubtless after discussions with his cabinet colleagues – to decide how he would proceed in this matter. Nevertheless, if he did proceed by way of parliamentary legislation to create a chivalric order, he must appreciate that by so doing he would have gone against all precedent in such matters. The customary form is for the sovereign to issue letters patent stating that an order is created, named such and such, of which he or she is the Sovereign Head; that it will consist of the following grade or grades, and that subsequently statutes will be issued setting down the details of the insignia of the said grade or grades as well as other details for the good governance of the said Order – and that is that: the Order exists.

For a few seconds Mr Pearson was silent – it seemed an eternity. Then he looked at me and one could almost see a very heavy weight fall from his shoulders. 'Dr Swan, that's obviously the way! Will you please be so good as to write for me a full memorandum as to how to proceed by the method you have just outlined. I shall be most grateful to you for this.'

I, naturally, agreed to do so. We discussed possible insignia and my recommendation to Colonel Matheson that these should not be bronze as originally suggested,[7] but in precious metal. This I felt more worthy of Canada, which is, after all, the largest country in the Americas. And this was agreed.

By now, Mr Pearson's luncheon engagement was pressing and RCAF *Yukon*[8] waited to take him back to Uplands Airport at Ottawa. I was anxious to catch my train. So I took my leave. He thanked me for coming, with a warmth of which I did not think he was capable. I took a cab from the hotel, as I needed to call in at the College of Arms on the way to Liverpool Street Station.

When we reached the College, the cab swung into the courtyard. I jumped out, sprinted up to my chambers on the first floor of the west wing, seized my copies of the statutes of the Orders of the Bath and of the British Empire, grabbed some paper and, cramming these into my brief case, cleared the stairs two at a time on the way down. Inside five minutes I was back in the taxi. I was soon at Liverpool Street Station, boarding my train home. On the train, notes towards the memorandum were jotted down, and over the weekend – between feeding the horses, washing interminable nappies (these were pre-disposable days) and winding Anastasia the latest genealogical addition, – work proceeded on the memorandum. Back at the College most of my following days were so occupied: drafting, considering, re-drafting. A cogent and practical scheme which could fit Canadian needs was gradually emerging.

By 28 September 1966, my Memorandum, comprising six and a half closely

[7] NAC: M26N4 File 001.42 File title General-Canada-Recognition for services to-Order of Canada: John R. Matheson, M.P. to Rt. Hon. L.B. Pearson, PC, MP, Prime Minister, 29 April, 1966.
[8] NAC: MG 26N8 Vol. 6. File: Pearson, L.B. Appointment Book, July-December, 1966 re Friday 16 September, 1966.

typed pages, was despatched to the prime minister's principal secretary. He acknowledged receipt on the following 3 October[9]. When the constitution[10] of the Order of Canada emerged it was gratifying to note how closely it followed points I had made in the memorandum.

Further information on certain matters was requested, and I complied by sending copies of the texts of the Patents of the Order of the British Empire and of the Royal Victorian Order.[11]

In due course by Letters Patent under the Royal Sign Manual of The Queen of Canada and the Great Seal of Canada, dated 21 March 1967 – and effective on the centenary of the establishment of Canada, 1 July 1967 – the Order of Canada was created with the constitution of the said order attached in a schedule thereto[12].

In order to obviate the problem of awards, considered by some as inappropriate, which had been made during World War I, giving rise to the Resolution of the House of Commons of 1919 – when one might say the baby was thrown out with the bath water – a Council of the Order, under the Chairmanship of the Chief Justice of Canada, was established to consider and advise on nominations.

The first awards were made on 1 July 1967; they have been bestowed at regular intervals ever since. There is no doubt that the Order has become a most prestigious award.

That the principal grade should be designated Companions was, in my opinion, brilliant. It continues a long tradition going back to the old Orders of the Garter, the Thistle, Bath, St Patrick's and St Michael and St George; it emphasizes the fact that the Order of Canada is, in accordance with its Letters Patent a '*society* [italics mine] of honour'. This was, I understand, first suggested by Colonel John Matheson and I heartily supported him in this. Further, in view of the fact that a Companion holds the highest grade of the highest Order in the

[9] SSA: Order of Canada file: Dr J.S. Hodgson, Principal Secretary to the Prime Minister to Dr Conrad Swan, Rouge Dragon Pursuivant of Arms, 3 October, 1966.

[10] Contained in the Schedule attached to the Letters Patent dated 21 March 1967 creating the Order of Canada.

[11] SSA: Order of Canada file: Western Union Cablegram: Dr J.S. Hodgson, Principal Secretary to the Prime Minister, to Dr Conrad Swan, 4 October 1966, requesting texts of Letters Patent establishing Order of the British Empire and Royal Victorian Order.

[12] The most serious of endeavours are not necessarily without the lighter side, as when I received a cable of 3rd September 1966 from Col. John Matheson, M.P., Parliamentary Secretary to the Prime Minister, addressed to 'Dr Swan, Rogue Dragon Pursuivant'. Had the operator decided that I was definitely 'non-U'? Was it a hint that I had not got my heraldic monster under control? Or was it a case of, 'the truth will out'? (SSA: Order of Canada file). Yet again, when discussions proceeded to consider appropriate post-nominals for members of the Order: for Companion of the Order of Canada 'C.O.C' and for Member 'M.O.C.' were passed on to me, I demurred vigorously, anticipating the opponents of all this saying 'what a COC(K) up!' and the 'MOC(K order)'! (SSA: Order of Canada file – D.F.Spink Esq to C.M.J.F. Swan, Esq. PhD. 20 September 1966).

country, and so is equivalent to a Knight Grand Cross, I was able to persuade the Earl Marshal that such should be entitled to have Supporters granted to their arms.[13]

By subsequent Letters Patent five years later[14] the grades of officer and member were added to that of companion. The insignia remain the property of the Order.

The establishment of the Order of Canada was simply one step further in the creation of such orders for the sovereign's Realms other than the United Kingdom. This is evidenced by the bringing into being of the Order of St Patrick, constituted in 1783 for Ireland;[15] the Royal Guelphic Order, founded 1815, in respect of Hanover; the Order of St Michael and St George, 1818, for the Ionian and Maltese Islands, and the Order of the Star of India for that sub-continent, 1861. Lord Monck, the first Governor General of Canada (1867-68), had in a sense foreshadowed the Letters Patent, effective 1 July 1967, with his suggestion of an Order of St Lawrence.

The Order of Canada was the first of those many that followed soon after, during the last quarter of the twentieth Century, as with the Order of Australia in 1975. One of my contributions to this antipodean decoration was to assure the Australian Cabinet – who sent a delegation before its creation to the College of Arms to discuss its establishment – that there was excellent precedent for the desire to have Wattle Flowers (the National Flower) embroidered in gold thread on the blue neck ribbon. This was to be found in the similar rendering of the Crown of Thorns on the black *moiré* neck ribbon of a Bailiff Grand Cross of the Order of Malta (one of the original military orders upon which, historically, all orders of Christian chivalry were initially modelled).

Further developments of this veritable constellation of chivalric distinctions within the Commonwealth at this time, with which I was intimately concerned, included my acting on behalf of the countries concerned in the establishment of entire systems of honours for Namibia (1992-94), and similarly for Antigua and Barbuda (1997), dealt with more fully in chapter XII.

II. PRO FIDE. PRO UTILITATE HOMINUM[16]

The first investiture of members of the Order of Canada took place on 24 November 1967 at the Governor-General's residence, Rideau Hall, Ottawa.

---

[13] C.A.R: Miscellaneous Enrolments I. 285 after due consultation with the Governor General and Government of Canada and in accordance with the Resolution of the Chapter of the College of Arms of December 1971. Supporters are beast, birds or human figures which stand on either side of the shield and support it. They are a great privilege in heraldry.

[14] 10 May, 1972.

[15] Ireland at this time was a separate kingdom. It did not become part of the United Kingdom until 1801.

[16] Mottoes of the Most Venerable Order of St John: For the Faith. For the Benefit of Mankind.

Despite the Resolution of 1919, this initial ceremony of the Order was not the first Investiture since what might be called the Bennett years of 1930-35, as such ceremonies of the Most Venerable Order of the Hospital of St John of Jerusalem[17] – frequently referred to simply as, 'St John' – had taken place at Rideau Hall at regular intervals since the foundation of the Canadian Commandery of that Order in 1934. This Order of the Crown, founded by Queen Victoria,[18] does have the grade of Knight, but as had been the case with the Royal Guelphic Order, founded for the Sovereign's Hanoverian Subjects – though frequently bestowed also upon those of the United Kingdom – the giving of that grade does not bestow the title of Sir upon the recipient. Presumably, in view of the excellent record of the hospitallery and similar work of the St John Ambulance, a foundation of that Order, it escaped the wrath the 'Resolutionists'. So for many years, it was the Order of St John that managed the drill and ceremonial of honorific investitures in Canada. As a member of that order I take great pride in this service it rendered for my compatriots.

In its Grand Priory[19], located in England, I had the honour of serving as Genealogist for some twenty years[20] and am a Knight of Justice of the Order.[21] In addition to helping with the direction of the order as a member of its chapter general, and on occasion providing heraldic advice and direction, there was also the duty of investigating and certifying the armorial entitlements of those Knights and Dames of Grace who were candidates for reclassification as Knights and Dames of Justice.

For orders located in England I was the Genealogist *en titre* for four, that is to say for St John, Bath[22], St Michael and St George[23] as well as the Order of Malta[24] (British Association); for the Garter I performed that function by virtue of being Garter Principal King of Arms.

With the Garter and Bath this meant supervising the making and setting up of armorial banners and Crests/coronets of the Knights/Ladies Companion, and of Knights Grand Cross, respectively; for St Michael and St George, Banners of the Knights Grand Cross – in all three Orders placed above the stalls of the holders; in addition, for all three Orders the stall plates comprising the Arms of the

---

[17] Sainty, Guy Stair. The Orders of St John. *The History, Structure, Membership and Modern Role of the Five Hospitaller Orders of St John of Jerusalem.* The American Society of the Most Venerable Order. New York, 1991

[18] 14 May 1888

[19] HRH. the Duke of Connaught was the Grand Prior when also Governor-General of Canada.

[20] 1976-95

[21] Officer, 17 May, 1972; Commander, 23 August, 1975; Knight 25 February, 1976.

[22] 1972-95

[23] 1989-95 as Honorary Genealogist, a position created for me, and designated as honorary as not occurring in the Statutes of the Order. Doubtless upon their revision the post will be included.

[24] 1975-95; of which Order I was also: Knight of Grace and Devotion; 1964 Knight of Honour and Devotion, 1979; Grand Officer of Merit, 1983.

Order of the Bath Installation Service, Henry VII's Chapel, Westminster Abbey. The Queen, as Sovereign of the Order, makes her offering of Gold and Silver kneeling before the altar. The Genealogist of the Order, York Herald of Arms, the Author (stands to the right, in front of steps) wearing the white mantle of an Officer of the Order. 28 October 1972. Credit: Hulton Archive: Getty Images.

person concerned along with name and date of award. These plates remain in the stall after the holders death as a permanent memorial of tenure, while the other armorial adjuncts about the stall are taken down upon demise to make way for the next occupant.

For the Order of Malta – the Sovereign and Military Order of St John of Jerusalem, of Rhodes and of Malta, commonly called the Order of Malta – the Genealogists' duties include certifying the armigerous status required for entry into various grades: three hundred years for Honour and Devotion; one hundred for Grace and Devotion; similarly for St John for reclassification as Knight/Dame of Justice, the person must be armigerous, whether by descent or personal grant by Letters Patent.

TRIA JUNCTA IN UNO[25]

The Most Honourable Order of the Bath is the Order for senior officers, both military and of the Civil Service. It was founded in 1725 by King George I, and has its chapel, Henry VII's Chapel, in Westminster Abbey[26]

Under the Sovereign of the Order there is a Great Master, always a prince of the blood – as with HRH the Duke of Connaught, who held that office when Governor General of Canada. At present the Great Master is the Prince of Wales. When his great-uncle and predecessor in that office, the old Duke of Gloucester died in 1974, we officers understood that the Earl Mountbatten of Burma had his eye on that position. Mercifully, the fact that though of royal blood he was not an HRH saved us, and we welcomed Prince Charles with open arms. From my India days I remembered how Mountbatten had taken an almost compulsive interest in minutiae, to the exhausted fury of many of his staff. Prince Charles was duly installed as Great Master on 28 May 1975. Several days before, he had attended the rehearsal for that occasion and its accompanying service. The Prince had just returned from taking part in a military exercise in Canada during which he had grown a full beaver, which was neatly trimmed. We had quite a long discussion about his Banner that I had recently had made. He wanted some adjustment of the overall tone. I often find it curious how so many want heraldry to look 'antique' – *eh bien, chacun à son goût*. I remember wondering, during our conversation, if he would parade for his installation complete with this splendid beard. In the event, he came sporting a moustache only; I think a certain august lady had had a word.

When a Knight Grand Cross has reached the necessary seniority – usually at present about fifteen years after appointment, – he becomes eligible for a stall, of which there are thirty-four in the chapel of the order. When one becomes vacant through death, at the next service of the order he will be installed by the Great Master. Apart from the Dean (an executive officer of the Order) saying certain prayers and issuing certain admonitions, all movements at the installations – and they are not uncomplicated – take place without any words of command. Instead there is a bow at particular moments, so previous rehearsals are essential. This is especially so when one remembers that Grand Crosses are very senior persons and unaccustomed to being moved around by others. However, the eyes of the officer responsible for a particular movement can become extremely expressive.

Between 1815 and 1913 there were no installations, and so no attaching of stall plates. Initially this was brought about by a sort of chivalric indigestion:

---

[25] Motto of the Order of the Bath: Three joined in one.
[26] For detailed history of the Order, vide Risk, James C. *The History of the Order of the Bath.* Spink & Son Ltd., London, 1972; and for the Chapel, Swan, Conrad. York Herald of Arms and Genealogist of the Order of the Bath. *The Order of the Bath: its Chapel, Ceremonial; Heraldry and Insignia.* Pitkins Pictorials, 1978

there were so many senior officers needing recognition because of the Napoleonic Wars, that installations were dispensed with. In time, this became a habit. As a result, no stall plates were put up for Sir John A. Macdonald, GCB, Canada's first Prime Minister; and Sir John Young (Lord Lisgar) GCB, its second Governor-General – a pity as his armorial bearings were among the first to bear the maple leaf – and many others.

Of these 'lost generations' the only one commemorated in the chapel so far is Sir John A. Macdonald. When I was the Genealogist, representations were received from Canada in the early 1970s asking if the Macdonald lacuna could not be remedied. Obviously a stall plate could not be placed in a stall, as this would falsify history; although entitled to one, he had never had one. In order to get round this problem, I suggested that a plate, in all ways the same as a stall plate, be prepared showing his armorial bearings, name, office and date of appointment, and that this be placed in the chapel as for a GCB, but that its actual location be on a stall end. This was readily agreed by my brother officers. What is more, although inscriptions in French, which had been customary for all stall plates prior to World War II, had ceased to be used, it was arranged that for Sir John A. Macdonald the inscription should be in both English and French.

Then with due ceremonial the plate was unveiled on Canada Day (1 July) of that year, 1974, by HE Mr J.H. Warren, High Commissioner for Canada to the Court of St James's, in the presence of the Honble Muriel Ferguson, Speaker of the Canadian Senate, and the Honble Lucien Lamoureaux, QC, MP, Speaker of the Canadian House of Commons.[27]

During the discussions of the officers leading up to their agreeing that a plate be raised, the Dean, the Very Reverend Eric S. Abbott, enquired: 'I trust he was not a Roman?' To which I replied: 'Dean – *carissimo* – this Roman can assure you that Sir John A. Macdonald was a copper-bottomed Protestant, though his appreciation of the decanter might have made some conclude otherwise' – at which everyone present laughed and we got on with deciding the details of the plate.

In 1913, George V put a stop to the long period of not adhering to the statutes which call for installations. Since then, they have taken place at regular intervals – the two World Wars alone causing interruptions.

Usually, everything goes off at these ceremonies as if each person performed the actions and moves involved every day – a sure sign of much planning and serious, previous rehearsal. However, being human, we cannot anticipate every contingency. So it was on Wednesday, 23 May 1990.

We had all just arrived, following the entry procession, at our places allotted: the clergy in the sanctuary (the Presbytery, in Abbey terms) and the remainder of

---

[27] For a good description of the ceremony, *vide The Calgary Herald* 'A Knightly tribute to Sir John' 10 July, 1974 p. 7.

us in choir. My place was immediately below The Queen's stall. We remained standing – as directed by the printed ceremonial – while the choir sang Psalm 68:

> Let God arise, and let his enemies be scattered;
> Let them also that hate him flee before him. …

most appropriate for such a predominantly military group. It was then that I felt the index finger of majesty forcing its determined way into my upper right shoulder blade. I turned towards Her Majesty with, I trust, a not too accusatory, yet definitely inquisitive look, but had my eyes re-directed, by her outstretched arm and pointing finger, towards an aged Grand Cross. He was swaying to and fro and looking as if he was about to faint. *Sotto voce*, yet with authority, she said into my ear: 'Tell that man to sit down.' So, with that military obedience acquired in the Indian Army, in a flash I was standing before the subject of her concern. 'The Queen says: 'sit down'' I said. There was no response. His flanking *confrères* echoed the royal command – to no avail. Fortunately, just then, two nurses from St Thomas's Hospital came forward from their discreet position beneath the choir screen, and we finally got the distinguished and antique Grand Cross to do as the Queen said.

After that, the service continued and the sovereign, officers and Knights Grand Cross were then led by Elgar's *Imperial March* towards Henry VII's chapel for the installation.

It was when moving forward, very slowly, at this point in the proceedings that one's mind might begin to wander just a little. Are we not told by some very holy people that they find it impossible to get to the end of even one *Our Father* without at least one distraction? So for us poor grosser souls, I suppose it was not too unusual for me sometimes to catch myself recalling my fellow Indian cadet at the Officers Training School, Bangalore, asking of the Order of the Bath:– 'What kind of bath is it, tin or what?'[28] This was, it seemed to me, a reasonable question if we Europeans must so designate one of our great honours. Catching myself smile, I would pull myself together, recognizing familiar faces to left and right among the Knights Commander and Companions who would remain in their places while the Grand Crosses proceeded through to the installation.

Amid this flanking sea of both service and civilian distinction one would note, here and there, a positive pharos of fidelity to his allies and compatriots. Their presence warned against the treacherous rocks of compromise. They had been made members of the order during World War II as an expression of gratitude for their gallantry and loyalty. Following VE Day in 1945 they remained in Britain in order to look after their like-minded compatriots, refusing to serve a nominally independent yet patently Communist government imposed by Moscow on the banks of the Vistula. Their resolute determination helped immeasurably towards

---

[28] SSA: IV CS, to EHS 20 August, 1944

the restoration of a freely chosen government for their country, a denouement much assisted by the agency of a trade union leader[29] and a Pope.[30,31] One could not miss them: amid a mass of British uniforms and morning suits, they – following the Continental custom for showing the greatest respect for the order – attended in white tie and tails, wearing the appropriate insignia of their grade.

Those in the procession having arrived in Henry VII's chapel took part in the installations (already described) and then returned to their places in choir, this time to Variation No 9 (*Nimrod*) from the *Enigma Variations,* once again by Elgar.

Then not having forgotten to pray for God's 'servants departed…members of this Most Honourable Order…the fair pattern of valiant and true Knighthood' we then sang *God Save the Queen* and processed out to the strains of:

For all the Saints who from their labours rest…

The gallant old gentleman who had tottered during the service was looked after all the while by the two nurses.

The Queen and the Officers then retired to the Deanery for well-deserved spirituous refreshment – a small G&T for HM; for the others something larger and stronger. Standing around below Canaletto's famous painting of the procession of the Knights of the Bath (1747) we discussed the day's events, and sympathized over the old unfortunate's turn. Following that, I remarked to Her Majesty: 'Yes, and this was the first time, ma'am, that I have been struck by my sovereign,' to which she replied: 'Just wait, York!', then laughed in that infectious way she has, and all joined in the laughter.

After that I thought I ought to have a small circle of purple velvet stitched to the upper right back of all my jackets in commemoration of the distinction of having been 'physically assaulted' by my sovereign – rather as the Royal Welch Fusiliers, to this day, have a flash of five silk swallow-tailed black ribbons stitched in fan-like formation to the back of their uniform collars following service in Nova Scotia at the time of the Peninsular War.[32]

---

[29] Lech Wałęsa, who later became a GCB when President of Poland.

[30] HH Pope John-Paul II.

[31] Lieutenant General Marian Kukiel, KCB, Minister of War within the Polish Government in Exile, Lieutenant General Tadeusz Komorowski, CB, Air Vice-Marshal Stanisław Ujejski, KCB, Lieutenant General Michal Tadeusz Tokarzewski – Karaszewicz, CB; Lieutenant General Stanisław Kopanski, CB, CBE, DSO; Major General Stanisław Maczek, CB; Major General Bronislaw Regulski, CB, and Major General Stanisław Tabor, CB, were among those I recall when I was the Genealogist of the Order.

[32] When men ceased to wear wigs, they tied their hair in a pony-tail or queue, as such was called, and the 'flash' kept the grease of their hair off the uniform. In July 1818 when the Peninsular War was about to open, the soldiers were told to cut their hair short. The Royal Welch Fusiliers, however, were on service in Nova Scotia at the time and continued to wear their flashes , which were confirmed by William IV as a distinction to the regiment in 1834. For further details *vide*, Edwards, Major J T *Military Customs.* 4th Edition. Aldershot, 1954 pp 110-111.

The Officers of the order also have armorial stall plates and stalls[33]. One of the Officers' stall plates that particularly interested me was that of Alexander Ochterlony. As Blanch Lyon Pursuivant of the Order, he was the first British North American to become an Officer of Arms, in 1784, aged twenty years.[34] He had been born in Boston, and was the step-son of Sir Isaac Heard, one of my predecessors as Garter Principal King of Arms.[35]

AUSPICIUM MELIORIS AEVI[36]

The Most Distinguished Order of St Michael and St George[37] was founded in 1818[38] conferring a mark of royal favour on the most meritorious of the Ionians and Maltese. The Ionian Islands were a British Protectorate at the time.[39] The Order is now the principal Order for Governors General and members of the Diplomatic Corps.

The annual service of this Order is, in my opinion, the most heraldic of all the Orders. When there is a banner to be affixed in the chapel (in St Paul's Cathedral) this is done, accompanied by prayers, at the beginning of the service. One such I particularly remember[40] was that of the Right Honble Sir John Kerr, AK, GCMG, GCVO, who, as Governor-General of Australia, had had the singular satisfaction of being able to dismiss an unsatisfactory Prime Minister. Upon completing an affixing, a procession leaves the chapel and makes its way up the nave to the high altar with everyone singing some such hymn as:

> Christ is the King, O friends rejoice!
> Brothers and sisters with one voice
> Make all men know he is your choice:
> Alleluia;

Stirring music, stirring words – and there's one thing one has to admit: those Anglicans do know how to sing. If Grand Crosses have died since the previous service, then their banners, having been taken down, are carried by Squires in this procession to be laid up on the high altar by the prelate. In the same

---

[33] The Stall of the Genealogist is Lower 5, South side.

[34] Lower 15, North side.

[35] (1784-1822). One of the first at the College of Arms to interest himself in North American genealogies. Visited the continent several times when working in Bilbao, Spain, 1751-57 prior to joining the College, 1759

[36] Motto of the Most Distinguished Order of St Michael and St George – Token of a better age.

[37] For a history of the Order see, De la Bere, Brigadier Sir Ivan. *The Queens Order of Chivalry*, Spring Books, London, 1964 p 139 ff and Abela, A E *The Order of St Michael and St George in Malta and Maltese Knights of the British Realm*. Progress Press Co. Ltd., Valetta, 1988.

[38] April, 27.

[39] Before becoming Governor-General of Canada, Sir John Young, later Lord Lisgar, GCMG, had been Lord High Commissioner of the Ionian Islands, 1855-59.

[40] On 17 July 1990.

procession, the King of Arms of the Order, the Chancellor and the Grand Master is each preceded by his banner, also carried by a Squire – it all makes a brave show of identification.

In my capacity as Honorary Genealogist I would attend the meetings of the Officers, almost always in the Foreign and Commonwealth Office – that splendid Italianate structure which on one side faces Whitehall, on the other overlooks St James's Park and Horseguards Parade. Much restoration work was going on during those years.

Foreign diplomats came and went, and my time coincided with that period when those from behind the Iron Curtain started to look much more human and, at times, not a little worried. One witnessed, as one passed along those corridors of diplomacy, the *accoucheurs* – willing or otherwise – attendant upon the birth pangs of a new life for Eastern Europe, which, naturally, interested and heartened me greatly.

Soon my new colleagues in the F & CO, were able to assist my family and myself in our first visit for over a century to our ancestral acres, but more of that later.

HONI SOIT QUI MAL Y PENSE[41]

The final Order of Chivalry with which I had an official and professional connection was the Most Noble Order of the Garter. That it was founded by Edward III[42] is certain; its exact date, not so. The year 1348 is usually taken as that of its foundation[43]. It is the oldest Order of Chivalry in Britain, and ranks among the oldest in Europe, along with that of the Golden Fleece (1429/30).

Members of the College of Arms became associated with the Order of the Garter from their earliest days. The most junior lead the processions of its members from the State Apartments of Windsor Castle down to St George's Chapel for the installation of new members and attendance at its services.

When I was first appointed to the College, as Rouge Dragon Pursuivant of Arms, I took my turn in leading the processions, along with my senior by a year (and soon to be very good friend), Rodney Onslow Dennys, then Rouge Croix Pursuivant of Arms – sometime of the Foreign Office; on the Nazi 'Death List' because of services to the Royal Netherlands Government during the German invasion of Holland, and brother-in-law of Graham Greene.

The heralds are summoned to attend upon their Sovereign and the Order at Windsor Castle for the ceremonies just mentioned. The present Queen has held them annually during her reign, except in 1984, and in view of her equine

---

[41] Motto of the Most Noble Order of the Garter – Evil to him who evil thinks (or literally: Evil to him who evil thinks of it).

[42] Reigned 1327-77.

[43] Begent, Peter J. and Chesshyre, Hubert, Clarenceux King of Arms and Secretary of the Order. *The Most Noble Order of the Garter 650 Years*. Spink, London, 1999 p. 15.

interests it has always been fairly safe to gauge that they will be required to be on duty on the Monday of Ascot Week – very convenient for forward planning.

On the day, most of the heralds, dressed in Royal Household uniform, usually have a picnic of champagne, smoked salmon and other simple gastronomic pleasures near the Thames at Runnymede. However, such was not my form, and I always repaired to some convenient hostelry near Windsor with my wife and the two guests we heralds were privileged to bring for these occasions. Such an arrangement ensured that one could have one's champagne and address one's victuals in reasonable comfort in all weathers. The heralds would then make for the Castle and, having dropped off their spouses and guests for the chapel, they would go to the State Apartments and be assisted into their tabards by Ede and Ravenscroft – the well-known London tailors.

Once so robed they went into St George's Hall and awaited the arrival of the members of the Order. When doing so, one might inspect the splendid display of the arms of the Knights, on the walls, or remark on the lines of the badminton court – used by the royal children – which peeked out from the edges of the carpets laid down for this occasion. A Guards' orchestra played in the background in another area, and when it stopped one knew that the luncheon the Queen had just given to her guests was over and that the Knights and Lady Companions would soon be in St George's Hall. The Officers of the Order were also entertained at these luncheons, which I attended when I became Garter. Of that for 15 June 1994 I noted in my diary:[44]

> It certainly was the most elegant 'meals on wheels' that I have ever had as the luncheon was, basically, brought down all the way from Buckingham Palace for this occasion – the real kitchens at the Castle not being in working order since the fire.[45]

As the members of the Order came into St George's Hall – all duly robed, complete with elaborate gold and enamel collars worn over their Garter blue velvet mantles – the heralds would start to invite them into their respective places according to seniority, *juniores priores*, for the procession outside down to St George's Chapel. After their excellent luncheon they were usually at their most biddable.

Some were especial friends and one would exchange some pleasantries, as with Lord de L'Isle who had been a fellow-guest at Government House, Perth. Then there were others, such as Field Marshal the Viscount Montgomery of Alamein, my father-in-law's first cousin, as mentioned before. He was one of the great and much-respected World War II generals. All who served under him recalled how he never had his men attack unless there was a real chance of

---

[44] SSA: Garter Swan Diary, 1992-95.

[45] There had been a serious fire not long before in the Castle.

victory: none of the carnage of World War I for him. He would even take the trouble to write personally to the families of his men. As a result he was adored by the families of the Other Ranks.

Respect for his professional qualities was also to be found among his officers, but there was not that same rapport between them and him as with the Other Ranks. I came to understand why. It so happened that he had asked me to add some of his immediate relations to the genealogical records on his family at the College of Arms. This I did and, as he requested, issued a certified extract from the records including the additions. When we next met up in St George's Hall prior to a Garter Service, the Field Marshal said in a loud voice: 'Rouge Dragon, you have made a grave error in my pedigree certificate.' Naturally, I was taken aback – especially being very junior at the time – and so simply replied: 'Field Marshal, if you will write and let me know what you consider incorrect I shall look into it and report to you. If I have made a mistake I apologize, without reservation.' In time he wrote and referred to a detail concerning an aunt. Before proceeding further with the story, I should explain that according to the Law of Evidence in England one is assumed to know something about one's grandparents and their descendants. Accordingly, if one provides precise details (such as full names, dates, places of birth, marriage or death) and attests these with a solemn affidavit signed before a witness, then such details are accepted until proved otherwise. Beyond grandparents independent evidences – such as official birth certificates and so on – are required.

So when I was back at the College of Arms, I looked into the detail about which he had complained. It turned out to be something he himself had provided in a solemn affidavit. Fortunately, such documents are carefully preserved at the College. Accordingly, I sent the field marshal a photocopy of this and, to do him credit, received a full apology in writing – an unusual possession to have from 'Monty', to say the least. The official College Record was subsequently corrected; I didn't charge the field marshal the usual fee for that, in view of his apology.

When we all met up again next year for Garter Day, I hoped that the field marshal would have said something, in an equally loud voice as on the previous occasion to put the record straight. One would not expect him to stand up and publicly confess his error – that would have been *de trop* – but what about something like: 'Thank you, Rouge Dragon, for that good work you did for me.' But, that was apparently hoping for too much – though how nice it would have been! Doubtless, the whole thing was good for my humility. I had come to understand why my father-in-law, and others, were a little reserved about him.

The character of the new member of the Order was often reflected in the manner of preparation for his/her installation. Usually, on the Friday before the Monday of that ceremony and the Service of the Order, a rehearsal would be held in St George's Chapel by Garter. These would not preclude unexpected problems on the day, but they do help to reduce them to a minimum. It is extremely helpful if those who have to lead a section taking part are present, so as to refresh memories over details; it is particularly useful for those about to be installed.

When a Royal is to be installed, they prove no problem. A competent and experienced *aide* is sent to note every move. He/she then goes through the procedure in private with his Royal master/mistress so as to be fully briefed for the occasion. So it was for the rehearsal and installation, for example, of HM Queen Margrethe II of Denmark.[46]

Non-Royals usually make a point of attending the rehearsal in person. However, when Sir Edward Heath was to be installed in 1992 he – though not Prime Minister for eighteen years – was 'far too busy' to turn up, and sent a young man to be his stand-in, who had never been sent on such an errand before. As a result, it was fortunate that the heralds allotted to look after Sir Edward on the day acted with their usual efficiency, and firmly guided him at all points, so avoiding an occasion of discontent.

On the other hand, someone who has the reputation of always knowing what to do, and doing so in a determined fashion, proved to be a model of docility in all this: Margaret, Lady Thatcher. When in 1995 she was about to become the second (in history) Lady Companion of the Order of the Garter she made an appointment to come and see me, I being then Garter Principal King of Arms. Upon arrival, she explained that she had never taken part in anything like an installation before and asked would I kindly tell her exactly what she had to do. So we had several private rehearsals in my chambers at the College of Arms before the usual Friday rehearsal in the Chapel. She was present in person and took part in the rehearsal, and so on the day acquitted herself splendidly.

After that digression, let us return to St George's Hall. Upon the arrival of The Queen and other members of the Royal Family, Garter would raise his sceptre as the signal to move off. At that the most junior heralds would start to lead the procession towards the Grand Staircase. That would be descended, passing on the landing, the Colours of the Southern Irish Regiments.

As we go out into the open air we are surrounded on either side by the members of the public who have received passes to witness the procession. If there is a breeze, the *ailettes* of our tabards are blown upwards. One wonders if they will live up to their name and soon have us air-borne. The Tudor hats worn by the heralds – velvet tam-o'shanter affairs – always seem to stay on. A Guards' Subaltern acts as left marker, keeping near by the two leading heralds. He is permitted to turn around so that he can advise the leaders whether to quicken, or more usually slacken, the pace – bearing in mind the maturity of some of the knights.

---

[46] Installation: 16 June, 1960.

A Guards' band plays, usually to the left, and the heralds walk along – almost ambling, no marching for the College of Arms, that sort of thing is left to the Lyon Court North of the Border. One hears snippets of conversation: 'Oh, look, there's the King of Spain. He's going to be installed today'; 'There's Churchill. He's enjoying himself;' 'the Queen Mother and the Emperor Haile Selassie are well matched for size, aren't they,' and so on.

Finally, one gets to St George's Chapel, through the cloister, up the West front steps and so inside. Having made a few paces inside, the trumpeters sound a salute as The Queen enters. The ladies curtsey as she and other Royals pass; the men give the Court bow, bringing the head forward so that the chin rests on the knot of the tie, nothing more.

With the Queen just inside the choir, *God Save the Queen* is sung, at the end of which she says:

It is Our pleasure that the Knight(s) Companion(s) (and Lady Companion(s) [if appropriate]) newly invested be installed.

The Chancellor of the Order then calls out the name of the first to be installed. By this time, he or she is standing before the Queen; and is then conducted to the stall by Garter. If there is another to be installed, the procedure is repeated and the Gentleman Usher of the Black Rod (an Officer of the Order as well as of Parliament) conducts that one to the designated stall; and so on, alternating between Garter and Black Rod.

When the installations are completed, Garter conducts the Sovereign to her stall; Black Rod the Chancellor to his, and upon Garter raising his sceptre the service commences. It includes prayers, a reading from Sacred Scripture, a hymn, perhaps 'Now Thank we all our God'[47] – followed by a Blessing, and the Service concludes.

A procession then proceeds down the nave, led once again by the heralds, and so out onto the broad, wide steps at the west end. The Guards are already there on either side. The heralds file out and place themselves in front of the Guardsmen, and finally the Knights place themselves in front of the heralds. The Sovereign and others of the Royal Family descend down the centre of the steps and mount carriages which will take them, once again, through the spectators on either side of the roadway back to the State Apartments.

The Knights and their ladies follow the same route in cars as do the heralds. Once back inside the State Apartments, off come the Tabards and so to tea in the Waterloo Chamber – much appreciated by everyone. Soon all disperse; summon their cars to the portico and are driven off home, after a long, yet good day's work.

⋆   ⋆   ⋆

---

[47] As at the Service on 15 June, 1988.

One innovation recently introduced in respect of the armorial identification of members of the Order concerns Lady Companions. Until 1995, according to the Law of Arms of England,[48] married ladies who were not Sovereigns identified themselves by marshalling their own arms with those of their husbands. However, this requirement concerning married ladies struck me as incongruous bearing in mind the part women play in contemporary society. Many hold the highest positions, and these positions are always considered as held absolutely in their own right and not that of their husbands.

Accordingly, I pressed that all married women be authorized to identify themselves with their own arms alone. In order to be so allowed, a Kings of Arms Ruling would be necessary. Now, the Kings of Arms tend to be rather like oil tankers sailing in a determined and serene manner through the ocean of life, and as a result they take a long time to change course. However, to change course on this point I felt was essential. Devoted as I am to precedent, I hold that it should only be the rock-bed of action if it meets the requirements of society; surely the inability to change is a sign of atrophy if not disease. Fortunately, I had the support of John Philip Brooke Brooke-Little, CVO, Norroy Ulster King of Arms[49], in my desire for this change.

A Kings of Arms Ruling, as the name implies, concerns the Kings of Arms alone. As a result, it was necessary for Garter, Clarenceux and Norroy and Ulster to agree, but, as I and Brooke-Little knew only too well, such would be more easily aspired to than achieved. This was due to the character of our brother King, Clarenceux, at the time that great scholar, Sir Anthony Wagner, KCB, KCVO, D.Litt, FSA. He had been at the College since 1931 and had previously been Garter for seventeen years. He was an heraldic monument, and he knew it. By now, however, he had become totally blind. Notwithstanding, he was determined to hold his own and continue to make his mark, even if, his age and physical condition often left him 'half a beat behind the conductor's baton'. 'The conductors' here were those who had succeeded him as Garter. Acutely sympathetic to his blindness, they were torn, between admiration for his heraldic, particularly genealogical, knowledge and the distraction to which such a 'dowager' drove them. Accordingly much persuasion was necessary. Yet Clarenceux put up a magnificent rearguard action with enfilade fire on the flanks, so to speak, all the way, as Norroy and Ulster and I gradually advanced. Finally, though, he gave way and the appropriate Kings of Arms Ruling was issued on 7 April, 1995.[50]

---

[48] Interestingly enough, because of its international implications based on Roman not Common Law.

[49] In my opinion, an enormous debt is owed to Brooke-Little in the way that he has brought home to the general public an appreciation of the relevance of heraldry in our lives. Through the Heraldry Society, which he founded along with its organ *The Coat of Arms*, he had his finger very much on the pulse of society, and the College of Arms benefited prodigiously from his presence in that naturally, and quite rightly, conservative body.

[50] CAR: Miscellaneous Enrolments II.40

As a result, the armorials about the stall in St George's Chapel of the second Lady Companion of the Order of the Garter, that is to say, Margaret, Lady Thatcher, displays her arms alone with a silver inescutcheon (very small shield) placed upon them to indicate that she is married.

VICTORIA[51]

The final Order of the Crown with which I have had an association, though not as one of its Officers, is the Royal Victorian Order of which I have been a member since 1978.[52]

Founded by Queen Victoria on 21 April 1896, the purpose of the Order is to recognise extraordinary or important or personal service 'to the Sovereign, or otherwise merit the Sovereign's Royal favour'[53]. Along with the Orders of the Garter, Thistle and Merit it is not subject to ministerial advice, and is bestowed at the personal instance of the Sovereign; the insignia is even paid for out of the Privy Purse and is not borne by a parliamentary grant.

IN HOC SIGNO VINCES

Any person with a drop of Polish blood in his veins thrills at the very mention of John Sobieski's victory at the Battle of Vienna, 12 September 1683 – surely Poland's 'Finest Hour'. It saved Europe from the, up to then, inexorable Western *Jehad* of Islam, and preserved Notre Dame and Westminster Abbey *et alii* from the fate of Constantinople's Santa Sophia.

And was it not the Sacred and Military Constantinian Order of St George which contributed so signally to that victory? As a result, in the following year on May 11th, the King issued a Decree at *Jaworów* recognizing all the privileges of the Knights of the Order within his Most Serene Commonwealth – in The Crown (Poland) from whence my paternal ancestors originally came, and also in The Grand Duchy (Lithuania) where, by the time of the Decree, they had lived for upwards of a century.

Yet the Polish connection does not stop there for today the Grand Master of this House Order of the Bourbons of the Two Sicilies, HRH. Prince Ferdinand, Duke of Castro, is himself half-Polish. His mother was Caroline, daughter of Andrew, Count Zamoyski. Further, almost all the cousins at Ferdinand's generation are also half-Polish as his uncle, Prince Gabriel, first married Margaret, daughter of Prince Adam Czartoryski and, following her death, Cecily, daughter of Prince Casimir Zubomirski.

As to origins, the Constantinian Order certainly existed in the second half of the sixteenth century. In 1570 one notes the first recorded investiture with, six

---

[51] Inscription on the Motto ribbon of the insignia of the Royal Victorian Order.
[52] Member (4th Class) MVO, 1978 (re-designated as Lieutant, LVO, 1984); Commander, CVO, 1986; Knight Commander, KCVO, 1994.
[53] Statutes of the Royal Victorian Order, 25 May 1936 Clause IV.

years later, the Holy See recognizing the Angeli not only as heirs of the Byzantine throne, but also as Grand Masters of the Order. From then on it has enjoyed the support of succeeding Pontiffs down to, and including, John Paul II[54].

Tradition has it that the Order descended from the Golden Militia formed by the Emperor Constantine to guard the Labarum or Imperial Standard, which displayed the cross and famous injunction: *In hoc signo vinces* as experienced in a vision by the Emperor just before his victory at the *Milvian* Bridge in AD 312.

Be that as it may, the insignia of the Constantinian Order – for as long as we have its recorded existence – has always included this type of cross, plus the Greek ☧ together with the injunction in abbreviated form: IHSV. As to the particular shade of blue of its ribbon, I feel sure that the Princess Clementina Sobieska, grand-daughter of the Vienna victor, and mother of Bonnie Prince Charlie, would have described, with a twinkle in her eye, as *True Blue*(!)

In 1697 the last of the Angeli Gian Andrea ceded the Grand Magistry to the Farnese Dukes of Parma. In 1734 this passed, by inheritance, to the Bourbons of the Two Sicilies where it remains today – and even so recognized by the Italian Republic[55].

The principal duty of the Constantinian Order is, and has always been, the defence of the Holy Roman Church, the fostering of the growth of religious principles among mankind and practical charity[56].

The advent of the Order among the English was relatively late. At the time it came very much to the fore the English Catholics were grappling, *usque ad sanguinem,* with the problems caused by the religious policies of certain Tudors.

However, in 1672 the Order was brought to the attention of their compatriots by that great scholar and yesteryear colleague of mine, Sir Elias Ashmole, Windsor Herald of Arms, in his *Institutions, Law and Ceremonies of the Most Noble Order of the Garter* where he refers to its members as the 'Constantinian Angelick Knights.'

Nevertheless, as a result of the 'Flight of Geese'[57], we find Irish officers serving in the armies of both Parma and The Two Sicilies, and entering the Order. An early example is Benedotto Hervey – 'Irlandese' – Captain in the Parmesan Bodyguard of Duke Antonio who was received as a Knight of Grace in 1728.

The first British knight normally resident in England to be brought into the Order was almost certainly Captain William D'arley. He commanded the Marines on board HMS *Vanguard* – Nelson's flagship – when she evacuated the royal family from Naples to Palermo in December, 1799 – not without running

[54] H.H. Pope John Paul II is represented in the order by an Ecclesiastical Counsellor – Cardinal Mario Francesco Pompedda.

[55] By Presidential decrees of 1963, 1973 and 1981.

[56] Statutes of the Constantinian Order of St George, 1982.

[57] See chapter III footnote 27

into a storm which almost sank the ship. He was created a Knight of Grace in 1801 (although probably a Protestant as Catholics were still prevented from serving as officers at the time). Later that year, on 7 December a Royal Licence of George III not only authorized him to wear the insignia appropriate to his grade, on his uniform, but also accorded him the title of 'Sir'[58].

As the nineteenth century wore on, and with the 'Second Spring' for Catholics, various United Kingdom subjects were received into the Order. Among these, one of my favourite *confreres* would have been a Canon of St Peters, the Reverend the Honble George Talbot, fifth son of the 3rd Lord Talbot of Malahide. His definition of the role of the Catholic laity was, 'To hunt, to shoot and to entertain' – *oh la, la*, what would the antagonists of our Countryside Alliance say to that?!

So we move on into the first three quarters of the twentieth century, but without any corporate organization of the British members. Then in 1975 four were brought in together: Major General the Viscount Monckton of Brenchley (who will be recalled from chapter V), the Viscount Furness, John Brooke-Little, Richmond Herald (later Clarenceux King of Arms, and also godfather of our no. 2, Juliana) and myself (then York Herald). This led, within a few years, to the establishment of the Constantinian Delegation of Great Britain and Ireland, on the Council of which I have the honour to serve as a Knight Grand Cross[59].

★   ★   ★

It is fascinating how to an extraordinary degree each of these Orders has a special character about it, all its own. This becomes especially apparent when members come together, usually for one of their Services.

When, for example, the Most Venerable Order of St John assembles, one gets a distinct impression of earnest efficiency. One knows that if someone suddenly falls sick, one will immediately, politely yet firmly, be asked to make room while the kiss of life is given, the femur set, the head put in the recovery position, or whatever is required. There is a whiff of the carbolic about.

If the Order of the Bath congregates, it is a matter of 'short back and sides', with a hint of discreet hair lotion from the best barbers on Jermyn Street, and a view of the situation, whether the problem is military or civilian, befitting those who make the real decisions in the country. The generals' ladies are adept at inspecting the mens' lines.

The Order of St Michael and St George on the other hand has the air of a garden party about it when they come to London, from the four corners of the globe, and foregather at St Paul's. Nostrils sense a touch of Chanel in the air, and

---

58 CAR: I. 36/191

59 For further information about this order see, Seward, Desmond. *Italy's Knights of St George. The Constantinian Order.* Van Duren Publishers, Gerrards Cross 1986, and Crispo, Michaele Basile, *L'Ordine Constantiniano di San Georgio: Storia, Stemmi e Cavalieri.* Parma, 2002.

large ladies' hats are the order of the day: members of the same club are coming together. One suspects that the apparent gaiety is a jovial front against some of the hard postings they are called on to endure. Some of the juniors of the Foreign Office attending, though not yet members of the Order, may lean over and with a smile say, 'You know, don't you, what the post-nominals of this Order really stand for? CMG: 'call me god'; KCMG: 'kindly call me god'; GCMG: 'god calls me god'.' Naughty young bucks – but its always amusing to learn the in-house jokes.

We are back to square one, as it were, when we come to the Order of Malta. It continues to be a religious order of the Church, and in 2013 will have reached its millennium. The higher echelons have taken the vows of chastity and obedience. It is, as I have noted, one of those that originally inspired the establishment of the Golden Fleece, the Garter and the other old temporal Orders. There is the Grand Priory of England for those who have taken the vows of religion, and the British Association for the others, both men and women.

Generally speaking the average age of the Order of Malta in England is younger than for those others we have been discussing, as recruitment is frequently at an earlier age. Further, the aristocratic element is higher in this than in the other Orders as there are nobiliary requirements for entry into the higher grades. Its members are fully conscious of belonging to families that represent the England of Chaucer and of Richard the Lion Heart, of Agincourt and of Crecy. Their attitude to their ancestral ways is quintessentially English. This means, if necessary, recusancy and, from time to time, the block – reflecting that characteristic of their compatriots: stubbornness or firmness (depending upon one's point of view).

The Order of the British Empire positively oozes merit from every pore. It is a huge five-grade Order which brings together a vast concourse of people from all walks of life and all gradations of society, who have contributed to the commonweal by their performance in life, be it in the arts, business world, science or any of the many legitimate walks of life, and they are brought into 'the British Empire', as the *cognoscenti* refer to this Order. It constitutes a throng of meritorious excellence.[60]

When the Royal Victorian Order meets up, the atmosphere is one of a family gathering. Every one there has served a particular person, or others related to that person; as a result they are bound together in a familial way. The principal private secretary will be seen talking with a gillie; a superintendent of police passes the time of day with a lady-in-waiting, and so on. Everyone knows that the other fits in, even if he does not know how, and every member of this familial Order is appreciated by the others for these qualities, and respected for them.

---

[60] The most recent resident Canadian to have been made a Knight Grand Cross of this Order appears to have been Edward W. Beatty, of Montreal, in the Birthday Honours of King George V, 23 June, 1935.

The atmosphere of a meeting of the Constantinian Order in Britain reminds me strongly of that of a Hunt or of a Cricket Club: devotion to ideals, principles and purposes held in common combined with catholicity of membership.

The Order is basically traditionalist as one would hope having a Bourbon as its Grand Master. As already noted, the basic ideals, principles and purpose of this Order focus on the support of the *Servitor servitorum Dei* for whom he is Christ's Vicar on earth. Its membership, as expressed in the Delegation of Great Britain and Ireland, includes members of old Catholic families, as well as of the Second Spring; of the peerage, as well as of 'the other place'; of barons of industry, diplomats, scientists; of Catholic members of the British Royal Family, and so on – its catholicity could hardly be more complete.

In addition to striving towards its *raison d'etre* it always remembers the necessity of practical help for the poor and the sick.[61]

Their Protestant compatriots, whose charitable work has Constantinian admiration are associated ecumenically with the Order by means of medals *Bene merenti*[62]. Other non-Catholics, including our Elder Brothers in Faith, those of the Hebrew Faith, and Muslims are enrolled in the order of Francis I which is not exclusively Roman Catholic[63]. The Grand Magistry of this order is also held by the Grand Master of the Constantinian Order.

Concerning the Order of the Garter, as the Duke of Wellington said, 'There's no damned merit about it; it's just distinction.' About their ladies lingers the essence of Yardley's.

Those are my impressions gained over a period of some forty years.

★   ★   ★

For the herald, it is significant that in respect of all these Orders just mentioned the vexillological aspect is always present: more with some less with others but it is there, the importance of flags. Flags in various forms play an important role not only in such societies of honour, but also in any grouping of associated people.

And so it is with countries. Each sooner or later requires symbolic identification in the form of a flag. Canada was no exception.

'An Unflagging Debate' The Canadian Almanac, 1896[64]

Following World War II, the designing of a national flag for the country became not just a pastime, but, for many, a compulsive hobby. In the sixties, as Canada

---

[61] Totalling some £600,000 in this current year (2003)

[62] A well-known recipient of such in gold was the historian, Sir Iain Moncreiffe of the Ilk, Bt., CVO, QC, DL.

[63] Such as The Baroness Thatcher, the Duke of Westminster and the Archbishop of Canterbury.

[64] Article on the subject of a distinctive Canadian flag by Edward Marion Chadwick a well-known Toronto Barrister and author of *Ontarian Families*.

approached the centenary of Confederation, as soon as it was known that the Federal Government was contemplating the adoption of a distinct national flag, Ottawa was inundated with suggestions – who could say heraldry was dead?! Rooms in the Parliament Buildings were filled with designs, some *naïve*, some primitive, some incomprehensibly complex, some excellent.

Because of this intense interest, coupled with the political passions it aroused, the way ahead would be something like a descent down the Larchine rapids. Colonel John Matheson, the Parliamentary Private Secretary to the Prime Minister, Mr Pearson, had to pilot it. However, as matters turned out, he was well up to the task, and there is little doubt that without him the ultimate successful denouement would not have been achieved.

As the College of Arms had assisted Canada, armorially, over the centuries[65], Ottawa considered it would be able to make a helpful contribution over a flag for the country. As a result, Matheson paid a courtesy call to the College in 1963, and was received amicably enough, by the senior herald, Sir Anthony Wagner, Garter Principal King of Arms. When he mentioned to Garter Canada's interest in a distinctive flag, 'Sir Anthony advanced the startling proposition that this was a subject over which he himself was vested by the Queen with complete jurisdiction and authority'.[66] Whereupon Matheson referred to the desire of successive Prime Ministers for this matter to be placed ultimately before the Parliament of Canada. At this 'Garter expressed visible annoyance at any such proposition, noting that intervention by Canada's Parliament was entirely unnecessary. A flag should constitute a grant from himself, the Queen's Principal King of Arms, to the Canadian people'.[67] Naturally, he would seek to please the government, but in the end he held that the decision lay with him. From his taking up such a position, one might have concluded that he had never heard of the Statute of Westminster (1931), or that if he had, he was unaware of its effect – let alone how matters had developed since its passage – *vis-à-vis* what might be termed the 'Old Dominions'.

It was obvious that, learned as Garter was in certain fields, he was not so in regard to the constitutional position of Canada: a completely separate and absolutely sovereign state. He was unaware that the Queen of Canada, as such, was in no way subject to the sovereign of the United Kingdom, or of the latter's officers, unless Canada chose to be.

Yet again, in the context of Canadian politics at the time Garter's approach was simply out of touch with reality. After this interview, Matheson and I discussed

---

[65] See for example, Swan, Conrad. *Canada: Symbols of Sovereignty*, University of Toronto Press, '1977, pp 3-13

[66] Matheson, John Ross. *Canada's Flag. A Search for a Country*. Mika Publishing Co. Belleville, Ontario, 1986 p. 121.

[67] *Ibid.*

the matter at length and we agreed to continue to co-operate closely: 'We would join forces against the Philistines on all sides'[68]

As a result, back in Ottawa, he continued to advance the cause of a National Flag, and to this end delivered his important 'Flag Speech' in the House of Commons on June 17 and 30, 1964. Hansard records it, in part, as follows:

June 30

Mr John R. Matheson (Leeds): Mr Speaker, tomorrow we celebrate another national birthday, our 97th, without a flag, 'Canada does not have an official national flag' ...

These are a few of the words carefully chosen by Dr Conrad M.J.F. Swan, Rouge Dragon, College of Arms, London, the first Canadian to be appointed by a sovereign to the College. They are taken from his published paper entitled 'The Canadian Arms of Dominion and Sovereignty'[69] which was presented at the fifth international congress of genealogical and heraldic science held in Stockholm, Sweden in 1960. This study is painstaking in its review of relevant authorities. Dr Swan was speaking to a world body of experts.[70]

Three months later, on September 10th, the Prime Minister announced the setting-up of an all-party Flag Committee. Nineteen days later, on 29 September, it wired the College of Arms requesting that I be permitted to appear before the Committee. Matheson knew that I was about to be on my way from London to visit my nonagenarian, maternal widowed grandfather, Alfred Edward Green, in Duncan on Vancouver Island, and that I could easily stop off in Ottawa.

To the considerable consternation of our Committee, a curt reply by cable was received from Sir Anthony Wagner on Monday, 5 October denying permission to Rouge Dragon to appear. Garter stated that he alone would appear for the college. The shocked reaction of the committee when this communication was studied destroyed utterly the influence in Canada of this historic authority. It was not helpful, at that vital and delicate juncture to be instructed from London whom we should and should not hear. Thereafter no member of the committee was interested in any advice from the London source, and Canada was completely on her own.[71]

Well, not quite alone. While conforming to Garter's prohibition against my

---

[68] *Ibid.*

[69] Colonel Matheson's speech was a precis of part of the author's paper 'Canadian Arms of Dominion and Sovereignty' as published in *Recueil du Ve Congrès International des Sciences Généalogique et Héraldique à Stockholm*, 1960.

[70] Canada. House of Commons Debates. Official Report. 'Flag Speech of John R Matheson, Member of Leeds. Queen's Printer, Ottawa, 1964 pp. 7-8.

[71] Matheson *op. cit.* p. 122.

appearing before the committee, I routed my journey to my grandfather through Ottawa, and had long discussions with Matheson – as a friend, and a Canadian wanting to help my country in a very difficult situation. We spent much time privately in the committee room and Matheson has been kind enough to record the outcome of our discussions, writing flatteringly of me: 'He was most generous and entirely uninhibited in his advice and unreservedly endorsed the design which was ultimately selected'.[72]

To me, it was obvious what was needed: a symbol clear in outline, simple, patently Canadian, and one that could unite us as a nation. The design finally chosen met in my opinion, all the criteria. The maple leaf is pre-eminently simple, clear in outline, and nothing if not Canadian. Having it red and placed on a white background – a vertical band, known in heraldry as a *pale* – shows up the maple leaf admirably. The wide red vertical bands that flank it give the whole design clear definition. That red and white, (*gules* and *argent* in heraldry), should be chosen was admirable, in that they are the livery colours of the Royal Arms of Canada as established by the Proclamation of 1921.

There was, however, a problem over the design when it came to the verbal, technical description known as a 'blazon' required in heraldry. Normally, if a design comprises three vertical stripes, *pales*, each pale should be about 1/3 of the total width, and if such were the case then the blazon of the flag would have been:

Gules on a Pale Argent a Maple leaf also Gules (or *of the 1ˢᵗ*, whichever one preferred).

However, the design was required *not* to be 1/3,1/3,1/3 but the centre *pale* was to be *square,* which precluded the customary width of each *pale*.

One could, of course, have gone in for a recitation of mathematical proportions in the blazon, but such would be totally against the simplicity of heraldry, against precedent and, indeed, clumsy. It therefore occurred to me to request that the Queen of Canada decree that a *pale* of specific proportions – different to its accompanying pales – in relation to a total design be given a particular name for the sake of identification and simplicity, and for this to be incorporated in the Sovereign's Proclamation establishing the flag. It was to be an historic occasion and one worthy of advancing that the armorial *pale* required for the flag – a square *pale* – be designated a 'Canadian Pale' and so my blazon ran: *Gules on a Canadian Pale Argent a Maple leaf of the first.* And this was duly incorporated in the Royal Proclamation, dated 28 January 1965, establishing the National Flag of Canada.[73]

Half way through the month following that of the Proclamation, that is to say on 15 February at noon, it took effect. Reactions in the country ranged from

---

[72] *Ibid.*

[73] *Ibid.* Appendix 3 for the text.

agony to ecstasy. Abroad, the reception was one of interest and, as far as I could gauge, general approval. Today, forty or so years on, it seems to be true to say that the flag has come to enjoy general respect, as a symbol to which all in the country can rally. Technically, from the heraldic point of view, it is an excellent design.

Nevertheless, despite the Queen of Canada having proclaimed her will and pleasure in establishing the new flag of her Canadian Realm, Sir Anthony publicly and characteristically expressed his disappointment.[74] An odd proceeding for an official in respect of the legitimate act of the head of a friendly state (especially when that head of state happened also to be his own sovereign).

As soon as Garter learned of the official blazon I had produced for the Proclamation he was almost puce with rage. It was presumption, as far as he was concerned, that a mere Pursuivant, Rouge Dragon, should take upon himself to advise a Government – quite overlooking the fact that it was not the government of the United Kingdom which had requested the assistance. I let down a long anchor and rode out the storm. In such situations Polish blood is an advantage. It knows how to say *nie* to those of this world who tend to exhibit tsarian tendencies!

Mistakes had, in fact, been made on both sides. We have noted, at some length, those of Garter Wagner. On the other hand, and this is quite understandable, the Flag Committee was unaware of the Byzantine complexity of a body, the College of Arms, which was then soon to celebrate the quincentenary of its foundation. Naturally, the Committee envisaged that Garter had over his colleagues of the College the same hierarchic, disciplinary authority as that of, for example, the chief executive of a corporation, or of a Permanent Under Secretary of State. The truth is that Garter – though holding an office of great prestige and armorial authority – is basically, as far as his brother heralds are concerned, *primus inter pares*. The sole person officially responsible for the discipline of the heralds is the Earl Marshal, pursuant to the Declaration of Charles II of 1673.[75]

As each herald is an independent, professional practitioner, – and the College is entirely dependent on all of them for its source of income – all that was necessary was for the Flag Committee to approach whomsoever among the heralds they wished to consult. It would then have been up to that person to decide to accept or refuse the invitation. Had he accepted, there might, ultimately, have been a Garterial pyromaniac display, but with certain types of Garters one gets used to such things. Bearing in mind the particular source of such an invitation, its acceptance could not be held to be in any way *ultra vires*.

---

[74] *Ibid*. p 122.

[75] For the text *vide,* Squibb, GD ed. *Munimenta heraldica MCCCCLXXXIV to MCMLXXXIV*. The Harleian Society. New Series, Vol. 4, 1985 pp.60-62.

When the sparks died down, I dusted off the ash, and got on with supporting the College by my work. Dragons rather like sparks – they are co-natural!

Wagner's extraordinary conduct throughout this entire episode did the College of Arms no good in the eyes of official Canada but, apparently, the converse for the 'presumptuous Pursuivant', judging by, among other examples, Prime Minister Pearson's request within two years, for his advice over the Order of Canada, as described earlier in this chapter.

To be fair, though, when the dust had settled down after the Wagnerian explosions, not only was Her Canadian Majesty's National Flag Proclamation entered in the Official Records of the College of Arms,[76] but I noticed that whenever, in future, any matter concerning the Commonwealth landed on Sir Anthony's desk, I was always consulted.

The Canadian Heraldic Authority
L'Autorité héraldique du Canada

The omens did not seem auspicious. The relationship between official Canada and the College of Arms had been soured by Garter Wagner. His reaction to the desire of the Canadian Parliament as to the establishment of a National Flag to mark the centenary of Confederation in 1967 had been as counter-productive as it was ill-informed; in short, a public relations disaster.

One year earlier, in the run-up to the celebrations marking this commemoration, The Heraldry Society of Canada La Société Héraldique du Canada had been established by a charter from the Federal Parliament; I had helped towards the charter. At the second annual General Meeting of the Society in November, 1967[77] none other than the Chief Justice of Canada, The Honble John R. Cartwright, PC, MC, LLB, addressed the meeting with a carefully prepared paper. In this he observed

> It is not seemly for anyone holding judicial office to make suggestions as to what he conceives would be a desirable policy to be adopted by the Government of the day, at all events if the matter is one which may become a subject of political controversy; but it is, I think, permissible for me to invite all the members of our society to give thought to the desirability of the creation in Canada of a body comparable to the College of Heralds, empowered to deal with this question of the right to armorial bearings. ...
>
> Her Majesty is of course our sovereign and all acts of government are done in her name. It is to her and her heirs and successors that we have sworn allegiance, but she reigns in this country as Queen of Canada, enacts laws by and with the advice and consent of the Senate and the House of Commons of Canada, and exercises her executive authority on the advice

---

[76] CAR: I. 83/46
[77] 4 November, 1967 held at the Skyline Hotel, Ottawa.

of Her Privy Council for Canada. There can be no doubt that if so advised by the Government of the day, Her Majesty, acting directly, or through His Excellency the Governor General, could set up an authority in this country clothed with all the necessary powers to adjudicate upon and grant the right to use armorial bearings.[78]

The official winds were clearly blowing one way/ beginning to swell the sails. Nevertheless, there was no unseemly rush on the part of the Federal Government to establish an independent authority. But consideration of this matter was moving forward, aided and informed by a series of well-mounted and impressive exhibitions organised in various parts of the country over the following years. Such a one was the 1983 exhibition in Vancouver held at the Robson Square Media Centre and entitled, 'Symbols of Splendour: Heraldry in British Columbia, 1778-1983'.[79] The play of the first three words of the title upon the motto of the Arms of that Province, *Splendor sine occasu*[80] will not have escaped the reader's notice.

This title had obviously also been influenced by that of my book, *Canada: Symbols of Sovereignty,*[81] published six years before. This work expounded, for the first time ever, the principles which governed the Arms of Dominion and Sovereignty, both in respect of the Arms of the United Kingdom and those of the Colonial territories and the Old Dominions (those independent, completely sovereign Realms of the Monarch). It apparently caused quite a stir in scholarly circles as well as the media[82] and Garter Wagner was generous enough to congratulate me publicly on the book. As a result, it brought home to many Canadians for the first time that a heraldic tradition – both French and British – existed in their country.

Heraldic ceremonies started to be observed in Canada which included the attendance of a Herald-in-Ordinary, first in 1980 in Toronto[83], and the second was seven years later in Vancouver[84]. Both are described in detail in the following chapter X, p. 265*ff* and p. 266*ff*, respectively.

In March, also of that same year (1987),[85] at the invitation of the Secretary of

---

[78] Text of the speech in *Heraldry in Canada*. The official organ of The Heraldry Society of Canada *La Société héraldique du Canada*. 1967 Vol. I no. 5 p. 5.

[79] 23-26 September, 1983

[80] The motto is capable of several interpretations but is obviously a play on the sun which figures in the Arms. The sun while apparently setting in the west never, in fact, decreases in its radiance and serves as a symbol of the Empire's glory which encircled the globe. Possibly, therefore, one might render the motto as, 'Brilliance without setting' – a characteristic to be shared by the province.

[81] Swan, Conrad. York Herald of Arms. *Canada: Symbols of Sovereignty*. University of Toronto Press, 1977.

[82] As in the Toronto *Globe and Mail*, 15 Nov. 1977, and Vancouver *Province*, 21 Nov. 1977.

[83] For an account *vide The Globe and Mail*, Thursday 25 Dec. p.3.

[84] 13-17 October, 1987.

[85] 26 March, 1987.

State of Canada, I took part in a 'National Forum on Heraldry' in Ottawa. The opening passage of the brief by the Heraldry Society of Canada *La Société héraldique du Canada* presented to the Secretary of State for this occasion, echoed the words of the Chief Justice of twenty years before. It brought together the ideas on this subject then being considered across the country. One cannot accuse Canada of rushing its fences! The brief observed:

> The purpose of this brief is twofold. First: to describe the nature of heraldry, the evolution of its use in Canada, the current dilemma posed by the need to use overseas granting agencies, and the absence of effective protection for Canadian heraldry under Canadian Law; and second: to make recommendations for the structure and administration of a Canadian heraldic authority, with an outline of the benefits which can be achieved by taking such action.[86]

It was obvious that Canada was about to establish its own heraldic arrangements. Despite the coolness of the official Canadian attitude towards the College of Arms as a whole since Garter Wagner's regrettable *faux pas*, an official delegation was sent to the College in order to inform it of the impending changes and to seek advice.

By this time Sir Colin Cole, KCVO, TD was Garter which was, probably, just as well bearing in mind the atmosphere of *froideur* existing, of late, between Ottawa and the College.

When faced with inevitable, legitimate changes, about which one can do nothing, there are two paths one can go down. One is the way of resistance and non-cooperation; the result in this particular instance would have been to brand the College for ever in Canadian history as obstructionist and ignorant of the constitutional position of Canada. The other path is that of willing assistance in the realization of the desired end; result, in this instance: the undying gratitude of Canada. Wisely, Sir Colin chose the latter course. Possibly, he remembered the opinion ventured in my memorandum to the Earl Marshal and all officers, following a world tour in 1976 that, 'in Canada, the college lives on borrowed time'[87].

After all, the delegation was made up of gentlemen. They remembered that it was the College of Arms which had continually served Canada in its heraldic needs during the previous three and a half centuries – since the establishment of arms for Newfoundland in 1638[88].

---

[86] Attachment no. 1 of the Distribution list by The Heraldry Society of Canada *La Société héraldique du Canada*. Ottawa, 2 March 1987.

[87] SSA. New Series X: York's World Tour 19 October-2 December, 1976.

[88] CAR. Heralds I.437. Obviously, the French Crown was responsible for matters armorial for New France until the Treaty of Paris, 1763. Following the charter of 1621 for a Scottish colony of Nova Scotia granted to Sir William Alexander there was a period of 'phantom rule' there with France disputing. Ultimately Nova Scotia was ceded to Britain by the Treaty of Utrecht, 1713

With the Canadian constitution patriated since 1982[89], the exercise of jurisdiction by the Earl Marshal in the intervening five years had been by leave of the authorities of that country.

But now, Her Canadian Majesty – as advised by Her Canadian Ministers – had decided to establish an heraldic authority of its own for this Her Realm of Canada. Despite all the recent problems, Canada still wanted to have an official heraldic office – could there have been a greater compliment to the College of Arms?

I was brought in on the discussions, and it was obvious to me that the delegates from the Federal government felt that Garter was one to whom they could relate. He was adept at getting on with people, doubtless from long military experience. He soon understood what they wanted and said he would do all he could to assist towards the new dispensation. In view of my knowledge of Canada he asked me to prepare a memorandum of points to be considered. This I did and, with nothing changed by Garter, sent the thirty-two typed pages of the memorandum off to the Department of the Secretary of State of Canada on 16 September, 1987[90].

It was obvious that the officials valued the College's five odd centuries of experience, and when, nine months later, the Canadian Heraldic Authority *L'Autorité héraldique du Canada* was finally established, it was gratifying to note that all the main points I had suggested were reflected in the new arrangements. The authority for these was achieved by Letters Patent dated 4 June, 1988. By these Her Majesty The Queen of Canada 'transferred the exercise of her heraldic prerogative to the Governor-General of Canada, thus fully patriating heraldry'.[91]

---

[89] Canada Act, 1982 Chapter II (Westminster Parliament); Constitution Act, 1982 and Proclamation dated 17 April 1982 by The Queen of Canada.

[90] Original now in the archives of the Office of the Governor-General of Canada: Dr Conrad Swan, CVO, PhD, FSA, York Herald of Arms, Registrar and Senior Officer of the College of Arms, to Kevin Macleod, Esq. Department of the Secretary of State of Canada, 16 Sept. 1987; copy in SSA. New Series X.

[91] H.E. and Rt Honble Ramon John Hnatyshyn, Governor-General of Canada and Head of the Canadian Heraldic Authority *L'Autorité héraldique du Canada* in his forward to *The Canadian Heraldic Authority*. Rideau Hall, Ottawa, August 1990; further it is asserted that 'Grants of arms are honours from the Canadian Crown' *vide, Granting Coats of Arms in Canada*. Public Information Directorate, Office of the Secretary of the Governor General, 1996 p.3.

CHAPTER X

A Herald at Home and Away
– Tours, Practice Matters, Appointment
as Garter and Retirement

'HAVE TABARD; WILL TRAVEL', was part of a telegram I sent in October '64 –
pre-facsimile and pre-e-mail days – to my brother, then the President and
Superior of St Thomas More College in the University of Saskatchewan. It was a
pun, obvious at the time, on the title of a well-known soap opera western: 'Have
gun; will travel'.

My wire was dictated over the telephone to the telegraph office in the local
railway station – the usual location then for such – from my hotel in Dodge City,
Kansas. The name of those comfortable lodgings escapes me now but its address,
never: corner of 1st Avenue and Gunsmoke.

This exchange took place during the first of a series of tours undertaken from
1964 onwards for the next thirty or so years that I was at the College of Arms,
and beyond.

This initial sally abroad as a herald kicked off with my giving the Woodward
Lecture for that year at Yale (already referred to in chapter V in connection
with the New England Governor of Madras after whom that university
was named). Oklahoma[1] was also included as well as the University of
Virginia[2].

Finally, I went north, to Portsmouth Priory on Rhode Island (founded from
Fort Augustus Abbey, Scotland) to call on my old friend, the Benedictine monk
who had danced with Pavlova, Dom William Wilfrid Bayne, OSB. Lest one
imagine this monk had broken his vows of religion, possibly I ought to explain
that Dom William started his lay adult life as a male ballet dancer, and had the
distinction of being chosen to dance with the great Russian; he was, apparently,
an expert lifter, as they say in ballet.

Premature arthritis cut short his dancing and, being good at graphic art, he
took up set-designing for ballet. This led to the development of his interest in
heraldry – his family had arms.

In the end he became a monk, and brought about a revolution in the

---

[1] *The Norman Transcript* (Oklahoma) 18 Oct. 1964.
[2] *Visiting Scholars of the University Center in Virginia* 1964-1965. U. of V. pp 1and 7.

ecclesiastical heraldic art of Catholic America: for its hierarchy, universities, colleges, societies and the like[3].

As a Southerner of the deepest dye, Dom William obviously regarded his time in New England as an opportunity to civilize the Yankees – 'in so far as one can,' he would observe!

★　　　★　　　★

So the tours went forward in '65[4], '66[5] and '67[6] – all along the same lines. During the last tour referred to it was remarked at St Thomas More College, Saskatoon, how pleased they were I had come when it was warm – I noted that the thermometer outside the Faculty Common Room windows registered 27° below freezing!

★　　　★　　　★

Next year, on 4 June 1968, I was promoted to be York Herald of Arms, the 39th holder of that office and title[7]. Four days later, 'London Day by Day' in *The Daily Telegraph* noted under the heading **Canadian Dragon** that he 'is probably the most travelled of the heralds…[8]'.

More tours and interest in the *'Canadian herald'* followed in this year of my promotion[9].

★　　　★　　　★

At the end of that year, one of the most gratifying situations in my whole career at the College occurred. An agency of the Stormont – that 'Protestant Parliament for a Protestant People' as it long described itself – invited the recently promoted York Herald – Roman Catholic and Knight of Malta (which Order has a special loyalty to the Holy Father) – to inaugurate the 'Sir William Scott Memorial Lectures', to be given annually thereafter.

Lord Craigavon, Prime Minister of Northern Ireland (1921-40) – following his many early visits to the United States – was convinced that some way must

---

[3] Many examples will be found in *No. 1 Heraldic Monograph Series of the American Society of Heraldry being a presentation of the heraldic art of Rev. Dom William Wilfrid Bayne, O.S.B., Ch. L.J.* The American Heraldic Society, 1967.

[4] *Post Despatch*, St Louis, Missouri, 8 March, 1965; *Regina Leader Post*, 17 March 1965.

[5] *Daily Oklahoman*, 18 April, 1966.

[6] *Shreveport Journal*, 20 Jan, 28 Feb 1967; *The Province* (Vancouver, B.C.), 3 Feb 1967; *The B.C. Catholic*, 26 Jan '67; *Edmonton Journal*, 3 Feb 1967.

[7] The first reliable evidence of its existence dates from 1484.

[8] 8 June 1968.

[9] *Kitchener Waterloo Record*, 2 March 1968; *Windsor Star*, 19 April 1968; *The St Catherine's Standard*, 19 April 1968; *The Chronicle Herald*, 20 April 1968; *Regina Leader Post*, 20 April 1968; *Times Mirror* (Leesburg, Virginia) 21 March, 1968.

Barclays Bulletin. Barclays Bank. No. 11, Summer 1968.

be found to assist those of Ulster descent, now living abroad, to learn something of the 'rock from which they were hewn' by providing, wherever possible, information regarding their forebears in Northern Ireland. Accordingly, the Ulster-Scot Historical Society (later Foundation) was founded with Sir William Scott, head of the Northern Ireland Civil Service as its Chairman.

The establishment of this historical society made it possible to provide, among other things, a professional genealogical research service especially for such Americans, and for this an appropriate fee could be charged. The society worked closely with the Public Record Office of Northern Ireland, which obviously could not, as such, carry out private genealogical research for non-tax-paying non-residents.

The general atmosphere which permitted this invitation to me was one in which the two sides in the province, Catholic and Protestant, were coming more and more together. This was evidenced by Catholic judges being appointed; Catholic priests being invited, from time to time, to conduct the prayers before the Stormont started its daily sessions; a good many Catholics starting to vote Unionist, and village Protestant football teams even starting to play against their Catholic counterparts.

In Irish terms these developments meant much: the two sides were gradually edging together. Further, the gentlemen, led by the reforming Prime Minister, Captain Terrence O'Neill – from whom one could expect some sort of civilized treatment – were still in power. They also included James Chichester-Clark[10], then holding the important portfolio of Agriculture and about to be Prime Minister of Northern Ireland[11].

In this context, it appears that a non-Ulster resident, non-Irish, Canadian Catholic member of the Royal Household was considered one who might be trusted to handle the invitation sensitively and so help forward the rapprochement between the two.

Accepting the invitation, I chose the theme 'Heraldry: Ulster and North American Connections' and delivered a lecture on this topic to the Foundation in Belfast during the evening of 2 December, 1968. It appeared to go down well. I made a point of staying with a Protestant family on the Ards Peninsula while in Ulster for this occasion.

Within a few weeks the Council of the Foundation asked if it might publish the text along with the specially prepared coloured illustrations of my lecture[12]. Can there be a greater honour for a lecturer? Naturally, I agreed immediately.

On the day following my lecture, 3 December, I attended upon the Lord Grey of Naunton at his inauguration as Governor of Northern Ireland.

[10] Later Lord Moyola and also later a client of mine.
[11] 1969-71.
[12] Swan, Conrad. York Herald. *Heraldry: Ulster and North American Connections*. Sir William Scott Memorial Lecture. Ulster Scot Historical Foundation, 1971.

The tenure of office of this last Governor of Northern Ireland coincided with the outburst of more 'troubles'.

It is probable that the two sides in Ulster were coming too close for the likes of the IRA and their loyalist counterparts to tolerate. With them stirring up trouble (past masters as they are at such), the tribal tendencies of Irish life began to reassert themselves.

As his tenure progressed, people would ask this Governor if each side was treating him well. To which he would reply, 'They treat me very well; but I do wish they'd be nicer to each other.'

★   ★   ★

From Belfast I returned to Boxford for Christmas. Soon, a situation without precedent arose: a herald was to function officially in Tabard for the first time in history on the other side of the Atlantic, (in Bermuda) and I was to have that distinction. From the outset it was made clear that all expenses would be met privately from Bermuda – such details always concentrate the official mind.

It was also to be the first time that a herald had appeared officially, outside the United Kingdom, since the Delhi Durbar in 1911. On that occasion a herald had not gone from Britain to India; instead two serving Indian Army officers were appointed Officers-of-Arms Extraordinary for that splendid ceremony alone[13]. The last official sortie of a herald from the United Kingdom had been in 1882, taking the Garter to the King of Saxony.

On 2 April Philip Howard, writing in *The Times*, summed up the situation well under the heading: '**Herald's Mission to Bermuda**.' He continued:

> The College of Arms, that citadel of scholarly precedent and tradition, is breaking precedent and making heraldic history. Next month York Herald of Arms, in tabard, cocked hat, old Lancastrian collar of SS's, grasping his white wand, and generally in full and glorious fig, is leading a mission to Bermuda. ...[14].

And so it was. On the following 5 May I set off by air for Bermuda (with £18-15-9 to pay on the excess luggage!). I was accompanied by my assistant, John George, as Secretary of the Mission. From that point on he kept a diary, almost hour by hour, of all we did[15]. Unless otherwise specified all the quotations concerning the Bermudan visit are taken from that record.

Upon arrival at Kinley Field we were greeted by Lt. CmDr David Blair, ADC

---

[13] Delhi Herald was Brigadier-General William Eliot Peyton, CVO, DSO (later Major General Sir William...KCVO, DSO); Assistant Delhi Herald was Hon. Captain and Hon. Malik Umar Hyat Khan, CIE, MVO (later Major General Sir Umar...GBE, KCIE) – both wore tabards, the former with a plumed topee; the latter a turban.

[14] *The Times*, 2 April 1969.

[15] SSA: in Bermuda file.

Primus in America. *The Author, York Herald of Arms, leads His Excellency the Governor of Bermuda, the Rt. Honble the Lord Martonmere, KCMG; the Mayor of the Town of St. George, Councillor N.R. Roberts; the Secretary of York's Mission, J.C.G. George, and (partially obscured) the ADC to the Governor, Lt. Cmdr. David Blair, to the King's Square, St. George's, for the presentation of the Patent of Arms for this original capital of Bermuda, 8 May, 1969 – the first occasion that an Officer of Arms, in tabard, carried out duties on the Western shores of the Atlantic. Credit: Courtesy of Government House, Bermuda.*

to His Excellency the Governor, Lord Martonmere. From there, we proceeded through roads lined with oleanders, to Government House: 'a most Italianate looking edifice (the Colonial Office had purchased the design from a Scots architect who had originally designed it as a Florentine Palazzo for an Italian noble who changed his mind).'

For the entire visit, this was to be our home where we enjoyed the generous hospitality and great kindness of our host and hostess, the Governor and Lady Martonmere.

The great day, Thursday, 8 May arrived and at 9a.m. it was time to dress. I put on a Herald's Royal Household scarlet, gold embroidered jacket, uniform overalls (black trousers with gold stripes down each outer side of the leg) and tabard. This was to be the first time that a herald had appeared in full uniform in the Americas, so I decided to follow the example of the Gentlemen Usher of the Black Rod of the Senate of Canada who wears trousers and not breeches and stockings.

When both of us were fully kitted out (HE, – in Governor's uniform complete with plumed hat) we posed for photographs on the terrace of Government House. As the Mission Diary recorded, 'a Herald of England standing in front of Palm Trees wearing his Tabard was a remarkably rare and probably unique sight and one of historic nature.' (The next governor and ADC to stand for the same purpose on that spot were assassinated[16]).

We (HE, ADC, Secretary to the Mission and York) then boarded the Governor's yacht, *Romay* and set sail for the Market Wharf, St George's where we arrived at precisely 11a.m. As the Governor stepped ashore, a fanfare of trumpets was sounded by the Band of the Bermuda Regiment, followed by the playing of 'God Save the Queen'. HE's flag, as well as that of my family arms, were broken from the cross-bar of the flag-mast in the square.

Greeted by the Mayor of the Town of St George, Counsellor N.R. Roberts, he then introduced to us the Town's Aldermen and Counsellors.

> The weather by now was beautifully warm and sunny with a cooling breeze blowing off the sea…The square was packed with people… local functionaries and the Bermuda Regiment dressed in scarlet and blue[17]. Colourful bunting festoons the houses and the streets which, with the blossoms on the trees, the pastel shades of the buildings, the bright-coloured clothes of the spectators, the regalia and uniforms of the officials, made up as pretty and charming a scene as one can imagine.

The official party then proceeded to a dais in the centre of King's Square. After prayers by the local Rector, the Mayor delivered his address of welcome to the Governor, who made reply, ending with a command to me to announce the terms of the Letters Patent conferring armorial bearings upon the Mayor and Corporation of this ancient capital (founded 1612). With my having done so, and having handed the patent to the Governor, he presented it to the Mayor. At that, a further fanfare sounded, and the arms of the Town in banner form broke from the cross-bar of the flag mast as well as from the Town Hall. Whereupon thunderous applause went up from the assembled crowd who, by this time, were thoroughly enjoying themselves.

---

[16] 10 March 1973: Sir Richard Sharples, KCMG, OBE, MC, Governor and Captain Hugh Sayers, ADC.
[17] No. 1 Dress Ceremonial – extremely smart turnout, if I may say so.

The Mayor then made an address of thanks to the Governor and York, concluding by making York an Honorary Freeman of the Town of St George – to the sound of a further fanfare. Apparently, this was the first time in the Town's history that such a distinction had been accorded.

The official party left the square in carriages. At Pigin Bay these were exchanged for automobiles which conveyed them to the Mayor's residence at Hoker Point for a reception.

Luncheon followed at government House and so on to the Bank of Bermuda head office for the further presentation. As at St George's that morning, when in procession at the Bank I proceeded HE, he 'thus became probably the first colonial Governor ever to have the privilege normally enjoyed exclusively by the Crown of having a Royal Herald officially in attendance.'

The presentation ceremony took place in the Great Banking Hall. Staff and other guests thronged the area, both on the ground floor as well as the half-mezzanine; all was filled to capacity.

With suitable speeches before and after by the Governor and Bank officials I announced the terms of the letters patent conferring armorial bearings on the corporation of the Bank of Bermuda.

Refreshments were then served, after which the Governor's party returned to Government House at about 6p.m. The day had been long but stimulating and:

In the cool of the evening, with the fragrance of the oleander, hibiscus and other semi-tropical flowers pervading the atmosphere, probably one of the most historic and colourful days in the annals of Britain's Island Colony in the Atlantic came gently to an end.

In the small drawing-room, after dinner, we watched the days' events on television – saw how we had done and made notes for the future.

Starting next day, the newspapers vied with each other to record the events of 8 May: '**Oyez! The splendid Mr York Herald in St George's pomp**' proclaimed the description by the local *Royal Gazette*[18]; and '**A Deed to Delight the 'Vexed Bermoothes**''headed the article in *The New York Times*[19]. However, possibly the most unexpected interest came, some time later, from the very heart of the United States, with the excellent article of the *Beatrice Daily Sun* (Nebraska) which commenced its enthusiastic account declaring, 'It had never happened before, and never would again.'[20]

After a further day of sight-seeing, and enjoying the all-pervading scent of cedar throughout Bermuda[21], the Mission Secretary and I returned, by air, to the United Kingdom on 10 May.

[18] 9 May 1969.
[19] 1 June 1969.
[20] *Beatrice Daily Sun*, 6 Sept. 1969.
[21] SSA: New Series I: C.S. to H.S. 7 May 1969.

Upon arrival there we then had to put our minds to the final preparations for the Investiture of the Prince of Wales – already described in chapter VIII.

Next year, 1970, saw the first of my many world tours. It lasted from 23 February to 11 April.

The route was:

From Britain to

Halifax, Nova Scotia	Melbourne, Victoria
Fredericton, New Brunswick	Canberra
Montreal	Adelaide, South Australia
Ottawa	Perth, Western Australia
Toronto	Johannesburg
Windsor, Ontario	Cape Town
Phoenix, Arizona	Port Elizabeth
Tuscon, Arizona	Pietermaritzburg
Sydney, New South Wales	Rome and back home.

During my first world tour, I had the pleasure of staying, for the first of many times, with Mr and Mrs Nigel Morgan at their most comfortable and commodious home in Toorak in Melbourne. Mrs Morgan (born Diana Manners) had been secretary to Richmond Herald (Ian de la Lanne Mirrlees) when I joined the College.

More lectures *en route* throughout the tour, and I was able to spend a few days in Perth as the guest of the Governor of Western Australia, Major General Sir Douglas Kendrew, KCMG, CB, CBE, DSO and his lady, which enabled me to inspect in Government House there (a veritable Knole in the tropics) what I consider to be one of the most important heraldic stained-glass windows in the Commonwealth[22].

From there the onward journey was a saddle-sore-back-breaking 14 hour flight to Johannesburg. As the Genealogist of the Most Venerable Order of St John, I was anxious to see how the training, and keeping up to date with new techniques, for the white, black and mixed-race members of the first-aiders/ambulance teams fared in view of *apartheid* which precluded mixed assemblies. Even I had to line up in the post office at a wicket marked 'Blank' (white) to buy a stamp.

Apparently, the one exception to this law was a religious service. So the members of the St John ambulance/first-aiders came together, said some prayers, and then got on with learning the new ways of bandaging, or whatever it was.

It all rather reminded one of the old army sergeant who said to the men, 'Right. Three more verses of 'oly, 'oly, 'oly, and then we bugger off'(!).

---

[22] Later in 1970, at the invitation of the then Governor, I wrote a memorandum on this amazing window, for the Government House Archives.

One of the problems of these long tours was that I missed Hilda terribly and towards the end of them my letter got more and more passionate. One such entry that I can, without a blush, allow others to read I wrote from Cape Town on this tour:

> I... can not wait to get back to you, my precious. My dreams at night of us together make 'Lady Chatterley's Lover' appear like something little better than a nursery tale! Every fibre of my body longs to hold you in my arms and give myself to you unreservedly with all my love as always

> Your adoring
> Conrad xxx[23]

The return flight by South African Airways was by way of the Portuguese African possessions – that company not being popular in the independent African countries – and by Rome back to Heathrow and so to the end of that tour[24]. Thence to Boxford and Hilda in our large four-poster (excellent scope for activity) with the nursery sleeping soundly nearby – the presents I had brought them tucked safely into their beds and cots.

In 1972, *The Daily Telegraph* noted that York Herald was '*Spreading his wings*'[25] for a tour from Reykjavik to Quito, by way of Toronto[26], Allerton (Pennsylvania)[27] and Washington, DC.[28]

The President of Iceland, Dr Kritján Eldjárn, an antiquary of note, wanted to have a lecture on the College of Arms.

Apparently, there is no word for 'herald' in Icelandic and so when the *Morgunbla* – Iceland's newspaper of greatest circulation – referred to my visit it had to describe me as '**Si ameistari Englandts-druttningar á Islandi**' ('a Chief of Protocol of the Queen of England in Iceland').

I delivered the lecture in the presence of His Excellency at the *Háskoli Islands* (alias *Universitatis Islandiae*(!)) – the only university in the world with a department of genealogy[29].

The occasion for my going on to Ecuador was the 150th anniversary of the conclusion of the county's war of independence in which the Albion Brigade of

---

[23] SSA. I: C.S. to H.S. 5 April 1970.

[24] *Ibid.* same to same 23 Feb 1970; *Ibid.* same to same 26 Feb 1970; *Ibid.* same to same 10 March 1970; *Phoenix Gazette* 11 March 1970; *The Star* (Melbourne) 16 March 1970; *The Herald* (Melbourne) 18 March 1970; SSA. I: C.S. to H.S. 20 March 1970; *Ibid.* same to same 25 March 1970; *The Canberra Times* 26 March 1970; SSA. New Series I: C.S. to H.S. 26, 27, 29, March 1970; *Ibid.* same to same 31 March, 1 and 3 April 1970; *Ibid.* same to same 4 April 1970; *Ibid.* same to same 6 April 1970; *Eastern Provinces Herald* (S. Africa) 7 April 1970.

[25] 29 March 1972.

[26] and *The Ottawa Journal*, 10 April 1972.

[27] *Allerton Chronicle,* 10 April 1972.

[28] *Sunday Star* (Wadington, D.C..) 23 April 1972.

[29] SSA new Series I: C.S. to H.S. 5 April 1972.

British mercenaries had participated. Many stayed on in Ecuador and their descendants were fiercely proud of their British blood so I was imported to give them a lecture on British historic ceremonial.

As the first serving Herald to visit South America[30], my return to Europe was by way of Madrid. There I stopped with my brother-in-law, Stafford by then 4th Earl of Iddesleigh, and his Spanish wife, 'Mima' (Maria Louisa Alvarez-Buillo y Uriquijo, Condesa del Real Agrado in Spain). There seemed something appropriate that the Herald who had blazed the trail to South America should make his first call in Europe upon the descendant and heiress of the first Conde del Real Agrado (cr.1771), Life Governor of Rio Banda in Peru[31].

★   ★   ★

It is always interesting to meet people in the same line of endeavour as oneself, so the Iddesleighs kindly arranged, on this occasion in Madrid, for me to meet the *Cronista Rey de Armas.*

Similarly, it was possible to call upon, when in Nairobi, the College of Arms of Kenya – an authority, duly constituted by the parliament of that country ten years after independence.

A little further south in Pretoria, another official body, the Bureau of Heraldry of South Africa, invited me to sit in on one of their executive meetings – the problems discussed sounded strikingly familiar to those aired at Chapter meetings back at the College of Arms[32]!

Possibly the most exotic exchange of heraldic views I have had so far was with the President of the Japanese Mon[33] Designs Association, one Mr. Sexiguchi at his home in Tokyo in 1973[34]. We got down to it in the local way and I admitted to my wife, 'this sitting on the floor is killing[35]!' He demonstrated his skills and having screwed up his courage asked, through the British Council interpreter, how we allowed our lions and other fauna in heraldic designs to be so impolite as to stick out their tongues?(!)

★   ★   ★

---

[30] Hugh Stanford London, F.S.A. (1884-1959) H.M. Consular Service, 1908-44 had served in South America for many years, but was not appointed Norfolk Herald of Arms Extraordinary until 1953 after having left that continent.

[31] For further details see Swan, Sir Conrad 'Peninsulares in the land of the Incas' *The Northcote Millennium Commonplace Book*. Heraldic Enterprises, Boxford House, Suffolk, 2000 pp 92-93.

[32] These meetings in Nairobi and Pretoria took place in 1979 between 10 Oct and 2 Dec.

[33] The only other hereditary system of symbolic identification of families – other than western heraldry – is the Japanese Mon. We would regard it as a series of badges – very simple devices such as the chrysanthemum of the Emperor.

[34] Friday 6 April 1973.

[35] SSA. New Series I: C.S. to H.S. 7 April 1973.

My first visit – and so of a herald – to New Zealand was in 1976[36]. On this happy occasion I stayed with my old friend of Cambridge days, and his wife, Dr and Mrs D.B.C. Taylor – he now being Vice-Chancellor of the Victoria University of Wellington.

Phillip Patrick O'Shea, Advisory Officer(Honours) to the Cabinet – an insignia designer of distinction – was seconded by the Government as my Officer-in-Waiting.

In a memorandum written upon the conclusion of this tour I was of opinion that in New Zealand

Governmental policy sees the Monarchy as a positive factor in creating cohesion in a state which is both multi-cultural as well as multi-national in origin.

The attitude of New Zealand is completely practical in this matter: if Monarchy will bind the country more and more together then Monarchy (and all that goes with it) must be fostered[37].

One result was that within eighteen months of this observation the office of New Zealand Herald of Arms Extraordinary was created appropriately enough on Waitangi Day, 6 February, 1978 with Phillip Patrick O'Shea as its first and present occupant[38].

In marked contrast when in Australia during the '76 tour I found that it was

Still licking its wounds of 11 November (1975) when the Governor General dismissed the Whitlam government.

That this act was completely constitutional seems only to infuriate the Socialists the more. The demonstrations against the Governor General are serious. The posters vilifying him have to seen to be believed looking, for all the world, as if designed and produced east of the Iron Curtain[39].

As a result

Really alarmed by the course and record of the Whitlam government, many States are actively seeking ways and means of making it even more difficult for any future Federal government to change the basic constitution of the country[40].

★　　★　　★

---

[36] 30 Oct. to 6 Nov. 1976

[37] SSA.New Series X: Memorandum, *York's Tour 19 October – 2 December 1976*, dated 21 Dec. 1976 and distributed to the Earl Marshal and all officers of the College of Arms.

[38] Until he could get one made the author was most happy to lend him his Royal Household Jewel which Officers of Arms wear at the neck.

[39] SSA. New Series X: Memorandum, *York's Tour... op.cit.*

[40] *Ibid.*

Sub Cruce Australe, primus. *The Author, York Herald of Arms proclaims the terms of the Royal Warrant, just signed by The Queen of Australia, granting Supporters to the pre-existing Arms of the State of Queensland, Seated, front row, the Honble Johannes Bjelk-Peterson, Premier of the State, and Her Majesty; rear row, Sir Martin Charteris, GCB, Principle Private Secretary to The Queen, and Lady Abergavenny, Lady-in-Waiting. 9 March, 1977 – the first occasion an Officer of Arms, in tabard, carried out duties South of the Equator. Credit:* Courier Mail, *Queensland Newspapers Pty Ltd.*

A reflection of all this was to be noted next year (1977) in the programme for The Queen's Silver Jubilee Tour of Australia in which I was included. It was the first time a herald had gone abroad from England – on such a happy occasion[41] – to accompany the Sovereign since Henry VIII met Francis I at the Field of the Cloth of Gold (1520)[42] and twelve years later at Calais[43]. Further, this antipodean sortie was to be the first time a herald had functioned *tabardé* in the Southern Hemisphere.

'Albany at Large', in the *Sunday Telegraph* of 27 February, 1977, picked this all up under the heading, **'Herald down under'**, noting 'Dr Swan and his gold embroidered tabard will be heavily insured'(!). The main purpose of all this was

---

[41] Sir Edward Walker, Garter (1645-77) had been in almost constant attendance on Charles II on the Continent, but that was during the monarch's exile – hardly a felicitous situation.

[42] Sir Thomas Wrythe, Garter (1505-34) & Thomas Tonge, York (1513-22).

[43] Wrythe was present.

to be the signing by The Queen of a Warrant granting supporters to the pre-existing arms of the State of Queensland[44].

Such was at the request of the then State Premier, the Honble Johannes Bjelk-Petersen[45].

So, with a steel uniform-case containing all my regalia, I set off by air from Heathrow on Friday, 4 March. Every customs office en route had been warned by the Queensland government that the potentially sinister looking metal box was harmless.

As Government House, Brisbane, is surprisingly small, Sir Martin Charteris, GCB, GCVO, Private Secretary, and I were put up, most comfortably, at Park Royal Hotel overlooking the Botanical Gardens and Brisbane River.

On Wednesday 9 March at about 7p.m., I dressed and Mr Gary Kross – my Aide, assigned by the State government – and I were driven to the site of the ceremony on the top of a hill which rejoiced in the name of 'Cloudland'.

Some 2,000 guests had already assembled and were enjoying a buffet supper. The men wore black tie and dinner jacket – the height of extreme formality in this semi-tropical area. The ladies were in their finest evening gowns. An orchestra of 150 members and a choir of 400 were in attendance.

The Queen – held up 15 minutes by the crowds, who wished to see and cheer her on her way – was wearing a sea-green gown with a diamond and ruby tiara and necklace, upon arrival.

As they entered the hall, the Royal Party formed up and we proceeded towards the dais on the far side, where we arranged ourselves as follows:

York	Queen's Australian ADC	Sir Martin Charteris	Lady Abergavenny Lady-in-Waiting
The Premier	HM	HRH	Mrs Bjelke-Petersen
Desk for signing the Warrant		X X X Microphones	Steps

Upon our arrival there, 'God Save The Queen' was sung, led by the orchestra, the choir and all the guests – most moving.

The Premier then welcomed Her Majesty, who made reply.

Whereupon the choir sang the specially composed Jubilee Hymn – well done, good voices.

I then conducted The Queen to the desk provided at the front of the dais and she signed the Warrant, and having returned to her seat, I read out the text of the

[44] Arms and crest of Queensland were granted in 1893 – the first for a colony since those of Jamaica, 1661.

[45] The description of this visit to Queensland is based upon the diary I kept, entitled, 'York's Mission to Brisbane, Queensland, 4th to 19th March, 1977 and held in SSA.

Warrant, at one of the microphones. With that completed, I returned the Warrant to The Queen, backed three paces, bowed and returned to my seat.

Following much applause, the dais party descended to the floor of the hall. The Queen went in one direction, and the Duke the other, so that as many as possible could be presented.

While standing, waiting, during this Royal 'walkabout', a very young journalist at one side asked me, 'Do you really take all this seriously, what you do?'

Before I give my reaction, let me mention that what I was wearing included the Royal Household uniform of a Herald – thick red material, padded on the inside, with much heavy gold embroidery and tabard. The customary sword was worn and wand carried.

Such are comfortable for a foggy, cold November day in London, but on this night in Brisbane the temperature was 90°F with humidity at 88° – and there was no air-conditioning in 'Cloudland'. I could feel sweat trickling down the pit of my back, and by the time of the journalist's question I had been on duty and standing around for about 3½ hours. York had known cooler conditions.

As a result, what I wanted to reply to my enquirer was, 'Get lost, you juvenile twit.' But that would not do. So by a triumph of grace over nature, I replied: 'Brother, we each have a job to do in life. As a journalist I am sure you do your best to live up to the highest standards of journalism. I try to do the same in my particular work, and I am sure you will afford me the same regard' – and moved on before I was tempted to strike him with my wand!

It was about 10.45p.m., when The Queen and the Duke completed their 'walkabout' and we left 'Cloudland'. When I undressed my originally white shirt, vest and underpants they were red from the dye of my uniform and wringing wet with sweat.

After my Aide and I had had a large nightcap each he went off to his home, and I to bed to be 'wrapped in the divine sweetness of sleep'[46] – but not for long.

At 6.30a.m. next day, I started off back home. Leaving Sydney on Thursday, 10 March at 20.00 hours and travelling for 23 hours, I arrived at San Francisco at 19.00 hrs on Thursday, 10 March!

By way of Vancouver, for a lecture, and three days of same at the University of Saskatchewan, I got back to Heathrow and so to Boxford after a memorable experience. But I resolved to suggest to a certain august lady, next time we met, 'Ma'm, if the appearance of heralds in the tropics becomes common, do please sanction a less punishing uniform!'

Sir Martin Charteris sent a very complimentary letter on my performance at Brisbane to the Earl Marshal, who was kind enough to show it to me.

It was gratifying that not long afterwards I was brought into the Royal Victorian Order as a Member, 4th Class (which grade was soon redesignated as Lieutenant); further promotion followed in due course.

★   ★   ★

Three years after the Brisbane ceremony further precedent was established when for the first occasion in any of the Old Dominions the personal representative of the Sovereign was attended by a herald-in-waiting. In this instance it was the Lieutenant Governor of the Province of Ontario, the Honble John Black Aird.

The occasion was the presentation, by the Lieutenant Governor, of Letters Patent of Armorial Bearings to the University of St Michael's College, Toronto, during Convocation after I had, at His Honour's command, proclaimed the terms of the patent[47].

★   ★   ★

At times, one's return coincided with some major undertakings at the College, as in the early '80s moving up to its quincentenary in 1984.

Chapter had decided that the building – riddled with dry rot, wet rot and boring beetles – was to be completely restored. As at the time I was the House Comptroller – responsible for the fabric – that involved me closely. We were fortunate in obtaining the services of Mr Christopher Mann as the Appeal's Director – work at which he excels – and of Cluttons – who had looked after the fabric for years. Both did us extremely well.

The proceedings included my setting an example to the other officers by moving out of my very comfortable chambers into a two tiered 'portakabin'[48]. This had been erected in the courtyard to house each officer in turn so that Cluttons could get into each set, take up the floor and perform radical yet essential repairs to the fabric. So as to amuse all involved I had a panel painted with my official badge as York Herald and inscribed: *Negotium ut Solet MCMLXXXII* (Business as Usual 1982). This hung outside the 'portakabin' when I moved in!

★   ★   ★

Going from the real world to that of make-believe, there was some rather amusing work as heraldic consultant for the James Bond film, *On Her Majesty's Secret Service*[49]. The Earl Marshal's Courtroom of the College of Arms was re-created at Pinewood Studios to such perfection, one might well have thought one was in the real thing. We spent a whole Sunday at the College for outside shots, such as George Lazenby, who played the part of 007, driving into the

---

[46] Homer, *Iliad*, book 2.

[47] 29 Nov. 1980.

[48] 'The Times Diary' *The Times* 2 April 1982: 'one of the Queen's heralds is sheltering in a Portakabin in the middle of a building site'. ' Temporary abode for the Herald' *The City Recorder*, 16 April 1982.

[49] In 1968, Richmond Herald (Robin de la Lanne-Mirrlees) at the request of his friend, Ian Fleming, wrote a memorandum on the College of Arms, and it was on this he based the College parts of the story.

courtyard, getting out and mounting the steps – again, and again, and again. It seemed to me extraordinary the number of people involved in the making of a film. They had much in common with one's servants in India – discussed earlier – the almost caste attitude of, yes, doing this, but never, ever doing that.

★   ★   ★

The James Bond film was a diversion which, fortunately, neither taxed the brain nor took up too much time. Rather more serious was the 10th anniversary of the foundation of the Heraldry Society of Canada[50] – a body of considerable significance – already mentioned. I was honoured to be asked to give the principal address in Ottawa.

★   ★   ★

1987 brought me the pleasure of returning twice to my natal province. The first was in March, to present a Patent of Arms to the Corporation of the District of West Vancouver. This was arranged to take place exactly on the 75th anniversary of its incorporation: the 15th of the month, notwithstanding it being a Sunday[51] that year.

The second coincided with the Commonwealth Heads of Government Conference (October 13-17) and has been touched upon in the preceding chapter. On this occasion I was the Herald-in-Waiting upon Her Majesty when she signed a Warrant granting Crest and Supporters[52] for the pre-existing arms of the Province[53]. The Supporters were a wapiti and an ovis montana[54], both long used but without due authority. The crest suitably differenced saved the Province from the solecism of continuing to proclaim itself to be the United Kingdom (whose crest *simpliciter* it had long used, doubtless out of loyalty to the Crown, but once again without due authority). This was achieved by the addition of a collar of dogwood flowers (the Provincial floral emblem) to the lion of the Royal Crest, and so rendered it technically different.

This was the happy resolution of a saga which had started some 20 years before, with a struggle I had with an eminent Provincial civil servant ('no names; no pack drill' as we say in the army!). He had asked my opinion concerning the unauthorized adjuncts external to the authorized Provincial shield. I told him I felt there would be no problem over the Supporters, as they were not already on record to any other person or authority. As to the crest, that was another matter,

---

[50] 1976.

[51] *North Shore News*, 13 & 18 March, 1987 and SSA New Series, misc. D.A.G. Lanskail, Mayor of West Vancouver, to Dr Conrad Swan, York Herald of Arms, 17 March 1987.

[52] CAR: I. 84-265.

[53] CAR: I. 75-5 (31 March 1906).

[54] Wapiti – a large North American deer (Cervus canadensis); Ovis Montana – a large mountain sheep ram with curling horns.

being, as it was, the crest of the United Kingdom. Some linear, not just chromatic, differencing would be needed.

At that, he publicly denounced me as 'obviously knowing nothing about the subject'(!), at a luncheon party given for me at Government House, Victoria, by the Lieutenant Governor, Major General the Hon. G.R. Pearkes, VC.

At which I resolved: 'Right, notwithstanding this man's intransigence – how typical of some civil servants when they stray into *terra incognita* – I shall see to it that my Province is better served'. Heralds bide their time and view matters from an historical perspective.

So worked diligently to that end[55], and it was in July 1987 that the Government of the Province of British Columbia, with the knowledge and concurrence of the Secretary of State of Canada, invited me to be the Herald-in-Waiting upon The Queen when she signed the Warrant augmenting the pre-existing Arms of the Province[56] as just mentioned.

The significance of the invitation was well summed up by the Provincial Premier, the Honourable William Vander Zalm, when after the actual ceremony he observed,

> this…has been a truly unique experience. In fact, a real first for Canada for there never has been an occasion before in Canadian history where both the Sovereign and one of Her Royal Heralds were personally present at such a ceremony[57].

All had to be arranged at break neck speed as there were only three months from the first notification to the ceremony on 15 October following. At that time Her Majesty would be in Vancouver for the Commonwealth Heads of Government Conference.

In meeting this dead-line, two factors assisted enormously: correspondence by facsimile, and the presence on the spot in the Province of Mr Robert Watt, President of the Heraldry Society of Canada – a fellow British Columbian. Little wonder that when in the following year, the Canadian Heraldic Authority was created, one leant decidedly and with confidence towards his appointment as Chief Herald of Canada.

I wore the Royal Household uniform of a Herald (without a tabard) as for the 1980 Toronto occasion. There being no Canadian tabard available, both the Federal and Provincial Authorities agreed to follow that precedent with the latter requesting that I wear the Herald's collar of S's to give 'added dignity to the occasion' as they phrased it[58].

---

[55] SSA. New Series IX: York to Sir William Heseltine, GCB, KCVO, 28 Sept. 1987 [office copy]

[56] Since 1906.

[57] SSA. New Series IX: *Court House Ceremony, October 15, 1987*. Ministry of Provincial Secretary and Government Service [British Columbia, 1987] p.9.

[58] Ministry of Provincial Secretary (British Columbia) to Garter Principal King of Arms, 23 Sept. 1987.

Armorial expectations mounted in the Province during the late summer as the date of the signing ceremony approached.

A discreet 'leak' had the *Vancouver Sun* observe:

> Some super-secret changes have been made to the B.C. shield of arms to satisfy the heraldry bigwigs in London, England[59].

– not exactly accurate, but reflecting the general rising interest.

Finally, with all in readiness, The Queen and the Duke of Edinburgh arrived, to a fanfare of trumpets, at the Court House in Vancouver at 4p.m. on 15 October where I awaited her. The Great Hall of this extremely modern, yet impressive, building was to be the scene of this historic ceremony.

In addition to the other distinguished guests it was especially fitting, bearing in mind the location of that day's proceedings, that the Supreme Court of British Columbia be present in force: 35 Justices robed in red and led by the Chief Justice. And while

> The Queen's Majesty is deemed always to be present in court…for the first time in the life of our own Province, the legal presumption becomes actual fact on this occasion,

as the Chief Justice elegantly expressed it in his speech of welcome[60].

I noticed that Her Majesty wore an attractive navy blue suit and white collar with a fetching white straw boater with blue trim. Against the robes of the Justices, the tunics of the RCMP, officers and my Royal Household uniform, there was not so much as a hint of a clash. (At which, York's thought: the intelligence service of HM's lady's maid i/c wardrobe on this tour is, obviously, in cracking form!)

The actual signing was not without complication. Each version of each of the three copies[61] of the Warrants (each in English and French) had first to be counter-signed at the end of the text – as an exercise in tending ministerial advice – by the Secretary of State of Canada, the Honourable David E. Crombie, PC, MP.

Then The Queen added the Royal Sign Manual – according to custom – at the upper right of the beginning of each version on each of the copies of the Warrant. A total of twelve signatures were required so I had to keep my wits about me in handing each document and indicating the appropriate place for the signature – discreet 'flags' helped!

With all this completed none could deny that Her Canadian Majesty had indicated her will and pleasure, as advised by her appropriate Canadian minister,

---

[59] 23 Sept. 1987 – article by Moira Farrrow.

[60] 'Coat of arms ceremony judged a rare affair' *The Vancouver Sun*, 16 Oct. 1987.

[61] One copy was to go to the College of Arms for official Recording; one was for the Provincial Archives, and one for Ottawa.

in respect of how she identified armorially her authority in right of British Columbia.

The issue of a Provincial Proclamation by the Lieutenant Governor, aided by the Premier and appropriate Provincial Ministers followed immediately; the Deputy Provincial Secretary applying the Great Seal of British Columbia which now bore the augmentation just assigned. All of this was completed before the assembled company.

As the final act of the Court House ceremony, The Queen was invited to unveil, by drawing aside large heavy dark blue velvet curtains, a massive high relief, coloured sculpture of the now legitimately complete armorial achievement of the Province. This she did by pressing an electric button – which worked perfectly! I was later told that the electricians who fixed it all up almost wore out the mechanism making sure it did work.

With this done, and the national Anthem sung, The Queen and the Duke left at 4.40p.m. for the Four Seasons Hotel and the further parts of their programme[62]. I made sure I collected up the copies of the Warrant that needed to be taken back to the College of Arms for recording there[63].

As I got into the car which took me back to my hotel, I still heard the chanting nearby, of a group of local First Peoples. This had gone on throughout the ceremony. They were, apparently, protesting. About what – despite several enquiries – I never discovered. The rhythmic sound they made brought back childhood memories of their potlatches and the like as referred to in chapter I.

That evening, as I walked in the Discovery Building to attend a dinner given by the Premier of British Columbia and Mrs Vander Zalm for The Queen and suite, the civil servant referred to earlier on came up to me and said, 'Wasn't the ceremony at the Court House wonderful! It was something we have all been working for, for years.' At which I smiled and replied, 'I leave that for you to say,' and made for my place at table no. 12.

At just about that same time, some 6,000 miles away, many villagers were battling their way up to Boxford House in the middle of the night, 'to see if Lady 'ilda was alright.' They met her out in the grounds in nightdress and dressing-gown checking on the animals. Britain was in the grip of its great storm of '87 with gusts up to 106 knots.

★ ★ ★

---

[62] For the details of this ceremony, see the official programme, *The Visit of Her Majesty The Queen and His Royal Highness the Duke of Edinbugh to British Columbia, Saskatchewan, and Quebec, October 9 to 24, 1987*. Minister of Supply & Services Canada, 1987 pp 67-70; *Court House Ceremony, October 15, 1987*. Ministry of Provincial Secretary and Government Services [British Columbia, 1987] and the printed ceremonial for *The Granting and Proclamation of the Complete Coat of Arms of the British Columbia by Her Majesty Queen Elizabeth II 15 October 1987. The Law Courts, Vancouver* – copies of all three in SSA. New Series IX.

[63] CAR: I. 84-265.

Next morning in Vancouver, when I heard about the terrible storm and damage in England – Boxford was no exception – and having done what I was in B.C. to do, I immediately leapt, with permission, onto the first Air Canada flight over the pole, and was back within hours to help cope with the mess, particularly among the trees on the property at Boxford.

Not long after this clean up was well forward, on the banks of the Box, there arrived the offer of an unusual appointment, on the banks of the Vistula: that of ambassador of the Sovereign and Military order of Malta to the Republic of Poland.

Permanent residence *en poste* was not necessary; a small chancery would be maintained by the Order in Warsaw; my presence was only required on certain specific occasions of national and Order importance.

In view of family and personal interests, acceptance was almost automatic and immediate. What was more, this potential Excellency had a wife who would add grace, charm and wit to any occasion at the Governor's Palace – the President's official residence – or at any other of the great houses of the Polish capital; and she a descendant of the Piast Kings of Poland, to boot[64]!

However, just before this request arrived, I had been told by the Earl Marshal to hold myself in readiness to be – some two years hence – the next Garter Principal King of Arms.

As a result, I thought long and hard, and had various consultations about these two highly important appointments. In the end, I came to the conclusion that I had to keep my eye on the main ball; and so declined. When I told the Earl Marshal, he summed up my own emotions and reasons when he wrote:

> I am really rather sad that you had declined the invitation to become SMO Malta Ambassador to Poland. But as you rightly say, you are about to become Garter and these might well clash, so your decision is wise and correct[65];

my good friend, Bill Heseltine (Principal Private Secretary to The Queen) concurred[66].

Had the invitation come somewhat earlier or later, acceptance, without problems, could have been a distinct possibility. Nevertheless, the invitation was a very great honour not only to me, personally, but also to the College.

Two years later (1992) I was advanced to be Garter Principal King of Arms, the 35th to hold that office and title. I thus became the most senior herald of the College of Arms and an officer of the Order of the Garter.

---

[64] See Appendix II.
[65] SSA. New Series XIII: The Earl Marshal to Dr Conrad Swan, York Herald of Arms, 16 February 1990.
[66] *Ibid*: Sir William Heseltine, G.C.V.O., G.C.B., A.C., to same 23 January, 1990.

The ingenious solution of the problem of the inevitable spaces left on either side of a basically vertical, columnar design within a circular seal shape, by the artist filling them up with the Author's family crest placed behind the shield, will be noted. Original design and brass seal engraved therefrom. Original seal design by John Bainbridge, Herald-Painter, College of Arms, for the seal of the Author as Garter Principal King of Arms. Photography by Peter Norris. SSA.

My Letters Patent of appointment, dated 5 October[67] were issued by 'Warrant under The Queen's sign manual'. When the document issued from the Crown Office in the House of Lords at Westminster arrived, the initial capital (the 'E' of Elizabeth II) of the document had been illuminated with a wreath of maple leaves (I being the 1st Canadian to hold that office) intertwined with white roses (I having been York Herald). There were sixteen fully open flowers to

---

[67] Preserved SSA.

correspond with the number of our grandchildren, plus one bud for the one the expected[68] at the time.

'The Times Diary'[69] anticipated this change of Garters with a piece headed, 'Swan upped' – a play on the annual swan-upping (marking the beaks) of the royal cygnets on the River Thames.

As the Earl Marshal had decided earlier on, most wisely in my opinion, that in future officers-of-arms must retire at 70, and as I was already 68, it was obvious that my time would be of short duration. But it was understood that I could stay on for a little after the new deadline in order to hold the fort until my juniors were experienced enough to take over. So I was, in fact, an SGG. ('stop-gap Garter')!

This attitude I explored in a memorandum[70] of early '93 for my brother-officers when I wrote.

> How do I see my position as Garter?
>
> I regard it as essentially that of a *locum tenens* – as one whose tenure allows the College to get into a position whereby in future all Garters will offer their resignations at 70.
>
> I for my part, will not seek popularity, I never have done so and have no intention of doing so now agreeing, as I do, with Adlai Stevenson, 'Popularity's OK, provided you don't inhale'!

With the passing of Empire, the clientele of the heralds – and so the potential income of both themselves and the College would be much reduced. Accordingly, I made various suggestions for consideration. One was the reduction of the number of Waiting Officers[71], but keeping the complement of 13 by filling the balance with distinguished Servicemen, Barristers and the like who would be honoured to be so appointed, and whose expertise would be invaluable to the College – such to be non-Waiters.

Naturally, although I would not be with them to see developments in full, whatever they were I wished the College a viable and vigorous future.

Upon discussion, some Officers showed imagination; others needed encouragement. Well, at least, I had possibly sown a seed.

In life my attitude is, if one has to mount a horse, whether one likes the beast or not, gather together and shorten the reins, let its flanks feel the determination of one's heels, lean slightly forward, and then go hell for leather at 90° straight for the hedge!

---

[68] Alicia Mary, Baroness Hatvany *b.* 10 Jan. 1993.

[69] *The Times*, 23 July 1992.

[70] SSA. New Series X Memorandum for the Officers, dated 15 Jan. 1993.

[71] As explained before a Waiting Officer is one who takes his turn to Wait (ie., be the Duty Officer) for a week at a time. Any work accruing from such periods he takes into his practice. Such Waits are the main source of income both for the Officer and the College.

Curiously enough, 'stop gap' holders of office have an odd way of being agents for major changes, as with Leo XIII and his encyclical *Rerum novarum*[72], and John XXIII summoning the Second Vatican Council. In my case it was the radical, if not revolutionary, change in heraldic terms – already discussed at length – which ensured that married ladies could henceforth identify themselves with their own arms alone and not be required to marshal them with those of their husbands.

I have already noted the work of Garter both within the College over general administration and in connection with the House of Lords, the Order of the Garter, and other external duties. Accordingly, it will not be necessary to go into those again. Garter's work as the Inspector of Regimental Colours has not been discussed.

This includes establishing Badges for regiments and the designing of the Sovereign's Colour and the Regimental Colour – two flags which identify the regiment as a whole.

By the time I became Inspector, Colonel John Walker (Lancaster Herald, then Clarenceux King of Arms sometime Deputy Inspector and latterly Inspector of Regimental Colours) had retired (1978). As a result, I had the good fortune to inherit his capable adjutant for the work involved, Mrs Margaret Marshall.

For all my work as Garter, I was able to move soon into Garter House as my predecessor, Sir Colin Cole, was considerate enough not to delay his moving out – that can not be said of some previous Garters unless they were carried out in a box! Garter House, complete with a Garter Blue front door, is a complete and separate house more or less in the middle of the College buildings. So I was happy for the other officers to use the upper floors as a passage way between the two parts of the building – especially in wet weather. Surely with gentlemen one need not be too concerned over security, they would not abuse the privilege.

The work kept one busy. One was rather amused, from time to time, to note criticism, in certain quarters, completely ignorant of the facts. But I suppose 'twas ever thus. The 'boss' is always fair game for the 'slings and arrows of outrageous fortune.'

In 1994 I was promoted to be a Knight Commander of the Royal Victorian Order (KCVO). So during the morning of 24 June Hilda, our son, Andrew, and our second daughter, Juliana Galvin, and I presented ourselves at Buckingham Palace for my Investiture. Security was very tight at the time so that even the under-side of our car was inspected with a looking-glass. The ceremony was arranged with military precision by military men: a triumph of a dignified occasion, economic in the time taken because of the ceremonial adhered to.

Placing myself on one knee before my Sovereign I, naturally, held my head

---

[72] 1891, which maintained the priority of man and his family over the state. It was considered so radical that it was never permitted to be promulgated in the Austro-Hungarian Empire – despite the Holy Father being a nobleman by birth!

very still as she administered the accolade by placing the sword first on my right
and then left shoulder, lest the blade came into contact with my ears! In addition
to the music provided by the orchestra present, there were other accompanying
background sounds: the nearby Israeli Embassy was bombed.

★   ★   ★

A few months later, after two thorough medical examinations, a malignant
condition was diagnosed. I decided to retire with effect from 5 October 1995.
Not having been able up to then to spend much time with Hilda during our
marriage, I thought it only right to try to make up the loss from then on. As I
was 13 years older than she, in the normal course of events, hers would have
been a long widowhood. It behoved me to concentrate, during the time left me,
upon making suitable provision for her. How – to vary Burns's words – 'the best
laid schemes o' mice an' men' in our case ganged tragically astray will become
clear in the next chapter of this book.

I had thoroughly enjoyed my time at the College. It was a marvellous
experience – yes, at times maddening, yet always stimulating. One's spectrum of
activity was not confined to the country of one's residence, but was world-wide.
No two practice cases were ever the same. By my tours, I think I could say that
knowledge of the work, and potential for everyone in respect of the College of
Arms had been widely disseminated.

It is always a challenge to fill the most important position of an establishment.
First as a Pursuivant and then as a Herald I had had a horizontal view of the
character of the College as initially gained from my work on the Garter Papers;
as Garter my view was vertical. There was much intelligence and much
commonsense in the heralds though upon occasion, during an observation of 33
years, I failed to find the two co-habiting in the cranium of one or two – or was I
not on the same wavelength?!

As we moved towards the date of retirement, Kenneth Rose in his *Daily
Telegraph* column, 'Albany at Large' wrote:

> Swan has served the College well for 33 years (after having first been a
> soldier and later an academic). The last three of them, as Garter King of
> Arms, has not always been easy. In some ways the College resembles the
> chapter of a cathedral – and not only in the time of Trollope – in the
> personal tensions and feuds[73].

I think that just about summed it up.

A time comes when a new regime must be allowed to see what it can do, and
not do – always a sobering experience.

---

[73] 21 May 1995.

As I moved towards handing over the sceptre of Garterial office, my brother-officers, in descending order of precedence, were:-

John Philip Brooke Brooke-Little, Esq., CVO, MA, FSA, FSG, FHS
49th Clarenceux King of Arms.
The sole survivor of the College of Arms which I joined in 1962.

David Hubert Boothby Chesshyre, Esq., LVO, MA, FSA
72nd Norroy and 28th Ulster King of Arms

Theobald David Mathew, Esq., MA
43rd Windsor Herald of Arms.

Peter Llewellyn Gwynn-Jones, Esq., LVO, MA
45th Lancaster Herald of Arms who succeeded me as Garter.

Thomas Woodcock Esq., BA, LLB, FSA
30th Somerset Herald of Arms.

Patric Laurence Dickinson, Esq., MA
42nd Richmond Herald of Arms.

Henry Edgar Paston-Bedingfeld, Esq., Chartered Surveyor
40th York Herald of Arms.

Timothy Hugh Stewart Duke, Esq., BA
40th Chester Herald of Arms.

Robert John Baptist Noel, Esq., MA, MPhil.
75th Bluemantle Pursuivant of Arms.

Major William George Hunt, TD, BA, FCA
39th Portcullis Pursuivant of Arms – the only Officer of Arms – apart from myself – with Service experience which compare with the situation when I joined the College of Arms in 1962.

Rouge Croix Pursuivant of Arms ⎫
Rouge Dragon Pursuivant of Arms ⎬ appointments vacant

The Officers of Arms Extraordinary were:-

Phillip O'Shea, Esq.,
1st New Zealand Herald of Arms Extraordinary.

Francis Sedley Andrus, Esq., LVO
1st Beaumont Herald of Arms Extraordinary
formerly Lancaster Herald of Arms.

Dr John Martin Robinson, DPhil., FSA
6th Maltravers Herald of Arms Extraordinary

Sir Walter Verco, KCVO
3rd Surrey Herald of Arms Extraordinary
formerly Norroy and Ulster King of Arms.

Major David Rankin-Hunt, MVO, TD
9th Norfolk Herald of Arms Extraordinary.

Dr Michael Powell Siddons, MA, MB, BChir, FSA
3rd Wales Herald of Arms Extraordinary.

Lt.Cmdr John Henry Bruce Bedells, JP, MPhil, RN
1st Howard Pursuivant of Arms Extraordinary.

Arundel Herald of Arms Extraordinary ⎫
Fitzalan Pursuivant of Arms Extraordinary. ⎭ appointments vacant

So upon taking my leave of my brother-officers of the College I prayed – and have so continued

Ut Deus, et Dominus noster Jesus Christus fratres meos quondam conservare dignetur, ac eos a votis promissus declinari non permittat
(that God and Our Lord Jesus Christ will deign to keep my former brethren safe from harm and will not permit them to be turned from their obligations).

All aficionados of chivalry will recognize this as an adaptation of a prayer of the Order of Malta.

Upon my retirement, the Earl Marshal[74], with whom I always got on extremely well – we were both soldiers and so spoke the same language – most generously and thoughtfully presented me with a gold watch engraved in facsimile of his own hand:

From Miles, E.M., to Conrad, Garter –
a token of your great friendship as
Garter with me. 1995.

---

[74] Miles, 17th Duke of Norfolk, K.G., Earl Marshal & Chief Butler of England, Premier Duke, died 24 June, 2002. *Requiescat in pace*

CHAPTER XI

Au foyer de la famille

I. 'Take this ring as a sign of my love and fidelity'

THE DOOR OF THE small drawing room at Pynes opened, and Lady Hilda Northcote walked in. I remember looking at her and thinking to myself, Now there's a woman I could marry – if she'd have me. I had never seen her before. Nevertheless, that's how it was that day – and how it all turned out in the end, to my eternal gratitude.

She was not tall, 5 foot something, but with a perfect figure – the sort one wants to touch, but mustn't. She was topped with a shock of naturally blond hair, which lasted like that for the rest of her life. I was to find out later that this colouring ran through the family from a marriage with Agnes Cockburn – of a family of Scottish nabobs of HEIC service. She had married Hilda's great-great grandfather, Henry Stafford Northcote, father of Sir Stafford Northcote, 8th Baronet and 1st Earl of Iddesleigh – Hilda's colouring was so good she needed no make-up, but a discreet application of lipstick just set off her fresh, generous face. She had that type of smile which lights up a whole room. She joined us in a glass of sherry and then led us all in for luncheon which she had cooked having just completed a Domestic Science course at the Exeter Technical College.

This was in October '54. I had got to one of those points in writing my doctoral thesis at Cambridge that I simply had to have a break and a complete change for a few days. This coincided with my mother being about to leave on tour for the West of England – Devon and Cornwall – to visit the branches there of the Catholic Women's League (CWL) – she being, at the time, its National President for England and Wales. So I offered to chauffeur her – as briefly mentioned in chapter VII.

Both Hilda's parents, Henry, 3rd Earl of Iddesleigh and 10 Baronet, and Elizabeth, Countess of Iddesleigh – already referred to in Chapter IV – were away but Lady Iddesleigh arranged that their sons, Stafford, Viscount St Cyres, and Edward, and their foster-son, Nicholas Maxwell-Lawford would entertain us at Pynes, a Queen Anne house overlooking the River Exe in Devon.

The luncheon was great success and I really liked Hilda so as we lived several hundred miles apart, a regular correspondence developed.

Cambridge May Balls (being in England they were, of course, held in June) and Balls down in Devon were excuses to get together, and were not missed.

Having finished my PhD at Cambridge I returned (in '55) to Assumption,

277

now Assumption University of Windsor as Lecturer in History. The correspondence continued.

For the whole of '56 I was busy with academic work in Canada. By May, next year, having been promoted to Assistant Professor, I was able to get to England – university vacations start early in Canada.

Hilda had, in the meantime, started a course at the Violet Melchiott Nursery Training College (the VM) London, specializing in the case of premature babies and young children with serious conditions.

The location of the VM was ideal as by a good train London was only 50 minutes from Colchester where I was staying with my parents. We saw much of each other: walked and lay on the grass in Battersea Park (near the VM); went to the theatre; laughed our way through Chinese meals, eaten with chopsticks (both first time for her).

We had the same sense of humour; enjoyed many things in common; she was a lovely sweet person – but with a definite character; we were both Catholics and socially out of the same drawer. If there are any signals for a successful marriage, they were showing for us. Further, I hoped – indeed had reason to believe – she liked me. I definitely liked her – hell, I was falling passionately in love with her.

I soon made up my mind to propose. But being the incorrigible romantic that I am, felt such must be done properly. So I suggested that we went to Covent Garden *en grande tenue*: Hilda in evening dress, and me in white tie and tails. This we did on 15 July to see a production of Mozart's *The Magic Flute*. That piece was particularly appropriate, it seemed, as anyone with a musical ear recognizes the opening bars of the second half which, had they not been by Amadeus, one would have sworn were by Calixa Lavallee, composer of the musical score of, 'O Canada terre de nos aieux…' rendered into English as, 'O Canada, our home and native land…' So we went to the opera, had a box, I proposed, and Hilda said, Yes. 'How such a glorious fate should have overtaken me, it is impossible to imagine, as I have done nothing to deserve it' was my reaction; and when taking her back to the VM, afterwards, 'I felt I could have torn the roof of the taxi off with my own hands[1]'.

Obviously, I then had to ask her father if we could marry. Quite apart from the form of the matter, as she was not yet 21, she was still then under age. It was arranged that I should do this at Iddesleigh's club, the Guards'. So he and I met on Tuesday 24 July over tea – helps to have things to fiddle with upon such occasions. We had not been conversing for long when he came straight to the point and asked what was my income. I told him. At which, like a shot out of a rifle, he came back with, 'Pounds or dollars?' Fortunately, I had already translated it into pounds! That was that. We shook hands and he invited me to dinner with

---

[1] SSA. New Series VI: C.S. to Lady Hilda Northcote, 16 July 1957. Unless otherwise indicated all the following references to letters from me to her are SSA. New Series VI. She – touchingly – kept almost all my letters to her for the rest of her life.

Lady Iddesleigh and Hilda. Apparently, they had been waiting for the outcome in the ladies' annexe. What would have happened if Iddesleigh had said, 'No!'?

By the end of the month, the announcement of our forthcoming marriage had appeared in the Court Circular of *The Times* as well as *The Daily Telegraph,* and congratulatory letters poured in to both of us.

The time soon came for me to return to Assumption for the Christmas term of that year. I got a larger flat in the same building in which I had been living: Windsor Court, 1616, Ouellette Avenue – a block built in the thirties with large, commodious apartments. The furniture from my smaller previous flat was brought around: nevertheless, one piece I looked into seriously: a double bed.

> 'I think we ought to have a fairly good one' I wrote to Hilda; I have no doubt that we'll put it through its paces: it would be too awful to have one of the springs go just at the critical moment! Which reminds me, are you going to have a diaphanous black nightie amid your trousseau for the honeymoon – you'd look terrific in one! What colour would you like my pyjamas to be for that occasion? What about black (not sheer!) with white lapels and collar – or do you think something more vivid, scarlet?[2]

Following one of her letters of October I felt it necessary to ask, 'What sort of articles, may I ask, do you read – how many pounds pressure people use when they kiss!!?! What do you think our average is – a really good ten pounder?!'[3]

Finally, and not without impatience, the date of departure for England had almost arrived. So the night before, in readiness, I made a small pile on my bedside table: passport, travellers cheques and wedding rings. These were essentials, but as my departure from Windsor was not to be until about noon next day, the clothes could be packed next morning.

So to bed and sleep – only to be roused at 5.30a.m., by the telephone. A voice said, 'Can you be ready in half an hour? We'll send a car to collect you. Fog is closing in on the airport here and if we don't get you airborne by 6.30a.m. it will not be possible to get you to Montreal for your 6p.m. flight, TCA 522 for Heathrow.' Like a gazelle I was out of bed, grabbed my morning suit and other clothes and stuffed them into a suitcase; picked up the little pile beside my bed and was ready downstairs at the front door of 1616, Ouellette waiting at 6.25a.m. – unshaved; that didn't matter and could be rectified later.

Upon arrival in England, I found I had brought everything that was necessary save the trousers of my dinner jacket, but those of a dark suit I had with me were a good enough substitute. Perhaps the great Dr Freud would have had something to say about this omission?!

Hilda and I had a joyful reunion for a few days in London: she staying with

---

[2] 20 Oct. 1957.
[3] 6 Oct. 1957.

'cousin Mary'[4], and I at the Challoner Club. We then returned to our respective families for Christmas.

The great day arrived: 28 December – the Feast of the Holy Innocents (!) which, in pre-Vatican II days, was the earliest for a nuptial Mass after Christmas. The day was unseasonably bright and warm. So much so that it was quite comfortable for the bride to be driven to and from the church in an open car (a luxurious affair once owned by a Maharaja and kindly lent by some friends).

The Exeter Sacred Heart – a red sandstone structure, typical of Devon – is a good sized church, and easily accommodated the 400 or so guests.

The actual wedding service was conducted by the Rt Rev. C.E. Restieux, Bishop of Plymouth, assisted by the Parish Priest of the church, the Very Rev. Canon P.J. Tobin. An old friend, whom I had known since Peterhouse days, the Rev. F.X. Martin, OSA, of University College, Dublin celebrated the Mass. The Rt Rev. Mgr A.N. Gilbey came over from the Cambridge chaplaincy to give the address.

The Mass was concluded for us with the reading out of the blessing of HH Pope Pius XII upon our marriage. He was held in high esteem by both families, not only as the Holy Father, but because he had also honoured each by receiving them, at different times, in special audience at the Vatican Palace[5].

Then Hilda and I, arm in arm, walked down the central aisle to the strains of the 'Grand March' from *Aida*, gathering behind us, as in the wash of a ship, our relations, new in-laws and old friends whom we led out of the church to photographs by the press, and so back to Pynes for the reception.

The receiving-line formed up in the small drawing-room – where I had first met Hilda. Each guest, having congratulated us, passed on to the drawing-room and ballroom for a champagne buffet luncheon – with the butler slipping Hilda and me the occasional sandwich and drink to stave off the pangs of hunger until all the guests had arrived.

After speeches and cutting of the wedding cake, Hilda and I changed into our going-away clothes and, amid a shower of confetti – not allowed by the city authorities outside the church – I drove her away for the first forty-eight hours of our honeymoon at nearby Lyme Regis in Dorset[6].

I had booked a suite there at the Alexandra – formerly a Georgian residence. A coal fire burning in the grate of our own sitting room, upon arrival, typified the warm welcome we received. Dinner that evening was served in that room.

---

[4] Mary Northcote, granddaughter of the Honble (Hugh) Oliver Northcote by his wife, Edith Livingston Fish, dau. of the Honble Hamilton Fish, Secretary of State of the U.S.A.. Edith and Hugh met and courted while their fathers negotiated the Treaty of Washington (1871).

[5] Concerning the author's parents, *vide*, *L'Osservatore Romano* 9 Sept. 1949 'Nostre Informazione'.

[6] The wedding was noted in the 'Court Circular' of *The Daily Telegraph*, 30 Dec. 1957 and in *The Tatler*, 22 Jan. 1958 and described in considerable detail in the *Express and Echo* (Exeter) 28 Dec. 1957 and in the *Windsor Daily Star* (Ontario) 28 Dec. 1957 and 7 Jan. 1958.

Wedding group in the Small Drawing Room at Pynes, Devon. From left to right: the Rt. Rev. C.E. Restieux, R. C. Bishop of Plymouth; the Earl of Iddesleigh (Bride's father); Mrs Edna H. Swan (Groom's mother); Daphne Aspden and Monica Bower (Bridesmaids, the latter the Groom's goddaughter); the Groom and the Bride; Lieut. John Hall, R. N. (Best Man); Preccelly Davies-Scourfield (Bridesmaid); the Countess of Iddesleigh (Bride's mother) and Dr. H.P. Swan (Groom's father).

Curled up on the sofa afterwards, we read the telegrams of congratulation. That was in the days when they existed.

It had been a wonderful, marvellous day, but we were utterly, if happily, shattered. This had been rather anticipated, so some days before I had put it to Hilda that if this was the case, might it be better to wait one more night before we consummated the marriage. Having persevered so long in single chastity, it would make little difference if we continued so for one more night before entering the united chastity of the marriage-bed. She agreed.

So when we couldn't keep our eyes open any longer, and the grate was burning low, I took her by the hand and led her into our bedroom. The question then was, which side of the double bed to sleep on? For me, the side nearest the door was what I preferred, and such became my custom ever after. 'That's so I can make a quick get-away if you don't satisfy me!' I would say, and then duck as a slipper or some other missile was hurled my way. Or was this some primeval urge to get between my woman and the cave-opening by adopting this position? Hilda was, in fact, easy as to which side.

Having got into our night clothes, we knelt down for the first time, each at the preferred side, and said our night prayers, as we did for the rest of our married life, that is when I was not dashing round the world. We never prayed together, but did so at the same time. The session was not long, though Hilda took a fraction more time, so I would remain on my knees until she finished. It seemed more polite.

When we had finished our prayers, we climbed into bed, and after a further goodnight kiss – if somewhat lingering – out went the lights, and we were off to the land of nod before head hit pillow. Sometime later, Hilda told me that she just came to consciousness once or twice during the night. On each occasion she found herself holding on to a certain part of my anatomy, and that I didn't seem to mind: just snuggled up closer in my sleep. Oh, those convent educated-girls!

Next day was Sunday, and so we went to Mass. The rest of that day was the slowest I have ever known. It never occurred to us that one didn't have to wait until night-time to do what we both longed to do. We soon learned otherwise.

Eventually, having finished our dinner, we decided to go to bed. Each of us seemed to take an interminable time in the bathroom. At last, we were both in our nightclothes and dressing gowns, on our knees on our chosen sides of the bed. When Hilda stood up, I knew: this is it, and slipped off my dressing gown. When she let hers drop, there was my beautiful Hilda with only a diaphanous black nightie and my silk pyjamas between us. I soon dispatched such impedimenta. At which both of us leapt into bed in a flash, and lights were out.

For each of us it was the first expedition into *terra incognita et pulchrissima*: mountains, valleys hills and unimagined (or at least so far) unexplored nooks and crannies.

When we were completely man and wife, we did not, as was traditional with Poles years ago, get out of bed and sing the *Magnificat*, but just lay back on our pillows in that soft after-glow of love – and agreed, if this is married love, it's terrific! One has to admit that God thinks up some cracking good things when He really puts his mind to it!

For the rest of our married life, this particular expression of love, devotion and complete surrender to each other was highly important. Of course, technique improved as time and practice followed, and all the other aspects of love developed alongside: the realization and appreciation of all the domestic, familiar and social virtues one found revealed in one's spouse starting with loyalty and generosity.

That is not to say we did not have our differences, from time to time – after all neither of us was a shrinking violet, and both had definite ideas – but all were of a prudential nature. However, our basic relationship was rock-solid. I didn't deserve Hilda, but she was generous enough to take me on, and put up with my idiosyncrasies. As a result, the rest of our married life together was the very best experience of my life. I hope I made Hilda happy – she appeared so.

The last few days of our time in England we spent in London. We sailed from Liverpool on the SS *Empress of England*, bound for St John's, New Brunswick – the St Lawrence being frozen up at that time of year.

II. Hilda – the don's wife and major's lady

Having disembarked, we made straight for Montreal, where Peter greeted us most warmly. We stayed at the Windsor, where my family always stayed when in that city. There we enjoyed the hospitality, as always, of Peter's and my good friends – soon to be Hilda's – Catherine (Shaughnessy[7]) Mrs L.O.P. Walsh, her daughter, Maria Teresa, and son-in-law, F.G.A. McCullough.

From Montreal, we went down through Toronto to Windsor, and so to our flat at Windsor Court. Hilda soon got the flat generally fitted out, combining some furniture the Faculty families kindly gave us as a wedding present with a few purchases she made herself. She got on well with the local people, and while some were a little surprised at her not wearing a coronet all the time, they soon took to her direct and cheerful manner.

One of Hilda's particular successes was with the army contingent of which I had been the commanding officer since 1956 as a major. It consisted, on the one hand, of young, already commissioned officers, and the army cadets. They were all a keen and very decent group of young men. From time to time we would entertain them at our flat, and they were amazed how Hilda was able to engage each in lively conversation. Well, of course, her father, brothers and foster-brother had all been in the army, so army talk was almost second nature. She was a great success as the major's lady.

After one miscarriage, we got things right and looked forward to the arrival of our first child, due in August '59. Hilda wanted the delivery to be at home. Such an idea was almost obscene as far as the local doctors were concerned: That sort of thing only happens in the Yukon, they said with pained disapproval. But they had met their match with Hilda, so she returned in the spring of that year to Pynes where she knew matters could be arranged easily.

I followed for the summer vacation to hover around as a distracted father when baby (Mary) Elizabeth Magdalen duly arrived on 5 August. For this delivery Hilda was attended by a most efficient young local doctor who took off his coat, tied on a large rubber apron and got on with the job. He considered the whole procedure quite normal.

We – 3 of us now! – returned to Assumption for the autumn term of the academic year '59/'60 which, as matters turned out, was to be our last there. After

---

[7] Niece of the 1st Lord Shaughnessy who, during the difficult World War I period in Ireland was seriously considered, by Westminster, as a possible Lord Lieutenant for that country (he being a Catholic).

that, the College of Arms was to be my next appointment, as already referred to in detail at the end of Chapter VIII.

III. English Language Summer School – Pynes

However, until I became a herald – and indeed for some time after that in view of the terms of appointment, as already explained – money coming in steadily would be needed. So Hilda decided that the answer was to start an English language school for foreign students during their holidays. Historically speaking, her foundation was one of the very first of the large number of such establishments up and down England today.

Soon after we had settled in at East Pynes (as we called the east wing of my parent's-in-law's house) our students for the season arrived: about 30 of them: Hilda looked after the commissariat and even did all the cooking; while I, plus an assistant, dealt with the academic side.

In general, the idea was to keep them busy all the time, and in one way or another learning English. Accordingly, there were formal lessons all morning; after lunch, organized games, riding, or swimming in the River Exe – despite a French girl protesting 'Oh, ze *salade!*' in reference to the aquatic plants near the banks! All these activities provided opportunities for further English lessons, for if any tuition was necessary it was all given in English. After the evening meal we had what are called 'drawing-room games' such as bingo, 'man and his object' and so on, – in fact anything to make them talk English. After all that they were ready for bed.

The summer of '61 rolled around, and we were expecting not only students but also another baby: due mid-July though. One of the students of the previous year, upon returning in '61, took one look at Hilda and told the new students, 'Lady 'ilda is suspecting a baby'. That was the understatement of the year, exquisite in its delicacy!

It was our custom with the students, that at bedtime Hilda and I also changed into our nightclothes and dressing gowns. We then paraded the dormitory-bedrooms to impress upon the students that when we said 'bed' we meant 'bed'. As very few had attended a boarding school before – such are a rarity on the Continent – this sort of life tended to excite them.

Now, it so happened at bedtime on 15 July that summer, when we were parading around in our dressing gowns that Hilda started to have contractions. So when a bout of them started, she would stand by a student's bed and hold onto its head or foot – it did not matter which for this exercise – for all her worth until the contraction subsided. Once over, she would continue on her perambulation until the next; all the while trying to give the impression that there was nothing unusual happening!

During the early hours of the next morning (16 July) (Hilda) Juliana Mary duly arrived: she came out with a Marcel wave and protesting at the top of her voice! This was the first delivery I had witnessed, so I fainted – well, it really is a terrible strain for the father! For the remaining three I behaved myself much better – though my doctorate didn't do me much good for any of them.

Later that morning at breakfast, as soon as the students heard that the baby had come during the night, they were full of curiosity. So before lessons began, it was arranged that they all trooped up into Hilda's and minute Juliana's bedroom. The attitudes of the students were most interesting. All the boys behaved impeccably and were extremely gentle, but were in such a state of excitement they were practically in bed with Hilda, so thrilled were they to see a baby of but a few hours. At home, when their mothers had their siblings in the local *clinique* they would not see the new arrival for a day or so. On the other hand the girls, though full of curiosity and also in the bedroom, hung back – as if anticipating the process for themselves?

Juliana's christening took place in the domestic chapel at Pynes amid a concourse of relations, friends and students. My brother, Peter, now President of St Thomas More College in the University of Saskatchewan, was over to baptize Juliana – which he did into a silver champagne bucket (well, one has to have something to catch the water, so why not something elegant?!)

It seemed that an *accouchement* was an added attraction offered by the English language school at East Pynes. Truth to tell, it was an advantage to have very young children about, as the students felt protective, and when they started to talk, were not embarrassed to practise their English on children younger than they.

IV. A place of our own: Boxford House, Suffolk and the English Language School there.

Since coming to East Pynes, we had been looking around for a place nearer London so that when I was appointed to the Royal Household I could go up and down, when necessary, easily. The journey from Exeter was too long to be practical on a daily basis.

In the end we discovered in Suffolk, Boxford House[8], a pleasant Georgian Gothic country house in the parish of that name, about 60 miles north east of London towards the sea. Following restoration it has proved ideal ever since for us.

The property, some 20 acres, was recorded in Domesday Book (1086)[9]. The house (built 1819-20) is near an Indian Cedar adjudged recently, by the Forestry Commission, to be between 700 and 800 years old – so there is a certain air of

---

[8] The Architect was Mark Greystone Thompson, see Bury St Edmunds West Suffolk Records Office: ACC.806/2/3. Thompson was a highly competent architect and was responsible for several important buildings in East Anglia.

[9] *Vide* under Coddenham (as Boxford was called at the time) in *Domesday Book – History from the sources*, Phillimore, Chichester, 1986 Vols. I and II.

Students of the English-Language School, Boxford House, Suffolk. Lady Hilda Swan,
Headmistress and Founder, stands in printed dress to the right holding the hand of Catherine
Swan, aged 3 years; the Author at extreme right. 1966.

stabilitas about the place. A wooded area marching along the entire boundary of
the property ensures seclusion.

With the roof made water-tight, Hilda (carrying Catherine, our third), little
Elizabeth and smaller Juliana, José (a 15-year-old Spaniard living with us for a
year) Hilda's old horse, 'General', and a donkey (which had become pregnant on
the way over from Ireland) plus myself all moved up from Devon in March '62.
It was so cold that, at night, the glasses of water on the bedside tables froze.

Room by room, the restoration progressed. In the end we had 32 rooms at our
disposal – a house can be too small, but never too large. It was ideal for a
growing family. Our three remaining children were all born here: Catherine
(October '62) Andrew (January '64) and Anastasia (July '66). In addition, we
could easily accommodate the 35 to 45 students we received in the summer from
then on down to 1995 when Hilda handed over the school to Catherine – by
then married with three children of her own, living about six miles away, also in
Suffolk, at Monks' Eleigh.

While I helped with the creation of an extensive new garden, when available,
it was really the result of Hilda's hard work, with the help of a single gardener.

The typical picture of her in the garden was of a woman in anorak, tweed skirt and wellingtons, a touch of leaf cinder from a bonfire in her shock of blond hair – or if it had settled on her lovely, cheerful face I regarded it as an 18th century patch!; at her heels a pair of Borzois – called 'Bolus' and 'Kroki' (the Polish version of the parish where my family had their property in Lithuania); then an Old English Mastiff – called 'Puppy Dog' (as a joke in view of its enormous size and weight); and finally an Irish Wolfhound – called 'Plunkette' (after Blessed Oliver Plunket[10] but, being a bitch, a feminine version). Andrew's Golden Labrador called 'Brandy' seemed to live for ever and was always about the place.

All manner of livestock were added and the stables increased gradually until we had eight horses and ponies so that the entire family could be mounted: Hilda, me and five children, with one mount over for a guest.

We rode to hounds and there were everlasting gymkhanas which engaged the children's attention – and parents' exhaustion trying to get that b… horse into the box!

When the students came in the summer, the stables proved a boon. Many wanted to ride but did not know how. This provided a marvellous English lesson – without them realizing it! In addition to all the things they would have to learn when actually riding, it was also essential to get them to realize that one end of the horse bites and the other kicks!

The regime for the students, academic as well as otherwise, at Boxford was very much as initiated at East Pynes: we kept them so busy, they often had to be reminded to pack at the end of their time with us, not having realized it was time to go home.

Some worked hard at their English and learned a good deal. When a boy once said, with a smile – after being with us for several sessions: 'Yes, Boxford House is Liberty Hall – so long as you do as you're told' – we felt we were getting somewhere!

Be that as it may, we soon had a question included on the entrance form: 'Reason for your son's/daughter's attendance at Boxford House?' The usual answer was, 'To learn English'. A pair of Norwegian parents once added: '… and to experience Dr Swan'(!).

It was possible for me to remain at Boxford for the entire summer school sessions because of the particular terms of appointment to the College of Arms – as detailed in Chapter VIII. Nevertheless, one kept one's eye on the practice at the College. At a fixed time each day, usually during the mid-morning break from lessons, the Secretary or other Staff would telephone with problems if there were any, or simply to report progress.

I was fortunate to have an excellent staff, several of whom have already been

---

[10] St Oliver Plunket, Archbishop of Armagh, executed 11 July, 1681 – the only Catholic priest from Ireland killed for religion during the Penal Period and he an Anglo-Irishman! His relics are preserved at Downside Abbey, near Bath – the school of our son, Andrew, and several of our grandsons.

mentioned. In addition there was Margaret Weld[11] – the most efficient of secretaries; later Rupert Fisher – a devoted Personal Assistant. Additional research assistants of note were: Elizabeth Dowman, Brenda Holroyd and Joyce Coulter, Oliver Hylton, (during university holidays); and John Tunesi of Liongam, Yr, was my Factor as Garter. So all the various aspects of my College of Arms practice moved forward like a well-maintained Rolls Royce.

With the students in the summer, College of Arms work throughout the whole year, as well as tours abroad, life was anything but monotonous: there was a new experience round every corner.

V. H.P.S. and E.H.S. move to their rewards

These experiences varied: some were thrilling and full of joy; others not so. Of the latter, a great sadness to me was that within a year of my appointment to the College of Arms, my father suddenly died of a massive heart attack on 23 November, 1963 – he was only 72.

That firm, ever-reliable rock of my life was no longer there. For a while the general sensation was rather like treading water. He had been anything but the life and soul of a party, but something infinitely better. If one had a problem, he was the one to go to for practical advice or real help – they were always given.

When the letters of condolence started to pour in from all over the world, the one phrase that occurred again and again was, 'he always had time to listen' – no bad epitaph for a doctor, I would suggest.

We buried his remains in the churchyard of our notable Catholic parish church of Our Lady Immaculate and St Edmund King and Martyr, Withermarsh Green, Suffolk. This is an historic church having been built, pursuant to the Relief Act of 1793 which permitted, for the first time since the Reformation, Catholic churches[12].

Thus began a twenty-five year widowhood for my mother.

Mother continued her work for the Sue Ryder Homes, a national institution on the English scene for many years now. She and the then Miss Sue Ryder[13],

---

[11] A Weld of Chideock, ultimately of Lulworth (in whose chapel John Carroll, 1st R.C. Bishop in the USA, was consecrated [1790]).

[12] 'provided it did not look like a church' – such a condition was music to the lawyers' ears! In the end, it was decided that if there was no tower then this condition was fulfilled. As a result, Catholic churches in England of this period look like Nonconformist chapels on the outside, and are then discovered to be all Sheraton or *Empire* within!

[13] Group Captain Leonard Cheshire, VC, OM, DSC, DFC, proposed to Miss Sue Ryder in my parents' house. At which my father, naughtily, said, 'That marriage will be consummated in heaven'(!) He was, in fact, wrong as they had two children. When about to be raised to the peerage in 1978 she wanted to be Baroness Ryder of Warsaw, in view of her work for the Poles, many being concentration camp victims. Such a *nomen dignitatis* with a foreign place in it had been permitted for the military, but not otherwise – as with Alexander of Tunis. However, putting on the 'poor little woman' act – at which she was a past master, she won the day; even the Communist Polish government gave its approval!

when both in BAOR, started to visit and help the concentration camp victims. The gates were open but, poor wretches, these former prisoners frequently had to stay on, as they had no home to go to; there was, at least a roof over their heads at the camps.

This joint work developed and issued, ultimately, in the foundation of the Sue Ryder Homes in Britain. In all this work, Mother's genius for fund raising proved invaluable.

For her monumental charitable work she was decorated by HH Pope John-Paul II with the highest award available to him at the time for women, the *Crux Honoris Pro Ecclesia et Pontifice*[14].

Chic, well groomed and completely *compos mentis* to the end, she was engaged on her charitable endeavours up to a short time before her death. This was hastened, doubtless, by a car crash in which she suffered.

It is said that if you want the maximum number to attend your funeral, then you must die at 40. If that is so, then it was as well that she soldiered on until two days before her 89th birthday (10 November 1988). As it was, at her requiem it was standing room only: she had touched so many lives. Interment was in my father's tomb in the churchyard at Withermarsh Green[15].

She was one of those rare people to whom many owed much; not least of all her immediate family.

Thus were gathered to their ancestors my two best teachers. May they rest in peace.

> Death is part of the future for everyone.
> It is the last post of this world,
> And the reveille of the next.
> (Pope John XXIII)

VI. The Cygnets

As mentioned before, our three remaining children were all born at Boxford House. Indeed, for a period we had five children under 7 years of age. Hilda's hands were especially full. The last to arrive, Anastasia, used to say, 'I wasn't a

---

[14] Papal Warrant dated 29 Oct. 1979.

[15] The inscription on the tomb (Portland Stone horizontal slab, 6' X 30') is as follows: Pray for the soul of Henry Peter Swan, MD,CM. 6 September, 1892. 23 November, 1963 and of that of his wife Edna Hanson Magdalen (née Green) Decorated with the Cross of Honour Pro Ecclesia et Pontifice. 12 November, 1899. 10 November, 1988. RIP.
PRAECLARUS VIR HENRICUS PETRUS CYGNUS NATU SWIECICKI ARMA JASTRZEBIEC BOLESTA ET NOBILIS RUSSIAE CODEX I PERSCRIPTIONES MDCCXIX, MDCCCLX ET SEQ. RIP.
(The distinguished man Henry Peter Swan born Święcicki. Arms Jastrzębiec Bolesta and a Noble of Russia Recorded Book I, 1799, 1860 and subsequently. May he rest in peace.

mistake; but I <u>was</u> a surprise!' Some of our friends nearby observed, as the family increased and multiplied, 'those b… Swans are trying to populate Suffolk'(!).

The children used to say that at one time they thought their father was a piece of red ribbon which gradually made its way across the map of the world in the nursery. That was when I was away on tour and would send back a stream of postcards so that they could plot the course of my route – and learn some geography in the process.

Upon my arrival back from a long tour abroad, there would be an immediate distribution of gifts I had collected en route for the children. Hilda and I would then retire to our bedroom and catch up on what we should have been doing together during the past long weeks. The children would give us about an hour. Then we'd hear a tap, tap; after which five little heads would appear round the bedroom door as it opened. One would be struggling to carry a teapot, the others cups, saucers, milk, biscuits and so on – one's heart melted! Hilda always seemed to have a bed-jacket under her pillow for such situations; as for Daddy sitting up in bed without a pyjama top, well that was quite a usual sight!

In due time, as with all good children, ours grew up and turned out remarkably well. They took after their dam and surmounted the disadvantage of such a sire! Hilda and I had every reason to be proud of them.

All our children married and being the offspring of a herald, had an appreciation of precedence. As a result, it was a case of 1st, 1st, 2nd, 2nd and so on; even our son, Andrew, who was the 4th in the family was the 4th to marry. All were country weddings, and all the girls were married from Boxford House, with a marquee on the lawn for the reception following the ceremony.

Elizabeth, the eldest (a Registered Nurse, trained at St Bartholomew's Hospital, London) married Roger Peter le Strange Herring in June '81. He is the son of Colonel Peter Herring, CBE, Provost Marshal, UK Land Forces; a collateral and heir of Thomas Herring, Archbishop of Canterbury (1745-57) who as Archbishop of York raised a large sum on behalf of the Hanoverian ascendancy during the Jacobite Rebellion (1745). Though Roger is a staunch Protestant of a somewhat Northern Irish hue, he is also a collateral of St Philip Howard who died for the Catholic Faith in 1595 – *dans la généalogie on ne…n'est ce pas,* as chorused so frequently in this book?![16]

Seven months later, Juliana (a nurse trained at St Thomas's Hospital, London) was married, in January '82, to Patrick David Thomas Galvin, an expert on Far East investment and partner in de Zoete and Bevan. His paternal family is Irish, descending from the Earls of Thomond and the Macgillicuddy of the Reeks; his maternal English descent is from the Earls of Derwentwater[17].

---

[16] For further details *vide,* Swan, Sir Conrad. *'Hiberniae Robur Lacrimaeque'* being chapter XXIII and 'Twice a Primate' being chapter XXIV in *The Northcote Millenium Commonplace Book.* Heraldic Enterprises, Boxford, Suffolk, 2000.

[17] *Ibid.* 'The Galvin Descent' being chapter XXX.

There was now a lull on the marriage front for four years, which provided opportunities to celebrate Silver Wedding and Golden commissioning anniversaries.

On 28 December, 1982 our children hosted a dinner party for us and old friends. Our first grandchild, Elizabeth Galvin, was able to come but, 'by reason of the tenderness of her years remained conveniently nearby, asleep' (aged 1 month) – as was noted in the list of guests on the reverse of the Bill of Fare prepared for the occasion by the late John Bainbridge, an extremely gifted herald-painter of the College of Arms.

Just about two years later, on 18 November 1994 – the anniversary of the very day upon which 20 of us were commissioned into the Indian Army – 14 of us met[18], appropriately enough at the Royal Overseas League premises, just off Piccadilly near the Ritz, for a most agreeable luncheon to celebrate this anniversary and our survival.

Upon entering the room reserved for us, 'I recognized immediately a good number. As for some of the others! I wonder what they made of me?!'[19]

Two years on, Catherine having returned from Hong Kong (and having trained as a nurse at Addenbrookes Hospital, Cambridge) she married in June '86, (John) Jeremy Walters, a partner in the well-known London solicitors, Charles Russell and Co. Jeremy was the son of a Captain, RN.

Three years later, in June '89, it was almost a case of marrying the girl next door when Andrew married Fenella, daughter of Air Chief Marshal Sir John Rogers, KCB, CBE. Although they met for the first time in London, the Rogers's home is at Little Hawkesly which is almost the next parish to Boxford.

Three months later, in September '89, Anastasia (a Registered nurse, trained at St Mary's Paddington, London) married Peter Galbraith Mark Hatvany (now a Judge), son of Baron Paul Hatvany, whose male-line family was raised to the peerage of the Kingdom of Hungary with a seat in the Upper House of Parliament in 1908[20].

There is, mercifully, no *fin de race* about our children. At the time of writing this book the grandchildren number 20 – at least when I last had them all on parade.

VII. Councillor Lady Hilda and Mistress[21] Rouge Dragon, York and Garter

When the grandchildren arrived, Hilda was always on hand, if needed. She also took her part following her family's tradition of public service, being elected as

---

[18] Bearing in mind the time span and our careers all over the globe, not to mention mortality, the gathering of this number was the result of a *tour de force* of sleuthing by the now late Rev. Roger Whitehead, Major S.R. O'R Shearburn and our distinguished barrister brother-officer, David Wade.

[19] SSA: Garter's Diary 18 Nov. 1994.

[20] Swan, *op. cit.* 'Continental Blockade and Golden Fleece' being chapter XXII.

[21] At the College of Arms the wife of an Officer of Arms is known as Mistress + her husband's heraldic title.

the Boxford representative on the Cosford Rural District Council[22]. A District Council, in non-urban England, is the middle stratum of Local Government; the County Council is at the top, and the Civil Parish council at the base.

For the Suffolk County Riding for the Disabled Association, she was the Chairman[23]. In connection with this, she ran a summer 'camp' as well for disabled carriage drivers at Boxford House: this swung into action immediately the foreign students left, as the beds were all up and everything was geared for large numbers. The disabled riders were mentally retarded children. Their faces would beam with delight as three helpers – none *dans sa première jeunesse*! – ran beside each child (one on either side to keep the child in the saddle and the third leading the mount: maximum speed the trot!). The drivers were simply physically disabled. One even was totally blind. With the aid of a seeing passenger she would immediately respond to, 'Tell Lightning to Walk on'; 'down on the left rein;' or whatever was needed, and she was off down the lanes with a look of sheer contentment on her face.

Hilda was also the President of the Suffolk St John Ambulance[24]. So what with all this, and more, including being the wife of a herald with various official social commitments – one could not say she stagnated.

One of the latter duties which amused us considerably was the Annual Diplomatic Reception at Buckingham Palace, usually in November. Hilda and I would attend in 'full fig': she in evening gown and tiara and I in white tie, tails and decorations.

We and the other non-Foreign and Commonwealth Office types were there to 'chat up' the foreign diplomats. An entry in my 1993 diary is typical:

> Hilda and I did our stuff with the Vietnamese Ambassador, his wife and two of the mission. They looked so pathetic and forlorn standing there in their 'no nonsense' Communist high-collared suits beneath the famous van Dyck portrait of Charles I advancing at one on a horse. Possibly they thought they were about to be trampled by this mass of counter-revolutionaries![25]

After such occasions it was a great convenience for both of us to be able to sleep in Garter House. Following an early breakfast, I would walk Hilda to Liverpool Street Station – a flood of bowler hats surging relentlessly against us! She would take the train, return to Boxford, feed the animals and get on with the day's work.

In fact, the College of Arms – and my chambers in particular – was, in a sense, an extension of Boxford House for the family.

[22] 1971-73.
[23] 1982-92.
[24] 1989 to her death in '95.
[25] SSA. Garter's Diary. 24 Nov. 1993.

From time to time, both as York and Garter, I had Mass offered in my chambers by various priests. I was not the first herald to do so since the Reformation; that was John Brooke-Little, Bluemantle, Richmond, Norroy and Ulster and, finally, Clarenceux. However, I was the first Garter to have arranged this in Garter House. One such early occasion there was in September '93, when my brother, Peter, in the 50th year of his ordination to the priesthood – referred to in chapter V – offered Mass, attended by other members of the family and of the College[26].

Upon the 510th anniversary of the foundation of the College by Richard III (2 March '94) His Excellency the Most Reverend Luigi Barbarito, then Apostolic Pro-nuncio[27] to the Court of St James's, celebrated Mass there. Before this I took the precaution of sending him a list of those expected to attend, and also drawing his attention to those who descended from English Catholic martyrs of the Reformation. As a result, he pointed out, during his address, something not always appreciated, 'that these English martyrs are the only martyrs that had died out of loyalty specifically to the Holy See' – although how true that is[28].

This Mass was attended by various family members, heralds and friends. Among the latter was the Gentleman of the Black Rod, Admiral Sir Richard Thomas, KCB, OBE, who came fully uniformed as Black Rod so that he could go on duty in the House of Lords immediately after the buffet luncheon which we served on these occasions.

Hilda and I held a series of sit down lunches to which all the heralds were invited in turn along with a number of people from outside we thought they might like to meet[29].

From about 1970 it had been the custom for the officers of the College to give a party at Christmas for all the various staffs, both of the college as well as of the heralds. This I attended for the first time as Garter in December '92.

VIII. Return after a century

That party at the College was a congenial, indeed a happy gathering. For the family, however, it would have been momentous had we known that at that very same time the Russian army was preparing to leave Lithuania completely. For over 50 years we had hoped and prayed to be able to walk upon Lithuania's green and pleasant land (with all due acknowledgements to the good Mr William Blake, who wrote *Jerusalem* in the year Boxford House was completed).

During the early nineties Lithuania, taking advantage of *glasnost* and *perestroika*,

---

[26] *Ibid.,* 2 September 1993.
[27] From December '94: Apostolic Nuncio.
[28] SSA. Garter's Diary, 2 March 1994.
[29] *Ibid*. 14 Oct. 1993.

gradually edged her way back to independence[30]. It was a triumph of argument and persuasion – Lithuania had no guns. During all this, we hoped we saw a possible visit dawning.

In '89 I was appointed the first Honorary Genealogist of the Order of St Michael and St George. This associated me closely with the Foreign and Commonwealth Office, and its Principal Under Secretary of State, Sir David Gillmore, and his colleagues proved towers of strength in helping us to achieve the desired visit.

So, on 20 April 1993 Hilda and I took off by air for the Lithuanian capital of Vilnius. There, at a broken-down much 'Sovietized' airport, we were most warmly welcomed by an academic, Dr Algis Tomas Geniušas, President of the United Nations Association of Lithuania. He, along with his wife, Dr Isolde Gabriele Geniušiene, took us in hand, and for the entire visit they could not have been more solicitous and helpful. H.E. Michael Peart, LVO, the British Ambassador, and his wife were also extremely hospitable.

A Soviet regime of atheistic Communism was the fate of Lithuania as the result of World War II[31]. Many of her sons and daughters, both at home and among the 300,000 exiled to Siberia (of whom only a fraction returned) surely often wondered, 'must the dove be the vulture's prey?'[32].

Notwithstanding, they put up a spirited defence of Christianity. They proved to be a thorn in the side of their oppressors, and refused to conform to the model of *homo Sovieticus*. Two Russian Orthodox, Alexander Solzhenitsyn in his *Gulag Archipelago*[33] and his fellow prisoner, Dimitri Panin, in his article in *Catacombes*[34] paid glowing tributes to the sterling Faith of their fellow prisoners from Lithuania.

This was the largest Catholic country directly under Moscow, and its clandestinely produced, *Chronicle of the Lithuanian Catholic Church* proved to be the main source for the West of the reality of Christian life under atheist rule[35].

On the other hand, from the material point of view Lithuania regained her independence with the national economy in shreds – thanks to the Soviet system (or more precisely, the Soviet lack of a viable, economic system) – and there was not a penny in the national coffers. The Russians might be prepared to leave the

---

[30] For an authoritative description of this process, see the account of one of its principal leaders, Landsbergis, Vytautas. *Lithuania Independent Again*. University of Wales Press, Cardiff 2000 (though not very well disposed towards the Lithuanian Poles!).

[31] Except 1941-44 when Lithuania was under the Nazis, but there was nothing to choose between the two regimes.

[32] Psalm 73.19.

[33] Solzhenitsyn, Alexander. *The Gulag Archipelago III* (English translation by H.T. Willets) Collins and Harvill Press, London, 1978 p.100.

[34] Panin, Dimitri. *Catacombes*. September 1975 p.5

[35] For a scholarly study, vide Bordeaux, Michael. *Land of Crosses. The struggle for religious freedom in Lithuania, 1939-78*. Augustine Publishing Co., Chulmeigh, Devon, 1979.

country – but not any money! When I gave my lecture at the University of Vilnius, it was the British Ambassador who had to provide the projector for the slides – the university was too poor to have one.

During our almost annual visits thereafter, it has been a joy to note the gradual, definite improvement so that by now, for example, in Vilnius – that Baroque gem – many ladies' shops would do London and Paris credit.

With my lecture, 'The Heraldry of Shakespeare' given at the university; we – Dr Geniušas, Hilda, myself and a driver – set off for Krakes in a clapped-out van; it was all that was available, but the engine worked.

As the crow flies, Krakes is about 50 miles north of the capital, towards Kaunas. The journey seemed longer, as we went not just on roads but along tracks beside fields as well. We wanted to see the *EURUPOS CENTRAS* stone on the way. A kind peasant farmer led us the last quarter mile across fields to this geographical centre of Europe.

Finally, we arrived at Krakes: a medium sized village, and soon found the parish priest, Fr Romualdas Ramašauskas – a big man, in his late thirties, I would have said, with bright enquiring eyes and a generous face. He welcomed us with open arms, and insisted upon personally showing us the way to Pasusvys, our family property, outside the village.

We were soon there. The servants' quarters still stood, as well as the huge barn – curiously enough built of flint and brick, as so often found in Suffolk. The house, however, originally built of wood in that classical style we would call Georgian, had long since disappeared. Nevertheless, its large brick cellars were still there but, upon close inspection, were found to be bereft of any vodka or Gloria (the excellent local brandy!). The house had overlooked a river bound bluff, with a view of fields and woods stretching off into the distance. One was immediately reminded of these lines in *Pan Tadeusz*:

> Among the birch trees on a little hill
> There stood a manor house, wood-built on stone;
> From far away the walls with whitewash shone,
> The whiter as relieved by the dark green
> Of poplars that the autumn winds would screen[36]

Under the Soviets, the property had been forced into the collective farm system. A number of peasant workers and their families were still living in the servants' quarters.

We were then taken towards an adjacent part of the original property. On the way we passed in the grounds a statue of St Anthony of Padua (*vere* Lisbon, as referred to in chapter VI). The four sides of the pedestal had inscriptions in Polish, Lithuanian, Russian and Latin, one on each. With the statue the total

---

[36] Mickiewicz *op. cit.* p. 2.

height was about 15 feet. During the Soviet period, the local government authority had ordered the statue destroyed. The peasants refused to join in this iconoclasm. This statue was in honour of the patron saint of my father's elder brother, Anthony, who was born at Pasusvys and, it will be recalled from Chapter III, spent a lifetime as an Oblate priest ministering to the Indians in the Rocky Mountains in British Columbia.

Fr. RR then took us to the orphanage, for which he had suddenly found himself responsible upon being appointed as parish priest. About 35 children were and are there, boys and girls, aged between 7 and 16. He has a group of lay people to look after them.

The conditions were spartan but spotlessly clean. I noticed teddy bears on the beds of several of the very young, so I felt the place had more than a mere touch of humanity about it. Upon Fr RR's arrival, several of the little ones ran out laughing to greet him, clutched him round the legs and made it difficult for him to walk. There was real affection there, and it was undoubtedly a happy place.

Some of the children were literal orphans. Others were from alcoholic parents: alcoholism is a serious problem in the country, much aggravated by the utterly bleak prospects for the population under the Soviets.

From this visit onwards, the Krakes orphanage has been high on our list of charities, if for no other reason than that most of the children there descend from the estate workers of our old home.

From Vilnius we flew down on 20 April to Warsaw, where we were looked after by Professor dr. hab. Stefan Kuczynski, president of the Polish Heraldry Society. I had been to Warsaw before in 1991 with our son, Andrew, when I lectured to the university there.

Having shown Hilda round, off we went – this time by train, for a change – further south to the old capital of Krakow. Here we were ably looked after, on the one hand by my confrère in the Order of Malta, Count Julius Ostrowski, head of that part of the Polish Association of the order which was in Poland while its headquarters was still in exile; and, on the other hand by, dr. hab. Marta Gibinska – Marzec, of the Institute of English Philology at the Jagellonian University, and later its Director.

Among the many delights of Krakow, high on the list, surely, is Wawal Hill. Upon it is located a combination, in a sense, of a Windsor Castle and a Westminster Abbey: the Castle and Cathedral.

The latter, scene of the coronations of the Kings of Poland, and burial place of the country's heroes, proclaims history from its every stone. Of especial interest to me, obviously, is the tomb of Kasimir IV, the only Polish monarch to have been a Knight of the Garter[37]. In his marriage with Elizabeth Hapsburg they had

---

[37] Reigned 1444-92; appointed K.G., 4 Aug. 1450 by Henry VI of England.

12 children. Through their 6 daughters they are ancestors of most of the royal houses of Europe. His sons comprised: 1 saint (Kasimir), 1 Cardinal and 4 Kings. At that recitation, I feel it is a case of: game, set and match!

With my lecture, 'The English Heralds in the 1990's: their Constitution and Function' delivered at the Jagellonian, Hilda and I returned by air to England.

Also in 1993 I served as Master of the Worshipful Company of Gunmakers of the City of London. Founded in 1637 – to *prove* not make guns, despite its title – the company, to this day, continues to carry out its original purpose; unlike many of the other Livery Companies of London whose *raisons d'être* have passed them by.

Although, originally, we proved all manner of guns, civil as well as military, with the increasing size of most of the latter we have, for many years, concentrated mainly on testing sporting guns. For this we maintain what is considered to be the leading ballistics laboratory in Europe.

When founded in the reign of Charles I, we were told that, as we were going to make an unconscionable racket, we must locate ourselves in the country. This we did and have stayed, ever since, on the same site. We now find ourselves in the East End on Commercial Road, surrounded by friendly Asiatic neighbours doing well in the 'Rag Trade'!

As a graduate Instructor of the Indian Army School of Small Arms at Sangor – as will be recalled from chapter V, the work of our company has always interested me intensely.

However, I think it time to say that my greatest contribution to the welfare of the Gunmakers Company was to obtain, for it, the legitimization of its Coat of Arms, previously used for some 300 years – doubtless with intense loyalty to the Crown – but illegitimately!

The case was further complicated by the fact that the Arms included insignia which require the personal sanction of the Sovereign, sparingly given, at the best of times, and only *one* to be asked for, whereas the Gunmakers had presumed to use two, that is to say, Royal Crowns (*oh la, la, comme on dit en Français!*)

In the end, a member of the Court of Assistants – the governing body – decided something must be done to save the Gunmakers from this embarrassing solecism, that is to say, Andrew, Count McMillan and Baron of Cleghorn. Accordingly, with the agreement of the Court he, personally, retained me professionally to see what might be done.

Pulling my heraldic cap down well over my ears, I beavered away, and – to cut a long story short – was, in the end, successful in obtaining from Her Majesty permission that the Arms of the same design henceforth be borne and used with all due authority. As a result, Letters Patent to that end were issued; the document beautifully illuminated – all made possible by the generosity of the one who had initiated the whole process by retaining me on the case in the first place. The effort required to achieve the end result was testing in the extreme, but it was completely worth it on behalf of such an honest and worthwhile Livery Company.

I thoroughly enjoyed my time as Master, and at all its social functions during my year of Office was, as always, most ably supported by the 'Master's Lady' who, obviously, enjoyed this expedition into a totally different world for her.

★   ★   ★

Later in '94 I received a request as to whether or not I would give the banner of the late Lord Shackleton, as a Knight of the Garter, to Christ Church Cathedral in the Falkland Islands. This followed from the fact that all such banners and crests, upon the death of a knight, are the perquisite of Garter. Usually, they find a place in some nook at the College of Arms, but it is entirely up to Garter to dispose of them as he sees fit. Naturally, I acceded immediately, as Shackleton was regarded as a 'champion of the Falkland Islands'[38].

The last year of my Gartership had started well, and continued much along such lines up to my retirement in the autumn. In fact, it might be described as a year of honours.

It will be recalled that King Harald of Norway had made me a Commander of the Royal Norwegian Order of Merit with Star. Accordingly, on 21 September of this year, the Norwegian Ambassador received me at the Residence on Kensington Palace Gardens – that hive of diplomatic Residences – and invested me with the appropriate insignia. He kindly invited Hilda and members of the family to be present, and held a reception afterwards during which His Excellency mentioned to me that it was a particular distinction for a Commander of the Order to be accorded a Star as well, which, naturally, added to the honour.

Then I had to go to Warsaw to receive further awards for which Hilda, Andrew and his wife, Fenella, Elizabeth, Juliana, and my brother, Peter, accompanied me.

First, we went to Lithuania on 23 September. It was the first time for all, other than Hilda and myself. We stayed in Vilnius at the *Mabre* – formerly a monastery and recently converted to be an hotel of the highest standard; the old *Astorija* of Hilda's and my first visit was being degutted and completely renovated at the time. In the capital, Hilda and I showed the family much that they should see, including the Gate of Dawn[39]: the chapel over the gateway in the fortifications of the city which houses the much venerated White Madonna painting.

Peter said Mass near the *Mabre* at St Anne's: that peak of Gothic architecture in Lithuania, built of lace-like brick. Napoleon, en route for Moscow, was so enchanted by it that he wanted to take it to Paris.

---

[38] See, for example, in the Bidding prayer in the printed ceremonial of the Service of Thanksgiving for the life and work of Lord Shackleton, 24 Feb. 1995 at Christ Church Cathedral, Falkland Islands.
[39] *Aušros Vartai* (Lithuanian) *Ostra Brama* (Polish). Built in 1671 by the Carmelites.

Naturally, we visited *Pasuvys*, called on Fr RR, and took presents to the orphans in Krakes.

We then flew down to Warsaw where, in the Royal Castle, on 28th of that month, I delivered, at the invitation of the Polish Heraldry Society[40], a paper entitled, 'English Heraldic Art in the 20th Century – some Thoughts by Garter.' At the end of which I was accorded the position of (literally) Honorary Member, which would be translated into English as Honorary Fellow of the Society.

With those proceedings completed, an emissary arrived at the Castle from the President of Poland, H.E. Lech Wałęsa, in order to invest me with the Cross of a Knight Commander of the Order of Merit of the Republic of Poland – in respect of cultural and protocol services to Poland.

While I felt these honours were completely undeserved, they were not only for that reason but also coming from an ancestral land, all the more appreciated. In a sense, they constituted for me a 'double first': as the first Garter to have been so honoured; yet again, this was the first time a member of my family had delivered a public address in the Royal Castle for over 200 years.

From Warsaw we took the train to Krakow. Where we stayed at the *Polski* just inside the Florianska Gate[41]: as central and convenient as it is delightfully Polish. Who wants to stay at a Hilton-like hotel when abroad?

Hilda and I guided the family to many of the sights. And so back to Warsaw and Heathrow after a memorable few days in the expanses of the former Most Serene Commonwealth of our ancestors. This got me back to England on 30 September, which allowed me to supervise the packing up of my 33 years' accumulation of office-gods at the College of Arms, ready for my retirement. On 2 October I left that ancient pile – never to return except when invited for a glass of sherry: there is nothing worse than the old colonel turning up, uninvited, on the parade ground when the new one is drilling the troops! Mary Tudor may have had Philip and Calais engraved on her heart; I had two 'dowagers', who stuck around like limpets, seared into my consciousness!

IV Dec[bris] MCMXCV: Dies irae, dies illa[42]

Two months had passed since my retirement. It was a wonderful time. Much got done at Boxford, long since promised 'when I don't have to go up to London'. Time was also devoted to sorting out the endless boxes used to bring down to Boxford my jackdaw accumulation of three decades at the College of Arms. This included my professional genealogical and heraldic library of over 1,000 titles, all

---

[40] *Polskie Towarzystwe Heraldyczne.*

[41] St Florian is the patron saint of those troubled by fire. When most houses in Poland were thatched he must obviously have been kept extra busy!

[42] 'Day of wrath! O day of mourning' – the opening phrase of the Sequence of a Tridentine funeral Mass.

of which had to be found a place at Boxford, which already had an enormous library of a bookish and literary family.

Christmas was not far off, and preparations for its celebration were well under way.

Monday, 4 December arrived. I got up, an especially fortunate husband of a heavenly wife; I went to bed, an incredulous widower with a wife on her way to heaven. Hilda had been killed in the late afternoon by a hit-and-run driver as she returned home from the village where she had gone to do a kindness for someone. 5.45p.m. or thereabouts arrived. She had not yet returned. I thought I would go down the hill to Boxford and walk with her back home. As I left the property by the gate nearest the village, police cars stood about with lights flashing. A local doctor broke off from the group standing by and approaching me said, 'Sir Conrad, I have very bad news for you. Lady Hilda has been killed.' My eyes followed his index finger.

There she was, for all to see, lying on the grass verge by the roadside: my wife; the object of my passionate devotion; the mother of our children; the one admired throughout the county for her many good works; and until a few moments ago, a living monument to so much English history.

Nearby, a papier-mâché box of six eggs rested on the grass, unbroken. Their fragility had been spared; Hilda's had not. For what seemed an eternity – but in fact only a minute or two – I stood there stunned; numb, yet feeling as if I had received a massive blow just beneath my belt. I wanted to stamp on those damned eggs. I refrained, not only knowing Hilda would never had approved of such a waste, but also not wishing to embarrass the general public standing near me: members of the Suffolk Police[43], the doctor and some villagers, by showing such emotion – one doesn't. The stiff upper lip learned at Honour's school in Duncan served well that day, as on a number of other occasions in my life.

Fr Michael Edwards, a local Parish Priest, was sent for so that he could come, anoint Hilda's body and say the appropriate prayers under such circumstances. He soon arrived from Sudbury where he lived. Both of us then knelt on the grass, and with me holding the printed *rituale* and a torch, Fr Edwards proceeded to carry out his sacred offices. The Police stood at a respectful distance, silent. When the parish priest and I stood up, they then carried on with their necessary procedures, which included arranging for Hilda's body to be taken to the undertakers.

By this time, it was obvious that even the Police were much affected by Hilda's death. She was well known to them by her work throughout the county. They reacted as if one of their own families had been struck down. All this was in marked contrast to the attitude of the driver who had killed Hilda. When he

---

[43] The police in England are not general for the whole country, but based on the county, city, borough and so on.

was finally caught, he attempted to sue me for the damage caused to his Porsche 924 by Hilda's body upon impact. I shall simply comment to the extent of saying that his impertinence did not succeed – nothing more.

When I went to bed that night, I wanted to cry, but couldn't. The whole situation seemed an unreal nightmare. How could it be so? But I knew perfectly well that it was. I sank to my knees on 'my' side of the bed and recited for the first, but by no means the last, time the *De profundis*[44] for the repose of her soul.

Never again would Hilda and I settle down for the night with arms entwined, conforming our bodies, the one to the other's as do two old pudding spoons, on their sides in a canteen of cutlery. The bed was the same late Georgian four-poster – the throne of such love, and the bed of much repose for decades – it would never be quite the same in future.

The national papers picked up her death within two days[45].

Messages of sympathy soon poured in, numbering over 1,000,[46] headed by a personal letter from Her Majesty herself who was 'aghast'[47].

Obituaries then made their appearance, in the local *East Anglian Daily Times*[48], and *The Suffolk Free Press*[49], those in the national papers included one in *The Daily Telegraph*[50] and that in *The Times*[51].

In the meantime the obsequies had to be arranged. No local Catholic church was large enough to accommodate the likely number of mourners. As a result, it is consoling to record that the two local bishops – Anglican and Catholic – as well as the other relevant authorities[52] gave their willing permission that we might have the requiem in the local Boxford Anglican Parish Church of St Mary the Virgin[53], conveniently situated at the foot of the hill down from Boxford House – *Floreat res oecumenica*!

The funeral took place on Saturday, 16 December. Additional chairs had been imported but, nevertheless, on the day it was standing room only in the church.

The concelebrating clergy for the Holy Sacrifice of the Mass were: as the principal celebrant, an old family friend, the recently retired Bishop of East

---

[44] The customary Catholic prayer for the repose of someone's soul: Psalm CXXIX, *De profundis clamo ad te, Domine…* Out of the depths I cry to thee, O Lord…

[45] For example, *The Times* and *Daily Mail* both of 6 Dec. 1995.

[46] SSA. New Series VIII: Death of Lady Hilda Swan.

[47] *Ibid.* From Buckingham Palace, 5 Dec. 1995.

[48] 6 Dec. 1995.

[49] 7 Dec. 1995.

[50] 6 Dec. 1995.

[51] 7 Dec. 1995.

[52] The Right Rev. John Dennis, (Anglican) Bishop of St Edmundsbury and Ipswich; the Right Rev. Peter Smith (Catholic) Bishop of East Anglia; the Rev. Canon Eric C. Hamlyn (Anglican) Priest in Charge of the church, and the St Mary's Parochial Church Council.

[53] The number of pre-Reformation churches in England, as is this one, dedicated to the Blessed Virgin is large: not unsuitable for a country known in Catholic days as 'The Dowry of Our Lady'.

Anglia[54] (and also representing the current bishop); Hilda's brother-in-law[55]; her Benedictine cousin[56]; the priest who gave her the last rites, on the roadside[57]; the new incumbent of the Catholic parish within which Boxford House is situated[58] – who was inducted on the day of the funeral; all assisted by a further priest from Sudbury[59]. One speaks of a flock of birds, a pride of lions, so might one speak of a competence of clergy, as in this case: a sextet.

In choir were the Lord Lieutenant of Suffolk[60] – representing HM The Queen – the Anglican Priest-in-Charge of the Boxford Parish[61]and another friend of long standing who had preached at our wedding, the Right Reverend Monsignor A.N. Gilbey[62].

A Suffolk St John Ambulance guard of honour was drawn up at the entrance to the church for the arrival of the coffin. This was draped with a banner of the matrimonial achievement of Hilda's arms: Swan and Northcote marshalled together. The Pall Bearers were her four sons-in-law[63]; grandchildren followed carrying her armorial escutcheon[64] as well as her chivalric insignia[65]; the immediate family wreath[66]and her brothers' and sister's wreath[67].

The choir and organist were of St Edmund's Catholic Church, Bury St Edmunds.

The requiem Mass then followed, during which the Earl Marshal of England, His Grace the Duke of Norfolk, read the first lesson, and Hilda's brother, Iddesleigh, the second; the choir singing their customary parts.

My brother gave the homily. He spoke of the significance in the Divine Economy of the Crucifixion and Resurrection in relation to all those who, through baptism, make up Christ's mystical body, and their ultimate destiny: union with Him in heaven.

The Mass being concluded – and upon one of the clergy proclaiming, 'In

[54] The Right Rev. Alan C. Clark, D.D.

[55] The Rev. P.J.M. Swan, CSB, PhD, President and Vice-Chancellor Emeritus of the University of St Michael's College, Toronto.

[56] Dom Philip Jebb, OSB, Prior of Downside Abbey.

[57] The Rev. Michael Edwards, Parish Priest of Sudbury, Suffolk.

[58] The Rev. Russell Frost, MA(Oxon), STh(Lambeth), Parish Priest of Hadleigh, Nayland and Withermarsh Green, Suffolk.

[59] The Rev. Paul Lewin.

[60] The Right Honble the Lord Belstead, P.C.

[61] The Rev. Eric Hamlyn, BA, Dip.Th.

[62] Protonotary Aposlotic to H.H. the Pope, Grand Cross Conventual Chaplain of the SMO of Malta, and chaplain to the Catholic students of Cambridge University when I was up.

[63] P.D.T. Galvin, Baron Peter Hatvany, R.J. le S. Herring and J.J. Walters.

[64] Edward Galvin, John Herring and Hugh Walters.

[65] Dame of Honour and Devotion, SMO of Malta; Dame of Justice, SMO Constantine St George and Serving Sister, Most Venerable Order of St John, carried by Thomas Galvin.

[66] Elizabeth Galvin.

[67] Nicholas Galvin.

peace let us take Hilda to her place of rest' – the coffin was borne out, followed by the clergy and congregation to the strains of the 'Grand Chorus' from *Aida*, as for the exit procession at Hilda's and my wedding.

The drive of about six miles followed to the churchyard at Withermarsh Green where, as the coffin was carried towards the grave, the Sisters of the Assumption[68] sang the hauntingly beautiful, 'May the choirs of angels come to greet you. May they speed you to paradise…'[69]

With the committal prayers concluded, the Polish – and so family – tradition of the breaking of Hilda's escutcheon took place. As the pieces were cast into the grave, the voices of the three young grandsons[70] performing this office pierced the bright and crisp winter air with, *sic transit gloria mundi*!

All having been invited to sprinkle the grave with holy water, they were then welcomed back at Boxford House for a substantial buffet lunch and copious spirituous refreshment – much needed.

In the meantime the Suffolk Police hunted the driver of the Porsche[71], and in just over a month of Hilda's death, a 27 year-old man, Martin Milne, was arrested and charged in court[72].

Finally, on 20 August '96, Milne was tried at the Crown Court in Ipswich, found guilty and sentenced to 9 months in gaol. It is not for me to say what I thought of such a sentence, but I may observe that the police were not pleased after all their hard work on the case.

One inevitably wonders, Why this death? As if we are the best judges in such matters. But then, Providence obviously chooses the best moment for our entry into life in order to fulfil a role unique to each, and of which the *terminus ad quem* is heaven. We used to learn these basic facts at an early age from the Penny Catechism[73]:

Question 1: Who made you?

Answer: God made me.

Question 2: Why did God make you?

Answer: God made me to know him, love him and serve him in this world, and be happy with him for ever in the next.

And so I would venture the opinion that Providence must know the best time for us to die with such a *terminus ad quem*: life in heaven.

The realization of this does not make the ache any less – especially at the

---

[68] From Hengrave Hall, Bury St Edmunds, Suffolk.

[69] By Ernest Sands. Hilda had attended schools run by this order, and to which her sister, Catherine (Sr. John Mary) belongs.

[70] John Herring and Hugh Walters, assisted by Edward Galvin.

[71] *East Anglian Daily Times*, 6 Dec. 1995; *Suffolk Free Press*, 21 Dec. 1995.

[72] *East Anglian Daily Times,* 12 Jan. 1996.

[73] The name given in English-speaking countries to the simple exposition of the Catholic Faith that was widely used, possibly for upwards of 100 years prior to the Second Vatican Council. It was first published, 1889.

outset, but it does provide a logical basis for reflection, starting with the necessary concomitant of our human condition that 'all good things must end'[74]. When facing up to this, the living monuments to that love we shared: children, can be, as ours are, towers of strength.

After the first terrible shock, while always missing one's wife, I remember more and more all the wonderful times enjoyed together; the shared interests; the bringing up of the children, and her devotion and selflessness towards them – and me; the admiration of her character; her humour; her delightful mannerisms; the smell of the scent she used, and so on.

I feel enormously privileged, and thankful to God, that I had not just one day of such experiences, but in fact years and years. That is not to say I do not find a tear welling up after many years when reminded of a shared delight or sorrow, I then blow my nose with vigour. I think one of my grandchildren summed it all up when he said, 'Why did Granny have to die? She was one of my favourite people.'[75]

---

[74] Psalm CXVIII. 96.

[75] The inscription on her tomb reads: Pray for the soul of The Lady Hilda Susan Mary Swan (nee Northcote) Dame of Honour and Devotion SMO of Malta, *dau.* of Henry Stafford, Earl of Iddesleigh. *b.* 23 July 1937. *k.* 4 December 1995 wife of Sir Conrad Marshall John Fisher Swan, KCVO, PhD, FSA, sometime Garter Principal King of Arms, son of Henry Peter Swan, MD, CM. *b.* 13 May 1924

RIP

MAGNOPERE AMAVERUNT DEUM, LIBEROS SUOS ET PROGENIEM LIBERORUM SUORUM QUI HUNC AMOREM CENTIPLICATUM REDDIDERUNT

(They greatly loved God, their children and the progeny of their children who gave back this love a hundredfold)

CHAPTER XII

Post Requiem – Dimidia Lux
or Light Emerging at the End of the Tunnel

As IN THE LUBYANKA, that infamous prison – the room, in which I sat, was badly lit, the windows were high up near the ceiling, and the doors strong, lest one had ideas of avoiding that cattle truck heading for Siberia. I waited, I thought. Of course, I knew that I was not in Moscow, but rather in London, SW1. Nevertheless, the room had that icon-stripped, God-forsaken look and atmosphere of such a soulless place.

This reverie was suddenly interrupted when the door – it didn't clang open, but there was a definite degree of suction when it swung on its hinges to let a grim-faced *fonctionnaire* through.

He handed me my visa to visit the domain of Slobodan Milosevic[1]. Evidently Belgrade had, at last, said Yes. The London Embassy of the Yugoslav-Federation was allowed no discretion in such matters.

No matter, like a shot out of a rifle I was off to Heathrow and, after interminable delays by Yugoslav Airlines, arrived on 18 May 1996 at the residence of the British Embassy, Belgrade at midnight, three and a half hours late. Notwithstanding, the Ambassador, HE Ivor Roberts, CMG[2] had stayed up to greet me. Such consideration set the tone of my visit to my client who had, most thoughtfully, invited me to visit his bailiwick as a distraction after Hilda's death.

While there, on behalf of the British Council I gave lectures on 'The Heraldry of Independence' and 'The Anatomy of Nobility' in Serbia and Montenegro, respectively.

Then the current problems of the Serbs expelled from Croatia and Bosnia – Hercegovina were all too obvious – even the gardener at the residence was a PhD (and not in horticulture) from Zagreb. Montenegro was like the Highlands of Scotland, but more so. No wonder they were never conquered by the Turks. Throughout my entire time travelling around this extraordinary area I had as my most efficient British Council aide one, Milan Aleksic who had learned his English – and very well, if I may say so – in Winnipeg and Halifax. Mrs Roberts,

---

[1] At the time of writing this chapter he now adopts a belligerent attitude towards the court in The Hague where his is being tried for crimes against humanity.

[2] Now HE Sir Ivor Roberts, KCMG, HBM Ambassador to Ireland.

my charming hostess, made sure that I had a squash ball (as a bath and hand-basin plug) and some towels when staying at the Sovietized hotels.

★   ★   ★

Upon my retirement as Garter, following the tradition of my immediate predecessors, I continued with my work as Knight Principal of the Imperial Society of Knights Bachelor[3].

Since the Middle Ages the dignity of Knight Bachelor has existed. It is the oldest form of knighthood we have.

However, such knights are not members of an Order of Chivalry and so, until the early part of the last century, lacked the cohesive, corporate existence, with a body to speak for them – with all the advantages which flow there from – which for Orders are provided by their Statutes. Accordingly, as the result of certain difficulties which arose from this situation at the turn of the century[4] one of their fellow knights, Sir William Bull, MP, called a meeting of Knights Bachelor in the House of Commons to discuss the problem. The result was the founding of the Society of Knights Bachelor (27 April 1908). Four years later, King George V accorded, by Royal Warrant, the Society the privilege of adding to it name the designation of 'Imperial'.

Before the creation of no less than seven Orders of Chivalry with knighthoods, in just under two centuries following the foundation of the Order of the Bath (1725)[5] – except for the Garter, Thistle, St Patrick and on rare occasions those designated Knights of the Bath (who were, basically, Knights Bachelor) – this knighthood was the only one available for general bestowal, so to speak.

As a result, throughout the history of this knighthood, one notes its many members who have made singular contributions to society. In addition to the many High Court Judges who – year in, year out – guard and interpret the law, a selection of personal interest to me would include, starting with the arts, Sir Henry van Dyke, Sir Joshua Reynolds, Sir Edward Elgar, Sir Ernest McMillan, and not forgetting – for his recent foundation of the Liverpool Institute of Performing Arts – Sir Paul McCartney; for the sciences and medicine, Sir Issac

---

[3] The author was Knight Principal, 1995-2000.

[4] In particular the case fought with the Walker Trustees in Edinburgh who, as holders of the ancient office of Usher of the White Rod (under the Walker Trust Act, 1877), claimed certain dues from persons receiving honours of the Crown. To this many knights objected.

[5] St Patrick (1783), St Michael and St George (1818), The Star of India (1861), The Indian Empire (1886), The Royal Victorian Order (1896) and The British Empire (1917). The Order of Hanover (1815) had knighthoods but such did not confer the title of, Sir. Though technically for Hanoverian Subjects it was given widely to British Subjects. So that the latter might have the title of Sir they had to be made Knights Bachelor. With the accession of Queen Victoria this Order was no longer bestowed on British Subjects. The Most Venerable Order of the Hospital of St John of Jerusalem (1888) has knighthoods but, as with the Order just mentioned they do not confer the title of Sir.

Newton and Sir Frederick Banting; for letters Sir Arthur Conan Doyle and Sir Charles Roberts; and for sport, Sir Roger Banister and Sir Henry Cooper.

And how many such groups of the great and the good can boast a canonized saint among their number, as can the Knights Bachelor with Sir Thomas More, Lord Chancellor of Henry VIII? In a typically English way, looking death in the face, and having asked to be helped up onto the scaffold, he remarked to his executioners, 'As for my coming down I'll shift for myself'(!)[6]

Although a number of Garters, not Knights Bachelor, have served as Knight Principal of the Society, the office has never been 'tied' to the Gartership. I was the third such in succession and I have reason to believe, in all humility, that we had served the Society well.

Nevertheless, when I mentioned to my fellow-members of the Council of the Society that, at such time as would be to their convenience, I would like to be allowed to retire, a move developed that the principal office of the Society should, once again, be filled by one qualified to be a member of the Society as a Knight Bachelor. To me this appeared to be completely logical and, indeed, desirable.

I did not take this desire as a reaction against the way I had performed my duties. Indeed, upon my retirement (2000) the Society presented me with a handsome crystal decanter engraved in the warmest terms of appreciation concerning my efforts on its behalf when Knight Principal. It had not only been an honour, but a real pleasure to serve such an admirable body of men.

★   ★   ★

ኢትዮጵያ እጆቿን ወደ እግዚአብሔር ታነሳለች

'Ethiopia Shall Reach Her Hand / Unto God...'[7]

'Of course, you do appreciate that you are eight years younger than you think', quipped His Grace, as I called on him in early November, 2000[8]. 'We haven't got to the Millennium yet as we're on the Julian Calendar, and for us it's the year 1992.' Thus spoke the Archbishop of Addis Ababa, Abune Berhaneyses Souraphiel, of the Ethiopic (Coptic) Rite in union with Rome, and Metropolitan of Ethiopia. As a Latin Rite Catholic I came under him – just as the Ukranian Rite Catholics in England come under the Latin Rite Archbishop of Westminster: a patent demonstration of the catholicity of the Catholic Church in each case.

I was in Addis – everyone usually refers to Addis Ababa in this way, rather

---

[6] Beheaded 6 July 1535, Tower Hill, aged 57. Canonized 1935.

[7] Psalm 67/68.32. A Song of David.

[8] 3 November 2000. This section of my autobiography is based upon my recollection, backed up by a detailed diary I kept while proceeding to, in and returning from Ethiopia, 30th October – 8th November, 2000. All quotations, unless otherwise specified, are from that manuscript, called here the *Ethiopian Diary* which is preserved in SSA.

than using its full name – for the formal and Christian burial of the late Emperor Haile Selassie I, KG[9]. After having been tortured and murdered by the *Degue* (literally 'Committee', in this instance, the Communist government) in August '75[10], he was buried under the lavatory in the bathroom of the then President, Mengistu Halemariam. This ruffian was the leader in the Red Terror and Cambodian-style mass murders which lasted for 17 years until the *Degue* was toppled in 1991 by the slightly rosier-red Tigré People's Liberation Front – which was part of the regime in power at the time of the Emperor's funeral in November, 2000.

In the year following the fall of the *Degue*, the Emperor's remains were sought out and exhumed[11] and for the next eight years kept temporarily in the church of the Baata Mariam Monastery in Addis. During this period, the new regime had to be persuaded to allow a formal funeral of the Emperor and his burial in the tomb, prepared for him during his reign, in the Cathedral of the Most Holy Trinity.

Naturally, the Imperial Family and all those associated with them, in any way, worked hard to this end. As the Heraldic Adviser to the Crown Council of Ethiopia; Grand Cross with Collar of the Order of the Most Holy Trinity (founded by the Emperor), and for several years responsible for his monument (his Stallplate) in St George's Chapel, Windsor Castle, as the only Knight of the Garter from Africa, in my capacity as Garter Principal King of Arms, I was, naturally, much concerned that suitable Christian burial of Haile Selassie be achieved. One of my early duties, as York Herald of Arms, was to attend upon the Emperor when he was Installed as a Knight of the Garter in St George's Chapel, Windsor Castle (19 June 1972).

The obsequies for Haile Selassie were spread out between Thursday 2nd and Sunday 5th November with a series of requiems in various churches and then the final entombment.

The lecture[12] I gave to the British Council and the English Department of the University of Addis Ababa[13] was a general introduction to heraldry, using for this purpose many examples from the heraldry of Shakespeare's historical plays so as to broaden the approach.

Naturally, I wanted to do some shopping – presents to take home to the

---

[9] Haile Selassie means 'the Power of the Holy Spirit'; born 23 July 1892, of the Solomonic line (his father was cousin to the Emperor Menelik who defeated the Italians at the battle of Adwa, 1896); declared Supreme Regent and Heir Apparent to the Empress Zauditu (at which he became *de facto* ruler of the country); crowned and anointed Emperor 2 Nov. 1930; Knight of the Garter, 14 Oct. 1954; seized and deposed by the *Degue*, 12 Sept. 1974; murdered Aug. 1975.

[10] The exact day is not known.

[11] 17 Feb. 1992.

[12] 2 November, 2000.

[13] Founded by the Emperor with the help of the Jesuits whom he invited to Ethiopia for this purpose.

family, and our local bishop and parish priest such an exotic gift as incense (produced in Ethiopia) and available in the Merkato Market (largest market in Africa).

Sunday, 5 November, the day of the final interment arrived. Up early and off with Mrs Frances Guy, the Chargé d'Affaires, to be at the parade ground on Addis's equivalent of Moscow's Red Square, more democratically renamed Meskel Square, by 8a.m. for the civic and civilian farewell. Back to her house for lunch

Then off again at 2p.m. for the cathedral. Thousands of people in the streets – some, of course, simply curious, but many obviously touched by the occasion.

Having arrived at the cathedral, the Chargé d'Affaires and I were whisked through the crowds to our seats on the stone platform at the top of the steep steps leading up to the church.

In addition to the Diplomatic Corps, a large number of representatives of different religious groups were present: Greek Orthodox, Catholic (Latin as well as Coptic rite, including the Metropolitan I had called on earlier) Protestants and Muslims.

Then the Coptic Patriarch arrived,

Abuna Paulo, resplendent in gold crown and vestments ... accompanied by a mass of Bishops of the Coptic Church, each garbed in marvellous vestments and with a variety of head-gear, mostly turban-like in various colours. Many were accompanied by an elaborate umbrella of velvet, heavily embroidered with representations of Our Lady and the Christ child and other religious symbols... each strand of the gold fringe of the umbrella was frequently tipped with a gold sequin. (Two of these magnificent objects – so useful in the sun here! – got entangled with their fringes and had to be sorted out!)

The coffin was placed on a catafalque in the centre of the square in front of the cathedral and the main part of the service conducted there – rather like a papal 'coronation' nowadays – so that the maximum can take part.

Much chanting interspersed with homilies by officials present and Abuna. When they said something of which the assembled approved, they clapped.

The grand scene in front of the cathedral, in the brilliant sunshine... was picturesque and exotic in the extreme. It was one of those days – rare in one's life – that one will always remember.

When the outside proceedings were concluded, the officiating clergy, Diplomatic Corps and I moved into the church. I had a few words with Abuna Paulo en route.

Inside, cables trailed, cameras flashed and – horror of horrors – the pulpit was crammed with television crews. As I made my way up towards the sanctuary, I met my friend, W.F. Deedes[14]. He was reporting the event for *The Daily Telegraph* – 70 years back, along with Evelyn Waugh, he had attended the Emperor's coronation. Viewing this unseemly scramble, he remarked to me, 'To deliver the sacred to the masses involves an unholy mess'[15].

We all then gathered in the area just outside the Holy of Holies. The coffin was carried in by members of the family, and one or two further speeches were made, in which I noted deliberate compliments to the British for their assistance to the late Emperor.

After that, the coffin was taken into a side chapel. The tomb had been prepared in happier days, but proved a tight fit for the coffin which was eventually got into position, but only just. The imperial remains were laid to rest, joining, among others in this church, those of Sylvia Pankhurst, the famous suffragette (!).[16]

> For the Earl Marshal and College of Arms…[the previous four days of obsequies]… would have been a nightmare. Not until almost the last minute did one know the place, date and time of each event. (Probably, this had been aggravated by the attitude of the present government only co-operating in so far as not actually opposing the occasion). Yet again, there were, obviously, no prior rehearsals. Upon each occasion, people would be moving all over the place; chairs would suddenly be provided, or moved from points A to B, held high over people's heads; groups of official guests would be moved from one set of chairs to another.
>
> Nevertheless, in the end the *terminus ad quem* of each exercise was achieved by some curious process which was not obvious…
>
> In a sense it could have been out of 'The Arabian Nights' but was not, as it was the actual laying to rest, with Christian rites, of a good man who tried to do his duty by his country.

He was not perfect, but who is? Notwithstanding, in respect of Ethopia he had abolished slavery, provided a constitution, a parliament, a codified legal system, a national bank, a university and so on. He had dragged Ethiopia – a mass of tribes, languages and religions – kicking and screaming into the 20th century – no mean achievements.

By Wednesday 8 November I was back in England but not without a marvellous visit to Lalibila and its 12 churches carved vertically out of the rock.

'These churches of Lalibila are monuments to a high state of civilization, and

---

[14] *Nom de plume* journalistic of The Rt Honble the Lord Deedes, MC, PC.

[15] W.F. Deedes. 'Amid a TV scrum, Haile Selassie is borne to his tomb' *The Daily Telegraph*, 6 Nov. 2000.

[16] Daughter of Emeline. She died 17 Sept. 1960 and is buried in that part of the cathedral reserved for Ethiopian Patriots of the Struggle of 1935-41 against the Italians. The Emperor attended her funeral.

coupled with their dramatic setting are, I feel, to be counted among the wonders of the world.', I wrote in my *Ethiopian Diary*.

★   ★   ★

An early African connection of mine was between 1992 and '95, when I designed the Great Seal of Namibia,[17] arranged a complete Honours system of several Orders, and drafted the parliamentary Bill of that Commonwealth state which brought them into being. All of this was done from my desk at the College of Arms. I would, naturally, have enjoyed a visit to Namibia, but that proved impossible because of other duties. It was one of those relatively short official tasks.

On the other hand, it is with their distant, transatlantic part-cousins of Antigua & Barbuda in the West Indies that I have had the longest association.

This started back in 1981, when it became a sovereign, independent, monarchial state within the Commonwealth. On that occasion I designed the official flag of The Queen's representative there, the Governor-General.

Later in the nineties, when a complete Honours system was required, I was appointed the constitutional adviser on Orders and Decorations to the Governor General, His Excellency Sir James Carlisle, GCMG.

The final result of a long and complicated period of advising on these matters was the creation, by the National Honours Act, 1998 being No. 23 of 1998 of the Parliament of Antigua & Barbuda, of the following four Orders:

1) The Most Exulted Order of National Hero
   One grade of Knights (KNH)   carrying the title
   Dames (DNH)   of Sir/Dame

2) The Most Distinguished Order of the Nation
   Knights/Dames Grand Collar (KGN/DGN)   carrying the title
   Knights/Dames Grand Cross (KGCN/DGCN)   of Sir/Dame
   Knights/Dames Commander (KCN/DCN)

3) The Most Illustrious Order of Merit
   Grand Cross (GCM)
   Grand Officer (GOM)
   Commander (CM)
   Officer (OM)
   Member (MM)

4) The Most Precious Order of Princely Heritage
   with 5 grades as for the preceding. (GCH; GOH; CH; OH; MH)

---

[17] Formerly a German protectorate, 1880-1915, then South West Africa administered by South Africa. Independent 1989.

The Governor-General is the Grand Master of each Order. There is an Honours Committee which considers proposed candidates. Each Order has a Chancellor and a Secretary-General[18] and there is a Chancery of the Orders situated in Government House.

At the same time as the Orders, just described, were brought into being, so were two offices of arms[19].

For such, there were precursive precedents already in the Caribbean of some two hundred years standing. These were to be found in the reign of the 'Black Napoleon'. Henry Christophe, King of Haiti (or Hayti as it was spelt then) 1811-1820.

Britain recognized this monarch and at his coronation on 2 June 1811 was represented by HMS *Reindeer*[20], under the command of Captain John Douglas, RN, who moored his ship in Capte Francis for the week of this very special event[21].

From all accounts, the King had a great respect for British ways and, as a result, moulded many of his arrangements accordingly. This even went to the extent of – despite being the ruler of a French-speaking nation and, similarly, of that language himself – his name on official documents and in his Royal Sign Manual was always spelt in the English manner: Henry, rather than the French: *Henri*.

Yet again, the most senior officer of arms among the total of fourteen[22] which he had as members of the Royal Household was designated, following the English manner; *roi d'armes*[23] rather then the French *Juge d'armes*.

Was the total of 14 heralds a case of royal 'one-upmanship' over the English 13? If so, *Oh la la. Quel méchant roi!* What is more likely is that he had been told there was a certain number at the College of Arms to which he simply added one more to keep them in order rather than with any thought of *lèse majesté* towards his brother monarch, George III – to whom King Henry referred specifically as such at his coronation[24].

Be that as it may, similar to the English heraldic titles those for Haiti had an

[18] Established, pursuant to the National Honours Act 1998, No 23 of 1998 of the Parliament of Barbuda & Antigua, by Statutory Instruments, 1999, Nos. 48, 49, 50 & 51

[19] *Ibid*.

[20] I am indebted to the Foreign Office Library for confirming this representation.

[21] 30 May to 5 June, 1811 – Public Record Office: ADM51/2775 (the ship's log).

[22] Prevost, Julien, le comte de Limonade, *Relations des glorieux evenements qui ont porté Leurs Majestés Royales sur le Trône d'Hayti, Suivi de l'Histoire du couronnement et du Sacré du roi Henry 1, et de la reine Marie-Louise*. Au cap-Henry, chez P. Rouse, imprimeur du Roi, 1811. p.101.[Prevost was the Foreign Minister; a highly intelligent mulatto who, naturally, had a great deal to do with foreigners. The *nomen dignitatis* of his countship, Limonade, referred to a district of Haiti.]

[23] *Ibid*.

[24] The author is indebted to the Foreign Office Library for confirming this detail.

ultimately territorial basis such as: *Héraut du Port-au-Prince*; *de Sans Souci*; *des Cayes* and so on[25].

When titles for the two Antiguan officers of arms were decided upon, once again, the Haitian precedent was followed. Thus the offices of Antigua Herald and of Barbuda Herald were instituted: the first Afro-Caribbean Heraldships of the British Crown. It will be recalled that the only other non-White Herald to have existed was Assistant Delhi Herald at the Delhi Durbar of 1911[26]. However, whereas his commission lasted for that one occasion, only, Antigua Herald and Barbuda Herald, on the contrary, are permanent officers of arms.

They are Heralds of the several Orders we have recently noted. In this regard, they are analogous to the Scottish officers of arms who are officials of the Order of the Thistle, as were the Irish ones of the Order of St Patrick; neither constituting a corporation as do the English officers of arms.

The first and present appointees of these offices are: Miss Julie Labadie, OM,[27] Antigua Herald, and Mr Atkinson Beazer, Barbuda Herald.

Is it not singular that the subject of Garter Bellew's 1934 *Illustrated London News* article – which fired my early heraldic interest (as referred to in chapter VIII) – should, almost three quarters of a century later, still concern me?

But enough of that for the moment. I must now get myself to Antigua to be made a Knight Grand Cross of the Most Distinguished Order of the Nation. Then upon my return, having just been appointed by HM King Abdullah II of Jordan as his Consultant on the Orders and Decorations of the Hashemite Kingdom, I must ready myself to cross the Jordan and make for Amman. Accordingly, bearing in mind the Caribbean climate – the investiture is to be out of doors – and the extremely dry heart of the Jordanian capital – where I shall be working – as EHS did in the garden at *Harrow Weald*, during that sultry evening some six decades ago, I, too, must consider in the very first words of this book, 'What shall I wear...?'

---

[25] Prevost, *loc. Cit.* where the complete list is given.
[26] See chapter X p 254 footnote 13.
[27] Order of Merit (Antigua & Barbuda) of a previous dispensation of honours of the country.

Descent from Saints and Sovereigns[1]

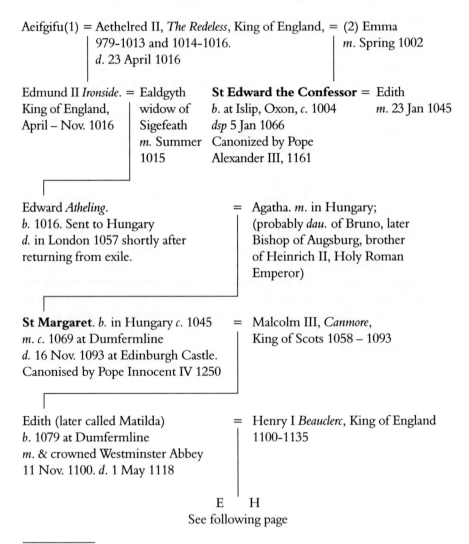

Aeifgifu(1) = Aethelred II, *The Redeless*, King of England, = (2) Emma
979-1013 and 1014-1016. *m.* Spring 1002
d. 23 April 1016

Edmund II *Ironside*. = Ealdgyth **St Edward the Confessor** = Edith
King of England, widow of *b.* at Islip, Oxon, *c.* 1004 *m.* 23 Jan 1045
April – Nov. 1016 Sigefeath *dsp* 5 Jan 1066
m. Summer Canonized by Pope
1015 Alexander III, 1161

Edward *Atheling*. = Agatha. *m.* in Hungary;
b. 1016. Sent to Hungary (probably *dau.* of Bruno, later
d. in London 1057 shortly after Bishop of Augsburg, brother
returning from exile. of Heinrich II, Holy Roman
Emperor)

St Margaret. *b.* in Hungary *c.* 1045 = Malcolm III, *Canmore*,
m. c. 1069 at Dumfermline King of Scots 1058 – 1093
d. 16 Nov. 1093 at Edinburgh Castle.
Canonised by Pope Innocent IV 1250

Edith (later called Matilda) = Henry I *Beauclerc*, King of England
b. 1079 at Dumfermline 1100-1135
m. & crowned Westminster Abbey
11 Nov. 1100. *d.* 1 May 1118

E H
See following page

---

[1] CAR: Arundel IV.3; G.E.C. *The Complete Peerage*, The St Catherine's Press, London, 1929 Vol VII pp. 42-43; 1936 Vol. IX pp 94-97 and 693; *Burke's Guide to the Royal Family*, Burke's Peerage Ltd; London, 1973 pp190-191, 193-200.

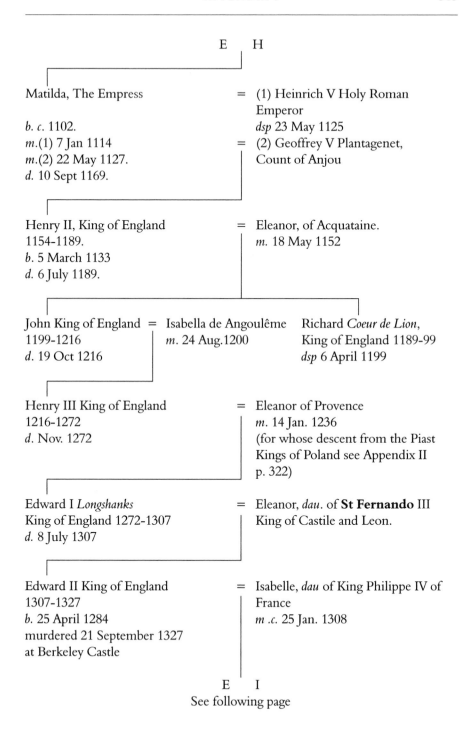

E   H

Matilda, The Empress   =   (1) Heinrich V Holy Roman
                                    Emperor
b. c. 1102.   *dsp* 23 May 1125
m.(1) 7 Jan 1114   =   (2) Geoffrey V Plantagenet,
m.(2) 22 May 1127.   Count of Anjou
d. 10 Sept 1169.

Henry II, King of England   =   Eleanor, of Acquataine.
1154-1189.   *m.* 18 May 1152
b. 5 March 1133
d. 6 July 1189.

John King of England = Isabella de Angoulême   Richard *Coeur de Lion*,
1199-1216   *m.* 24 Aug.1200   King of England 1189-99
d. 19 Oct 1216   *dsp* 6 April 1199

Henry III King of England   =   Eleanor of Provence
1216-1272   *m.* 14 Jan. 1236
d. Nov. 1272   (for whose descent from the Piast
                                    Kings of Poland see Appendix II
                                    p. 322)

Edward I *Longshanks*   =   Eleanor, *dau.* of **St Fernando** III
King of England 1272-1307   King of Castile and Leon.
d. 8 July 1307

Edward II King of England   =   Isabelle, *dau* of King Philippe IV of
1307-1327   France
b. 25 April 1284   *m .c.* 25 Jan. 1308
murdered 21 September 1327
at Berkeley Castle

E   I
See following page

E   I

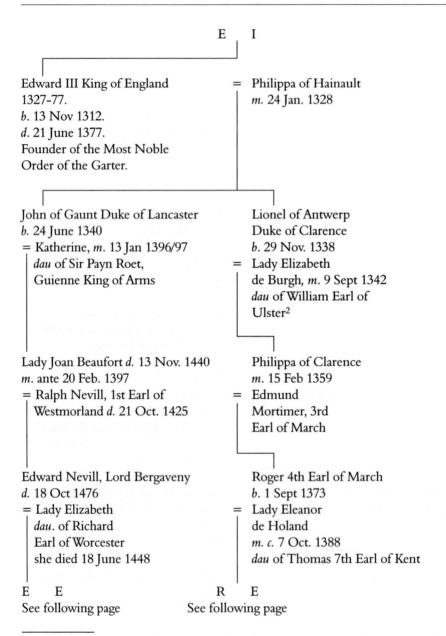

Edward III King of England
1327-77.
b. 13 Nov 1312.
d. 21 June 1377.
Founder of the Most Noble
Order of the Garter.

= Philippa of Hainault
m. 24 Jan. 1328

John of Gaunt Duke of Lancaster
b. 24 June 1340
= Katherine, *m.* 13 Jan 1396/97
   dau of Sir Payn Roet,
   Guienne King of Arms

Lionel of Antwerp
Duke of Clarence
b. 29 Nov. 1338
= Lady Elizabeth
   de Burgh, *m.* 9 Sept 1342
   dau of William Earl of
   Ulster[2]

Lady Joan Beaufort *d.* 13 Nov. 1440
m. ante 20 Feb. 1397
= Ralph Nevill, 1st Earl of
   Westmorland *d.* 21 Oct. 1425

Philippa of Clarence
m. 15 Feb 1359
= Edmund
   Mortimer, 3rd
   Earl of March

Edward Nevill, Lord Bergaveny
d. 18 Oct 1476
= Lady Elizabeth
   dau. of Richard
   Earl of Worcester
   she died 18 June 1448

Roger 4th Earl of March
b. 1 Sept 1373
= Lady Eleanor
   de Holand
   m. c. 7 Oct. 1388
   dau of Thomas 7th Earl of Kent

E   E   R   E
See following page   See following page

---

[2] From whom descends Roger Peter le Strange Herring husband of Mary Elizabeth Magdalen Swan, eldest *dau.* of the author by his wife Lady Hilda Northcote; and also St Philip Howard, *d.* in Tower of London, 1595, canonized 25 Oct. 1970 & St Philip's grandson, Blessed William Howard, Viscount Stafford, executed 29 Dec. 1680 – the last official execution in England for adhesion to Roman Catholicism. For details *vide* 'The Royal Descent of Herring' *The Northcote Millennium Commonplace Book*, Heraldic Enterprises, Boxford House, Suffolk, CO10 5JT. 2000 p. 158*ff*.

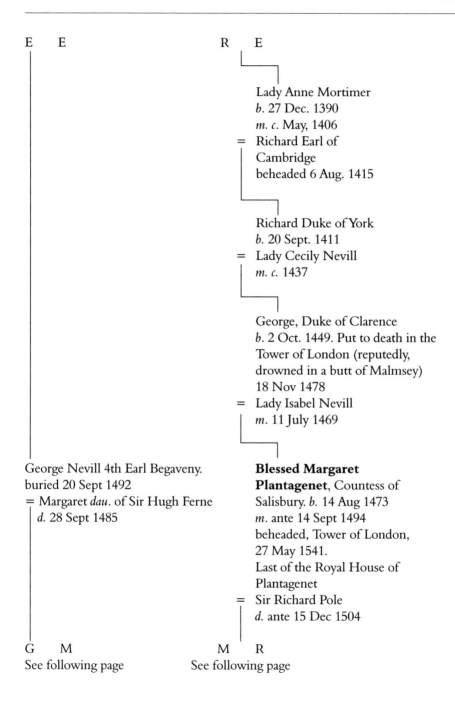

E   E   R   E

                                          Lady Anne Mortimer
                                          b. 27 Dec. 1390
                                          m. *c*. May, 1406
                                       = Richard Earl of
                                          Cambridge
                                          beheaded 6 Aug. 1415

                                          Richard Duke of York
                                          b. 20 Sept. 1411
                                       = Lady Cecily Nevill
                                          m. *c*. 1437

                                          George, Duke of Clarence
                                          b. 2 Oct. 1449. Put to death in the
                                          Tower of London (reputedly,
                                          drowned in a butt of Malmsey)
                                          18 Nov 1478
                                       = Lady Isabel Nevill
                                          m. 11 July 1469

George Nevill 4th Earl Begaveny.   **Blessed Margaret**
buried 20 Sept 1492   **Plantagenet**, Countess of
= Margaret *dau*. of Sir Hugh Ferne   Salisbury. *b*. 14 Aug 1473
   d. 28 Sept 1485   *m*. ante 14 Sept 1494
                                        beheaded, Tower of London,
                                        27 May 1541.
                                        Last of the Royal House of
                                        Plantagenet
                                     = Sir Richard Pole
                                        d. ante 15 Dec 1504

G   M   M   R
See following page   See following page

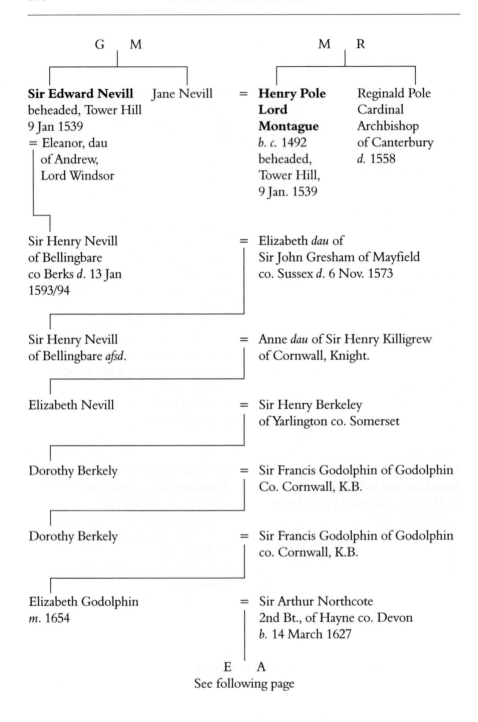

G   M   M   R

Sir Edward Nevill   Jane Nevill   =   **Henry Pole**   Reginald Pole
beheaded, Tower Hill   **Lord**   Cardinal
9 Jan 1539   **Montague**   Archbishop
= Eleanor, dau   *b. c.* 1492   of Canterbury
  of Andrew,   beheaded,   *d.* 1558
  Lord Windsor   Tower Hill,
                                          9 Jan. 1539

Sir Henry Nevill   =   Elizabeth *dau* of
of Bellingbare   Sir John Gresham of Mayfield
co Berks *d.* 13 Jan   co. Sussex *d.* 6 Nov. 1573
1593/94

Sir Henry Nevill   =   Anne *dau* of Sir Henry Killigrew
of Bellingbare *afsd.*   of Cornwall, Knight.

Elizabeth Nevill   =   Sir Henry Berkeley
                                          of Yarlington co. Somerset

Dorothy Berkely   =   Sir Francis Godolphin of Godolphin
                                          Co. Cornwall, K.B.

Dorothy Berkely   =   Sir Francis Godolphin of Godolphin
                                          co. Cornwall, K.B.

Elizabeth Godolphin   =   Sir Arthur Northcote
m. 1654   2nd Bt., of Hayne co. Devon
                                          b. 14 March 1627

E   A
See following page

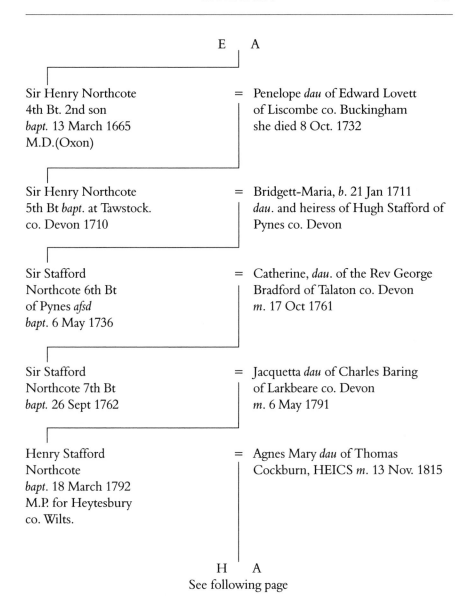

E   A

Sir Henry Northcote   =   Penelope *dau* of Edward Lovett
4th Bt. 2nd son   of Liscombe co. Buckingham
bapt. 13 March 1665   she died 8 Oct. 1732
M.D.(Oxon)

Sir Henry Northcote   =   Bridgett-Maria, *b.* 21 Jan 1711
5th Bt *bapt.* at Tawstock.   *dau.* and heiress of Hugh Stafford of
co. Devon 1710   Pynes co. Devon

Sir Stafford   =   Catherine, *dau.* of the Rev George
Northcote 6th Bt   Bradford of Talaton co. Devon
of Pynes *afsd*   *m.* 17 Oct 1761
bapt. 6 May 1736

Sir Stafford   =   Jacquetta *dau* of Charles Baring
Northcote 7th Bt   of Larkbeare co. Devon
bapt. 26 Sept 1762   *m.* 6 May 1791

Henry Stafford   =   Agnes Mary *dau* of Thomas
Northcote   Cockburn, HEICS *m.* 13 Nov. 1815
bapt. 18 March 1792
M.P. for Heytesbury
co. Wilts.

H   A
See following page

H   A

Sir Stafford Henry
Northcote 8th Bt &
1st Earl of Iddesleigh,
G.C.B. *b.* 27 Oct. 1818.
Chancellor of the
Exchequer, 1874-80;
Governor of the
Hudsons Bay Company
1869-74 etc.
d. 12 June 1887 at
no. 10 Downing Street

= Cecilia Frances *m.* 5 Aug 1843
dau. of Thomas Farrer and sister of
Thomas 1st Lord Farrer of Abinger

Henry Stafford, 1st & last
Lord Northcote, 2nd son.
b. 18 Nov. 1846. Governor
of Bombay, 1900-03;
Governor General of Australia
1903-08, G.C.M.G., G.C.I.E.
d.s.p 29 Sept. 1911
= Alice, adopted *dau.* of
   George, 1st Lord Mount
Stephen, President C.P.R.

The Rev. Prebendary the Honble
John Northcote, 3rd son. *b.* 3 Jan
1850. Fellow of Kings College,
London; Hon. Chaplain of Queen
Victoria, Edward VII & George V.
d. 5 June 1920.
= Hilda Cardew, *m.* 14 June 1881
dau. of the Very Rev. Frederic Farrar,
Dean of Canterbury.

Henry Stafford
3rd Earl of Iddesleigh,
10th Bt.
b. 19 Nov. 1901. M.A.(Oxon)
Major, Welsh Guards
d. 16 Feb. 1970

= Elizabeth Susan Angela Mary
m. 14 May 1930 *dau.* of
Frederic Sawrey Archibald Lowndes
by his wife Marie Adelaide Julia
Renee Belloc

H   E
See following page

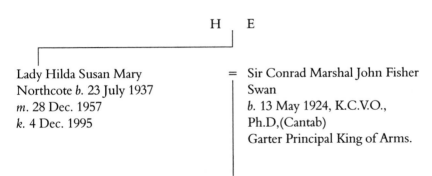

H   E

Lady Hilda Susan Mary   =   Sir Conrad Marshal John Fisher
Northcote *b.* 23 July 1937   Swan
m. 28 Dec. 1957   *b.* 13 May 1924, K.C.V.O.,
k. 4 Dec. 1995   Ph.D,(Cantab)
                                     Garter Principal King of Arms.

For the continuation of the descent see Chapter III p 72

Descent from the Piast Kings of Poland[1]

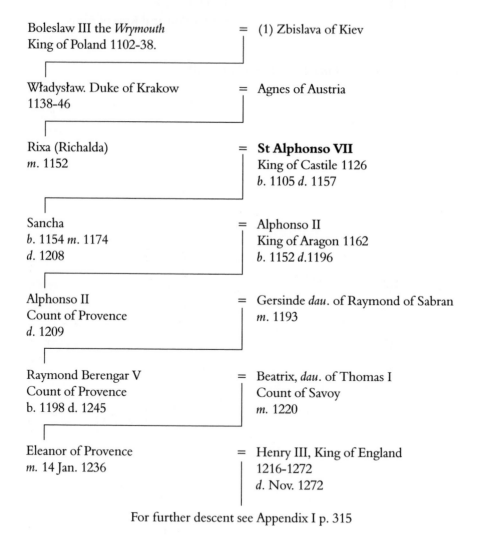

Boleslaw III the *Wrymouth*   =   (1) Zbislava of Kiev
King of Poland 1102-38.

Władysław. Duke of Krakow   =   Agnes of Austria
1138-46

Rixa (Richalda)   =   **St Alphonso VII**
m. 1152   **King of Castile 1126**
                                    b. 1105 *d*. 1157

Sancha   =   Alphonso II
b. 1154 *m*. 1174   King of Aragon 1162
d. 1208   *b*. 1152 *d*.1196

Alphonso II   =   Gersinde *dau*. of Raymond of Sabran
Count of Provence   *m*. 1193
d. 1209

Raymond Berengar V   =   Beatrix, *dau*. of Thomas I
Count of Provence   Count of Savoy
b. 1198 d. 1245   *m*. 1220

Eleanor of Provence   =   Henry III, King of England
m. 14 Jan. 1236   1216-1272
                                    d. Nov. 1272

For further descent see Appendix I p. 315

---

[1] Dworzacek, W. Genealogia. Institut Historii Polskiej Akademii Nauk. Warsawa, 1959 Tables 1 and 5; Louda Jiri and Maclagan, Michael. *Lines of Succession*, Orbis Publishing, London, 1981 Tables 45 and 132.

Priestley–Belloc–Swanton Descent[1]

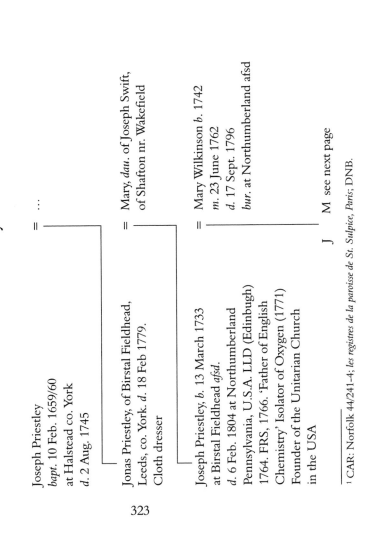

Joseph Priestley
bapt. 10 Feb. 1659/60
at Halstead co. York
d. 2 Aug. 1745

=   …

Jonas Priestley, of Birstal Fieldhead,
Leeds, co. York. *d.* 18 Feb 1779.
Cloth dresser

=   Mary, *dau.* of Joseph Swift,
of Shafton nr. Wakefield

Joseph Priestley, *b.* 13 March 1733
at Birstal Fieldhead *afsd.*
d. 6 Feb. 1804 at Northumberland
Pennsylvania, U.S.A. LLD (Edinbugh)
1764. FRS, 1766. 'Father of English
Chemistry' Isolator of Oxygen (1771)
Founder of the Unitarian Church
in the USA

=   Mary Wilkinson *b.* 1742
m. 23 June 1762
d. 17 Sept. 1796
bur. at Northumberland afsd

J   M   see next page

[1] CAR: Norfolk 44/241–4; *les registres de la paroisse de St. Sulpice, Paris*; DNB.

Joseph Priestly
b. 24 July 1768
at Leeds
d. 2 Sept 1833
at Exeter

= Elizabeth Ryland
b. 25 Oct. 1769
m. 13 Apr. 1792
d. 8 May 1816

Other issue

Hilaire Belloc = Jeanne Henriette
deceased by   Belzons
1821   living 1821

James/Jacques Swanton Lieut. Col. Commandant, Berwick Brigade in which a Cadet, 1769, Commissioned, 1776; wounded in Service (lost an eye). Chev. de l'Ordre de St. Louis (1790). b. 1 Jan. 1753 (ex Cork to France aged 11) d. 28 Jan. 1823 in France.
= Marguirite Louise Josephe Chasserain. m. 10 Jan. 1785

= (Anne) Louise. Authoress, aged 21 yrs in 1821 when on June 1st she married in St. Sulpice Church, Paris

Elizabeth Rayner
b. 28 Aug. 1797
m. 29 June 1824
d. 10 Oct. 1877

= Joseph Parkes, of George Street, Westminster
b. 22 Jan. 1796
d. 17 Aug. 1865
Solicitor.
Drafted Reform Bill, 1832
From 1833 Parliamentary Solicitor, From 1847 Taxing-Master in Chancery.

Jean Hilaire Belloc
s. and h. Portrait Painter.
Aged 34 years in 1821 when recorded as a land owner & also of rue des Franc Bourgeois no. 18, Parish of Blancs-Monteaux, Paris, & La Celle St. Cloud

Armand Justin Swanton. Staff Officer with Napoleon through Lithuania to Moscow 1812. Commissioned 1812; wounded in Service (lance to the head) Russian prisoner of War; escaped and survived The Retreat. b. 10 Nov. 1792 d.s.p. 4 Sept 1844
= Marie Cesarina Jauberd de Beaujeau (widow) m. 26 Jan. 1836

AL see next page

J

E   J see next page

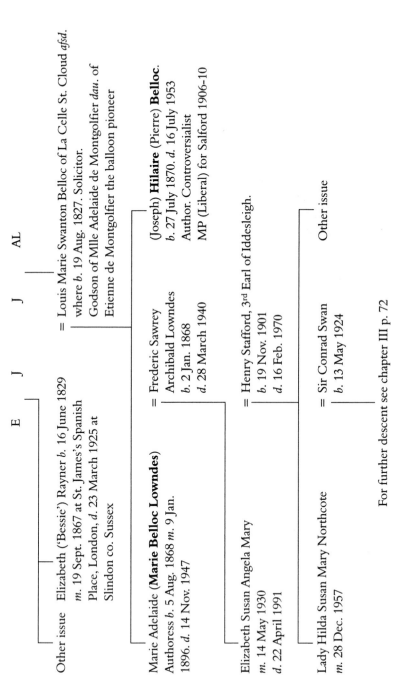

E   J   J   AL

Other issue   Elizabeth ('Bessie') Rayner *b.* 16 June 1829 *m.* 19 Sept. 1867 at St. James's Spanish Place, London, *d.* 23 March 1925 at Slindon co. Sussex

= Louis Marie Swanton Belloc of La Celle St. Cloud *afsd.* where *b.* 19 Aug. 1827. Solicitor. Godson of Mlle Adelaide de Montgolfier *dau.* of Etienne de Montgolfier the balloon pioneer

Marie Adelaide (**Marie Belloc Lowndes**) Authoress *b.* 5 Aug. 1868 *m.* 9 Jan. 1896. *d.* 14 Nov. 1947

= Frederic Sawrey Archibald Lowndes *b.* 2 Jan. 1868 *d.* 28 March 1940

(Joseph) **Hilaire** (Pierre) **Belloc**. *b.* 27 July 1870. *d.* 16 July 1953 Author. Controversialist MP (Liberal) for Salford 1906-10

Elizabeth Susan Angela Mary *m.* 14 May 1930 *d.* 22 April 1991

= Henry Stafford, 3rd Earl of Iddesleigh. *b.* 19 Nov. 1901 *d.* 16 Feb. 1970

Lady Hilda Susan Mary Northcote *m.* 28 Dec. 1957

= Sir Conrad Swan *b.* 13 May 1924

Other issue

For further descent see chapter III p. 72

Abbreviations & Symbols

In addition to the abbreviations commonly used,
those below are also relevant to this book.

CAR   College of Arms Records (London)
CS   Sir Conrad Swan – author of the book
EHS   Edna Hanson (Magdalen) Swan – mother of the author
HPS   Dr Henry Peter Swan – father of the author
NAC   National Archives of Canada
PS   The Rev. Dr Peter (Julian Michael) Swan – brother of the author
REG   Rose Elizabeth Green – maternal grandmother of the author
SSA   Święcicki Swan Archives (located at Boxford House, Suffolk)
=   married
∗   issue of this union not shown

Index